I0211756

EVIDENCES OF CHRISTIANITY

Evidences of Christianity

Parts 1–4

J. W. McGarvey

DeWard™
for your journey

This edition of *Evidences of Christianity,* by J.W. McGarvey is published in 2017 by:

DeWard Publishing Company, Ltd.
P.O. Box 6259, Chillicothe, Ohio 45601
www.deward.com

J.W. McGarvey's work is in the public domain. This edition, its layout, and the new forew is © 2017. All rights reserved.

Printed in the United States of America.

ISBN: 978-1-947929-02-9

FROM THE PUBLISHER

A word should be said about a few changes to this edition of McGarvey's *Evidences*. When Parts 3–4 were added and the work was published as a single volume, the table of contents for the latter section was kept separate from the original table of contents—appearing more than 190 pages into the work. Although it may offend the purist, in the interest of being the most helpful to the most readers, this edition has combined to two tables of contents at the beginning of the work. Second, McGarvey's original work included postils in the margins. Although they were incredibly useful, their reproduction here was beyond the scope of this project. Finally, and less significantly, Scripture citations were modernized to use Arabic numerals rather than Roman.

This edition also includes a foreword by Dr. Timothy McGrew, chair of the Philosophy Department at Western Michigan University and Director of the Library of Historical Apologetics. Our thanks to him for taking the time to supply this valuable addition to our volume.

DeWard Publishing Company
January, 2018

FOREWORD

John William McGarvey (1829–1911) ranks as the foremost intellectual leader in the second generation of the Restoration movement begun by Alexander Campbell in the early Nineteenth Century. He was not raised as a Christian. When his father died in 1833, McGarvey's mother remarried, and his stepfather intended the boy for a career in industry. But in 1848, while he was a student at Bethany College, he was persuaded of the truth of Christianity and baptized by professor W. K. Pendleton, who had himself been baptized by Campbell just eight years earlier. The change in his convictions demanded a change in his education, and McGarvey, who had never made any study of the Christian Scriptures, set out to rectify that problem. "The prodigious amount of reading which he did," his son wrote after his death, "was done for the purpose of acquiring the fullest possible knowledge of the Book."

That study shaped the rest of his life. Through more than a decade of pastoral ministry and more than four decades as a professor at two institutions, he honed his knowledge both of the content of the Scriptures and of the grounds of their credibility. Those who heard him from the pulpit or in the classroom remembered his rare gift of clarity. He was a speaker, as one biographer put it, who was easy to hear and hard to forget. His extensive writings give us evidence of that gift. In ten commentaries on books of the New Testament, in two volumes of sermons, and in scores of essays on biblical criticism and modern biblical scholarship written for the *Millennial Harbinger*,

American Christian Review, the *Christian Standard*, and *Lard's Quarterly*, McGarvey left a legacy of clarity and conviction that few scholars of his generation could rival.

McGarvey wrote his *Evidences of Christianity* out of the belief that existing works on the subject were not suitable as textbooks. By this he did not mean that existing works were of no value. His copious references to the apologetic literature of the previous century and a half leave no doubt that he saw in the history of apologetics a storehouse of much that was of permanent value. But for those who are making a study of the evidences, McGarvey's text has notable advantages over even the best of earlier works. It is more systematic than anything by Thomas Chalmers or Charles Pettit McIlvaine, more readable than Nathaniel Lardner's sprawling *Credibility of the Gospel History*, broader and more up to date in its treatment of the manuscript evidence of the New Testament and the patristic witnesses than William Paley's *View of the Evidences of Christianity*.

McGarvey's standpoint in the *Evidences* is that of a scholar who is thoroughly familiar with the most skeptical criticism of his day but at the same time completely persuaded that traditional views of the authorship, historical trustworthiness, and inspiration of Scripture are rationally defensible. He believed that Moses wrote the Pentateuch, Daniel wrote Daniel, and Isaiah wrote Isaiah. He held that Jonah was swallowed by a great fish and that Balaam's ass spoke Hebrew as well as his master did. But he organizes the work in a way that does not presuppose these convictions. Only in the third part does he mount a defense—a vigorous defense—of the verbal inspiration of the Scriptures. His approach predates and might have influenced the position of B. B. Warfield, who wrote in 1893:

> Inspiration is not the most fundamental of Christian doctrines, nor even the first thing we prove about the Scriptures. It is the last and crowning fact as to the Scriptures. These we first prove authentic, historically credible, generally trustworthy, before we prove them inspired. And the proof of their authenticity, cred-

ibility, and general trustworthiness would give us a firm basis for Christianity, prior to any knowledge on our part of their inspiration, and apart, indeed, from the existence of inspiration.

The position McGarvey holds is more conservative than that held by most mainstream New Testament scholars today. But the change in the sociology of New Testament scholarship has been driven far more by philosophical fashion than by any change in the evidence itself. The explosion of the number of manuscripts for the New Testament has done nothing to weaken the case McGarvey makes; quite the contrary. Our modern researches in archaeology and the deep advances of the Twentieth Century in our understanding of Second Temple Judaism tend more to emphasize than to detract from his argument. And on many points, he emphasizes the evidence we are inclined to overlook.

For just that reason, McGarvey's book affords a much-needed counterbalance for contemporary readers whose only exposure to the evidences of Christianity has been filtered by a seminary education that discounts the patristic evidence for the authorship of the Gospels, or that rules out *a priori* the credibility of reported miracles, or that accepts without demur the often fanciful conjectures of redaction criticism. These are contested points. McGarvey contests them, and he does so with evidence and argument. And for anyone who has never made any study of the evidences for the Christian faith, this book provides a point of entry that balances rigor with clarity. In many respects, it still provides a model introduction to the subject. It would be a significant gain for the cause of the kingdom if every minister of the Gospel today would read this book.

Timothy McGrew
Kalamazoo, MI
January 23, 2018

PREFACE

On no other subject have so many thoughtful volumes been written within the last hundred years, as on the Evidences of Christianity. This is true as regards both sides of the question at issue; for while the uninspired friends of Christ have never before defended his cause with ability so consummate, they have never before encountered opponents with learning so extensive or with talents of so high an order. But among the army of writers whom the deepening conflict has called into the field, very few have attempted to reduce the arguments *pro* and *con* to a form suitable for class-room instruction. Scarcely one of these writers has failed to widen the field of investigation, or to direct attention to some of the new phases which the controversy is ever assuming; but since the appearance, a century since, of Lardner's immortal work, no English author has attempted an exhaustive discussion of the whole subject. Of the few works in which a general though not exhaustive discussion of the subject has been presented with a view to the instruction of College classes, not one has continued in general use to the present day. As a consequence, instructors are now limited to the unsatisfactory method of teaching by lectures alone on this important theme.

These considerations furnish the ground on which the author excuses himself for offering to the public the work of which this volume is the first installment. The work is intended, not for those who are already proficient in the knowledge of Evidences, but for those who have given the subject little attention or none: hence its elementary character. The young persons of both sexes who make up the classes in our high schools and colleges, have been constantly before the mind of the author in preparing it, and he has enjoyed the advantage of actually testing much of the matter contained in it by the oral instruction of classes in Kentucky University. He trusts that the simplicity at which he has aimed in both style and arrangement, will bring the subject, though usually considered difficult, within the easy comprehension of every student.

The author has indulged the hope that he would be able by this time to publish the whole of his projected work; but so pressing have been the demands of other duties that in this he is disappointed, and now it is probable that several years will pass before the work is completed; he therefore sends forth the two Parts contained in this volume, in the hope that if they shall meet with a favorable reception, he may be enabled, by the kind providence which he recognizes in all the affairs of life, to finish his undertaking at some future time. He sends these forth the more willingly, because each Part presents an inquiry complete in itself, and not dependent on any other Part for its intelligibility or its value.

Subjoined to Part 2 the reader will find an Index to the whole volume, which, while serving the usual purpose of such a document, will be found especially valuable as a means of readily collecting into a single view all that is said throughout Part 2 on the genuineness of any book of the New Testament.

Of the works which are cited or referred to in this volume, only a few need be mentioned here. The citations from Scrivener's Introduction to the Critical Study of the New Testament, which abound in Part I., are all taken from the third and latest edition of this invaluable work. Those from the Ecclesiastical History of Eusebius follow the very imperfect translation of Cruse, except when otherwise indicated. For the writings of the Christian Fathers earlier than Eusebius, the author has used the Ante-Nicene Library, published by T. & T. Clark, Edinburgh; and he has used the American edition of Farrar's Early Days of Christianity.

Lexington, Ky., January, 1886

CONTENTS

INTRODUCTION

The divine origin of the Christian religion depends for its proof on the evidence that Jesus of Nazareth is "the Christ, the Son of the living God." As he is the author of this religion, if it be proved that he is that Christ whose coming and workwere predicted by the prophets of the Old Testament, and that he is the Son of God miraculously begotten, his religion is proved to be of divine origin, and to be for this reason possessed of divine authority.

But should we succeed in establishing the fact that Jesus is the Christ, the Son of God, and fail to show the authenticity of the writings on which we depend for a knowledge of his religion, the fact established would be of no practical value, seeing that we could not know how to secure to ourselves the blessings which the religion might offer. For this reason it is necessary to the practical value of an inquiry into the evidences of Christianity, that it furnish conclusive proof not only of the claims of Jesus, but of the authenticity of the Christian Scriptures.

Moreover, an authentic account of the Christian religion which should fall short of infallibility, would leave the mind a continual prey to doubt in regard to its exact teaching and requirements. If we have in the Christian Scriptures nothing more than an authentic account, such as wise and good but fallible men could give, we must be content, and not pretend that we have more. But our inquiry will not reach the result that is desirable unless we find proof that the Scriptures are infallible.

The importance of this inquiry, whether to the believer or the unbeliever, can scarcely be overestimated. As respects the unbeliever, it may be estimated in part by the following considerations:

1. The rejection of the Christian religion is the rejection of all religion. The adherents of any other faith may lay aside their own and accept the Christian, and many have done so; but no man who studies the evidences of the Christian religion and fails to find proof of its divine origin, can find such proof in favor of any other. As Richard Watson has well said, "It is universally acknowledged among us, that there is but one book in the world which has claims to divine authority so presumptively substantial as to be worthy of serious examination."[1] It is clear, then, that the Christian communities of the earth would be stripped of all the blessings which religion brings to a people should they decide against the religion of Jesus, seeing that the alternative; would be no religion at all.

2. The Christian religion offers to every man who properly accepts it the forgiveness of sins and life everlasting, two blessings with which, in our present state, no others conceivable are worthy to be compared. The importance of an inquiry into its truth is proportionate to the value of these blessings.

3. If it is true, every man who disbelieves it will suffer final and eternal condemnation. This its founder repeatedly declared, and in the declaration he assumed that the evidence which would attend the gospel would be such that no man could disbelieve without guilt, and such guilt as requires final condemnation. As surely as the religion is true, disbelief is a fatal sin.

To the believer the inquiry is only less important than to the unbeliever. It is important, first, for his own good. If his faith has not a sure foundation it may fail in the hour of trial; and what foundation is sure except a knowledge of the evidences. It is important, secondly, for the good of others. We are required to give to others, for their good, a reason of the hope that is in us, and this we can not do with satisfaction to them or to ourselves, unless we know the evidence on which our hope is based.

---

[1] Theological Institutes, Vol. I., 105.

In order that our conclusions on any subject may be safe and satisfying, our investigation of it must be conducted in a proper frame of mind. Inquirers into the evidences of Christianity are exposed to dangers at this point, varying according to their preconceptions on the subject. Unbelievers are in danger of so earnestly wishing that the evidence shall appear inconclusive, as to underestimate the force of every proof, and to overestimate the force of every objection. Such a frame of mind is inimical to the reception of truth. Unfortunately, many persons who are not committed to unbelief, approach this subject more or less affected by this bias; for the Bible condemns all men who are not obedient believers, and thus it arouses a degree of antagonism within them at the very time that they are investigating its claims. He who would avoid an unjust judgment against the Bible must suppress this tendency, and be perfectly willing that the Bible shall prove itself the word of God.

The believer, on the other hand, is in danger of pursuing the inquiry with so fixed a determination that the Bible shall be found true, as to lead him to accept shallow sophisms for sound arguments, and to disregard the force of serious objections. Such an inquirer, should he afterward exercise a calmer judgment, must look back with distrust upon his former conclusions and experience a consequent weakening of his faith.

There is a proper place and work for the zealous polemic on the subject, especially in the field of controversy where bold and often unscrupulous assailants are to be met; but the student and the teacher should assume the spirit of an inquirer or a judge, rather than that of an advocate. By this must not be understood a spirit of indifference.[2] The judge before whom a man of previous good char-

---

[2] "If indifference to the result be an essential qualification for an investigator of the Scriptures, then I must give up all hope of ever being one. To the result I can not be indifferent if I would; for there are all my hopes." (Calvin Stowe, *History of the Books of the Bible*, 254).

"When I hear some youth telling me, with a simpering face, that he does not *know*, or pretend to *say*, whether there be a God or not; or whether, if there be, He takes any interest in human affairs; or whether, if He does, it much imports us to know; or whether, if He has revealed that knowledge, it is possible or impossible for us to ascertain it; when I hear him further saying, that meantime he is disposed to make himself very easy in the midst

acter is being tried under the charge of an infamous crime, would be unfit for his high office, if, while enforcing with impartiality the rules of evidence, he should have no wish to see the man's innocence established. So, in prosecuting an inquiry into the evidences of Christianity, while the student must guard vigilantly against self-deception, he should most earnestly wish that a religion which confers upon men so much good in this life, and promises so much more in the life to come, may prove to be unquestionably true.

Many persons, in studying the claims of Christianity, take up the objections that are urged against it before they learn what it is, or examine the evidences in its favor.[3] They hear the negative in the debate before the affirmative; they allow the witnesses for the defendant to testify before they hear the plaintiff state his case; they read books and attend lectures in opposition to the Bible, when they know but little of its contents and still less of its evidences. They often decide the question after hearing only one side, and that the side which should be heard last, not first. This is a reversal of the order established in all courts of justice, in all well conducted discussions, in all scientific investigations. Common sense and the maxims of justice alike demand that we hear first the arguments in favor of a proposition, and afterward those against it. He who reverses this order prejudges the case, and comes to the consideration of the affirmative evidence, in a frame of mind unfavorable to a candid hearing or a just decision. If we hear much evil said of a man before we form his acquaintance, we are prejudiced against him; whereas, had we known him first the

---

of these uncertainties, and to await the great revelation of the future with philosophical—that is, being interpreted, idiotic— tranquility, I see that, in point of fact, he has never entered into the question at all; that he has failed to realize the terrible moment of the questions (however they may be decided) of which he speaks with such amazing flippancy." (Henry Rogers. *Eclipse of Faith*, 31.)

[3] We have a striking example of this in the notorious Thomas Paine, who says, in reference to the composition of Part I. of his Age of Reason, which he published in advance of Part 2: "I had neither Bible nor Testament to refer to, though I was writing against both." After this confession, it is not surprising to hear him say, in Part 2: "I have now furnished myself with a Bible and a Testament, and I can say also that I have found them to be much worse books than I had conceived." (*Preface to Age of Reason, Part 2*) A man so unjust as to assail a book which he had never read, would be expected to read it, if at all, for the purpose of finding it worse than he had represented it.

evil speech that we heard might seem to be only calumny. Unfortunately for the great majority of unbelievers, they have pursued this improper method, and then after forming their opinions, have either neglected the Bible and its evidences entirely, or have come to the study of them with an unfriendly spirit.

In the investigation of any question which is a subject of controversy, it is desirable to begin with admitted facts, and to take the successive steps of the inquiry in such an order that neither shall in any degree involve its successor. In the present instance we may begin with the undisputed fact that we now have a collection of writings making up the Bible, and that these are said to have been composed many centuries ago by men divinely inspired for this purpose. Should we first inquire as to the divine origin of the Bible as a whole, and then inquire as to the canonicity of its several books, our first inquiry would overlap and involve the second. But should we first inquire as to the uncorrupted preservation of the books; then, as to their authorship; then, as to their authenticity; then, as to the inspiration and infallibility of its writers, we would have a series of inquiries, every one of which would have an intrinsic value independent of the others, and no one of which would overlap its successor. We would also have in this series of inquiries all that is necessary to the discussion of both the divine origin of the Christian religion and the infallibility of the Holy Scriptures. We would then be at liberty to give attention to any other evidences not included in this line of argument, and also to objections not thus far encountered. Such is the plan of the present work. It proposes an inquiry into the following topics, in the order here given:

    I.   The Integrity of the New Testament Books
    II.   Their Genuineness
    III. Their Authenticity
    IV. The Inspiration of Their Writers
    V.   Other Evidences of the Divine Origin of Christianity
    VI. The Integrity, Genuineness, Authenticity and Inspiration of the Old Testament Books

In conducting all of these inquiries it is proposed to state fully and to consider fairly the principal objections and counterarguments of unbelievers.

It is also proposed to collect in this volume, in the form of foot-notes and appendixes, many valuable documents from the pens of both ancient and modern writers, which have important bearings on the subject, but which are now inaccessible except to those who have the use of costly libraries. These documents, it is thought, will add great value to the work, independently of its line of argument.

PART I

Integrity of the
New Testament Text

ONE

Nature and Limits of the Inquiry

1. By the integrity of an ancient book is meant its wholeness, or its uncorrupted preservation. The integrity of a book is preserved when it has been transmitted without material change; that is, change which affects its meaning. We may also affirm the integrity of a document, when, though material changes have been made in it, we shall have detected these and restored the original readings. The branch of science which treats of this subject is called Textual Criticism, and sometimes, when applied to the books of the Bible, Biblical Criticism. Its province is to ascertain, first, what differences of reading, if any, are to be found in the various copies of the book; and second, to determine which of the various readings is the original one.

2. This inquiry became necessary from the fact that all books of which many copies were made before the invention of printing, underwent changes through the mistakes of copyists, and were liable to intentional alterations. There is not a writing of antiquity which has come down to our age without many such changes. A large part of the labor of the editors of Greek and Latin classics consists in correcting as best they can the erroneous readings thus introduced into these works. It was stated by Dr. Bentley, a celebrated English scholar of the eighteenth century, that he had himself seen in a few copies of the comedies of Terence, a Latin writer of the second century before Christ, as many as 20,000

various readings, although the work is not near so large as the New Testament, and the few copies compared were not examined with very great minuteness. Yet Terence, he declared, was in a better condition in this respect than almost any other classic.[1] The same writer mentions several smaller works in which the variations are as numerous as the lines, and some which on this account have become a "mere heap of errors."[2] Ancient authors were well aware of this liability to change, and they had a wholesome dread of it when publishing their books. Thus, Irenaeus of the second century appended to one of his books an earnest entreaty in the name of the Lord, that his transcriber shall correct his copy by the original, and transmit this entreaty to subsequent copyists; and this entreaty is quoted by Eusebius of the fourth century, and adopted with reference to his own books.[3] The Jewish copyists of the Old Testament were aware of the same danger, and, as

---

[1] "Terence is now in one of the best conditions of any of the classic writers; the oldest and best copy of him is now in the Vatican Library, which comes nearest to the poet's own hand; but even that has hundreds of errors, most of which may be mended out of other exemplars that are otherwise more recent and of inferior value. I myself have collated several, and do affirm that I have seen twenty thousand various lections in that little author, not near so big as the whole New Testament; and am morally sure that, if half the number of manuscripts were collated for Terence with that niceness of minuteness which has been used in twice as many for the New Testament, the number of variations would amount to above fifty thousand." (From *Phileleutherus Lipsiensis,* quoted by Tregelles, *Hist. of Printed Text,* 51.)

[2] "In the late edition of Tibulus, by the learned writer Mr. Broukhuise (1708), you have a register of various lections in the close of that book, where you may see, at the first view, that they are as many as the lines. The same is visible in Plautus, set out by Pareus. I myself, during my travels, have had the opportunity to examine several MSS. of the poet Manilius, and can assure you that the variations I have met with are twice as many as all the lines of the book." (*Ib.,* 52.)

"In profane authors (as they are called) whereof one manuscript only had the luck to be preserved, as Velleius Paterculus among the Latins and Hesychius among the Greeks, the faults of the scribes are found so numerous, and the defects so beyond all redress, that, notwithstanding the pains of the learnedest and acutest critics for two whole centuries, these books still are, and are like to continue, a mere heap of errors." (*Ib.,* 51.)

[3] "Irenaeus also wrote the treatise on the Ogdoad, or the number eight.... At the close of the work we found a most delightful remark of his, which we shall deem incumbent upon us also to add to the present work. It is as follows: 'I adjure thee, whoever thou art that transcribest this book, by our Lord Jesus Christ and by His glorious appearance when He shall come to judge the quick and dead, to compare what thou hast copied, and to correct it by this original manuscript from which thou hast carefully transcribed, and that thou also copy this adjuration and insert it in the copy.'" (Eusebius, *Eccles. Hist., c.* 20.)

stated in the Talmud published about AD 350, they adopted for themselves very minute regulations to preserve the purity of the sacred text. They numbered the verses, words and letters of the Scriptures, by books and sections, marking the middle verse and letter of each, so that by counting these in any copy they could determine whether a word or a letter had been added or omitted.[4] We have no account of the rules adopted by copyists of the New Testament, but we know that they had every inducement to copy with care. The author of the Book of Revelation had given the warning, that to anyone who should add a word to his book God would add the plagues written in it, and that if any one should take away a word God would take his name out of the book of life; and that this solemn warning was accepted by Christians at an early date as applying to other books as well as to this, is known by the fact that Irenaeus thus applied it to some who were charged with altering the text, though he expresses the opinion that those who do so without evil intent may receive pardon.[5] But notwithstanding the vigilance of Jewish copyists, and the solemn warnings addressed to Christian copyists, a large number of erroneous readings found their way into the manuscript copies of both Testaments, and the existence of these gave rise to the science of Biblical Criticism.

3. It was known, from a very early period of Christian literature, that errors of transcribers had crept into the sacred writings,[6] but

---

[4] Davidson, *Biblical Criticism, I.* 116.

[5] He is speaking of a change which had been made in some copies, by which 616 was found in Revelation 13.18, instead of 666; and he says of those who had made the change or had received it: "Now, as regards those who have done this in simplicity, and without evil intent, we are at liberty to assume that pardon will be granted them by God. But as for those who, for the sake of vainglory, lay it down for certain that names containing the spurious number are to be accepted, and affirm that this name, hit upon by themselves, is that of him who is to come; such persons shall not come forth without loss, because they have led into error both themselves and those who have confided in them. . . . As there shall be no light punishment upon him who either adds to or subtracts anything from the Scripture, under that such a person must necessarily fall." (*Against Heresies*, B. V., c. xxx., § 1.)

[6] Origen, at the beginning of the third century, says: "But now great in truth has become the diversity of copies, be it from the negligence of scribes, or from the evil daring of some who correct what is written, or from those who in correcting add or take away what they think fit." (*Com, on Matthew*, quoted in Scrivener's Int., 509.)

it was not until after printed copies had come into circulation, and the copies issued by different publishers had been compared, that scholars began to realize the magnitude of the evil and to search for the means of correcting it. Printing from movable types was invented in 1438, and the first book printed was the Latin Bible about 1452.[7] In the last quarter of the same century several editions of the Hebrew Bible were printed by wealthy Jews in Italy,[8] but it was not until the beginning of the sixteenth century that the Greek New Testament was given to the world in this form. It was first printed at Complutum (Alcala) in Spain, under the direction of Cardinal Ximenes, in the year 1514; but on account of delay in obtaining the consent of the Pope, this edition was not published until 1522. In the meantime an edition was prepared by Erasmus and published at Basle in Switzerland, in 1516. After this, editions and copies were multiplied rapidly; the Protestant Reformation, which began about the same time, stimulated the work, and the attention of scholars was drawn more and more to the differences among the printed editions, and between them and the manuscripts, until Biblical Criticism, to which printing gave birth, grew to its present maturity. As a result of these investigations, the number of various readings, that is, readings different from those in the text commonly used, which are to be found in the hundreds of existing manuscripts, is now estimated at not less than 120,000.[9]

4. But while the art of printing brought into clearer light the various readings of manuscripts, and gave rise to the inquiries of Biblical critics, it also brought the multiplication of various readings to an end, and fixed a limit to the field in which these inquiries are to be prosecuted. Such is the perfection to which the art of printing has attained, that when the types for a book are once

---

[7] It was published at Mentz, by Gutenberg (the inventor of printing) and Faust; and Scrivener states that eighteen copies of the edition are still preserved, "a splendid and beautiful volume." (*Int.,* 351.) One of these was sold at auction in London, in March, 1885, for the enormous price of $19,500.

[8] For an account of these, see Davidson's *Bib. Crit.,* I., 137–141; Tregelles, *Hist. of Printed Text.* 1, 2.

[9] This is Scrivener's estimate (Int. 3). The number is placed higher by some other authors.

set, and stereotyped plates are made from them, all the copies printed therefrom, however numerous, are alike in every word and letter; consequently, the mere multiplication of copies, which is the chief source of error in manuscripts, originates no errors in printed copies. It is also practicable, by means of proof-reading, which is a part of the art of printing, to secure perfect accuracy in the types or plates from which the printing is done, and to perpetuate this accuracy in making duplicates of the plates. It is claimed, for instance, by the American Bible Society, that there is not a single misprint in any of the myriads of copies of the English Bible which they are annually printing in various editions. It follows, that since the art of printing has been perfected, the multiplication of various readings in the original Scriptures has ceased, and that when the errors which crept in before the invention of printing shall have been corrected, the Bible will be no longer exposed to such errors, the Science of Biblical Criticism will have completed its task, and the subsequent generations of men will have no care concerning the purity of the sacred text. Our inquiry into the integrity of the New Testament is therefore limited to the period which preceded the invention of printing, or to the first fifteen centuries of our era.

TWO

Character of the Various Readings

1. A bare statement of the number of various readings in the sacred text is calculated to excite surprise and alarm; but when the character of these variations is considered these feelings quickly subside. Dr. Hort, one of the most competent of living authorities on the subject, declares, that in regard to the great bulk of the words of the New Testament, there is no variation, and no other ground of doubt. He estimates the number of words admitted on all hands to be above doubt, at not less than seven-eighths of the whole. When, of the remaining one-eighth, we leave out mere differences of spelling, the number still left in doubt is about one-sixtieth of the whole; and when we select from this one-sixtieth of those which in any sense can be called substantial variations, their number he says, can hardly form more than a thousandth part of the entire text. That is, only about one thousandth part of the New Testament is so variously expressed in the various copies, as to make any substantial difference of meaning.[1]

---

[1] "With regard to the bulk of the words of the New Testament, as of most other ancient writings, there is no variation, or other ground of doubt, and therefore no room for textual criticism; and here, therefore, an editor is only a transcriber. The same may be said in truth with respect to those various readings which have never been received, and in all probability never will be received, into any printed text. The proportion of words virtually accepted on all hands as raised above doubt is very great, not less, on a rough computation, than seven-eighths of the whole. The remaining eighth, therefore, formed in great part by changes of order and other trivialities, constitutes the whole area of criticism. . . . Setting aside differences in orthography, the words in our opinion still subject to doubt only make up about one-sixtieth of the New Testament. In this second estimate, the proportion of comparatively trivial variations is beyond

2. The various readings consist mainly in differences of Greek orthography; in the form of words not affecting the essential meaning; in the insertion or omission of words not essential to the sense; in the use of one synonym for another; and in the transposition of words whose order in the sentence is immaterial. It is obvious that such variations, however numerous, leave the text uncorrupted as regards its thoughts. An essay might be written in English with almost every word misspelt and every sentence ungrammatical, which would still express its meaning as clearly as the most accurate and elegant composition. The writings of "Josh Billings" are as clear as those of Addison. It is only then, in the one-thousandth part of the New Testament, or the part in which the variations affect the meaning, that the text has undergone corruption worthy of any serious inquiry.

3. To illustrate still further the nature of these variations, we open the Critical New Testament published by Tregelles, at the second chapter of Matthew. He has collected the various readings, not from all the ancient authorities, but only from those of the more ancient class; yet in the first seven verses of this chapter his notes exhibit twenty-five various readings. So insignificant are they, however, that only four of the twenty-five can be represented at all in an English translation. One of the four is a case of transposition, and the other three of the omission or insertion of words not essential to the meaning. They are as follows:

v. 3.	"The king Herod."	"Herod the king."
v. 3.	"Jerusalem with him."	"All Jerusalem with him."
v. 4.	"All the priests and scribes."	"All the chief priests and scribes."
v. 4.	"Inquired from them where the Christ should be born."	"Inquired where," etc.

Should we submit to like examination the entire work of Tregelles, or any similar work, we would find the changes throughout

---

measure larger than in the former, so that the amount of what can in any sense be called substantial variation is but a small fraction of the whole residuary variation, and can hardly form more than a thousandth part of the entire text." (*Introduction to Greek New Testament,* Westcott and Hort, 2.)

of the same character, with the exception of about the one-thousandth part mentioned by Dr. Hort.

4. Some of the changes which affect the meaning of particular passages by introducing ideas not originally expressed in them, are nevertheless immaterial as regards the general teachings of the scriptures, because the ideas introduced are found in other passages. For example, in Luke's account of the conversion of Paul, the words, "It is hard for thee to kick against the goads," and the words, "Lord, what wilt thou have me to do?" are interpolated in many copies, and they give expression to ideas not penned by Luke in this place; but still these words were spoken on the occasion, as we learn from Paul's accounts of the same incident in his speeches reported in other chapters of Acts.[2] Again, the entire thirty-seventh verse of the eighth chapter of Acts, as found in some MSS., is an interpolation, adding to the original the statement, that Philip said to the eunuch "If thou believest with all thy heart thou mayest," and the eunuch's response, "I believe that Jesus Christ is the Son of God"; yet the fact that such a confession of faith was required of converts as a prerequisite to baptism is taught in other passages,[3] and this interpolation is not misleading. Another example of the same class is the well-known passage in 1 John 5.7–8, where the statement about the three witnesses in heaven is interpolated, yet it states what is known by many other passages to be true.

5. Put besides the changes which are not material to the general teaching of scripture, there are a few that are so, and there are two passages of considerable length, the genuineness of which has been brought into doubt by the investigations of critics. Of the former class we mention the statement of John 5.4, that an angel went down into the pool and troubled the water, and that the first person who stepped in afterward was healed of whatever disease he had.[4] The two long passages brought into doubt are the last

---

[2] Acts 9.5–6; comp. Acts 22.7–10; 26.14–15.

[3] Romans 10.9–10; Mark 16.16.x7

[4] The evidence for and against the genuineness of this passage is fully given in Scrivener's Intro., 607.

twelve verses of Mark, and the account in John's Gospel of the woman taken in adultery. The genuineness of these is doubted by some critics, though confidently defended, especially the former, by others.[5] Further investigation will doubtless bring all to the same judgment concerning them.

6. While it is evident from the preceding statements that some interpolations are found in the MSS. and printed editions of the New Testament, it has yet been ascertained by a careful examination of all these, that they contain nothing contradictory of the parts which are genuine, and nothing subversive of faith or duty. In the language of Dr. Davidson, "No new doctrines have been elicited by the aid of Biblical criticism, nor have any historical facts been summoned by it from obscurity. All the doctrines and duties of Christianity remain unaffected"[6]; and in the still more specific language of Dr. Hort, "The books of the New Testament as preserved in extant documents assuredly speak to us in every important respect in language identical with that in which they

---

[5] The genuineness of Mark 16.9–20 is most ably discussed by Westcott and Hort on one side, and Scrivener on the other. The conclusion reached by the former, after an elaborate dissertation, is stated in these words: "There is no difficulty in supposing (1) that the true intended continuation of verses 1–8 either was very early lost by the detachment of a leaf, or was never written down; and (2) that a scribe or editor, unwilling to change the words of the text before him, or to add words of his own, was willing to furnish the Gospel with what seemed a worthy conclusion by incorporating with it unchanged a narrative of Christ's appearances after the resurrection, which he found in some secondary record then surviving from the preceding generation. If these suppositions are made, the whole tenor of the evidence becomes clear and harmonious. Every other view is, we believe, untenable. . . . It [the passage] manifestly can not claim any apostolic authority; but it is doubtless founded on some tradition of the apostolic age." (*Introduction to New Testament, Appendix I.,* p. 51.)

In opposition to these conclusions, Scrivener speaks with equal confidence. He says in regard to both of the passages mentioned above: "We shall hereafter defend these passages, the first without the slightest misgiving, the second with certain reservations, as entitled to be regarded as authentic portions of the Gospels in which they stand." He redeems this pledge by furnishing an elaborate answer to all the arguments made by Dr. Hort. (*Scrirener's Introduction,* 583–590). The positions taken by other able critics are given in the same note.

In regard to John 7.53–8.11, opinions of critics are not so conflicting. All agree that it can not have been a part of John's original MS., but it is held by some of the ablest that it is nevertheless an authentic piece of history, and that it was probably inserted by John in a second edition of his Gospel. (Scrivener, 610.)

[6] *Biblical Criticism,* ii. 147.

spoke to those for whom they were originally written."[7] If these statements are true, as they undoubtedly are, then all the authority and value possessed by these books when they were first written belong to them still. The case is like that of a certain will. A gentleman left a large estate entailed to his descendants of the third generation, and it was not to be divided until a majority of them should be of age. During the interval many copies of the will were circulated among parties interested, many of these being copies of copies. In the meantime the office of record in which the original was filed was burned with all its contents. When the time for division drew near, a prying attorney gave out among the heirs the report that no two existing copies of the will were alike. This alarmed them all and set them busily at work to ascertain the truth of the report. On comparing copy with copy they found the report true, but on close inspection it was discovered that the differences consisted in errors of spelling or grammatical construction; some mistakes in figures corrected by the written numbers; and some other differences not easily accounted for; but that in none of the copies did these mistakes affect the rights of the heirs. In the essential matters for which the will was written the representations of all the copies were precisely the same. The result was that they divided the estate with perfect satisfaction to all, and they were more certain that they had executed the will of their grandfather than if the original copy had been alone preserved; for it might have been tampered with in the interest of a single heir, but the copies, defective though they were, could not have been. So with the New Testament. The discovery of errors in the copies excited alarm leading to inquiry, which developed the fact that he who has the most imperfect copy has in it all that the original contained of doctrine, duty and privilege.

---

[7] *Introduction to Greek New Testament*, 284.

THREE

The Sources of the Various Readings

The student can scarcely realize how the number of various readings can be so great and yet the number of serious differences so small as we have represented in the preceding chapters, until he becomes acquainted in detail with the sources whence the various readings have arisen.

Much the greater part of the variants, as the reader must already have perceived, is the result of accident; but there are some which must be regarded as intentional alterations. They are therefore divided into the two general classes of accidental and intentional alterations; and in seeking to trace them to their more especial sources we will consider these two classes separately.

The sources of the accidental alterations may be classified as follows:

1. *Momentary Inattention.* Every person who has had experience in copying knows that it is difficult to keep the attention closely fixed on the task for a protracted period, and that if it is diverted even for a moment, mistakes are almost certain to occur. This is a prolific source of such mistakes as the omission of letters and words, the repetition of the same, the substitution of words for others composed chiefly of the same letters, the substitution of letters for others of similar form, and the transposition of words.

2. *Diversion of attention from the words to the subject matter.* An intelligent copyist must unavoidably follow the train of thought

in that which he copies, and the moment that he becomes more absorbed in this than in the exact words employed, he is exposed to such mistakes as the omission of particles not necessary to the sense, the substitution of one synonym for another, and the addition or omission of pronouns, and the insertion of nouns where their pronouns were understood.

3. *Writing from dictation.* The task of the copyist was a very tedious one, and he naturally resorted to every available means of hastening his progress. One of these was to employ an assistant who would read a few words at a time while he copied. In this case he had only the sound of the words to guide him, and he was exposed to errors through his reader's fault as well as his own. If the reader mispronounced a word, or pronounced it indistinctly, it was likely to be misspelt or mistaken for another. If he omitted or repeated a word, it was omitted or repeated by the copyist.[1]

4. *Homoioteleuton.* For want of a suitable English word critics have adopted this Greek word for another source of clerical errors, the similar ending of clauses, sentences and lines. The copyist, when he finishes a certain clause, or sentence, or line, bears in his mind as he turns his eye back to the manuscript before him, the ending of what he has just written, and seeing a similar ending close by he starts from it, omitting some words, a whole clause, the whole of a short sentence, or possibly the whole of a line.

5. *Change of pronunciation.* Words in a living language undergo many changes of pronunciation; and when a dead language is employed by scholars of different tongues it is subjected to as many different modes of pronunciation as the tongues employed; and in all these cases there is a constant tendency toward the misspelling of words to suit the changed pronunciation.

---

[1] Dr. Scrivener remarks in regard to this source of error: "One is not very willing to believe that manuscripts of the better class were executed on so slovenly and careless a plan"; and he thinks that "the confusion of certain vowels and diphthongs having nearly the same sound" can be accounted for on other suppositious. Doubtless he is correct; and it may be added, that no scribe would trust himself to this method who did not regard himself as very proficient in Greek orthography; yet, while all this is true of manuscripts of the "better class," it may not be true of those of inferior classes, and a supposition so natural in itself, and adopted by all other critics, can not be set aside entirely by the counter-supposition of a single critic. See Scriv. Int., 10.

6. *Trusting to memory.* The copyist necessarily carries words in his memory from the moment that his eye turns away from the text before him until the last word of the number thus carried is written. The greater the number of words thus carried at once the more rapid his progress and the less wearisome his task. He is therefore tempted to trust too much to memory. The same is true in writing from dictation. From this cause must have sprung a large number of errors of nearly all the kinds mentioned above.

7. *Absence of spaces and punctuation.* Early manuscripts were written in continuous rows of capital letters, without spaces between the words and sentences. The earliest example of separated words is found in a manuscript of the ninth century, and it was not until about this period that the punctuation marks now employed came into use, the earliest existing Greek manuscripts having no stops at all, and the oldest existing manuscripts of the New Testament having only a single point here and thereat the top of the letters to denote a pause in the sense.[2] That such a mode of writing must have been a prolific source of mistakes in copying, and must have aggravated the effects of the other causes mentioned above, is obvious. The English scholar will have a more lively appreciation of it if he will imagine himself copying a book printed as follows:

HOWBEITTHATWASNOTFIRSTWHICHISSPIRI-
TUALBUTTHATWCHICHISNATURALANDAFTER-
WARDTHATWHICHISSPIRITUALTHEFIRSTMANI-
SOFTHEEARTHEARTHYTHESECONDMANISTHE-
LORDFROMHEAVENASISTHEEARTHYSUCHAREAL-
SOTHEYTHATAREEARTHY

The sources of intentional alterations are not numerous, and the number of such alterations is comparatively small. All these sources are to be found in the various purposes for which the alterations were made, and all may be included in the following:

1. *To correct a supposed mistake.* Every copyist, knowing that preceding copyists were liable to mistakes, was tempted to correct

---

[2] Scrivener's *Int.*, 46, 47.

such mistakes when he discovered them, or when he thought he discovered them. These supposed mistakes were of two kinds: first, errors in grammatical construction; and second, errors of omission, addition, or substitution. When a sentence appeared to the scribe ungrammatical, or even inelegant, he sometimes corrected it without altering the sense. Sometimes, also, MSS. were thus corrected by interlineation, and copies of these MSS. perpetuated and multiplied these corrections.[3] Errors of the other kind originated chiefly from confounding marginal notes with marginal corrections. It was quite common for owners of MSS. to write notes and comments on the margin, or between the lines; and it was also common for copyists when they had accidentally omitted a word or a number of words, to insert these in the same way. Now and then, a subsequent copyist would mistake one of these marginal notes for a marginal correction, and purposely put it into the body of his text. It is supposed, for example, that the portion of 1 John 5.7 relating to the Heavenly Witnesses, the whole of Acts 8.37, the doxology to the Lord's prayer, and John 5.4, as represented in King James' version, were interpolated in this way.

2. *To secure fullness of expression.* In many instance the scribes have copied into a passage in one of the Gospels words which belong to the parallel place in another, but which appeared to him necessary to fill out the sense. Thus, in the sentence, "I came not to call the righteous, but sinners to repentance," the words "to repentance" are copied into Matthew 9.13 and Mark 2.17, from Luke 5.32 where they are genuine. Again, the prophetic citation in Matthew 27.35 is interpolated from John 19.24.[4] In other instances, separate narratives of the same event, written in the same book, are made to supplement one another. In the account of Paul's conversion given in Acts 9.3–6, the words, "it is hard for thee to kick against the goad," were taken from 26.14; and the

---

[3] The student who understands Greek syntax may find a number of examples of this class of corrections in Scrivener's Introduction, 13 (12).

[4] Scrivener makes the very apposite remark, that the tendency to thus fill up one narrative from another must have been aggravated by the laudable effort of Biblical scholars (beginning with Tatian's Diatesseron in the second century) to construct a satisfactory harmony of them all. Int., 12 (9).

words, "Lord, what wilt thou have me to do," from 22.10. In other instances, the transcribers, in copying quotations made from the Old Testament by New Testament writers, have extended the quotations. The words, "draweth nigh to me with their mouth" (Matt 15.8); "to heal the broken hearted" (Luke 4.18); "him shall ye hear" (Acts 7.37), are examples. In these instances the added words are found in the Old Testament, and the New Testament writers had seen fit to omit them, but the transcribers took the liberty to insert them.

3. *To support a doctrine.* There is only a very small number of variations which can be suspected of a doctrinal origin; and fortunately none of these affects materially the doctrine of the Scripture as a whole on the subject involved. Yet the difference between manuscripts in regard to the following readings can scarcely be accounted for on any other hypothesis. In Matthew 19.17, some MSS. read: "Why callst thou me good? There is none good but one, that is God." Others, "Why askest thou me concerning that which is good? One there is who is good." In John 1.18, some read "the only begotten son"; others, "the only begotten God." In Acts 20.28 some read "the church of God which he hath purchased with his own blood"; others, "the Church of the Lord," etc. It is highly probable that, no matter which of the readings in each of these instances is the original, intemperate zeal on the question of the Trinity led to the insertion of the other in the copies which have it. It is possible that in some of them the scribe regarded the objectionable reading as a mistake of his predecessor, yet doctrinal prejudice is the most probable cause of his so thinking.

When we consider all of the foregoing sources of corruption to which the sacred text was exposed for fourteen hundred years, the multitude of accidental mistakes to which a long line of copyists were exposed, the constant temptation of ambitious scholars to make what they might think improvements in the style, and the almost irresistible inclination on the part of sectaries engaged in fierce controversy to make the Scriptures conform to their dogmas, we have reason to be surprised, not that there are so many

various readings, but that they are so few and of so little importance. Nothing short of a miracle could have prevented their existence, and nothing short of reverence for divine things can have
so limited their number and character.

FOUR

Means of Restoring the Original Text

The materials employed by Biblical critics for the restoration of the original text are the same ancient documents in which the various readings are found. Though imperfect and conflicting they contain the evidence by which the perfect original is to be restored. These materials are

I. Ancient Greek Manuscripts,
II. Ancient Translations,
III. Quotations made by Ancient Writers,
IV. Internal Evidence.

We will consider these materials or sources of criticism separately in the order in which we have named them, and will then show briefly and in general terms the manner in which a decision is reached by means of their combined testimony.

I. Ancient Greek Manuscripts. The autographs of the New Testament writers perished in all probability at an early day. Unless they were written on the best of parchment or vellum,[1] and were kept with special reference to long-continued preservation, their destruction was inevitable. While parchment was certainly used by the apostle Paul, as we see from a remark in 2 Timothy 4.13, yet paper (the Egyptian papyrus, made from the inner bark

---

[1] The term "parchment" is confined to the writing material made from the skins of sheep and goats, and "vellum" to that from the skins of very young calves or antelopes. The latter is the more costly and the more durable.

of a reed), was used by the apostle John in writing his shorter epistles. 2 John 1.12. It is highly probable that on this latter material, which is quite brittle and perishable, much of the New Testament was written; and although some specimens of very ancient papyrus manuscripts, having been buried in Egyptian tombs or in the ruins of Herculaneum, have been preserved, yet documents like the apostolic writings, which must have passed rapidly from hand to hand, for the purpose both of reading and copying, could scarcely fail to perish in a short time. Even those written on parchment would soon be defaced by this process and cease to be prized on account of the superior freshness of the copies taken from them. The thought of serious errors in the copies was not entertained, and consequently the idea of preserving the originals as a standard of accuracy was not suggested.

Not only have the autographs most probably perished, but all the copies made directly from them, and indeed all made during the first three hundred years of the church's history have met with the same fate so far as we know. Multitudes of the sacred books were hunted and destroyed by the heathen in the various persecutions through which the early church passed, and this must have created a tendency to the use of cheap and perishable materials in making copies of them.

As we have remarked in a previous chapter, the earliest Greek manuscripts were written entirely with capital letters; but during the ninth and tenth centuries a change in the size and form of the letters was gradually introduced to lessen the labor of copying. The new style was called the *cursive,* or running hand, while the old was named *uncial,* or inch long, an exaggeration of the size of the letters.[2] Manuscripts written in the old form are called Uncials; those in the new form, Cursives. The cursive style of writing seems to have been employed on other works much earlier than

---

[2] "Speaking generally, and limiting our statement to Greek manuscripts of the New Testament, uncial letters prevailed from the fourth to the tenth or (in the case of liturgical books) as late as the eleventh century; cursive letters were employed as early as the ninth or tenth century, and continued in use until the invention of printing superseded the humble labors of the scribe." (Scrivener, *Int.,* 58.)

on the Scriptures; for the earliest cursive manuscript of the New Testament now known to exist bears date AD 978.[3]

Of uncial MSS. of the New Testament only eighty-three are now known to critics;[4] but this is a large number compared with that of classical works of like antiquity. Of Homer, for example, only a few fragments exist in this form, while the oldest complete copy of his works is a cursive of the thirteenth century.[5] There is but one uncial copy of Virgil, and one each of Æschylus and Sophocles.[6]

Of these eighty-three uncial MSS. there are but few that originally contained the whole New Testament, and only one that contains it now. Much the greater part were originally copies of single books, or of groups of books, and most of these are now fragmentary. The four Gospels are found in a good degree of completeness in four of them, Acts in nine, the Catholic epistles in seven, the epistles of Paul in nine, and the Apocalypse in five.[7]

The cursive MSS. are far more numerous. Scrivener gives a catalogue and description of 1,997;[8] and of these about thirty contain all of the New Testament,[9] while the remainder, like the uncials, are copies of single books, or of groups of books, many of them in a mutilated condition. Thus we see that while the Scriptures existed only in manuscript, the number of complete copies was comparatively small.

Besides the manuscript copies of New Testament books, a class of works called Lectionaries (reading lessons), were anciently in common use, which serve the purposes of criticism in a similar way. These consisted of passages selected from the historical books

---

[3] *Ib.* 40, note 1.

[4] This is the whole number of distinct manuscripts given in Scriveners list (*Int.* 87–177), though the number as he counts them, repeating several times the count of those containing large portions of the New Testament, is 97.

[5] Scrivener, *Int.* 4.

[6] Dr. Philip Schaff, Int. to American Edition of Greek Testament by Westcott and Hort, p. xiv.

[7] Westcott and Hort, *Int.* 75.

[8] Introduction, 307 cp. Appendix xxx. *note.*

[9] Westcott and Hort, *Int.* 76.

and the epistles, for public reading in the churches on consecutive Sundays throughout the year. Of these about 540 have been preserved, of which about eighty are uncials.[10] The cursives of this class are included in the 1,997 mentioned above, but the uncials must be added to the eighty-three mentioned before, making all the uncial MSS. of portions of the New Testament about 163.

Ancient manuscripts were preserved through the dark ages, not so much by the care as by the neglect of their owners. After being used for a comparatively short time, they were laid away in libraries, because their owners had ceased to read them, and their very existence in many cases passed out of human knowledge. The immense library of the Vatican palace in Rome, founded in 1448, now occupying a room 2,100 feet in length, is one of the largest depositories of such documents, but the most of them have been found in the neglected libraries of convents and monasteries which were established in large numbers throughout southern Europe, northern Africa, and western Asia, during the fourth, fifth and sixth centuries. In these places they have been found by Biblical critics, who have made their contents known to the learned world.

Manuscripts when thus discovered were named after their discoverers, or after the places in which they had been kept; or they were distinguished by the numbers which they bore in the library catalogues. Most of the cursives are now designated by numerals, though some are known by the small letters of the Roman alphabet. The uncials, while still bearing the names first given, are now more conveniently designated by the capital letters of the Roman and Greek alphabets, while one of them is known by the first letter of the Hebrew alphabet. In some instances one capital letter is made to stand for several MSS. by appending small letters to its upper right hand curve. Thus, O O^a O^b O^c O^d O^e O^f represent seven distinct MSS. Unfortunately the letters are not applied to them in the order of their age or that of their discovery.

The age of an ancient MS. is not determined, like that of a modern book, by a date on its title page; for the custom of dating

---

[10] Scrivener's Int. 280 cp. Appendix xxx. *note.*

books did not originate till the tenth century. The earliest Biblical manuscript bearing a date is the copy of the Gospels known as S in the Vatican library, which was written AD 949. But an uncial MS. shows by the very fact that it is one, that it was written previous to the tenth century, while a cursive shows in the same way that it was written since that century. This is the most general classification of MSS. with respect to age. But while all scripture MSS. before the tenth century were written in capital letters, the forms of the letters underwent some changes from time to time, and by these changes the dates of MSS. can be proximately determined.[11] The gradual introduction of punctuation marks, of abbreviations for words of frequent occurrence,[12] of larger letters at the beginning of sections, and of spaces between the words, are among the other marks of date. By such means, and the use of the skill acquired by protracted and minute observation, a critic is enabled to determine, within very narrow limits, the date of any MS. There is a striking analogy to this in the history of printed books. If we open a book in which the letter s is printed *f*, we know that it was printed not later than about the year 1830, after which this form of the letter passed out of use. If we open one, however old in appearance, and find steel engravings in it, we know that it can not have been printed earlier than the beginning of the present century, for engraving on steel was first invented in the year 1805.[13] Again, if we find in a book the capital V used for both v and u, the small u used for both u and v, we know that it belongs to the earliest period of printing; for such was then the custom in regard to these two letters. So accurately are the indications of date in ancient MSS. now interpreted, that there is no serious disagreement among competent critics regarding the century, or even the half century in which any well known MS. was written.

---

[11] See Scrivener's Introduction, § 10, pp. 29–39, where these changes are minutely traced with respect to every letter of the alphabet.

[12] Among the most common of these are θς, κς, ις, πνα, for θεός, κύριος, ἰησοῦς, χριστός, πνεῦμα.

[13] New American Cyclopedia, Art. *Engraving.*

There are four uncials whose antiquity is so great and whose value is so preeminent that every student of the Scriptures should have at least a general knowledge of them, and this we now proceed to give:

1. The *Codex Sinaiticus,* or Sinaitic Manuscript, usually designated by ℵ (*aleph)* the first letter of the Hebrew alphabet. This is the one uncial MS. which contains all the books of the New Testament. It also contains a large portion of the Greek version of the Old Testament, and it has appended to the New Testament the Epistle of Barnabas, and a portion of The Shepherd by Hermas, two documents of which we shall have occasion to speak in Part Second of this work. It is written on vellum, and its leaves are 13½ inches wide by nearly 15 in length. It is supposed that before it lost the absent portions of the Old Testament and of The Shepherd, it contained 730 leaves, or 1460 pages—a very large book. But now it contains only 790 pages. It was found by Tischendorf in the Convent of St. Catharine at the foot of Mt. Sinai, in the year 1859, and it is now kept in the imperial library at St. Petersburg; but through the munificence of the late Czar Alexander three hundred *fac simile* copies of it have been distributed among the public libraries of Europe and America.[14] Biblical critics unite in ascribing it to the middle or the first half of the fourth century. In point of value it has but one rival for the highest place among all existing manuscripts of the New Testament.

2. *Codex Alexandrinus,* or the Alexandrian Manuscript, designated by A. It is in four volumes, of which the first, three contain the Septuagint version of the Old Testament almost complete, and the fourth the New Testament with some wide gaps. It lacks all of Matthew up to xxv. 6, two leaves of John's Gospel, including vi. 50–viii. 52, and three leaves from II. Corinthians, including iv. 13–xii.6. Appended to the New Testament are the first Epistle of Clement, and a portion of the second. Its leaves, of which there are 793, are about 13 inches long and 10 broad,

---

[14]There is a copy each in the Congressional Library at Washington, the Astor Library, New York, the libraries of the Union Theological Seminary, Harvard University and the Andover Theological Seminary.

and the writing is in two columns to the page. It was sent as a present to Charles I. of England, in 1628, by Cyril Lucar, the Greek Patriarch of Constantinople, who had previously brought it from Alexandria. It is kept in the British Museum, where the open volume of the New Testament portion can be seen under glass by every visitor. Its date is assigned by the common judgment of critics to the beginning of the fifth century or the close of the fourth. It occupies the third place in point of value among the great manuscripts.

3. *Codex Vaticanus*, or the *Vatican Manuscript*, known as B. This, like the two preceding, was originally designed for a complete Greek Bible; but it now lacks the first forty-six chapters of Genesis, and thirty-two of the Psalms (105137.); and the New Testament part terminates at Hebrews 9.14. The remainder of the New Testament has been appended by a later hand. It is written on very thin and delicate vellum, supposed to have been made from the skins of antelopes, and it makes a volume ten and a half inches long, ten broad, and four and a half thick, with 1518 pages. It was placed in the Vatican library shortly after its first establishment in 1448, and there it is still very carefully preserved. Of its previous history nothing is known. Few persons have been allowed to handle it, though the open volume is kept on exhibition under glass in a magnificent hall filled with other rich treasures of the Vatican. In point of antiquity, it is the rival of the Sinaitic, both belonging to the middle or the first half of the fourth century, and the opinions of scholars being divided as to which is the older. The narrow jealousy of the Popes and their Councils has prevented minute examination of it by Protestant critics, and it was not until the year 1881 that a printed edition of the New Testament portion, marked by many imperfections, was given to the world by some Italian scholars.[15] But notwithstanding the imperfect knowledge

---

[15] In Scrivener's Introduction, 105–116, there is a full account of the futile efforts made during nearly half a century to obtain an accurate acquaintance with the readings of this venerable document. The jealousy of the Papal authorities has to this day excluded Protestant scholars from the privilege of carefully collating it, and the collations made by Catholics have proved unsatisfactory.

of it which has been obtained it is now regarded by some critics as the most reliable of all existing manuscripts.

4. Next in point of antiquity and value is Codex Ephraemi, C, in the National Library of Paris. It contains a small portion of the Old Testament in Greek, and fragments of every book of the New Testament except 2 Thessalonians and 2 John, amounting to about two-thirds of the whole New Testament. It is written, like the three preceding, on vellum, and its leaves are about the size of those in A. It is what is called a *palimpsest* manuscript, or a *codex rescriptus;* that is, a copy on which another work has been written over the faded letters of the original writing. This MS. consists of detached leaves of an ancient Greek Bible written over with some works of a Syrian Christian of the fourth century called St. Ephraem, whence its name. The new writing was done about the twelfth century, but it did not entirely efface the original. Where the latter had faded too much to be read it has been restored by the use of chemicals, and the contents of the manuscript have been copied and printed. Its date is about the same as that of A, and it is believed by some to be more accurate. It was brought from some unknown library in the East to Florence in 1535, and was soon afterward brought to Paris together with a number of other ancient MSS. which are still kept in the National Library of France.

It is evident at a glance that the ancient Greek MSS. which we have now mentioned, and especially the four which we have just described, must constitute the most reliable class of witnesses concerning the exact reading of the original Scriptures. Where they all agree, as they do according to Dr. Hurt's estimate quoted in a former chapter, in seven-eighths of the whole New Testament, there can be no room for doubt that we have the original perfectly preserved. Where they differ in sense, it is the business of the critic to estimate the preponderance of their testimony in favor of this reading or that. In most instances this preponderance is so great as to leave little if any room for doubt. In estimating it reference is had not merely to the *number* of MSS. on either side, but also to their antiquity and their known accuracy.

When a MS. has been found by comparison with others to be generally accurate, its testimony in a particular place has greater weight, and *vice versa*. And when a MS., though not very ancient itself, contains evidence of having been copied from one that is ancient, its readings are enhanced in value. It has also been found that MSS. are distributable into groups called families, each family having sprung from a parent copy of more ancient date. Those of the same family are known by having certain variant readings in common which are not found in members of other families. Critics are on this account led to the study of the genealogy of MSS.; for it is evident that the testimony of a whole family in favor of a certain reading, is no stronger than that of the parent of the family.[16] These remarks are sufficient to show that many years of study, combined with a well balanced judgment, are necessary to proficiency as a Biblical critic.

II. Ancient Versions. A translation of the Scriptures from Greek into another language, enables a scholar who understands both languages to determine approximately the wording of the Greek text from which the translation was made. It enables him especially to determine whether a given clause or sentence, or a leading word in a sentence, was absent or not from the Greek copy that was used.[17] The MSS. of ancient translations, however, have suffered, like the Greek MSS., at the hands of transcribers; and consequently in the use of them the critic has to make due allowance for the changes thus introduced. Though this detracts from what would otherwise be the authority of these witnesses, it still leaves them with an authority second only to that of the Greek MSS., and the authority of some of them is enhanced by the fact

---

[16] Dr. Hort has given more attention to the subject of genealogies than any other critic since Griesbach, and the student who wishes to be fully informed on the subject should consult his Introduction to the Greek New Testament of Westcott and Hort, Sec. iii.

[17] "While versions are always of weight in determining the authenticity of sentences or clauses inserted or omitted by Greek manuscripts, and in most instances may be employed even for arranging the order of words, yet every language differs so widely in spirit from every other, and the genius of one version is so much at variance with that of others, that too great caution can not be used in applying this kind of testimony to the criticism of the Greek" (Scrivener, *Int.*, 310).

that they are older than any known MS., and testify to readings correspondingly more ancient. Modern versions are of no value for this purpose, seeing that they are made either from comparatively modern MSS., or from ancient MSS. which can themselves be consulted.[18]

The ancient versions, which are chiefly used by critics, are the following:

1. The Peshito Syriac. This is a translation of both the Old and the New Testament into Syriac or Aramean, the language anciently spoken in Northern Syria and Upper Mesopotamia. Many evidences combine to prove that it was made in the second century of our era, and that it was therefore derived, as regards the New Testament, from a Greek text which had been transmitted not quite one hundred years from the pens of the original writers.[19] From its date to the present time it has been the common Bible of the Syrian Christians, and they have used it exclusively in their public worship. It must have received the name Peshito (*simple*) from a comparison with some versions not so simple, yet there is another and later Syriac version that is more literal.[20] It lacks four of the smaller Epistles (2 Peter, 2 and 3 John, and Jude) and also the Apocalypse. It is the most valuable of all versions for the purposes of Biblical Criticism.

2. The Old Latin. This is a translation of the Bible into Latin, made in the second century, as is known from its being cited by Latin writers as far back as Tertullian, who lived from about 150 to 220 AD It was made, not in Italy, as would be naturally supposed, but in North Africa, where the Latin language prevailed,

---

[18] Tregelles rejects the use of all versions made this side of the seventh century (*History of the Printed Text*, § 13). But the majority of critics allow the readings of some versions of more recent date to be considered.

[19] Dr. Hort has propounded the theory that the original underwent a revision in the third century, and that the Peshito is the result of this revision, while a MS. in the British Museum known as the Curetonian Syriac represents the original unrevised Syriac Version (Int. to Greek New Testament, 84, 132–135). This theory, though accepted by some critics, is strongly contested by others, especially by Scrivener (Int. 319 ff, 533 ff); but while the question at issue is one of importance, its decision either way will not modify materially the statements which we make concerning the version in this treatise.

[20] The Philoxenian, or Harclean (Scrivener, *Int.* 318–325).

and where there was a vast multitude of Christian converts at a very early day. It was superseded in both public and private use by a later Latin version, and consequently it has not been preserved entire; but thirtyeight fragments of it, representing portions of almost every book of the New Testament, are yet in existence,[21] and large portions of it are quoted in the writings of the early Latin fathers. It was made about the same time as the Syriac version, and they both represent Greek copies two hundred years older than the oldest existing Greek manuscripts, the one answering to the Greek scriptures current in Syria, and the other to those current in Africa.

3. The Latin Vulgate. When the old Latin version had been in use about two hundred years, it was found that different copies of it contained many variations, and to remedy the evil Damasus, Bishop of Rome, ordered a revision of it to be made. The task was entrusted to Jerome, in the year 382, and he completed it in 385. This version gradually took the place of the Old Latin, and at length acquired the title Vulgate, or Common Version. This is the version, which, after passing through some later revisions, was canonized in 1546 by the Council of Trent, which decreed that "in public readings, disputations, preaching and exposition it should be held as *authentic.*" Since that time all Roman Catholic translations into other tongues are made from it, and not from the original Greek. As Jerome, in preparing it, made use of what he then called "ancient Greek manuscripts," it represents a Greek text much older than itself, and older than the earliest MSS. now extant. The manuscript copies of it of which many have been preserved, are considered more valuable than the Old Latin, as aids to criticism.[22]

4. The Egyptian or Coptic Versions. When the Arabs conquered Egypt in the seventh century, they gave the name Copts to the Egyptian Christians, and their language has been called Coptic ever since. It had been written in alphabetic characters since about the time of the first establishment of Christianity in Egypt.

---

[21] A catalogue and description of these fragments is given in Scrivener's Introduction, 342 ff.

[22] Scrivener, *Int.,* 360.

Before that time the common written language of the people had been partly alphabetic and partly hieroglyphic. The language was spoken in two dialects, one in Lower Egypt, called the Bahiric, from Bahirah, the Egyptian name of Lower Egypt, and the Memphitic, from Memphis, the principal city; and the other, in Upper Egypt, called Sahidic, from Sahid, the name of the district, and Thebaic, from Thebes, the principal city. The scriptures were translated at a very early period into both of these dialects, and it is the opinion of Bishop Lightfoot, the most proficient student of the Coptic dialects in Great Britain, that at least portions of them were thus translated before the close of the second century.[23] Both these versions contain all the books of the New Testament, though the Apocalypse is usually in a separate volume, as if it were not considered an undoubted part of the New Testament. They are almost as ancient as the Peshito Syriac and the Old Latin, and Lightfoot regards them as of superior value in Biblical criticism to those venerable versions.[24] Thus it appears that we have four translations of the New Testament that were made previous to the date of our oldest existing Greek copies.

5. The Æthiopic Version. The Æthiopia language is closely related to the Arabic, and was anciently spoken in the country now called Abyssinia, where the Christian religion became prevalent in the fourth century. A vernacular translation of the New Testament soon became a necessity, and one was made near the end of the fourth century or the beginning of the fifth. All the books of both Testaments were included in it.

---

[23] The section on The New Testament in Coptic, in Scrivener's Introduction, was prepared by Lightfoot, then a Professor at Oxford, and from it the above account of the Coptic versions is derived. He expresses the opinion quoted above on p. 371.

[24] He says: "Of all the versions, the Memphitic is perhaps the most important for the textual critic. In point, of antiquity it must yield the palm to the Old Syriac and the Old Latin; but, unlike them, it preserves the best text as current among the Alexandrian fathers, free from the corruptions which prevailed so widely in the copies of the second century" (Page 392). Of the Thebaic he says: "Its textual value is perhaps only second to the Memphitic among the early versions. It unquestionably preserves a very ancient text, but it is less pure, and exhibits a certain infusion of those readings which were so widely spread in the second century, and which (for want of a better term) are often called Western, though to nothing like the same extent as the Old Latin and the Old Syriac" (Page 400).

6. The Gothic Version. While the Goths were invading Southern Europe, they were in turn invaded by the missionaries of the cross, and so many of them were turned to the faith, that Ulphilas, a Cappadocian, who had gone among them in the year 345, made an alphabet of their language and translated into it both the Old Testament and the New. As he died in the year 388 his version belongs to the latter half of the fourth century. There is still extant an uncial manuscript of this version, made near the beginning of the sixth century, written on purple vellum in letters of silver with occasionally some in gold. It belongs to Sweden, and is kept in the library of the University of Upsal.

7. The Armenian Version. The Armenians claim to have been the first people who accepted the gospel as a national faith, but they were then without an alphabet of their own language. They read the Scriptures in Syriac, using the Peshito version until the fifth century, when Miesrob, one of their own countrymen, invented an Armenian alphabet, and with the assistance of other scholars, translated into the native tongue the whole Bible. Unfortunately, no very ancient manuscripts of this version have been preserved.

The versions which we have now named represent in the aggregate the copies of the Greek Scriptures which were known and used in every part of the world that had been evangelized up to the close of the fourth century. Their value for the purpose of determining the condition of the original during the two hundred and fifty preceding years can scarcely be overestimated.

III. Quotations made by Ancient Authors. Ancient Christian writers were in the habit of quoting the scriptures in their Writings very much as we quote them now, and it is clear that every literal quotation made by one of them from the Greek Testament shows the reading in that place of the manuscript which he used. Even an allusion to a certain passage may sometimes enable the critic to determine whether a clause now in doubt was present in the passage or not. In a few instances these writers expressly mention differences of reading, and then their testimony is explicit, and, to the extent of their information, reliable. This source of evidence, so far as it can be safely used, is of very great value, and the more so from the fact that some of these writers lived at a period preceding the date of our earliest manuscripts. Had their writings come down to us entire they would have been still more valuable, but some of the best of them have reached our day in a very fragmentary form.[25] Their value has been further depreciated by the fact that their MSS., like those of the scriptures and of the versions, have undergone some changes, and that none of a very early date have been preserved.[26] Much has yet to be done in the way of thoroughly searching those that remain to us, before all the evidence from this source will be in hand.

IV. Internal Evidence. The evidence furnished by the readings of Greek manuscripts, ancient versions, and quotations made by ancient authors is called external evidence. When it is decisive, that is, when the preponderance of evidence for a certain reading from all of these sources is so great as to leave no room for doubt, there is no occasion for evidence from any other source. But when the evidence from these three sources is indecisive resort must be had to what is called internal evidence. This is the evidence found by exercising the judgment on two questions of probability; first, which of two conflicting readings is the more likely to have been substituted for the other by a transcriber; and second, which is the more likely to have been employed by the original writer. In judging of the former question, we are to consider all the sources of error to which copyists were exposed. In judging of the latter, we are to consider the usual style and mode of thought of the writer, and also the bearing of the context. Dr. Hort, with fine discrimination, styles this kind of evidence internal evidence of readings, and he distinguishes the two questions of probability just mentioned by the terms intrinsic probability, referring to what the au-

---

[25] For example, of Origen's continuous Commentary on the Greek New Testament, written at the beginning of the third century, only about one sixth has been preserved in the original Greek. The whole of it would now be invaluable (Hort, *Int.*, 88.).

[26] "Codices of the Fathers are for the most part of much lower date than those of the Scriptures which we desire to amend by their aid; not many being older than the tenth century, the far greater part considerably more modern."(Scrivener, *Int.*, 418.)

thor would have written, and transcriptional probability, referring to the work of the transcriber.[27] When these two kinds of probability are in conflict they tend to neutralize each other; but when they unite, that is, when the reading which is most likely to have been used by the author is at the same time most likely to have been exchanged by transcribers for the other, the internal evidence exists in its strongest form, and it is often indispensable in determining questions in which the external evidence is conflicting. Recent critics are agreed, however, that corrections of the text should seldom or never be made on this kind of evidence alone.[28]

We now have before our minds all the materials which are employed by Biblical critics in restoring the original text, and it is evident that a large amount of patient labor and a sound judgment are necessary in order to the skillful application of them all to the noble end proposed. For examples of this application the student is referred to the critical works to be mentioned in the following chapter.

---

[27] Dr. Hort's own words on these distinctions are remarkably clear. After introducing the expression Internal Evidence, he says: "As other kinds of Internal Evidence will have to be mentioned, we prefer to call it more precisely Internal Evidence of Readings. Internal Evidence of Readings is of two kinds, which can not be too sharply distinguished from each other; appealing respectively to Intrinsic Probability, having reference to the author, and what may be called Transcriptional Probability, having reference to the copyists. In appealing to the first, we ask what an author is likely to have written; in appealing to the second, we ask what copyists are likely to have made him seem to write" (New Testament in Original Greek, *Int.* 20).

[28] On this point Dr. Scrivener speaks very positively: "It is now agreed among competent critics that Conjectural Emendation must never be resorted to even in passages of acknowledged difficulty; the absence of proof that a reading proposed to be substituted for the common one is actually supported by some trustworthy document being of itself a fatal objection to our receiving it" (*Int.* 490). Dr. Hort expresses himself less positively. Speaking of Transcriptional Probability he says: "But even at its best this class of Internal Evidence, like the other, carries us but a little way toward the recovery of an ancient text, when it is employed alone. The number of variations in which it can be trusted to supply by itself a direct and immediate decision is very small, when unquestionable blunders, that is, clerical errors, have been set aside" (*Int.* 25).

FIVE

The Labors of Biblical Critics, and the Results Obtained

We are now prepared for a brief sketch of the history of Biblical Criticism, showing particularly the successive stages of its progress, and the results which have thus far been attained.

As we have stated before, the art of printing is the parent of this science, seeing that it was by means of printed copies that the attention of scholars was first awakened to the importance of the subject and led to the study of it. The early printed editions, being copied from different manuscripts and printed in different countries, at first produced confusion by their differences, and afterward led to the adoption without very good reasons of a "Received Text," which became a standard for all others. The steps by which this result was reached were briefly as follows: The Greek Testament of Erasmus, published in 1516, at Basle, Switzerland, and the Complutentian Polyglott, printed at Complutum (Alcala) in Spain, in 1514, but not published till 1522, were, as we have said before, the first printed editions of the New Testament. These editions had circulated about a quarter of a century without rivals, when Robert Stephen, a celebrated printer at Paris, brought out an edition in 1546, followed rapidly by three others, the last in 1551. In this last the Greek Testament was first divided into verses numbered on the margin, the division into chapters having been introduced in the Latin Bible in 1248. The purpose of both divisions was to facilitate references to particular passages.[1] His third edition (1550) became the standard or received text in England, and from it chiefly the English version was made in 1611. In 1633 a very small Greek Testament was published at Leyden in Holland, by two brothers named Elzevir, in which the verses were marked by breaks in the text, and not merely by numbers in the margin as before. In a somewhat boastful spirit, the Elzevirs remarked in their preface, "Now you have a text received by all, in which we give nothing changed or corrupted." The words helped forward their own fulfillment, and this edition became the Received Text on the Continent of Europe. The differences between its readings and those of the edition of Stephen are not very numerous nor very important. Neither of these standard editions was prepared with such care and skill as to entitle it to special preeminence, yet each in the course of time gained such a hold upon the public mind that to change it was considered almost sacrilegious.

It was not until the year 1707 that an edition of the Greek Testament was published containing a really serious attempt to apply the materials of Biblical Criticism to the restoration of the original text. This was the critical edition of John Mill, of Oxford University. He spent thirty years in preparing it, and he died just two weeks after its publication. In preparing it he collated a large number of Greek MSS., versions, and ancient quotations, and printed in his notes their various readings, amounting to about 30,000. He also discussed the value of the evidence adduced, and pointed out the corrections which it indicated, but he printed in the body of his work the text of Stephen without correction. This work excited alarm and opposition among the friends of the Bible, and some infidel writers took advantage of the facts to inveigh against the reliability of the Scriptures;[2] but the final result of the discussion was to render Christian scholars more favorable to the

---

[1] For a detailed account of the origin and progress of these divisions, see Scrivener, *Int.* 60–68.

[2] The leader of this attack was Anthony Collins, the most noted infidel writer of that age. See Farrar's *History of Free Thought*, 132–135.

prosecution of critical studies. It was perceived that discovering various readings was not creating them, but that it was a necessary preparation for correcting them. Scrivener expresses the common judgment of critics when he says, "Dr. Mill's services to Biblical Criticism surpass in extent and value those rendered by any other, except perhaps one or two men of our own time."[3]

The attack upon Mill's work, of which we have just spoken, having been made after his death, its defense was taken up by Dr. Richard Bentley, one of the most accomplished scholars and brilliant writers of that age. His defense of Mill increased his own interest in the work of Biblical Criticism, and directed the attention of others to his qualifications as a critic, so that he was at length induced to attempt the preparation of a critical edition of the New Testament. A large amount of preparatory work was done, and many valuable contributions were made to the development of the science, but other engagements diverted his attention to such a degree that, to the regret of subsequent critics, he left his work incomplete.[4]

Thus far the work of criticism on the New Testament had been prosecuted almost exclusively in Great Britain; it was now transferred to Germany, and but little more was done in England for about a century. The next critical edition after Mill's was the work of John Albert Bengel, which appeared in 1734, twenty-seven years later. When Mill's work appeared Bengel was a student at the University of Tübingen, and in common with thousands of other pious men he was excited and alarmed by the multitude of various readings which had been brought to light. He commenced the collection of critical materials merely to satisfy his own mind, but was encouraged by others to complete the work and give it to the public.[5] The characteristics of his edition were the following:

---

[3] For an account of the discussion and its results, see Tregelles, *History of the Printed Text,* 46–57.

[4] Both Tregelles (Printed Text 57–65) and Scrivener (453–456) give interesting accounts of the career and critical labors of Bentley.

[5] Tregelles, *History of Printed Text,* 69.

He made some changes in the Received Text, but only such as he found in some previous printed edition; he printed the text in paragraphs, instead of the detached verses used by the Elzevirs; he printed in the margin the various readings which he thought worthy of notice, with signs to indicate their relative value; he gave the evidence in favor of a received reading as well as that against it; and he was the first critic to point out the fact that MSS. are distributable into families. He was a man of undoubted piety and great faith in the inspiration of the Scriptures. Besides his critical work he wrote a valuable commentary called The Gnomon of the New Testament, a revised edition of which in English has been recently published.

John James Wetstein was the author of the next critical edition, published at Amsterdam in two folio volumes, 1751-2. He was a native of Basle in Switzerland, where he was ordained to the ministry at twenty years of age. He had already become so enamored with critical studies that his ordination sermon was on the subject of Various Readings of the New Testament, and "his zeal for this fascinating pursuit," says Scrivener, "became at length with him a passion, the master passion which consoled and dignified a roving, troubled, unprosperous life." He visited both England and France in his search for MSS., and in the midst of his labors he was deposed from his "pastorate" on account of Unitarian sentiments. He finally obtained a Professorship at Amsterdam, where his work was completed and where, two years later, he ended his life. He was the first to employ the method now in use of designating uncial MSS. by capital letters, and the cursives by Arabic numerals. He collated 102 MSS.,[6] and his collations were more accurate than those of his predecessors. Scrivener expresses the opinion that in the critical portion of his work he must be placed "in the very first rank, inferior (if to any) to but one or two of the highest names."[7]

---

[6] Scrivener, *Int.* 460. Tregelles (Printed Text 77) states the number at *twenty.* The discrepancy is due to different methods of counting. MSS. of the Gospels, of Acts, of Paul's Epistles, of the Catholic Epistles, and of the Apocalypse, are sometimes counted separately even when they are parts of one copy of the New Testament. In this way a MS. containing all would be counted as five if cited for every part, and yet it may be counted as one.

[7] Scrivener, *ib.* 460. To this testimonial may be added the statement of Davidson (Biblical Criticism ii. 125): "Notwithstanding the defects and inaccuracies observable in the

The next eminent critic after Wetstein was John James Griesbach, whose name stood for many years at the head of the list of Biblical critics. His principal edition appeared in two volumes, the first in 1796 and the second in 1806. While he was engaged in its preparation many MSS. hitherto unnoticed were collated by other scholars. The libraries of Russia, Austria, Italy and Spain were ransacked in search of them, and the results published in various volumes were appropriated by Griesbach. He also himself collated quite a number of MSS., versions and ancient authors. The materials before him were therefore more abundant than those possessed by any previous critic, and he used them with a skill hitherto unprecedented. The distinctive purpose of his edition was to place before his readers such evidence from the materials of criticism as would enable the student of his work to decide for himself on the genuineness of any given reading. He also carefully laid down the principles which should guide us in reaching a decision. Following the suggestion of Bengel, he attempted to make a distribution of MSS. into three great families, which he called the Alexandrian, the Western and the Byzantine, according as he thought that their parentage could be traced to Alexandria, to Europe, or to Constantinople. This was the most distinctive feature of his critical theory, and it is the one which has received the greatest amount of adverse criticism from more recent critics. He devoted forty years to constant labor in his chosen field, and died in the year 1812.[8]

The edition of Scholz, a Roman Catholic Professor in the University of Bonn, is the next in order of time. It was the result of twelve years' labor and was published in two volumes, one in 1830, the other in 1836. Scholz is noted among critics for two things

---

work, it is still indispensable to all who are occupied with sacred criticism; and will ever remain a marvelous monument of indomitable energy and diligence, united to an extent of philosophical learning rarely surpassed by any single man"; and the following passage from Tregelles: "Bishop Marsh says of Wetstein, what that critic said of Mill, that he accomplished more than all of his predecessors put together. If this character be too high, it is but little more than the truth" (*History of Printed Text*, 77).

[8] For a fuller account of his career and of the estimate in which his labors are held by later scholars, see the works of Tregelles, Davidson and Scrivener, already referred to so frequently, and Dr. Hort's Introduction.

of contrasted merit—for the vast number of new MSS. which he brought to the notice of scholars (six hundred and sixteen) and in part collated, and for the extreme inaccuracy with which all his work was executed.[9] In search of MSS. he visited the old libraries of France, Italy, Switzerland, Palestine and the Archipelago, doing much service in the way of gathering materials for future critics, but exhibiting little skill in using them.

The next year after the appearance of Scholz's first volume (1831) Charles Lachmann published at Berlin a small Greek Testament, which was followed by a larger edition in two volumes, the first in 1842 and the second in 1800. In the first of these editions he startled the world by the boldest and most original adventure yet made in Biblical Criticism. He cast aside the Received Text entirely as being entitled to no authority other than that of the MSS. from which it was printed, and formed a text from ancient documents alone. This appeared sacrilegious to those who had learned to regard the Received Text almost with the reverence due to the apostolic autographs, and it aroused against its author a storm of denunciation. But true critics at once accepted the principle involved as correct, and from that time all prescriptive claims set up for the Received Text have been disregarded.[10] Another distinctive feature of Lachmann's work was not so well received by critics. His

---

[9] "It is our duty," says Scrivener, "to express our sorrow that twelve years and more of hard and persevering toil should, through mere heedlessness, have been nearly thrown away" (*Introduction, 475*). "His collations have been hasty and superficial. They are often incorrect" (Davidson, *Bib. Crit.* ii. 137). "If Scholz' text is compared with that of Griesbach, it will be seen that it is a retrograde step in the application of criticism; and thus though he maintained a truer system of families than Griesbach did, yet his results are even less satisfactory, because he applied a theory to the classification of authorities by which their respective value was *precisely reversed*" (Tregelles, *History of Printed Text*, 97).

[10] The following remarks of Tregelles on this subject are worthy of notice even at the present day by persons who are but partially informed on the subject of Biblical criticism, and who are prejudiced against what they style changes in the text: "It is in vain to call such a labor 'wholesale innovation,' or to say that it manifests 'want of reverence for Holy Scripture;' for it is not *innovation* to revert to the first sources; it is not *irreverence* for God's word to give it forth on the best and most attested basis. It is not *canceling* words and sentences, when they are not inserted because the oldest and best authorities know nothing of them. Honest criticism has to do with *facts as they are*, with evidence as it has been transmitted, and not with some subjective notion in our own minds of what is true and right—a notion that has no better basis than recent, ill-grounded tradition."

aim was to reproduce, not necessarily the true text, but the text as it existed in the fourth century. He used only such documents as he thought necessary to this result, and where they united in an unquestionable error, he printed this error, because it was a part of the text which he was aiming to reproduce. Subsequent critics agree in the opinion that the documents which he used were insufficient even for the purpose which he had in view,[11] and many have condemned the purpose itself, because they have understood him as aiming at a restoration of the true text.[12] After all that can be said against it "still the fact will remain," says Tregelles, "that the first Greek Testament since the invention of printing, edited wholly on ancient authority irrespective of modern tradition, is due to Charles Lachmann." Like so many of his fellowlaborers he ended his critical labors with his life. He died in 1851, the year following the completion of his second edition.

The name of Constantine Tischendorf stands next in the list of great Biblical critics, and it was the first to tower above that of Griesbach. He published eight editions of the Greek Testament, of which the first appeared in 1841, and the eighth was completed in 1872. On this last edition, which was published in parts, from 1865 to 1872, his fame as a critic chiefly rests, and of it Scrivener remarks: "This is beyond question the most full and comprehensive edition of the Greek Testament existing; it contains the results of the latest collations and discoveries, and as copious a body of various readings as is compatible with the design of adapting it for general use."[13] But while thus extolling the edition as a whole, the same author speaks unfavorably of Tischendorf's stability of judgment, and shows that he paid too much deference to the authority of the Sinaitic MS., of which he was the discoverer.[14]

---

[11] Tregelles, his greatest admirer and zealous defender, says on this point: "A wider scope of ancient evidence should have been taken" (*Ib*. 100).

[12] Davidson, after stating Lachmann's real purpose, says: "Had this, his *true* purpose, been perceived, it would have saved a great deal of misapprehension on the part of his censors, who have written against him through ignorance" (*Bib. Crit.*, ii. 141).

[13] Introduction, 481.

[14] "The evidence of *Codex* ℵ, supported or even unsupported by one or two authorities of any description, proved with him sufficient to outweigh all other witnesses, whether manuscripts, versions, or ecclesiastical writers" (*Int.* 529). "The result of this excessive and

Tischendorf's fame rests not merely on the number and value of the editions of the Greek Testament which he edited, but also and perhaps chiefly on the large number of valuable manuscripts which he caused to be carefully printed, thus relieving scholars who wished to examine them of the necessity of visiting the libraries in which they were kept.[15]

The career of this great critic, from the time that he commenced his critical labors until he attained world-wide celebrity, has been candidly related by himself.[16] It possesses all the interest of a romance, and it is full of encouragement to young men, who, under the crushing weight of extreme poverty, aspire to a life of eminent usefulness. He resolved, in 1839, to devote his life to the textual study of the New Testament, and to attempt, by using all the acquisitions of his predecessors, to reconstruct the exact text which came from the hands of the sacred writers. After publishing his first edition (1841) he was convinced that to accomplish his purpose it would be necessary for him to examine the original documents for himself, and to give them a closer scrutiny than they had yet received. But this required a protracted and expensive tour to foreign lands, and money he had none. He applied to his Government (that of Saxony) and obtained a grant of one hundred dollars a year for two years. With this meager sum, insufficient to allow the purchase of an extra suit of clothing, he started on a literary tour which was destined to occupy four years. He spent two years in Paris, and thence went successively to Holland, England, Italy, Egypt, the Libyan Desert, Mt. Sinai, Palestine, Smyrna, the isle of Patmos, Constantinople and Athens, everywhere searching

---

irrational deference to one of our chief codices, that which he was so fortunate as to bring to light twenty-five years ago, appears plainly in Tischendorf's eighth edition of the New Testament. That great critic had never been conspicuous for stability of judgment" (*ib.* 528).

[15] "It may be truly asserted that the reputation of Tischendorf as a Biblical scholar rests less on his critical editions of the New Testament than on the texts of the chief uncial authorities which in rapid succession he has given to the world" (*ib.* 483).

[16] The narrative was published in Germany in 1864, and a translation of it into English was published by the London Tract Society in 1866, followed by a reprint of the American Tract Society, in the same year. The little volume bears the rather cumbrous title: *"When were our Gospels Written: An Argument by Constantine Tischendorf, with a Narrative of the Discovery of the Siniatic Manuscript."*

through collections of ancient manuscripts and collating many of them. The journey and his purchases cost him about five thousand dollars, which came to him through the use of his pen, and through the gifts of persons who became interested in his work, thus verifying the conviction with which he set out, that "God helps those who help themselves, and that which is right must prosper." His labors on this tour were full of important results, one of the most important of which was the restoration, by chemical applications, of the faded manuscript C, at Paris, and the printing of its text. While visiting the convent of St. Catharine, in 1844, he saw a basket of old parchment leaves, which the monks had set aside to be burned as worthless, and to his great delight he detected among them some sheets of a very ancient copy of the Old Testament in Greek. He obtained about forty-five of the leaves without difficulty, but the ignorant monks inferred from his lively satisfaction that they must be of great value, and they refused to let him have more. These were published when he returned home, and their great antiquity was so clearly demonstrated that he resolved to leave no effort untried to obtain the whole volume to which they belonged. In 1853, nine years later, he was at the convent again, but he could find no trace of the coveted treasure. In 1859 he went again, backed his time by commendations from the Czar of Russia, and supported by his money. After searching in vain for a few days, and almost despairing of success, he found the whole of the precious document in the hands of the steward of the convent. It proved to be the Sinaitic manuscript of the whole Bible in Greek which we have described in Chapter IV. It was with the utmost difficulty, after bringing to bear the influence of high officials in the Greek church, and making several journeys back and forth, that he succeeded in obtaining permission to carry it to Cairo and copy it. He copied its "one hundred and ten thousand lines, many of which were so faded as to be almost illegible, in the months of March, April and May, when the thermometer was never below 77° in the shade. He finally succeeded in obtaining the manuscript itself for the imperial library at St. Petersburg, and on the 19th of November, 1859, he proudly laid it at the feet of Alexander 2, in his winter palace. By the munificence of his imperial patron he was also furnished with the funds necessary to make a large number of *fac simile* copies in four volumes each, which were distributed gratuitously among the more noted libraries of Europe and America. This task was completed in 1802, but Tischendorf afterward published the New Testament part of the manuscript in ordinary type, with critical notes which exhibit its variations from the Elzevir text and from Codex B.

The surprising and gratifying results of his life-long industry secured to Tischendorf from time to time the most flattering encomiums from learned men, University Faculties, and crowned heads in every part of Europe, but he concludes his narrative by saying: "That which I think more highly of than all these flattering distinctions is, the conviction that providence has given to our age, in which attacks on Christianity are so common, the Sinaitic Bible, to be to us a full and clear light as to what is the word written of God, and to assist us in defending the truth by establishing its authentic form." After thirty-four years of unremitting and exhausting labor in his chosen field, his strong frame was prostrated by a stroke of paralysis in 1873; his work was thus brought suddenly to an end, and his useful life closed on the 7th of December, 1874, when he had nearly completed his sixtieth year.

Though Biblical Criticism, which had its birth in Great Britain, as we have seen, soon afterward left her shores, after an absence of more than a hundred years it returned, and English critics, with the clearness of thought and even balance of judgment which characterize their race, seem destined to the high honor of bringing it to perfection.

While Tischendorf was prosecuting his Herculean labors on the continent, S. P. Tregelles, his only rival as a critic, his friend and correspondent, was quietly toiling at the same task in England. Born in Falmouth of Quaker parentage in 1813, just two years before the birth of Tischendorf, at an early age he joined the body called Plymouth Brethren, with whom he was connected the greater part of his life. In 1838, when he was only twenty-five years of age, he published a specimen page of a proposed Critical Greek Testament, the plan of which had been formed as a result of several years of study undertaken at first for his own satisfaction. The distinctive feature of the plan, much like that of Lachmann's, of whose edition he then knew nothing, was the formation of a text based exclusively on ancient manuscripts, but allowing ancient versions a determining voice in regard to clauses and longer passages.[17] He afterward modified his plan so as to admit the testimony of ancient versions without limitation, and to include also the evidence of quotations made during the first three and a half centuries.[18] In 1844 he published the first fruits of his labors in the form of a corrected text of the Apocalypse, accompanied by an English translation. In further prosecution of his studies, he found it necessary in order to settle points of difference among his predecessors, and to guard against repetition of any of their mistakes, to recollate all the MSS. and versions on whose authority he proposed to rely. For this purpose he visited the principal libraries of Europe, conversed much with Lachmann, and compared notes with Tischendorf. After more than twenty years of such toil, he published Part First of his work, containing Matthew and Mark, in 1857, and Part Second containing Luke and John, in 1861. In neither of these parts had he the opportunity of using the Sinaitic MS., which, though found in 1859, had not yet been published. The remainder of the New Testament was brought out in three other parts from 1865 to 1870. Part Fifth was published for him by other editors, who sadly state in

---

[17] There had arisen before my mind a plan for a Greek New Testament, in which it was proposed,—

1st, To form a text on the authority of ancient copies, without allowing the "received text" any prescriptive right;

2nd, To give to the ancient versions a determining voice as to the insertion or non-insertion of clauses, *etc;* letting the order of words. *etc.,* rest wholly on MSS.;

3rd, To give the Authorities for the text, and for the various leadings, clearly and accurately, so that the reader might at once see what rests on ancient evidence (*Account of Printed Text,* 152, 153).

[18] *Ib.* 173.

their Introduction, that in the early part of that year while Dr. Tregelles was in the act of revising the concluding chapters of Revelation, he was visited by a second and very severe stroke of paralysis, which, though it left his intellect unclouded, disabled him from a further prosecution of his work.[19] Thus did another great Biblical critic pay the oft-inflicted penalty of an overtaxed brain, and cease from labor when the noon of life had little more than passed. His assistant editors bear witness to his faith and piety in these words: "For many long years he has reverenced the Scriptures as being veritably the word of God. His prayer has been that he might be the means of protecting it from the consequences of human carelessness, and presenting it as nearly as possible in that form in which it was first given us by God."[20] His personal friend, Dr. Scrivener, who always refers to him in terms of tender regard, says that he met with much disquietude and some mild persecution among the Plymouth Brethren, and adds: "His last years were more happily spent as a humble lay member of the Church of England, a fact he very earnestly begged me to keep in mind."[21] He lingered in helplessness for several years, and died at Plymouth April 24, 1875.

The principles by which Tregelles was guided in forming his text are regarded by other critics as defective, on the ground that they exclude the use of nearly all the cursive MSS. He allowed only such of these to be heard as can be proved to have been copied from ancient uncials, while it is held by the objectors that all the witnesses should be heard, and the testimony of each taken at its proper valuation.[22] But it is conceded on all hands that he performed the tedious work of collation with more accuracy than

---

[19] Advertisement to Part Fifth, 1.

[20] *Ib.*, 2.

[21] *Introduction*, 487.

[22] "Tregelles' 'ancient authorities' are thus reduced to those manuscripts which, not being Lectionaries, happen to be written in uncial characters, with the remarkable exception of Codd., 1, 33, 69 of the Gospels, and 61 of the Acts, which he admits because they preserve an 'ancient text.' We shall hereafter inquire (Ch. vii.) whether the text of the New Testament can safely be grounded on a basis so narrow as that of Tregelles" (Scrivener, *Int.*, 485). In Chap, vii., as promised, the question is discussed elaborately.

did any of his predecessors, and that the text which he produced was the nearest approach yet made to the identical words of the sacred writers.[23]

In the spring of 1853, when Lachmann's text and Tischendorf's second edition had but recently appeared, two Professors at Cambridge, B. F. Westcott and F. J. A. Hort, undertook the preparation of a manual text for their own use, "hoping at the same time that it might be of use to others." For twenty-eight years their labors were continued with some delays and interruptions occasioned by other occupations, and their edition was not published till May, 1881. It bears the title, "The New Testament in the Original Greek"; and in harmony with the title the first sentence of the Introduction reads as follows: "This edition is an attempt to present exactly the original words of the New Testament, so far as they can now be determined from surviving documents." The two editors worked independently, but compared their results from time to time, and discussed their differences. Such differences as they could not adjust they have indicated on the margin. As a reason for this procedure they say: "This combination of completely independent operations permits us to place far more confidence in the results than either of us could have presumed to cherish had they rested on his own sole responsibility."[24] And it may be added that it permits the student also to receive them with a proportionate degree of confidence. The text was published in one volume, and the Introduction and Appendix shortly after-

---

[23] "Having followed Tregelles through the whole of Cod. 69, I am able to speak positively of his scrupulous exactness; and in regard to other manuscripts now in England it will be found that where Tischendorf and Tregelles differ, the latter is seldom in the wrong" (Scrivener, *Int.* 486).

"We believe that his accuracy in making collations and faithfully recording them is superior to that evinced by any of the great editors, Mill, Wetstein, Griesbach, Lachmann or Tischendorf" (Davidson, *Bib. Crit.* ii. 146).

"Of the services of Tischendorf in collecting and publishing materials it is impossible to speak too highly, but his actual text is the least important and least satisfactory part of his work. Dr. Tregelles, to whom we owe the best recension of the Gospels, has not yet reached the Epistles of St. Paul" (J. B. Lightfoot, *Preface* to *Commentary on Galatians,* iii). This testimonial from one of the ripest of living scholars was written in February, 1865, when Parts First and Second of Tregelles' Edition were all that had been published.

[24] New Testament in Original Greek, Introduction, §§ 1, 20, 21.

ward in another. Both were promptly republished in America by Harper & Brothers.

These editors made no attempt at a general collation of manuscripts, though they have done some valuable work in this department. Their work is distinguished by a more careful research into the genealogy of documents than has been attempted hitherto, and by a consequent more discriminating judgment as to the weight of evidence which should be attached to each. They are accused of ascribing too much authority to Codex B, and their views in some other particulars are called in question, but Dr. Scrivener, who urges these objections, bears hearty testimony to the general value of their work, and says of the Introduction that it is "a very model of earnest reasoning, calling for and richly rewarding the close and repeated study of all who would learn the utmost that can be done for settling the text of the New Testament on dogmatic principles."[25] In their text they depart more widely from the received text than any previous editors have thought allowable, and some of the most important changes which they have made are contested. The qualifications of the two editors for their task are of the highest order. They are pronounced by Scrivener "two of our best living scholars."[26] Dr. Westcott is best known in America by his Introduction to the Four Gospels, his admirable work on the New Testament Canon, and his Commentary on the Gospel of John, part of The Bible Commentary.

We are now prepared to sum up briefly the results thus far attained by the labors of Biblical critics. We have mentioned only those critics who have prepared editions of the Greek Testament, omitting many who have made invaluable contributions in the way of collating particular manuscripts, editing portions of the text, and taking part in the discussion of the facts and principles involved; but we have mentioned enough to show in a general way how the results have been attained which we mentioned in Chapter Second. Besides demonstrating that the text of the New

---

[25] Introduction, 530, § 15, and see the entire chapter on Recent Views of Comparative Criticism.

[26] *Ib.* 488.

Testament has been so well preserved that only in one place in a thousand, and that a place on which we can put our finger, is there any doubt as to the original reading, we are able to name the following results which have been placed within the reach of all:

1. The "Revised Version" of the English New Testament puts into the hands of all who read the English language, the maturest results of Biblical Criticism in an English dress. Its text, where there are no references made to different readings, represents the settled Greek text that is known to have been composed by the sacred writers, while the marginal readings point out all the words in reference to which there is any difference worthy of notice among ancient documents. Not only so, but the relative degree of probability in favor of the reading adopted in the text is approximately indicated, so that the least educated English reader can see for himself the broad ground of certainty and the narrow ground of doubt.

2. The Revisers, who were selected from among the most eminent scholars in Great Britain and America, had before them all the critical editions which have been mentioned above, including advanced sheets of Westcott & Hort's text, and where these differ they made an intelligent choice of readings. The Greek which they followed in translating has been published by Dr. E. Palmer, of Oxford, and also by Dr. Scrivener, thus placing in the reach of every one who can read the Greek Testament a far purer text than has been seen by any previous generation since the sacred autographs disappeared.

3. The materials for criticism which have been collected by the diligence of the noble men whom we have mentioned are now so ample, and the number of thoroughly accomplished critics yet engaged in the work so great, that we have every reason to expect a speedy consummation of their hopes in a restoration of the original text which shall approach very nearly to perfection. Then the science of Biblical Criticism, having finished her task, may lay aside the implements of her toil and rest under the benediction, well done!

PART II

Genuineness of the
New Testament Books

ONE

Evidence From Catalogues

Having discussed in Part First the history and present condition of the text of the New Testament, we now inquire whether its books can be severally traced back to the writers whose names they bear. In order to begin, as in Part First, with admitted facts, we make the date of the oldest existing copy of the Greek New Testament the starting-point of the present inquiry. It is an axiomatic proposition that every book is as old as its oldest existing copy; but the acknowledged date, as we have before stated (page 30), of the Sinaitic Manuscript, the oldest complete copy of the New Testament now in existence, is the first half of the fourth century; and consequently all of the books in question were certainly in existence at that date. This conclusion is universally admitted, and the task before us is to trace these books back through the two and a half centuries which lie between that date and the age of their reputed authors.

Our first evidence is that of catalogues. If the inquiry had reference to Shakespeare's plays, and we should find in a document written AD 1600, a list of them as existing works, we would know from this that they were written at least that early. Now it so happens that writings of ancient authors have come down to us which contain lists or catalogues of such books both of the Old and the New Testament as were known and used in their day. These catalogues furnish demonstrative proof that the books which they mention were already in existence.

Some of these catalogues are found in the acts of various eccle-siastical assemblies, which, like the assemblies that drew up the creeds of the several Protestant churches, set forth the books of the Old Testament and the New which they regarded as the true word of God. The earliest of these assemblies in whose acts such a catalogue is found, is the Council of Carthage, which met AD 97.[1] It was composed of the Bishops of Africa, representing all the churches in the Roman province of that name. The rule ad-opted on the subject begins with these words: "It was also deter-mined, that beside the canonical[2] Scriptures nothing be read in the churches under the title of divine Scriptures." It names all the canonical books of the Old Testament, including all in our pres-ent Bible and some of those in the Apocrypha, and then gives the New Testament books in the following order: "Four books of the Gospels, one book of Acts of Apostles, thirteen Epistles of the Apostle Paul, one of the same to the Hebrews, two Epistles of the Apostle Peter, three of John, one of James, one of Judas, one book of the Apocalypse of John." It concludes: "We have received from our fathers that these are to be read in the churches."[3]

This document shows not only that all of the books of our pres-ent New Testament were in existence and in use as "divine Scrip-tures" at the close of the fourth century, but that they had been held in the same esteem by the "fathers" of the venerable men who composed this assembly. These "fathers" must have lived in the earlier part of the fourth century, and the books had then been in use so long as to be regarded by them as having proceeded from

---

[1] The Council of Laodicea, which met AD 363, is commonly quoted as having made a catalogue, but there are good grounds for believing that the catalogue appended to the report of its proceedings was added at a later date. The evidence is given by Westcott, *Canon of New Testament*, 428–432.

[2] The word *canon* is the Greek word κανών anglicized, and means a rule. Paul employs the original term in Gal. vi. 16. and it continued in use among the Greek writers of the early church. Applied to the Scriptures, it represents them as the *rule* of faith and practice. *The* Canon is the whole Bible, and a book is said to be canonical when it is entitled to a place in this Canon. The term was also applied to the various rules adopted by councils. For a full account of its use, see Appendix A to Westcott's *Canon of New Testament*.

[3] For the original Latin text of this catalogue, see Westcott on the Canon, 533, or Charteris, *Canonicity*, 18; and for an English translation of it, see Lardner's Credibility, v. 78.

the Apostles. This testimony pushes the history of the books back
to at least the beginning of the fourth century—farther back than
the date of the oldest existing copy of them.

The next catalogue which we cite is from the pen of Athanasius, who was Bishop of Alexandria from 326 to 373 AD, and
one of the most noted Greek writers of the fourth century. In an
epistle addressed to the disciples under his oversight, he gives, for
the purpose of guarding "some few of the weaker sort" from being deceived by apocryphal books, a list of the true books of the
whole Bible, those of the New Testament being the same that we
now receive. He declares that these books had been "delivered to
the fathers" by those who were "eye-witnesses and ministers of
the word," and that he had learned this "from the beginning." He
appends to his list this warning: "These are the fountains of salvation, that he who thirsts may be satisfied with the oracles contained in them: in these alone the doctrine of religion is taught: let
no one add to them or take anything from them."[4] This testimony

---

[4] The Greek text of the extract is given by Westcott (*Canon,* 546) and by Charteris, 13,
and the following is Lardner's translation of it: "But since we have spoken of heretics as
dead persons, and of ourselves as having the divine Scriptures for salvation; and I fear lest,
as Paul wrote to the Corinthians, some few of the weaker sort should be seduced from their
simplicity and purity by the cunning and craftiness of some men, and at length be induced
to make use of other books called apocryphal, being deceived by the similitude of their names
resembling the true books; I therefore entreat you to bear with me if I by writing remind
you of things which you know already, as what may be of use for the church. And for the
vindication of my attempt, I adopt the form of the Evangelist Luke, who himself says:
Forasmuch as some have taken in hand to set forth writings called apocryphal, and to join
them with the divinely inspired Scriptures of which we are fully assured, as they delivered
them to the fathers who were eye-witnesses and ministers of the word: it has seemed good
to me also, with the advice of some true brethren, and having learned it from the beginning,
to set forth in order these canonical books which have been delivered down to us, and are
believed to be divine Scripture: that every one who has been deceived may condemn those
who have deceived him, and that he who remains uncorrupted may have the satisfaction
to be reminded of what he is persuaded of." Here follows the list of the Old Testament
books, and the writer proceeds: "Nor do I think it too much pains to declare those of the
New. They are these: The four Gospels, according to Matthew, according to Mark, according to Luke, according to John. Then after them the Acts of the Apostles, and the seven
Epistles of the Apostles called catholic: of James one, of Peter two, of John three, and after
them of Jude one. Besides these, there are fourteen Epistles of the Apostle Paul, the order
of which is thus: the first to the Romans, then two to the Corinthians, after them that to
the Galatians, the next to the Ephesians, then to the Philippians, to the Colossians, after
them two to the Thessalonians, and the Epistle to the Hebrews, then two to Timothy, to

sets forth both the personal knowledge of Athanasius as far back as he "could remember, and that of his early instructors. As he was made Bishop in 326, we may fairly presume that he remembered the books in use as far back as AD 300, and that his early teachers remembered far into the third century. All remembered them as books believed to have been delivered to the first generation of "the fathers" by the "eye-witnesses and ministers of the word." They must have existed long before, in order to acquire this reputation.

Our next catalogue is that of Cyril, who was Bishop of Jerusalem a part of the time in which Athanasius was Bishop of Alexandria. He lived from 315 to 386 AD. Jerome, who wrote his life, says that while yet a youth he composed catechetical lectures for the instruction of candidates for baptism.[5] In one of these he gives a list of the books which were to be read as the inspired Scriptures, and it agrees precisely with ours except that he omits Revelation. He says to his pupil: "The Apostles and ancient Bishops, governors of the church, who have delivered these to us were wiser and holier than thou. As a son of the church, therefore, transgress not these bounds."[6] This shows that all the books of the New Testament except the Apocalypse were in use in Palestine, the birthplace of Christianity, at the beginning of the fourth century, and that they had been in use a sufficient length of time to be regarded as having come down from the Apostles through the ancient overseers of the church.

Titus one, the last to Philemon; and again the Revelation of John. These are the fountains of salvation, that he who thirsts may be satisfied with the oracles contained in them. In these alone the doctrine of salvation is taught; let no man add to them or take from them." (*Lardner's Credibility*, iv., 282–284.)

[5] Quoted by Lardner, iv., 299, *note* a. His catechetical lectures which he wrote in his youth are extant.

[6] Quoted in the original by Westcott, *Canon of New Testament*, 541, 542. I translate the part concerning the New Testament as follows: "Of the New Testament, receive the four Gospels. But the others are falsely written and injurious. The Manicheans have also written a gospel according to Thomas, which, as by the fragrance of its evangelical title, corrupts the souls of the simple-minded. And receive also the Acts of the twelve Apostles; in addition to these, also, the seven Catholic Epistles of James and Peter, John and Jude, and the seal of all, the last work of the disciples, the fourteen Epistles of Paul."

Eusebius, called the Father of Ecclesiastical History, because he wrote the first church history that has come down to our day, is our next witness. He lived from 270 to 340 AD, and was Bishop of the Church of Caesarea in Palestine. He was 45 years old when Cyril was born, and 56 when Athanasius was made Bishop of Alexandria; his testimony, therefore, reaches back about half a century earlier than that of our last two witnesses. He lived through the persecution under the Emperor Diocletian, which continued from AD 303 to 311, and Books viii. and ix. of his history are devoted to an account of this persecution. The edict under which it was inaugurated required that all the churches be razed to their foundations, and that all copies of the Scriptures be burned.[7]

The edict was universal, and it was executed with especial zeal in Africa, Egypt, Palestine, Syria, Asia Minor, Italy and Spain.[8] Its promulgation shows that at this period the Christian Scriptures were in use throughout the Roman Empire, and that they were well known to the heathen authorities as the foundation and support of the Christian faith.[9]

Eusebius leaves us in no doubt as to the books which made up the Scriptures whose wide-spread use and influence are thus in-

---

[7] "It was the nineteenth year of the reign of Diocletian, and the month Dystrus, called by the Romans March, in which the festival of our Saviour's passion was at hand, when the imperial edicts were everywhere published, to tear down the churches to their foundations, and to destroy the sacred Scriptures by fire, and which commanded also that those who were in honorable stations should be degraded, but those who were freedmen should be deprived of their liberty, if they persevered in their adherence to Christianity." "All this has been fulfilled in our own day, when we saw with our own eyes our houses of worship thrown down from their elevation, the sacred Scriptures of inspiration committed to flames in the markets, the shepherds of the people basely concealed here and there, some of them ignominiously captured and the sport of their enemies." (*Eccles. Hist.,* vii. 1, 2.)

[8] The extent of the persecution, and the varying degrees of severity with which it was conducted, are traced by Gibbon in the celebrated Sixteenth Chapter of his Decline and Fall of the Roman Empire.

[9] "The philosophers, who now assumed the unworthy office of directing the blind zeal of persecution, had diligently studied the nature and genius of the Christian religion; and as they were not ignorant that the speculative doctrines of the faith were supposed to be contained in the writings of the prophets, of the evangelists, and of the apostles, they most probably suggested the order that the bishops and presbyters should deliver all their sacred books into the hands of the magistrates, who were commanded under the severest penalties to burn them in a public and solemn manner." (Gibbon, *Decline and Fall,* ii., 64.)

dicated. He mentions every one contained in our New Testament. He says, however, of seven, that though they were well known and recognized by most persons, they were controverted by some. These were Hebrews, the Epistles of James and Jude, 2 Peter, 2 and 3 John and the Apocalypse.[10] He says of the same books in another passage, that "though they are not canonical but controverted, they are nevertheless constantly recognized by most of our ecclesiastical authorities."[11]

The force of this evidence depends not merely on the personal knowledge of Eusebius, which reached back into the last quarter of the third century, but still more upon the fact that he had gleaned all the Christian literature which had come down to his age. He constantly refers to "the ancients," and "the ancient writers" for what he says of these books.[12] If we suppose that by "ancient writers" he meant those who lived as far back as 200 years before his own time, he included among them the cotemporaries of the Apostles. His testimony, therefore, traces at least the uncontroverted books to the apostolic age, and he gives no hint that the others had originated at a later date.

Eusebius lived to see the Christian religion established by law throughout the Roman Empire. He was commissioned by

---

[10] "Among the controverted books, which are nevertheless well known and recognized by most (τοῖς πολλοῖς), we class the Epistle circulated under the name of James, and that of Jude, as well as the second of Peter, and the so-called second and third of John, whether they really belong to the evangelist, or possibly to another of the same name. . . . And moreover, as I said the Apocalypse of John, if such an opinion seem correct, which some, as I said, reject, while others reckon it among the books generally received." *Translated by Westcott (Canon, 415) from Eccles. Hist.*, iii., 25. Of Hebrews he deposes as follows: "Of Paul the fourteen Epistles commonly received are at once manifest and clear. It is not right, however, to ignore the fact that some have rejected the Epistle to the Hebrews, asserting that it is gainsaid by the Church of Rome as not being Paul's." (*Canon of New Testament*, 412. *Eccles. Hist.*, iii. 3.)

[11] Eccles. Hist., iii., 25.

[12] "But as I proceed in my history, I shall carefully show, with the succession of the apostles, what ecclesiastical writers *in their times* made use of any of the disputed writings." (iii. 3). "At a more proper time we shall endeavor also to state, by a reference to some of the *ancient writers*, what others have said respecting the sacred books. But, besides the Gospel of John, his first Epistle is acknowledged without dispute, both by those of the present day and also by the *ancients*. The other two Epistles, however, are disputed. The opinions respecting the Revelation are still greatly divided. But we shall, in due time, give a judgment on this point also, from the testimony of the *ancients*" (iii. 24).

Constantine, the first Christian Emperor, to have transcribed fifty copies of the Bible for the use of the Churches in Constantinople, and he wrote a Life of Constantine whom he survived but a few years.[13]

We now go back to Origen, who was born at Alexandria, AD 185, and died in 254. He was the most voluminous and one of the most eminent of the Greek writers of the early church. He wrote commentaries and homilies on the principal books of both Testaments, besides volumes on various other subjects; and his defense of Christianity against Celsus, the first infidel writer, is one of the most noted works of antiquity.[14] In his exposition of the first Psalm he incidentally names the books of the Old Testament, and in a homily on the book of Joshua he names those of the New Testament as we now have them.[2] The original of this homily has perished, and we are dependent for this evidence on a Latin version of it, but there is no reason to doubt the substantial correctness of the version.[15]

In other passages also he mentions all of our books. In his Commentary on Matthew he says that the four Gospels alone [as Gospels] are uncontroverted in the Church, and that they were written by Matthew, Mark, Luke and John, in the order here given to their names.[16]

---

[13] Book X. of Ecclesiastical History gives an account of the final triumph; and for the facts concerning the fifty Bibles, see *Life of Constantine*, iv., 34, 35.

[14] A brief sketch of his life and a list of his works is appended to the second volume of his extant writings in the Ante-Nicene Christian Library.

[15] After describing the fall of Jericho, when the trumpets were blown by the priests, he says: "So, too, our Lord, whose advent was typified by the son of Nun, when he came, sent his apostles, bearing well-wrought trumpets. Matthew first sounded the priestly trumpet in his Gospel. Mark also, Luke and John, each gave forth a strain on their priestly trumpets. Peter, moreover, sounded loudly on the two-fold trumpet of his Epistles; and so also James and Jude. Still the number is incomplete, and John gives forth the trumpet-sound in his Epistles and Apocalypse; and Luke, while describing the Acts of the Apostles. Lastly, however, came he who said, 'I think that God hath set forth us Apostles last of all,' and, thundering on the fourteen trumpets of his Epistles, threw down even to the ground the walls of Jericho, that is to say, all the instruments of idolatry and the doctrines of philosophers." (*Homily on Joshua vii.* 1, quoted and translated by Westcott, *Canon of New Testament*, 358.)

[16] His words, as quoted by Eusebius, are as follows: "I have understood from tradition respecting the four Gospels, which are the only undisputed ones in the whole Church of God throughout the world, that the first is written according to Matthew, the same that

In his commentary on the gospel of John, after speaking in general terms of Paul's epistles, he says: "But Peter, upon whom the church of Christ is built, against which the gates of hell shall not prevail, has left one epistle undisputed. Suppose, also, the second was left by him, for on this there is some doubt."[17] But although he thus declares that there was some doubt about 2 Peter, preventing him from styling it like 1 Peter, "undisputed," he shows his own judgment of it not only by the passages cited above from one of his homilies on Joshua, but also by quoting 2 Peter 1.4, with the formula, "Peter said"; and 2 Peter 2.16, with the words, "As the Scripture says in a certain place"; and by citing what Peter said in his "first" epistle, implying a second.[18]

Eusebius quotes him as saying in the same commentary, that John wrote the Apocalypse, that he left one epistle and perhaps a second and a third, "for all do not allow that they are genuine."[19]

Concerning the epistle to the Hebrews he expresses the opinion that the thoughts are Paul's, but that the diction and phraseology are those of another. He says that some ascribed the writing to Clement, and others to Luke; but he shows that he had himself formed no opinion on this point by saying, "Who it was that really wrote the epistle, God only knows."[20]

---

was once a publican, but afterwards an apostle of Jesus Christ, who, having published it for the Jewish converts, wrote it in Hebrew. The second is according to Mark, who composed it as Peter explained to him, whom he also acknowledges as his son in his general Epistle, saying, 'The elect church in Babylon salutes you, as also Mark, my son.' And the third according to Luke, the Gospel commended by Paul, which was written for the converts from the Gentiles; and last of all, the Gospel according to John." (*Eccles. Hist.*, VI., xxv., p. 245.)

[17] Ib. VI., xxv., p. 246.

[18] Quoted by Westcott, *Canon of New Testament*, 359, *n. 7;* from Homily on Leviticus iv. 4; Commentary on Romans iv. 9; Homily on Numbers xiii. 8; and De Principiis Viris, 2, *n.,* 3.

[19] "What shall we say of him who reclined upon the breast of Jesus? I mean John, who has left one Gospel, in which he confesses that he could write so many that the whole world could not contain them. He also wrote the Apocalypse, commanded as he was to conceal and not to write the voices of the seven thunders. He also left an Epistle consisting of a very few lines; suppose also that a second and third are from him, for not all agree that they are genuine; but both together do not contain a hundred lines." (Quoted by Eusebius, *Eccles. Hist.*, VI., xxv., p. 246.)

[20] "I would say, that the thoughts are the Apostle's, but that the diction and phraseology belong to some one who has recorded what the Apostle said, and one who noted down

We now see that Origen's catalogue contained all the books of the New Testament; and that although he says of 2 Peter, and 2 and 3 John, that they were held in doubt by some, he expresses no such doubt as existing in his own mind. It should also be carefully noted, that he does not intimate as the ground of the doubt which he mentions a supposed recent origin of any of these epistles. As respects Hebrews, the only doubt he expresses has reference to its composition; he had none as to its apostolic origin.

The value of this testimony is enhanced by a consideration of Origen's opportunities for correct information. His father, Leonides, suffered martyrdom at Alexandria in the persecution under Septiraius Severus, who reigned 193–211, and not long after his father's death Origen was made teacher of the Catechumens in Alexandria. This was in the year 203, when he was but eighteen years of age. The intimate knowledge of the Scriptures which this appointment implies, shows that his personal acquaintance with the sacred books reached back into the second century; and the information that he derived from his martyred father reached back to a still earlier date. It was only by the stern command of his father that he was dissuaded from joining the latter in martyrdom. Later in life he visited Palestine, Syria and Greece; and he made his home at Caesarea during the last twenty-four years of his life, though he died in Tyre after suffering extreme torture at the hands of persecutors. His life was full of trial and self-denial, and he acquired a world-wide fame while he yet lived. His testimony to the New Testament books is therefore that of a competent and unimpeachable witness.[21]

Clement of Alexandria, so called to distinguish him from an

---

at his leisure what his master dictated. If, then, any church considers this Epistle as coming from Paul, let it be commended for this; for neither did those ancient men deliver it as such without cause. But who it was that actually wrote the Epistle, God only knows. The account, however, that has been current before us is, according to some, that Clement, who was Bishop of Rome, wrote the Epistle; according to others, that it was written by Luke, who wrote the Gospel and Acts" (*Eccles. Hist.* vi. 25, pp. 246, 247).

[21] Eusebius gives a disconnected account of his career in Ecclesiastical History, Book vi.; Lardner gives a connected account in Vol. II. of his Credibility; and a brief account is given in the volume of the Ante-Nicene Christian Library containing his extant writings.

earlier Clement, of Rome, is the next writer whose testimony we cite. He lived from about 165 AD to 220.[22] In early life he was a student of pagan philosophy, but on becoming a Christian he visited eminent teachers of Christianity in Greece, Syria, Egypt, Palestine and other countries, to receive their oral instruction.[23] Such was his proficiency in these studies that he was made catechetical teacher in Alexandria in 189, and continued to hold the position till 202, when he left Alexandria, and was succeeded by his pupil Origen.[24] His extant writings fill two of the octavo volumes of the Ante-Nicene Library, but one of his most important works, which bore the Greek title Hypotuposes (Outlines) has perished. Eusebius, who had this work before him, says that in it Clement gave concise explanations of all the canonical scriptures, "not omitting the disputed books."[25] This statement is confirmed so far as the epistles are concerned by Photius, a Latin writer of the ninth century, who also had read the lost work, and who says that it contained interpretations of Paul's epistles and the Catholic epistles, the "disputed epistles" being included in the latter expression.[26] According to these statements, while Clement made no formal catalogue of

---

[22] Neither the place nor the exact date of either his birth or death is certainly known (see Lardner, Vol. n. c. 22), but the above are the dates accepted by the best scholars as the most probable. See Westcott on the Canon, 350.

[23] That he was proficient in pagan philosophy is apparent throughout his works from his frequent references to it. Of his Christian teachers, he speaks as follows: "My memoranda are stored up against old age, as a remedy against forgetfulness; truly an image and outline of those vigorous and animated discourses which I was privileged to hear, and of blessed and truly remarkable men. Of these the one in Greece, an Ionic, and the other in Magna Grecia: the first of these from Coele-Syria, the second from Egypt, and others in the East. The one was born in the land of Assyria, and the other a Hebrew in Palestine" (*Stromata*, B. I., c. i., *Ante-Nicene Library*, iv. 355).

[24] *Eccles. Hist.*, vi. 6; *Ante-Nicene Library*, iv. 9, and references there given.

[25] "In the work called Hypotuposes, to sum up the matter briefly, he has given us abridged accounts of all the canonical Scriptures, not even omitting those that are disputed. I mean the book of Jude and the other general Epistles. Also the Epistle of Barnabas and that called the Revelation of Peter" (*Eccles. Hist.* vi. 14).

[26] "Now the whole scope of the book consists in giving, as it were, interpretations of Genesis, of Exodus, of the Psalms, of the Epistles of St. Paul, and of the Catholic Epistles, and of Ecclesiasticus" (Quoted by Westcott, *Canon*, 352).

This statement differs from that just quoted from Eusebius (Note 25) as to the number of books treated in the work, but the two statements are alike in regard to the Catholic Epistles.

the books in question, he did what was equivalent, he gave explanations more or less elaborate of them all.[27]

Eusebius quotes Clement as saying concerning the Epistle to the Hebrews, that it was written by Paul in the Hebrew tongue, and translated into Greek by Luke. In this way he accounts for its similarity in style and phraseology to Acts, and he supposes that Paul left it anonymous lest the prejudices of the Jews against him might prevent them from reading it.[28]

But in addition to this second-hand testimony, we find in his extant writings that he names and quotes from every book in the New Testament except Philemon, James, 2 Peter and 3 John.[29]

This evidence is furnished by a man who was born within sixty-five years of the death of the apostle John, and had received instruction from eminent teachers who, to use his own words, "Preserving the tradition of the blessed doctrine derived directly from the holy apostles, Peter, James, John and Paul, the son receiving it from the father (but few were like the fathers) came by God's will to us also to deposit those ancestral and apostolic seeds."[30] How few generations of transmission are here alluded to

---

[27] Lardner (II. 228, 229), followed by Westcott (Canon of New Testament, 352–4), expresses doubt as to the strict correctness of Eusebius and Photius (Notes 25, 26) concerning the Catholic Epistles, basing the doubt on a statement of Cassiodorus, a writer of the sixth century, who says that Clement made some comments on the Canonical Epistles, "that is to say, on the First Epistle of St. Peter, the First and Second of St. John, and the Epistle of St. James." He says further that he had been solicitous concerning the other Canonical Epistles, when he met with a book of one Didymus giving an exposition of the seven. This shows that Cassiodorus knew of comments by Clement on only four of the seven Catholic Epistles. This can be accounted for by supposing either that those on the other three were absent from his manuscript of Clement, or that Eusebius and Photius were both mistaken. It seems to us that the former of these alternatives is more probable than the latter, and that the positive statement of the two writers is to be accepted.

[28] "But the Epistle to the Hebrews he [Clement] asserts, was written by Paul to the Hebrews in the Hebrew tongue; but that it was carefully translated by Luke and published among the Greeks. Whence one also finds the same character of style and of phraseology in the Epistle as in Acts. But it is probable that the title, Paul the Apostle, was not prefixed to it. For as he wrote to the Hebrews who had imbibed prejudices against him, and suspected him, he wisely guards against diverting them from the perusal by giving his name" (*Eccles. Hist.*, vi. 14).

[29] The citations are too numerous for our space, but they may be found in Lardner's Credibility, 2 210–230, and in the two volumes of Clement belonging to the Ante-Nicene Christian Library.

[30] *Stromata, I.* i. (*Ante-Nicene Lib.* Vol. iv. 355).

can be realized, if we remember that a man eighty-five years of age could have lived ten years with the apostle John and ten years with Clement. The interval was too brief for books originating within it to be transmitted as having been known since the days of the apostles.

Tertullian, a famous Latin writer of Africa, was born in Carthage about AD 160, and died about AD 240.[31] He was, therefore, a contemporary of Origen and Clement, and his personal knowledge of the New Testament books extended through the last quarter of the second century. He left no formal catalogue, but his extant writings contain statements concerning the gospels and Paul's epistles that are equivalent to a catalogue, and he mentions all the other books except 2 Peter, James, and the two shorter epistles of John. He names our four gospels, and says that Matthew and John[32] were written by apostles, and Mark and Luke by "apostolic men." In the last book of his work against Marcion, he names all of Paul's epistles to churches in regular order, drawing an argument from each one separately, thus refuting Marcion out of the very books on which he relied to support his heresy. He does the same with Philemon, and twits Marcion for accepting, as he did, this personal epistle, yet rejecting the two to Timothy and the one to Titus.[33] Thus he arrays the thirteen epistles of Paul as authorities in debate. He was also acquainted with Hebrews, but he represents it as having been written by Barnabas.[34] He frequently quotes Acts of the Apostles by its title, ascribing it to Luke, and asserting

---

[31] See the evidences and opinions adduced by Lardner, 2 253, and also Westcott, *Canon,* 341.

[32] "Of the Apostles, therefore, John and Matthew first instill faith into us; whilst of apostolic men, Luke and Mark renew it afterward" (*Tertullian against Marcion,* iv. ii. 280).

[33] "To this Epistle alone did its brevity avail to protect it against the falsifying hands of Marcion. I wonder, however, when he received this letter which was written to but one man, that he rejected the two Epistles to Timothy and the one to Titus, which all treat of ecclesiastical discipline. His aim was, I suppose, to carry out his interpolating process even to the number of Epistles" (*Tertullian against Marcion,* v. xxi. 478).

[34] He says: "For there is an Epistle of Barnabas, inscribed to the Hebrews, written by a man of such authority, that Paul has placed him with himself in the same course of abstinence: 'Or I only and Barnabas, have we not power to forbear working?'" Then follows a quotation from Hebrews 6.4–8. See the passage cited from *De Pudicitia,* by Lardner, *Credibility,* ii. 270.

that those who do not receive it have no means of showing when, or with what beginnings the church was formed.[35] He quotes by name 1 Peter and Jude.[36] He also quotes frequently from 1 John and the Apocalypse, ascribing the latter to John.[37]

In addition to the testimony given in this indirect way, Tertullian, in opposition to Marcion who rejected all the Gospels except Luke's, and was charged with mutilating this, insists that the Gospels came down "from the very beginning," "from the apostles," and that they had been kept as a sacred deposit in the churches planted by the personal labors of the Apostles, as well as in others.[38] He furthermore refers such persons as would indulge their curiosity, to the churches to which letters were written by Apostles, and affirms that in these "their own authentic letters are read, uttering the voice and representing the face of each of them

---

[35] "Accordingly, in the Acts of the Apostles we find that men who had John's baptism had not received the Holy Spirit, whom they knew not even by hearing" *(De Baptismo,* x. 243). "Moreover, since in the same Commentary of Luke, both the third hour of prayer is pointed out, at which, when entered by the Holy Spirit, they were held to be drunk, and the sixth, at which Peter went up on the house-top," etc. *(De Jejuniis,* c. 10). "And assuredly He fulfilled His promise, since it is proved in the Acts of the Apostles that the Holy Spirit did come down. Now they who reject that Scripture can neither belong to the Holy Spirit, seeing they can not acknowledge that the Holy Spirit, has been sent as yet to the disciples, nor can they pretend to claim to be a church themselves who positively have no means of proving when and with what infant nursing this body was established" *(Prescription against Heretics,* xxii. 26).

[36] "Peter says to the people of Pontus, How great glory it is, if, when ye are punished for your faults yet take it patiently," etc. (1 Pet 2. 20–21). *Lardner, 2* 274 *n. f.* In arguing for the genuineness of the Book of Enoch, he says: "To these considerations is added the fact that Enoch possesses a testimony in the Apostle Jude" (Jude 14–15). *On Female Dress,* iii. 708.

[37] "John exhorts us to lay down our lives for our brethren, denying that there is any fear in love; for perfect love casteth out fear" (1 John 3.16; 4.18). *Lardner, 2* 275: "John in his Apocalypse is commanded to chastise those who eat things sacrificed to idols and commit fornication" (Rev 2.14). *Prescription against Heresies,* xxxiii. 40.

[38] "On the whole, then, if that is evidently more true which is earlier, if that is earlier which is from the beginning, if that is from the beginning which has the Apostles for its authors, then it will certainly be quite as evident that that comes down from the Apostles which has been kept as a sacred deposit in the churches of the Apostles." He then refers to the writings of Paul, Peter and John, and to Luke's Gospel, and with reference to the latter he adds: "The same authority of the apostolic churches will afford evidence to the other Gospels also, which we possess equally through their means and according to their usage—I mean the Gospels of John and Matthew—whilst that which Mark published may be affirmed to be Peter's, whose interpreter Mark was. For even Luke's form of the Gospel men usually ascribe to Paul, and it may well seem that the works which disciples publish belong to their masters." *(Against Marcion,* v. 186–187).

separately."[39] There has been much dispute over the word "authentic" as used in this passage. If Tertullian meant by it only to affirm that well authenticated *copies* of the Epistles were in those churches, the remark could scarcely have been worth making; for the same was equally true of other churches. He must have meant that the autographs themselves were still preserved. In this he may have been mistaken, or have indulged in rhetorical exaggeration; yet it is not at all incredible that the autographs had been preserved until that time. But the value of the testimony depends not so much upon the accuracy of this statement, as upon the fact which it makes manifest that the churches referred to believed themselves to have received such letters from Apostles, and in this belief they can not have been mistaken.

The earliest formal catalogue of the New Testament books now extant, is that of a document called the Muratorian Canon. The manuscript of this document was found in 1740 in an old library in Milan, by an Italian named Muratori, whence the title Muratorian. The MS. belongs to the seventh or the eighth century, and is a Latin translation from a Greek original. It claims to have been composed by a cotemporary of Pius, Bishop of Rome, who died in the year 157, and it is not therefore of later date than AD 170.[40] The existing MS. is fragmentary, having lost some lines from both the beginning and the end. It begins with the last words of a sentence of which there is not enough left to make complete sense, and continues thus: "In the third place is the book of the Gospel according to Luke."[41] After a brief account of Luke, it states that John's Gospel is the fourth. This enumeration makes it quite

---

[39] "Come now, you who would indulge a better curiosity, run over the Apostolic churches, in which the very thrones of the Apostles are preeminent in their places, in which their own authentic writings are read, uttering the voice and representing the face of each of them severally. Achaia is very near you, you find Corinth. Since you are not far from Macedonia, you have Philippi, you have the Thessalonians. Since you are able to cross to Asia, you get Ephesus. Since, moreover, you are close upon Italy, you have Rome" (*Prescription against Heresies,* xxxvi. 42).

[40] "Hermas wrote The Shepherd very recently in our own time in the City of Rome, while his brother Pius was occupying the Bishop's chair in the church at Rome." See the Canon quoted by Westcott, *Canon of New Testament,* 200. n. 1.

[41] "Quibus tamen interfuit et ita posuit. Tertio Euangelii, librum secundo Lucan."

certain that the part torn away spoke of Matthew and Mark. It contains all the other books except the two Epistles of Peter, 1 John, James and Hebrews. As these important Epistles are absent, while 2 and 3 John, and Philemon, far less important, are present, it is more probable that the former have been lost from it than that they were originally omitted.[42]

The author of this catalogue wrote when Tertullian, our last witness, was but ten years of age. His personal knowledge of the books, if he was a middle-aged man when he wrote, reached back into the first half of the second century, and be may have conversed with men who had lived in the midst of the Apostles, and his information concerning the origin of our books may have been derived to some extent from original witnesses.

The earliest writer who set forth a formal list of the books which he accepted as authoritative, was Marcion, who came from Pontus to Rome about the year 140,[43] and was then a teacher of great notoriety. He was the founder of a heretical party called Marcionites after his own name. While the Ebionites, an intensely Jewish-Christian sect, the theological offspring of the Judaizers against whom Paul waged so constant a warfare, rejected all of Paul's writings, and also the writings of Luke, because he was under Paul's influence, Marcion took the opposite extreme, and claiming that Paul was the only Apostle who understood the gospel correctly, he rejected all the New Testament writings except ten of Paul's Epistles, and Luke's Gospel. The two Epistles to Timothy and the one to Titus he rejected for reasons that are not known, and also Hebrews. His teaching demonstrates the previous general recognition of this Gospel and these ten Epistles, while his antagonism to the other Gospels and to the writings in general of the other Apostles, demonstrates the existence of those. Moreover, the ground on which he rejected the latter was not their want of genuineness, but, admitting their genuineness, he denied the apostolic authority

---

[42] Westcott gives the whole Latin text of this document, and discusses it exhaustively (*Canon of New Testament*, 208–218, and *Appendix C*).

[43] Westcott (*Canon of New Testament*, 309), fixes the date between 139 and 142; Davidson (*Canon of the Bible*, 85), at 140.

of their authors.[44] Thus the direct and indirect evidence from this source combine to show that at least the greater part of our books were known to Marcion, and his knowledge reached back into the first quarter of the second century.

The five writers last quoted, Marcion, the author of the Muratorian Canon, Tertullian, Clement and Origen, unitedly mention by name all the books of the New Testament. They are the earliest group of writers who do so, and they all lived within the second century, spanning with their personal knowledge the whole of this century from the beginning of its second quarter to its close. They declare that these books had been handed down "from the fathers," "from the ancients," "from the Apostles"; and they speak from Rome, from Africa, from Egypt, from Palestine. The age of a single man may have overlapped the early days of the latest of the five and the latter part of the life of John. We have therefore traced the existence of these books by unquestionable evidence to the second generation after that of the Apostles, and we find them at that time widely circulated over the world as apostolic writings. Can they have gained this circulation and this reputation if they had originated by forgery within the intervening generation? We find also these unimpeached witnesses asserting that they had received these books from their fathers, who had received them from the cotemporaries of the Apostles. Is it credible that all of these were deceived, or that they all, in widely separated parts of the world, conspired together to impose upon their fellow-men as apostolic, books which their fellow-men must have known to be of recent origin? If it is not, then the evidence from catalogues alone is credible proof that all of the New Testament books originated in the days of the Apostles.

---

[44] This is implied in the following extract from Tertullian's reply: "But Marcion, finding the Epistle of Paul to the Galatians, wherein he rebukes even Apostles for not walking uprightly according to the truth of the Gospel, as well as accuses certain false apostles of perverting the Gospel of Christ, labors very hard to destroy the standing of these Gospels which are published as genuine and under the name of Apostles, in order, forsooth, to secure for his own gospel the credit which he takes away from them" (*Against Marcion,* iv. 3). A brief account of the career of Marcion and of his teaching is given by Westcott (*Canon of New Testament,* 308–315).

TWO

Evidence from Versions

It is self-evident that every book must be as old as any translation of it into another language, and that so far back as we can find a translation of the New Testament books, we trace their existence by this fact to the same date. Moreover, a book is seldom translated until it has acquired such a reputation in its original tongue as to create a demand for it in some other country where a different tongue is spoken. The period necessary for this was comparatively long in ancient times, when literary intercourse between nations of different languages was not so free as in this age of travel, of newspapers and of printed books. The New Testament books, therefore, must have been in existence for a considerable period previous to the earliest translation of them. As we have already traced their existence by evidence indisputable into the second century, we need not start with this new evidence at a later period, but we shall begin with it where the other terminated.

We have already given evidence in Part First,[1] that in the last quarter of the second century two versions were made into the two dialects of the Coptic language, the dialects of Lower and of Upper Egypt, and that both of these versions contained the whole of our present New Testament. This shows that all of these books had existed long enough in the original Greek to become known throughout the land of Egypt, and that they had such a reputation

---

[1] See p. 35.

as created a demand for their translation into the native tongues of that country. It should be remembered, too, that Greek was the prevailing language in Alexandria, the literary and political center of the country, and that consequently the demand for a vernacular version in Egypt was not so prompt as it otherwise might have been. When made, the version contained the same books which were used, as we have seen, by the two famous Greek teachers at Alexandria, Clement and Origen, who continued their labors after these versions had gone into use. Is it credible that these books were of recent origin, and that the scholars and churches of Egypt were deceived in thinking that they had been in use from the days of the Apostles?

The Peshito Syriac version carries the evidence to a still earlier date. It was made, as we have seen in Part First, about the middle of the second century, and it contained all the books of the New Testament but five, viz.: 2 Peter, 2 and 3 John, Jude and Revelation.[2] It was made for the people of Syria, of which Antioch was the principal city. Its existence implies the Conversion to Christ of so many persons in that country who could read only the Syriac tongue, that a translation of their sacred books was demanded. The fact that the Greek language was prevalent in Syria among the educated classes, would naturally retard the rise of such a demand, yet it existed and was supplied within fifty years of the death of the last apostle. Among the persons for whose use the version was made were many whose fathers, or whose aged friends, had been baptized by Apostles and their fellow-laborers. They believed these books to have been written by those men, and to have been handed down to themselves by their own fathers. It must be conceded that they could not have thus believed if the books were recent forgeries which their fathers had never seen. It seems scarcely possible to doubt that this evidence alone traces the books contained in this version to the apostolic age.

Almost simultaneously with the Peshito Syriac in Syria appeared the Old Latin Version in Africa. By some scholars its date

---

[2] See p. 34.

is fixed a little earlier; by others a little later; but the very latest date that can be assigned it is the year 170.[3] It was not made in Italy, as one would naturally suppose, but in the Roman province of Africa, of which Carthage was the principal city, and where Latin was the prevalent language. The church in Rome itself continued thus far to use Greek literature.[4] As Greek was but little known in Africa, a translation of the Greek scriptures became indispensable as soon as the disciples became numerous. This accounts for the fact that although Africa was among the latest of the Roman provinces to be evangelized,[5] it was among the first to possess a translation of the Christian scriptures. The publication of this translation so soon after the conversion of the people, makes it probable that they received the translation from the same persons who brought them the gospel. But these persons lived at a period early enough to know what books had come from the apostolic age, and books of recent origin could not have been palmed off on them as apostolic. The version included all of our present

---

[3] See p. 35, where the evidences are given.

[4] "At first it seemed natural to look to Italy as the center of the Latin literature of Christianity, and the original source of that Latin version of the Holy Scriptures which, in a later form, has become identified with the Church of Rome. Yet however plausible such a belief may be, it finds no support in history. Rome itself, under the Emperors, is well described as a Greek city, and Greek was its second language. As far as we can learn, the mass of the poorer population—to which the great bulk of the early Christians belonged—was Greek either in descent or in speech. Among the names of the fifteen bishops of Rome, up to the close of the second century, four only are Latin, though in the next century the proportion is nearly reversed. When St. Paul wrote to the Roman Church, he wrote in Greek, and in the long list of salutations to its members, with which the epistle is concluded, only four genuine Latin names occur. Shortly afterward Clement wrote to the Corinthian Church, in Greek, in the name of the Church of Rome; and, at a later period, we find the Bishop of Corinth writing in Greek to Soter, the ninth in succession from Clement.... The apologies to the Roman emperors were in Greek.... The first sermons that were preached at Rome were in Greek... Meanwhile, however, though Greek continued to be the natural, if not the sole language of the Roman Church, the seeds of Latin Christianity were rapidly developing in Africa.... Carthage, the second Rome, escaped the Grecism of the first. In Africa Greek was no longer a current dialect." Westcott, *Canon of New Testament*, 244–247.

[5] "Nothing is known in detail of the origin of the African churches. The Donatists classed them among 'those last which shall be first'; and Augustine in his reply merely affirms that 'some barbarian nations embraced Christianity after Africa, so that it is certain that Africa was not the last to believe.' The concession implies that Africa was late in being evangelized. Tertullian adds that it received the gospel from Rome." Westcott, *Canon of New Testament*, 246.

New Testament books except Hebrews, James and 2 Peter. But Hebrews and James were both in the Peshito Syriac, and all the books absent from that except 2 Peter were present in this. Consequently we find the existence of every book of the New Testament except 2 Peter attested by translations as early as the middle of the second century. They were translated because they were the authoritative books of the churches, and they were authoritative because the churches believed them to have come from apostolic hands. Is it possible that these churches could have been totally mistaken about such facts when the interval had been so short?

When we remember that the gospel was preached and the churches were established before the close of the second century in all the nations of the Roman empire, we are led to inquire why so few translations of the Christian scriptures were then made. But the small number should excite no surprise. In the first place, the Greek language was the universal language of literature, known and read by educated persons throughout the world except in Africa. In the second place, most of the nations not closely connected with Greece or with Rome were as yet without an alphabet. Even in Egypt the Christian translators were compelled, as we have stated, to enlarge and otherwise change the native alphabet, and in Armenia as well as among the Goths, an alphabet had to be invented.[6] Moreover, in all countries the masses of the people were unable to read, and were dependent for knowledge of books on the public and private readings of their teachers. The latter could translate as they read, and thus the demand for written translations was delayed. This universal spread of the Greek language, which had resulted from the conquests of Alexander and the dominion of his successors, served three important purposes of divine providence: it facilitated the preaching of the gospel and the intercourse of remote Christian communities with one another; it obviated for some generations the necessity of translating the scripture into the vernacular tongues; and it led to the composition of the New Testament Scriptures in the language best

---

[6] See page 37.

adapted of all that had been spoken among men to the expression of the nicer distinctions in religious thought.

THREE

Evidence from Quotations

Quotations from a book, like copies of it, catalogues of its parts, and translations of it, are self-evident proofs of its previous existence, seeing that it is impossible to make quotations from a book not yet written.

Quotations are divided into three distinct classes:

I. Those in which the words quoted are credited by name to the book whence they are taken, or to its author. These are called express quotations.

II. Those in which the source of the quotation is not given. These are called anonymous quotations.

III. Those in which an idea, a figure of speech, or a form of expression, is borrowed from another writer without credit. These are variously styled coincidences, allusions, reminiscences; but they are really quotations from memory, and we think it better to treat them as such.

As we proceed, we shall refer to these classes of quotations by their numbers.

In the second and third classes, and especially in the third, the fact that a quotation is actually made is usually a matter of probability, not often one of certainty. It depends on the probability that two writers used the words, ideas, or figures of speech in question, independently of each other; and the degree of this probability depends upon the character of the matter used by them in common. Such ideas, figures and phrases as are commonplace, and such as have become common property, may be used in common by two writers unacquainted with each other's productions; but such as are strikingly characteristic of a certain author are known, when found in the works of another, to be borrowed property. The identification depends on the well known fact, that as every man has his own peculiar features, so every writer of any originality has his own peculiar mode of expression, and his peculiar thoughts. For example, if in the works of any writer since Shakespeare there should be found the words, "to be, or not to be, that is the question," there could be no reasonable doubt that he obtained them directly or indirectly from Shakespeare's Hamlet. On the other hand, if they should be found in the works of some author previous to Shakespeare, it would be morally certain that Shakespeare had borrowed them from him. In like manner the characteristic phraseology, figures of speech, or thoughts of any New Testament writer, when found uncredited in the work of another author, furnish proof that the latter borrowed directly or indirectly from the former, except when the New Testament writer can be regarded as the later of the two.

We now propose to draw upon this source of evidence, by presenting not all, but a few of the quotations made from the New Testament books by early authors, and we have selected those on which the force of the evidence from this source chiefly depends, and which for this reason should be familiar to every student of Evidences.

The writers whom we have already mentioned, such as Origen, Clement, Tertullian, and others of a later date, made many and copious quotations from the books of the New Testament, so many and so copious that the opinion has sometimes been expressed that the whole New Testament, if it were lost, could be reproduced out of the Christian writings of the first four centuries. But as we have already seen that these men mention the books by name, it would be but reiteration to cite their quotations. It is needful only that we begin at the point of time already reached by means of the latter evidence, and cite the quotations made by writers who lived at a still earlier period. If the period between the writers just named and the apostles can be spanned by a succession of writers making quotations from the books in question, the existence of these books will be traced to the age of the apostles by evidence absolutely conclusive.

We begin this line of evidence with Irenaeus, a writer who mentions so many of the New Testament books by name that he might almost be classed with those who have left catalogues. The exact date of his birth is not known, nor is that of his death; but both are fixed within very narrow limits, and we adopt as certainly quite close to the truth the date 135 as that of his birth, and 200 as that of his death.[1] He speaks of having seen Polycarp in Smyrna in his early youth, and from this it is supposed that Smyrna, or some adjacent part of Asia Minor was his native place.[2] Later in life his home was at Lyons, in Gaul, where he was made a Bishop in the year 177. Previous to his ordination he visited Rome as the bearer of a letter from certain members of the church at Lyons who were in prison and awaiting martyrdom, to the Bishop of the church at Rome.[3] From all this it is apparent that he had means of knowing what books of the New Testament were in use within the period of his remembrance, in Asia Minor, in Gaul and in Rome. His memory reached back within the first half of the second century. His quotations and citations may be classified as follows:

---

[1] These are the figures adopted by Westcott (*Canon of New Testament*, 379) while Donaldson (*Ante Nicene Library, Int.* XVIII., XIX.), says that "the general date assigned to his birth is somewhere between AD 120 and AD 140," and that "he is supposed to have died about AD 202."

[2] "But Polycarp was not only instructed by apostles, and conversed with many who had seen Christ, but was also by apostles in Asia appointed bishop of the church in Smyrna, whom I also saw in my early youth, for he tarried a very long time, and, when a very old man, gloriously and most nobly suffering martyrdom, departed this life, having always taught the things which he had learned from the apostles, and which the church has handed down, and which alone are true." Irenaeus, *Against Heresies*, 262, 263.

[3] "But these same martyrs recommending also Irenaeus, who was then a presbyter of the church at Lyons, to the Bishop of Rome, before mentioned, bear abundant testimony in his favor, as the following extracts show: 'We pray and desire, father Eleutherus, that you may rejoice in God in all things and always. We have requested our brother and companion, Irenaeus, to carry this epistle to you, and we exhort you to consider him as commended to you as a zealous follower of the testament of Christ.'" Eusebius, *Ecclesiastical History*, v. 4.

1. He says that what the Apostles first preached they afterward "handed down to us in the Scriptures"; that they were filled with the Holy Spirit before they preached; that Matthew "issued a written gospel" while Peter and Paul were preaching at Rome; that Mark, "the disciple and interpreter of Peter," wrote what had been preached by Peter; that Luke, "the companion of Paul, recorded in a book the gospel preached by him"; and that "John, the disciple who had leaned on the Lord's breast, published a gospel during his residence in Ephesus."[4] He further claims that the ground on which these Gospels rest was so firm that even the heretics against whom he wrote and whose doctrines were condemned by them, were constrained to acknowledge them, some acknowledging one, and some another.[5] He makes other remarks concerning the Gospels equally explicit, and his quotations from them are very numerous.

2. Irenaeus makes many quotations from Acts, and repeatedly speaks of it as a work of Luke. For instance, he quotes the account of Simon the sorcerer (Acts 8.8–11) as the words of Luke;[6] he

---

[4] "We have learned from none others the plan of our salvation, than from those through whom the gospel has come down to us, which they did at one time proclaim in public, and at a later period, by the will of God, handed down to us in the Scriptures to be the ground and pillar of our faith. . . . For after our Lord rose from the dead the apostles were invested with power from on high when the Holy Spirit came down, were filled from all his gifts and had perfect knowledge. Matthew also issued a written gospel among the Hebrews in their own dialect, while Peter and Paul were preaching at Rome and laying the foundations of the church. After their departure, Mark, the disciple and interpreter of Peter, did also hand down to us in writing what had been preached by Peter. Luke also, the companion of Paul, recorded in a book the gospel preached by him. Afterwards, John, the disciple of the Lord, who had also leaned upon his breast, did himself publish a gospel during his residence at Ephesus in Asia." *Against Heresies,* iii. 1.

[5] "So firm is the ground on which these gospels rest, that the very heretics themselves bear witness to them, and, starting from these each one of them endeavors to establish his own peculiar doctrine. For the Ebionites, who use Matthew's gospel only, are confuted out of this very same, making false suppositions in regard to the Lord. But Marcion, mutilating that according to Luke, is proved to be a blasphemer of the only existing God from those passages which he still retains. Those again who separate Jesus from Christ, alleging that Christ remained impassible, but it was Jesus who suffered, preferring the gospel by Mark, if they read it with the love of truth, may have their errors rectified. Those, moreover, who follow Valentinus, making copious use of that according to John to illustrate their conjunctions, shall be proved to be totally in error by means of this very gospel." *Against Heresies,* III. 7.

[6] "Simon, the Samaritan, was that magician of whom Luke, the disciple and follower

credits in the same way the account of Paul's interview with Jesus on the way to Damascus;[7] and he cites the passages in Acts where the author uses the first person, as proof that Luke was with Paul on the occasions referred to.[8]

3. Twelve of Paul's Epistles are quoted by this author, some of them many times, and the authorship[9] of all is especially ascribed to Paul. The two not thus quoted are Philemon and Hebrews. The former he neither quotes nor mentions—an omission readily accounted for by the brevity and personal character of this document. Of the latter there is no mention in his extant writings, but Eusebius gives a list of some of his works now lost, in one of which this Epistle was both named and quoted;[10] while Photius, a writer of the ninth century, quotes a still earlier writer as saying that Irenaeus denied the Pauline authorship of Hebrews.[11] The

---

of the apostles, says: 'But there was a certain man, Simon by name, who before time used magical arts in that city, and led away the people of Samaria, declaring that he himself was some great one, to whom they all gave heed, from the least to the greatest,'" etc. *Against Heresies*, I. 23,1.

[7] "But again, we allege the same heresies against those who do not recognize Paul as an apostle; that they should either reject the other words of the gospel which we have come to know through Luke alone, and not make use of them; or else, if they do receive all of these they must necessarily admit also that testimony concerning Paul when he tells us that the Lord spoke at first to him from heaven: 'Saul, Saul, why persecutest thou me? I am Jesus whom thou persecutest;' and then to Ananias, regarding him: 'Go thy way; for he is a chosen vessel unto me, to bear my name among the Gentiles, and kings, and the children of Israel.'" *Against Heresies*, III. 15, 1.

[8] "But that this Luke was inseparable from Paul and his fellow laborer in the gospel, he himself clearly evinces, not as a matter of boasting, but as bound to do so by the truth itself. For he says that when Barnabas and John who was called Mark, had parted company from Paul and sailed to Cyprus, 'we came to Troas'; and when Paul had beheld in a dream a man of Macedonia, saying, 'Come into Macedonia, Paul, and help us;' 'immediately,' he says, 'we endeavored to go into Macedonia, understanding that the Lord had called us to preach the gospel unto them.'" In this manner he proceeds to cite all the passages in which the author of Acts uses the pronoun of the first person plural. *Against Heresies*, III. 14, 1.

[9] The citations necessary to verify this statement are too numerous for our space, but they can be readily found by glancing through the footnotes of the English Version of the works of Irenaeus, and they are collected in a group in Lardner's Credibility, III. 163, 164.

[10] In naming some of the minor works of Irenaeus, Eusebius says: "There is a book also of various disputes, in which he mentions the epistle to the Hebrews." *Ecclesiastical History*, v. 26.

[11] "Moreover, by Photius we are informed that Stephen Gobar writes thus: 'Hippolytus and Irenaeus say, the epistle of Paul to the Hebrews is not his'; by which, perhaps, we need not understand that Irenaeus had expressly said so anywhere." Lardner, *Credibility*, 2 185.

sum of the evidence then is, that Irenaeus made use of all of the Epistles commonly ascribed to Paul except Philemon.

4. Irenaeus[12] quotes by name the First Epistle of Peter,[13] and the First and Second of John.[14] The Third of John, and the Epistles of James and Jude he neither mentions nor quotes. In two places he makes a quotation of the third class from the Second Epistle of Peter. In trying to show that Adam died the same day that he ate the forbidden fruit, he states as the opinion of some, that he died within a thousand years, and he argues that since "a day of the Lord is as a thousand years," he died within the time stated in the sentence.[15] In another place he assumes that the six days of creation are a prophecy of the earth's duration, and argues that as "the day of the Lord is as a thousand years," in six thousand years the world will come to an end.[16] This bold and startling statement that "a day of the Lord is as a thousand years" is found in almost the identical words in 2 Peter 3.8, and it is there employed in connection with the very subject to which Irenaeus in the last instance applies it, the end of the world. The

---

[12] By this expression is meant the epistles of James, Peter, John and Jude, called catholic, (general) because they were not addressed (except 2 and 3 John) to any particular person or congregation. The expression originated at an early period, and is very convenient as a brief designation of this group of epistles.

[13] "Peter says in his epistles, 'Whom, not seeing, ye love; in whom, though now ye see him not, ye have believed, ye shall rejoice with joy unspeakable'" I. Peter i. 8. *Against Heresies*, IV. 9, 2.

[14] After quoting a statement of John in his gospel, Irenaeus adds: "For this reason also he has testified to us in his epistle: 'Little children, it is the last time; and as ye have heard that antichrist doth come, now have many antichrists appeared; whereby we know that it is the last time'" (1 John 2.18.) *Ib.* iii. 5. "These are they against whom the Lord has cautioned us beforehand; and his disciple, in his epistle already mentioned, commands us to avoid them when he says: 'For many deceivers are entered into the world who confess not that Jesus Christ is come in the flesh'" (2 John 7.8) *Ib.* iii. 8.

[15] "And there are some, again, who relegate the death of Adam to the thousandth year; for since a day of the Lord is as a thousand years, he did not overstep the thousand years, but died within them, thus bearing out the sentence of his sin." *Ib.* v. 23, 2.

[16] "For in as many days as this world was made, in so many thousand years shall it be concluded. And for this reason the Scripture says: Thus the heavens and the earth were finished, and all their adornment, and God brought to a conclusion upon the sixth day the works that he had made, and God rested on the seventh day from all his works. This is an account of the things formerly created, as also it is a prophecy of what is to come. For the day of the Lord is as a thousand years; and in six days created things were completed: it is evident, therefore, that they will come to an end at the sixth thousand years." *Ib.* v. 28, 3.

thought is strikingly original, and it could not have occurred independently to Irenaeus and the author of 2 Peter. We conclude then that it was borrowed by the former, and that he not only knew this Epistle, but accepted it as an authority on this high subject, the mysterious relation which God sustains to time.[17] In the use which he makes of the passage he follows Justin Martyr, a writer yet to be mentioned.[18]

5. Our author makes many quotations from the Apocalypse, and he ascribes it to the Apostle John. He also states approximately its date, saying that it was written "toward the end of Domitian's reign."[19] Domitian died AD 96.

We now see that Irenaeus quoted, and was familiar with all the books of the New Testament except the three short Epistles, Philemon, Jude and 3 John, and the longer Epistle of James. As his own personal remembrance reached back within the first half of the second century, this evidence traces all these books at least that far. But his opportunities for information were such that we must grant for his evidence even more than this. The Bishop of Lyons who preceded him, and under whom he held the office of presbyter, was Pothinus, who suffered martyrdom at ninety years of age in the year 177.[20] He was consequently thirteen years of

---

[17] The only ground for doubting, as many eminent authors do, that Irenaeus here quotes 2 Peter, is based on the possibility of his having obtained the thought from Psalm 90.4. But the thought of the Psalmist is quite different from that of Peter and Irenaeus. The latter speaks of God's absolute relation to time, and interprets his language accordingly; while the Psalmist is considering God's long existence in the past, and speaks of it as being so long that a thousand years dwindle in comparison to the length of a day or a watch in the night. Moreover, the words of Irenaeus are almost identical with those of Peter, and they vary materially from those of the Psalmist. "A day of the Lord is as a thousand years," Irenaeus. "One day with the Lord is as a thousand years," Peter. "A thousand years in thy sight is but as yesterday when it is past, and as a watch in the night," Psalmist.

[18] See below, under quotations from Justin Martyr.

[19] "We will not, however, incur the risk of pronouncing positively as to the names of antichrist; for if it were necessary that his name should be revealed at the present time, it would have been announced by him who beheld the apocalyptic vision. For that was seen no very long time since, but almost in our day, toward the end of Domitian's reign." *Against Heresies*, V. 30, 3.

[20] "Pothinus, having died with the other martyrs of Gaul, in the ninetieth year of his age, was succeeded by Irenaeus in the episcopate of the church at Lyons," Eusebius, *Ecclesiastical History*, v. 5. This occurred, as the same writer states, in the seventeenth year of the reign of Marcus Antoninus, which was AD 177. *Ib.* v., Preliminary.

age when the Apostle John died in the year 100, and his memory spanned all the period between that event and the mature years of Irenaeus. He must have known whether any of the books represented as apostolic had come into existence in his own day; and his knowledge on this subject was imparted to Irenaeus, his pupil and subordinate. Furthermore, when Irenaeus was a boy in Smyrna he saw Polycarp, who was instructed by Apostles,[21] and who had conversed with many persons who had seen Jesus. He had also conversed with another person whom he styles "a certain presbyter," who had been taught by men who had seen the Apostles.[22] From his boyhood, then, he had known the New Testament books as they were known by men who had seen the Apostles, and this renders it in the highest degree improbable that any of them had originated since the apostolic age.

Before we leave the writings of Irenaeus it may be well to notice the reverence paid to the New Testament books by the disciples of his day, as it appears in the titles which he familiarly applies to them. He calls them "the Sacred Scriptures," "the Oracles of God."[23] He speaks of the New Testament as containing "the writings of the Evangelists and the Apostles," as the Old Testament contains "the law and the prophets."[24] He holds these Scriptures

---

[21] "But Polycarp also was not only instructed by apostles, and conversed with many who had seen Christ, but was also by apostles in Asia appointed bishop of the church in Smyrna, whom I also saw in my early youth, for he tarried a very long time, and, when a very old man, gloriously and most nobly suffering martyrdom, departed this life, having always taught the things which he had learned from the apostles, and which alone are true." *Against Heresies*, iii. 3, 4.

[22] "As I have heard from a certain presbyter, who had heard it from those who had seen the apostles, and from those who had been their disciples, the punishment in the Scripture was sufficient for the ancients in regard to what they did without the Spirit's guidance." *Ib.* iv. 27, 1.

[23] "In like manner do these persons patch together old wives' fables, and then endeavor by violently drawing away from their proper connection, words, expressions and parables whenever found, to adapt the oracles of God to their baseless fictions" *Ib.* i. 8, 2. "These things are such as fall under our observation, and are clearly and unambiguously in express terms set forth in the sacred Scriptures. And therefore the parables ought not to be adapted to ambiguous expressions" *Ib.* ii. 27, 1.

[24] "And it is not only from the writings of the evangelists and the apostles that they endeavor to derive proofs for their opinions by perverse interpretations and deceitful expositions: they deal in the same manner with the law and the prophets, which contain many parables and allegories that can frequently be drawn into various senses, according to the

to be perfect, since they were spoken by the Word of God and his Spirit;[25] and he declares that no light punishment awaits him who either adds to or subtracts anything from them.[26] Is it possible that books thus esteemed in the middle of the second century and believed to have been in use in the church from the days of the Apostles could have been written but a few years previous?

We next go back to Justin, a native of the ancient city of Shechem in Palestine, which was called Flavia Neapolis by the Romans, and is now called Nablus by the Arabs.[27] His nationality was uncertain. He calls the Samaritans his people,[28] but this may be only because he was born among them. His name, and that of his father and his grandfather, are Roman, indicating the probability of a Roman lineage. His principal writings which have come down to us are two Apologies, and a Dialogue with one Trypho, a Jew. One of the former was addressed to the Emperor Antoninus Pius, and the other to the Roman Senate. The Dialogue, which is by far the most elaborate of his works, is an attempt to state and to answer the arguments of the Jews against the Christian faith; and the Apologies are remonstrances against the persecution of Christians by the Roman authorities. The exact date of his birth is not known, but it was not much later than the

---

kind of exegesis to which they are subjected." *Ib.* i. 3, 6.

[25] "We should leave those things of that nature [things we can not explain] to God who created us, being most properly assured that the Scriptures are indeed perfect, since they were spoken by the Word of God and his Spirit" *Ib*. ii. 28, 2.

[26] Speaking of a change in the number 666 (Rev 13.18) which had been made by some heretics, he says: "Now in the first place, it is loss to wander from truth, and to imagine that as being the case which is not; then again, as there shall be no light punishment on him who either adds to or subtract anything from Scripture, under that such a person must necessarily fall." *Ib*. v. 30, 1.

[27] "To the emperor Titus Ælius Adrianus Antoninus Pius Augustus Caesar, and to his son, Verissimus, the philosopher, and to Lucius, the philosopher, the natural son of Caesar and the adopted son of Pius, a lover of learning, and to the sacred senate, with the whole people of the Romans, I, Justin, the son of Priscus and grandson of Bacchius, natives of Flavia Neapolis in Palestine, present this address and petition in behalf of those of all nations who are unjustly hated and wantonly abused, myself being one of them." *First Apology. Address.*

[28] "For I gave no thought to any of my people, that is the Samaritans, when I had a communication with Caesar, but stated that they were wrong in trusting to the magician Simon of their own nation, who, they say, is God above all power and authority and might." *Dialogue, c.* 120.

beginning of the second century.[29] The date of his death is involved in equal uncertainty, but that of his first Apology is stated in the work itself as about one hundred and fifty years after the birth of Jesus, and it is agreed among scholars that it was written in 146 or 147.[30] He suffered martyrdom at Rome,[31] and from this circumstance he is usually called Justin Martyr. In regard to these dates it is sufficient for our present purpose to know that he lived through the first half of the second century.

In his dialogue he gives an interesting account of his own early inquiries on the subject of religion. Being desirous of obtaining a knowledge of God, he sought personal instruction from Greek philosophers. His first teacher was a Stoic. After spending much time with him and learning but little, he resorted to a Peripatetic, then to a Pythagorean, and finally to a Platonist. Under the latter he says that his mind was "furnished with wings," and that he was elated with the thought that he would soon look upon God; but at this juncture, while enjoying a solitary walk by the seashore he met an aged Christian through whose conversation he was brought to the true knowledge of God."[32] He was the more easily converted on account of his previous knowledge of the patience with which Christians endured persecution.[33] From this time he went about in the garb of a philosopher, contending earnestly for the gospel in various countries, especially in Ephesus and at

---

[29] See Westcott on the Canon, p. 95, 98, *n.* 1, and the authorities quoted by Lardner, *Credibility 2* 112, 116.

[30] "But lest some should, without reason and for the perversion of what we teach, maintain that we say that Christ was born one hundred and fifty years ago under Cyrenius, and subsequently, in the time of Pontius Pilate, taught what we say he taught; and should cry out against us as though all men who were born before him were irresponsible, let us anticipate and solve the difficulty." *First Apol. c.* 46. Westcott, following Dr. Hort, gives the exact date as 146 (Canon of N.T. 98, *n.* 1), and the author of the infidel work called Supernatural Religion, makes it no later than 147. Vol. i. 284.

[31] An interesting account of his martyrdom by an unknown writer has come down to us, and an English version of it may be found in the Ante-Nicene Christian Library, vol. 2 367.

[32] *Dialogue* c. ii.-viii.

[33] "For I myself, too, when I was delighting in the doctrines of Plato, and heard the Christians slandered, and saw them fearless of death and of all other things which are counted fearful, perceived that it was impossible that they could be living in wickedness and pleasure." *Second Apology,* c. 12.

Rome. According to Eusebius, "he was the most noted of those who flourished in those times."[34]

As Justin's argument in all three of his works pertains not to the doctrine or discipline of the church, but to the person and character of Jesus, and to the moral status of Christians, his quotations from the New Testament are necessarily confined almost entirely to the gospel narratives. From these he makes about one hundred and twenty quotations setting forth all the characteristic teachings of Jesus, and nearly all of the prominent events of his life. For a very obvious reason he nowhere mentions any of our gospels by the name of its author; for the author's name would amount to nothing with the heathen emperor or the unbelieving Jew; but he designates the books in such a way as to give them their full weight of authority. He refers to them constantly as the sources of his information and the authority for Christian ordinances; and he designates them by such titles as these: "The Gospel," "The Memoirs of the Apostles," "The Memoirs composed by the Apostles, which are called Gospels," "The Memoirs which were drawn up by His Apostles and those who followed them." There are sixteen instances of this kind, two in the First Apology, and fourteen in the Dialogue.[35] By an examination of

---

[34] "But Justin was the most noted of those who flourished in those times, who, in the guise of a philosopher, preached the truth of God, and contended for the faith also in his writings." *Eccles. Hist.* IV. 11.

[35] "Among us the prince of the wicked spirits is called the serpent, and Satan, and the devil, as you can learn by looking into our writings." *First Apol.* c. 28. "For the Apostles, in the memoirs composed by them, which are called Gospels, have thus delivered to us what was enjoined on them; that Jesus took bread, and when he had given thanks, said: 'This do ye in remembrance of me; this is my body;' and that, after the same manner, having taken the cup and given thanks, he said: 'This is my blood;' and gave it to them alone." *IBC* 66. In describing the regular order of service in the meetings of the Christians, "on the day called Sunday," he says, "The memoirs of the apostles, or the writings of the prophets, are read so long as time permits." *IBC* 67. He represents Trypho the Jew as saying to him: "I am aware that your precepts in the so-called Gospel are so wonderful and so great, that I suspect no one can keep them; for I have carefully read them." *Dialogue*, c. 10. "But also in the gospel it is written that He said: 'All things are delivered unto me by my Father'... we find it recorded in the memoirs of His apostles that He is the Son of God." *IBC* 100. "For they that saw Him crucified shook their heads each one of them, and distorted their lips, and twisting their noses to each other, they spoke in mockery the words which are recorded in the memoirs of His apostles: He said he was the Son of God: let him come down; let God save him." *Ib.* c 101. "He kept silence and chose to return no answer to any one in

those passages, copied in the footnote below, it will be seen that while Justin names the title Gospels as being in common use he prefers the title Memoirs, and uses it more frequently than all others. In this he showed excellent judgment, and at the same time he makes it more certain to us that he refers to our four hooks; for they are in the strictest sense Memoirs, or personal reminiscences. This title describes them exactly, while the title Gospels does not. Furthermore, his description of them as Memoirs composed by the apostles and their followers, corresponds precisely to the authorship of our four, two of them having been composed by apostles, and the other two by their followers. Indeed it is when he is about to make a quotation from Luke that he designates the latter two in this way.[36]

These citations not only show that our gospels were in existence and in use in the days of Justin, but that they were in wide circulation among both Jews and Gentiles, and that they were used as authorities in the churches. His remark to the heathen emperor, "Among us the prince of the wicked spirits is called the serpent, and Satan, and the devil, as you can learn by looking into our writings," shows that they were well known among the

---

the presence of Pilate, as has been declared in the memoirs of His apostles." *IBC* 102. "For this devil, when Jesus went up from the river Jordan at the time when the voice spoke to him, 'Thou art my son; this day have I begotten thee,' is recorded in the memoirs of the apostles to have come to Him and tempted Him." . . . "For in the memoirs which I say were drawn up by the apostles and those who followed them, it is recorded that his sweat fell down like drops of blood while he was praying and saying, 'If it be possible, let this cup pass.'" *IBC* 103. "And this is recorded to have happened in the memoirs of His apostles." *IBC* 104. "For I have already proved that he was the only-begotten of the Father of all things, being begotten in a peculiar manner, word of power by Him, and having afterward become man through the virgin, as we have learned from the memoirs." "For when Christ was giving up his spirit on the cross, he said, 'Father, into thy hands I commend my spirit,' as I have learned also from the memoirs." "And these words are recorded in the memoirs: 'unless your righteousness shall exceed that of the scribes and Pharisees, ye shall not enter into the kingdom of heaven.'" *IBC* 105. He stood in the midst of his brethren, the apostles, and when living with them sang praises to God, as is made evident in the memoirs of the apostles." "And when it is said that he changed the name of one of the apostles to Peter; and when it is written in the memoirs of Him that this so happened, as well as that he changed the names of other two brothers, the sons of Zebedee, to Boanerges." *IBC* 106. "And that He would rise again on the third day after the crucifixion, it is written in the memoirs that some of your nation, questioning him, said, show us a sign." *IBC* 107.

[36] Dialogue, c. 103.

heathen. The remark of Trypho, "Your precepts in the so-called Gospel are so wonderful and so great, that I suspect no one can keep them; for I have carefully read them," shows that they were well known among unbelieving Jews His reference to them as authority for observing the Lord's Supper, and his statement that they were read, together with the writings of the prophets, in the weekly meetings of the churches, shows that they were held by Christians as authoritative writings.

Now, as all this testimony is given by a man who spoke in the middle of the second century, whose memory reached back to near the beginning of that century, and who spoke to men with memories reaching back as far as his own, it is quite certain that those Memoirs had come down to them from the age of the Apostles with the credit of apostolic authorship.

Of the other New Testament books Justin quotes by name only the Apocalypse. This he cites by the name of its author to show that the prophetic gifts which had existed among the ancient Jews had appeared among the Christians.[37] He has quotations of the third class from five of Paul's epistles, viz., Romans, First Corinthians, Colossians, Second Thessalonians, and Hebrews.[38] There is evidence, moreover, apart from quotations, that he was acquainted with the body of Paul's epistles and with Acts, in the fact that he

---

[37] "There was a certain man with us whose name was John, one of the Apostles of Christ, who prophesied by a revelation that was made to him, that those who believed in our Christ would dwell a thousand years in Jerusalem; and that thereafter the general, and in short the eternal revelation and judgment of all men, would likewise take place." *IBC* 61.

[38] "For when Abraham himself was in uncircumcision, he was justified and blessed by reason of the faith which he reposed in God, as the Scripture tells. Moreover, the Scriptures and the facts themselves compel us to admit that he received circumcision for a sign, and not for righteousness." *IBC* 22, *comp.* Romans 4.10–12. "For the passover was Christ . . . and as the blood of the passover saved those who were in Egypt, so also the blood of Christ will deliver from death those who have believed." *IBC* 111; *comp.* 1 Corinthians 5.7. "For every demon, when exorcised in the name of this very Son of God, who is the first-born of every creature." *IBC* 85, *comp.* Colossians 1.15. "He shall come from heaven with glory, when the man of apostasy, who speaks strange things against the Most High, shall venture to do unlawful deeds on the earth against us the Christians." *IBC* 110, *comp.* 2 Thessalonians 2.1–10. "That all these things should come to pass, I say our Teacher foretold, He who is both Son and Apostle of God, the Father of all and the Rider, Jesus Christ; from whom also we have the name Christians." *First Apol.* c. 12 *comp.* Hebrews 3.1. the title Apostle given to Jesus.

wrote against Marcion's heresy,[39] the most striking peculiarity of which was the acceptance of the writings of Paul and Luke, with the exception of Titus and 1 and 2 Timothy, while he rejected the writings of all the other apostles.[40]

As to the Catholic Epistles, it is conceded by some of the most eminent writers on the Canon, that Justin quotes from none of them;[41] but there are two passages which have every appearance of being quotations of the third class from the Second Epistle of Peter. Speaking of the decree that Adam should die in the day that he ate of the tree, he says: "We have perceived, moreover, that the expression, 'The day of the Lord is as a thousand years,' is connected with this subject."[42] This remark shows that there was a well known expression, "The day of the Lord is as a thousand years," an expression which is found in almost the identical terms in 2 Peter 3.8, but nowhere else in the Bible.[43] In the other passage, he gives as a reason why God had delayed to send Satan and those who follow him into their destined punishment, that it was because of his regard for the human race: "For he knows that some are to be saved by repentance, some even, that are not

---

[39] "And there is Marcion, a man of Pontus, who is even at this day alive and teaching his disciples to believe in some other God greater than the Creator. . . . But I have a treatise against all the heresies that have existed, already composed, which, if you wish to read it, I will give you." *First Apol.* c. 26. "And there is Marcion, a man of Pontus, who is even at this day alive and teaching his disciples to believe in some other God greater than the Creator. . . . But I have a treatise against all the heresies that have existed, already composed, which, if you wish to read it, I will give you." *First Apol.* c. 26.

[40] This is made very clear in Tertullian's work against Marcion. His fifth book is an attempt to refute Marcion out of the very epistles of Paul, which he acknowledged as genuine, and in other books, especially the fourth, he refutes him out of Luke's, which alone he accepted in a corrupted form. He says: "The same authority of the apostolic churches will afford evidence to the other gospels also, which we possess equally through their means, and according to their usage—I mean the gospels of John and Matthew—whilst that which Mark published may be affirmed to be Peter's, whose interpreter Mark was. . . . When, then, Marcion ought to be called to a strict account concerning these also, for having omitted them, and insisted in preference on Luke, as if they had not had free course in the churches, as well as in Luke's gospel, from the beginning 4.5.

[41] "It will be found that the Catholic Epistles, and the Epistles to Titus and Philemon, alone of the writings of the New Testament, have left no impression on the genuine or doubtful works of Justin Martyr." Westcott *On the Canon*, 170.

[42] Dialogue with Trypho, c. 81.

[43] Compare what I have said of the use made of the same passage by Irenaeus, page 88.

yet born."[44] Now this is the identical reason, expressed in different words, that is given for this delay in 2 Peter 3.9: "God is not slack concerning his promise, as some men count slackness; but is long-suffering to youward, not wishing that any should perish, but that all should come to repentance." It is far more likely that Justin obtained this thought from Peter than that he originated it himself and propounded it on his own authority, as an interpretation of God's mind.

To sum up the evidence from the writings of Justin, we may state, that it proves beyond question the general and public use within the first half of the second century, of the four Gospels, of all of Paul's Epistles except Titus and 1 and 2 Timothy, of the Apocalypse, and almost certainly of the Second Epistle of Peter.

The next author whose testimony we employ is Papias. He was an overseer of the church at Hierapolis, a city which stood in the vicinity of Laodicea and Colosse, and whose well preserved ruins continue to attest its ancient magnificence. It was the last home and burial place of the Apostle Philip and two of his three daughters.[45] The church is mentioned by Paul, Colossians 4.13.

All that we know of Papias personally is derived from the writings of Irenaeus and Eusebius. He was the author of a work in five books entitled An Exposition of Oracles of the Lord.[46] The whole

---

[44] "For among us the prince of the wicked spirits is called the serpent, and Satan, and the devil, as you can learn by looking into our writings. And that he would be sent into the fire with his host, and the men who follow him, and would be punished for an endless duration, Christ foretold. For the reason why God has delayed to do this, is his regard for the human race. For he foreknows that some are to be saved by repentance, some even that are, perhaps, not yet born." First Apology, c. 28.

[45] Eusebius quotes from Polycrates, a bishop of the church at Ephesus, the following statement made in a letter to Victor, a bishop of Rome: "For in Asia also, mighty luminaries have fallen asleep, which shall rise again at the last day, at the appearance of the Lord, when he shall come with glory from heaven, and shall gather again all the saints. Philip, one of the twelve apostles, who sleeps in Hierapolis, and his two aged virgin daughters. Another of his daughters who lived in the Holy Spirit, rests at Ephesus." *Eccles. Hist.* III. c. 31; v. 24. Some have supposed that in this quotation Philip the apostle is substituted for Philip the evangelist, but its correctness is successfully argued by Lightfoot, *Com. on. Colossians*, 45–47.

[46] Irenaeus, *Heresies*, v. 33, 4; Eusebius, *Eccles. Hist.* III. 39. The above is Westcott's translation of the title (*Canon*, 70) followed by Lightfoot, *Com. on Colossians*, 47. Donaldson (*Hist. Chris. Lit. and Doc.* I. 314) renders it, An Exposition of the Lord's Sayings. The original words are Λογίων Κυριακών Εξήγησις.

work has perished except a few quotations made from it by early writers, chiefly Eusebius; consequently we have but very limited means of knowing what use he made of the New Testament writings. The work was based, as its title indicates, on sayings of Jesus, and consequently we should expect its references to be confined to the four Gospels.

The period at which he lived is determined by the following statements: Eusebius says that he claimed to have conversed with the daughters of Philip;[47] Irenaeus says that he was a companion of Polycarp;[48] and he says of himself that he had conversed with various persons who had been followers of the Apostles; that he had inquired of them what the Apostles taught, and that he thought he derived more benefit in writing his Exposition from the living voice of these persons than from books.[49] These statements show that he was separated from the Apostles by only a single generation, and that his knowledge of apostolic teaching derived from books was supplemented by the recitals of original hearers. Eusebius considers him a man of weak judgment,[50]

---

[47] "That the apostle Philip continued at Hierapolis with his daughters has been already stated above. But we must now show how Papias, coming to them, received a wonderful account from the daughters of Philip." *Eccles. Hist.* III. 39.

[48] "These things are borne witness to in writing by Papias, the hearer of John, and a companion of Polycarp, in his fourth book, for there were five books compiled by him." *Heresies*, v. 33.

[49] Eusebius quotes him as follows: "But I shall not regret, to subjoin to my interpretations also for your benefit, whatsoever I have at any time accurately ascertained and treasured up in my memory as I have received it from the elders, I have received it in order to give additional confirmation to the truth of my testimony. For I have never, like many, delighted to hear those that tell many things, but those that teach the truth; neither those that record foreign precepts, but those that are given from the Lord to our faith, and that come from the truth itself. But if I meet with one who had been a follower of the elders anywhere, I made it a point to inquire what were the declarations of the elders. What was said by Andrew, Peter, or Philip. What by Thomas, James, John, Matthew, or any other of the disciples of the Lord; for I do not think I derive so much benefit from books as from the living voice of those that are still surviving." *Eccles. Hist.* III. 39.

[50] "He says there would be a certain millennium after the resurrection, and that there would be a corporeal reign of Christ on this very earth, which things he appears to have imagined, as if they were authorized by the apostolic narrations, not understanding correctly those matters which they propounded mystically in their representations. For he was very limited in his comprehension, as is evident from his discourses; yet he was the cause why most of the ecclesiastical writers, urging the antiquity of the man, were carried away by a similar opinion; as, for instance, Irenaeus, or any other that adopted such sentiments."

but this, if true, does not detract from his testimony concerning facts.

Of Matthew's Gospel he makes the following statement: "Matthew composed the Oracles (*Ta> Lo<gia*) in the Hebrew dialect, and every one translated it as he was able."[51] The manner in which the book is mentioned implies that it was then well known, while the declaration concerning the dialect in which it was written implies that it had not continued to circulate in that dialect: for if the Matthew still in use was written in Hebrew it would have been very idle to inform the public that it was composed in that dialect. Moreover, the statement that every one "translated it as he was able" implies that such translation was of the past and belonged to the earlier period of the book's existence.[52] When Papias lived it was known only in the Greek.

Concerning our second Gospel, Papias states, on the authority of one of the elders above referred to whom he calls "John the Presbyter," that Mark was Peter's interpreter, that what he recorded was written with great accuracy though not in chronological order, and that Peter gave him such instruction as was necessary.[53] His language implies, as in the case of Matthew, that this Gospel

---

Eccles. Hist. III. 39. Perhaps this low estimate of the man's comprehension was suggested by the poor opinion which Eusebius entertained concerning the doctrine of the millennium; yet in the very expression of this opinion he shows that Papias exerted a very decided influence over the views of later writers.

[51] *Ib.*

[52] "When 'every one interpreted' the Hebrew Matthew 'as he could,' he means and implies in his language, that the necessity of rendering the Hebrew into Greek *had* once existed, to be sure, but existed no longer." Prof. Geo. P. Fisher, *Supernatural Origin of Christianity*, 162. Meyer, speaking on this subject says: "The original Hebrew writing, however, from which our present Matthew proceeded through being translated into Greek, must, apart from the language, have been in contents and in form, in whole and in part, substantially the same as our Greek Matthew. The general evidence in favor of this view is, that throughout the ancient church our Greek Matthew was already used as if it had been the authentic text itself." *Com.* on *Matthew, Int.* § ii. (3).

[53] "And John the presbyter also said this: Mark being the interpreter of Peter, whatsoever he recorded he wrote with accuracy, but not, however, in the order in which it was spoken or done by our Lord; he was in company with Peter, who gave him such instruction as was necessary, but not to give a history of our Lord's discourses. Wherefore Mark has not erred in anything by writing some things as he has recorded them; for he was carefully attentive to one thing, not to pass by anything that he heard, or to state anything falsely in these accounts." Quoted by Eusebius, *Eccles. Hist.* III. 39.

was well known in the days of Papias, and was believed to have come from the pen of Mark.

The Gospel of John is not mentioned in any of the extant fragments of Papias, but a manuscript of John in the Vatican library has a Latin "argument" prefixed to it which was written in the ninth century, when the works of Papias were still extant, and it states that Papias described this Gospel and related that it had been given to the churches by John.[54]

Besides these three Gospels, Eusebius says that Papias made use of testimonies from the First Epistle of John and also from that of Peter;[55] and Andrew of Caesarea, a Greek writer of the fifth century, declares that he bore testimony to the inspiration of the book of Revelation.[56]

These are all the books mentioned or quoted by Papias, so far as our meager information extends. They include all the Gospels but Luke's, 1 Peter, 1 John, and the Apocalypse. It is probable, from the nature of his work, as before intimated, that if we had it all, the list would not be greatly extended. It is altogether certain that the books which he does use were not only recognized in his day as apostolic, but that they were so recognized by the elders who were his instructors and who had known the Apostles. This traces them to the Apostles and their companions by evidence that can not fairly be called in question.

Polycarp of Smyrna is one of the most conspicuous characters of the church in the second century. Irenaeus, who when a boy was personally acquainted with him, says of him that "he was instructed by Apostles"; that he had "conversed with many who had seen Christ"; that he was appointed an overseer of the Church

---

[54] The passage as given by Westcott (*Canon of N. T.* 76, *n.* 1) is thus translated: "The Gospel of John was published and given to the churches by John while yet in the body. So relates Papias, a man of Hierapolis, in the last of his five books. He has rightly described the gospel as being composed by John."

[55] *Eccles. Hist.* III. 39.

[56] Westcott, *Canon of N. T.* 443. The words of Andrew are as follows: "With regard to the inspiration of the book (Revelation) we deem it superfluous to add another word; for the blessed Gregory Theologus, and Cyril, and even some of still older date, Papias, Irenaeus, Methodius and Hippolytus, bore entirely satisfactory testimony to it." *Fragments of Papias*, VIII., *Ante-Nicene Library*, vol. I.

in Smyrna by Apostles; that he lived to be a very old man; and that he suffered "a glorious martyrdom." "To these things," adds Irenaeus, "all the Asiatic churches testify, as do all those men who have succeeded Polycarp down to the present time."[57]

His martyrdom occurred Feb. 23, AD 155, or 156,[58] and in an account of it written in the name of the church at Smyrna he is represented as claiming to have served the Lord Jesus eighty-six years.[59] This dates his baptism as early as the year 70, the date of the destruction of Jerusalem. If we suppose that he was 100 years old at his death, a supposition quite in harmony with the statement of Irenaeus, he was baptized at fourteen, and he was twelve years old when Paul was beheaded, AD 68. He may have seen that Apostle when he was a child. After his baptism he lived thirty years cotemporary with the Apostle John, and as John spent the latter part of his life at Ephesus, only fifty miles from Smyrna, Polycarp may have seen him and heard him. Furthermore, as Philip's home in the latter part of his life, was at Hierapolis, only about 100 miles east of Smyrna,[60] Polycarp may have seen that Apostle, and he may, in the course of his life have met with others. It is not improbable that Irenaeus is correct in saying that he was instructed by Apostles, and by Apostles appointed to office in the church. His long life, reaching back into the very midst of the apostolic age, and extending down to the middle of the sec-

---

[57] *Against Heresies,* 262, 263.

[58] "His death is variously placed from 147–176. The recent investigations of M. Waddington as to the date of the Proconsulship of L. Statius Quadratus, under whom Polycarp suffered, fix the true date [Feb. 23], 155–6 AD" *Westcott, Canon of N. T.* 39, n. 5.

[59] "Then the proconsul urging him and saying: 'Swear and I will set thee at liberty, reproach Christ;' Polycarp declared, 'Eighty and six years have I served him, and he never did me an injury, how then can I blaspheme my King and my Savior?" *Martyrdom of Polycarp,* c. IX., *Ante-Nicene Library,* vol. I. There has been much discussion as to the authenticity of the document called the Martyrdom of Polycarp. Donaldson, after pointing out many unauthentic details in it, reaches this conclusion: "The hypothesis by which we can give the most probable account of this production is that it really was, as it professes to be, a letter from the church in Smyrna, that it was a short summary of the principal circumstances of the martyrdom; and that as this letter went down to posterity it gathered length and absurdities." *Hist. of Christian Lit. and Doc.* I. 160–169. Westcott says of it: "The authenticity of this narrative has been called in question, but there seems to be no sufficient reason for doubting its general truthfulness." *Canon of N. T.* 40 n. 3.

[60] See page 98.

ond century, enabled him to know what writings of the Apostles were in use almost from the beginning, and it made him familiar with the first appearance of all their later productions. The books which he recognized as apostolic must have been so, and what he taught concerning them was propagated in Gaul by his pupil Irenaeus, in Asia by other pupils, and in Rome by himself; for in the imperial city he in person defended the faith against heresy.[61]

Polycarp wrote a number of epistles to neighboring churches,[62] of which that to the Philippians alone has been preserved. It is quite brief, occupying in print not much more than five ordinary octavo pages. It is written in the name of "Polycarp and the presbyters with him," and it is addressed to "the church of God sojourning at Philippi."[63]

As one would naturally suppose, the writer makes allusions to Paul's Epistle to the Philippians, and exhorts the brethren to observe its precepts.[64] His citations of other books are made anonymously, and they are interwoven with one another and with his own words in such a way as to form continuous sentences. In the first of the fourteen very short chapters into which the epistle has been divided, he in this way quotes Philippians, Acts, First Peter and Ephesians.[65] Several whole chapters, and large parts of others

---

[61] "He it was who, coming to Rome in the time of Anicetus, caused many to turn away from the aforesaid heretic. The church of God, proclaiming that he had received this one and sole truth from the apostles—that, namely, which is handed down by the church." Irenaeus, *Against Heresies,* III. 3, 4.

[62] "From his [Polycarp's] epistles also which he wrote to the neighboring churches in order to confirm them, or to some of the brethren in order to admonish and to exhort them, the same thing may be clearly shown." Irenaeus quoted by Eusebius, *Eccles. Hist.* v. 20.

[63] "Polycarp and the presbyters with him, to the church of God sojourning at Philippi: Mercy to you, and peace from God Almighty and from the Lord Jesus Christ our Saviour, be multiplied." *Salutation of the Epistle. Ante-Nic. Lib.* vol. I.

[64] "Neither I nor any other such one, can come up to the wisdom of the blessed and glorified Paul. He, when among you, accurately and steadfastly taught the word of truth in the presence of those who were then alive. And when absent from you he wrote you a letter, which, if you carefully read, you will find to be the means of building you up in that faith which has been given you, and which, being followed by hope, and preceded by love toward God and Christ and our neighbor, is the mother of us all." c. iii. "But I have neither seen nor heard of any such thing [covetousness] among you, in the midst of whom the blessed Paul labored, and who are commended in the beginning of his Epistle. For he boasts of you in all those churches which then knew the Lord; but we [of Smyrna] had not yet known Him." c. xi.

[65] "And because the strong root of your faith spoken of in days long gone by, endureth un-

might be styled a patchwork of quotations, the quotations being taken from the first three Gospels, Acts, all of Paul's Epistles except Titus and Philemon, the First Epistle of John, and the First of Peter.[66] The genuineness of all these books is therefore supported by this invaluable evidence.

Barnabas is the author of an Epistle giving mystical and fanciful interpretations of many facts and laws of the Old Testament. He was until recently thought to be the Barnabas mentioned in the New Testament, but this has been disproved beyond reasonable doubt by the contents of the epistle.[67] The latter was known only in a Latin version, until a copy of the Greek original was found by Tischendorf attached to the Sinaitic manuscript.

The date of this document is not very definitely fixed. It was written after the destruction of Jerusalem, as appears from the fact that this event is mentioned in it;[68] and it was written long enough before the days of Clement of Alexandria to have acquired the reputation of having been written by the New Testament Barnabas.[69] The majority of competent critics agree in assigning it to the first quarter of the second century.[70]

---

til now [Phil. i. 5] and bringeth forth fruit to our Lord Jesus Christ, who for our sins suffered even unto death, whom God raised from the dead, having loosed the bands of hades. [Acts ii. 24]. In whom, though now you see Him not, ye believe, and believing, rejoice with joy unspeakable and full of glory [I. Pet. i. 8]; into which joy many desire to enter, knowing that by grace ye are saved, not of works, [Eph. ii. 8, 9] but by the will of God through Jesus Christ."

[66] See appendix "A" for three of these chapters and the scripture references. Only by examining these can the student see the full force of the remarks made above.

[67] It contains many gross blunders in regard to the Levitical law, of which Barnabas, the Levite, can not have been guilty, many silly interpretations which a man of his sense can not have accepted, and many misstatements about matters of fact which can not have been made by a man of his information. These are pointed out abundantly by Donaldson (*Hist. Christ. Lit.* and *Doct.* I. 201–210), and they may be seen by the most casual reading of the epistle itself.

[68] "Moreover, I will tell you concerning the temple, how the wretched Jews, wandering in error, trusted not in God himself, but in the temple as being the house of God. * * * Moreover, He again says: Behold, they who have cast down this temple, even they shall build it again. It has so happened. For through their going to war it was destroyed by their enemies; and now they, as the servants of their enemies, shall rebuild it." *Epistle of Barnabas,* c. xvi.

[69] Clement quotes it several times as the work of "the apostle Barnabas," and he says that Barnabas was "one of the seventy and a fellow worker of Paul" *Stromata* ii. 6, p. 19; 7, p. 22; 15, p. 41; 20. p. 66, v. 8, p. 252; 10, p. 258.

[70] "We therefore come to the conclusion that it must have been written after the destruction of Jerusalem, that it could not have been written after the close of the second century, but that there is no certain way of fixing on any intervening date as the period of

If this is correct, the writer's personal knowledge reached back into the first century.

Its subject matter being an interpretation of portions of the Old Testament, we could not expect to find in it many quotations from the New. Its chief value for our present purpose is found in its quotation of Matthew with the formula, "It is written:" "Let us beware lest we be found, as it is written, many are called, but few are chosen."[71] As this is the formula with which Christian writers and speakers introduced quotations from the Scriptures, its use by Barnabas in quoting Matthew shows that he regarded this book with the same reverence as the older Scriptures. This is the earliest known instance of the use of this formula in citing a New Testament book.

There was no document from an uninspired pen so highly prized by the church of the early centuries, as the Epistle of Clement to the Corinthians. Only three manuscript copies of it are now known to exist. One of these, long supposed to be the only one, is attached to the Alexandrian MS. of the New Testament, as if it were a part of the sacred volume; one was discovered in Constantinople in the year 1875; and the third, in Syriac, was found in Paris in 1876, bound in a Syriac MS. of the New Testament immediately after the Catholic Epistles.[72]

The Epistle does not bear the name of Clement, but is written in the name of "The Church of God which sojourns at Rome, to the Church of God sojourning at Corinth." There is abundant ev-

---

its composition. Most have been inclined to place it not later than the first quarter of the second century. The whole cast of the letter seems to me to require a later date, but this is a matter of personal feeling." Donaldson, *Hist. Chris. Lit and Doc.* I. 220. "The letter contains not only an allusion to the destruction of the Jewish Temple, but also affirms the abrogation of the Sabbath and the general observance of the Lord's day, which seems to show that it can not have been written before the beginning of the second century." Westcott, *Canon of N. T.,* 41.

[71] *Epistle of Barnabas c.* iv. *comp.* Matthew 22.16.

[72] "In 1875 critics and students were startled by the appearance of a careful and complete edition published in Constantinople from a MS. discovered in the "library of the Holy Sepulcher" in that city. Its editor is Philotheos Bryennios, Metropolitan of Serrae. Six new chapters, containing among other interesting matter a prayer of singular beauty are added by this new MS. to the text of Codex A." "Scarcely was this discovery realized when a Syriac MS. of the "Two Epistles" was also found (1876) in Paris." Charteris, *Canonicity, Int.* viii., ix.

idence, however, from the statements of other writers, that Clement, who was then the principal bishop of the Church at Rome, was the writer.[73]

Clement is said by both Irenaeus and Eusebius to have been the third Bishop of the Church in Rome, and the date of his appointment as given by Eusebius is the twelfth year of Domitian's reign, which was AD 93. He died in the third year of Trajan, which was AD 101.[74]

The epistle was written, according to its opening statement, after some "sudden and calamitous events" had just happened to the Church of Rome, commonly supposed to have been a local persecution.[75] Such persecutions frequently occurred under the reign of Domitian, and the most probable date assigned to the epistle is AD 90 or 97.[76] But the date of the epistle is not so important for our purpose as the period in which the author lived. If he was old enough in the year 93 to be appointed Bishop of a

---

[73] "Of this Clement there is one epistle extant, acknowledged as genuine, of considerable length and of great merit, which he wrote in the name of the church at Rome to that at Corinth, at the time when there was a dissension in the latter. This we know to have been publicly read for the common benefit in most of the churches, both in former times and in our own; and that at the time mentioned a sedition did take place at Corinth, is abundantly attested by Hegesippus." Eusebius, *Eccles. Hist.* III. 16.

[74] "The blessed apostles, then, having founded and built up the church [at Rome] committed into the hands of Linus the office of the episcopate. * * * To him succeeded Anacletus; and after him, in the third place from the apostles, Clement was allotted the bishopric. This man, as he had seen the blessed apostles, and had been conversant with them, might be said to have the preaching of the apostles still echoing in his ears, and their traditions before his eyes." Irenaeus, *Heresies*, III, 3, 3. "In the twelfth year of the same reign [that of Domitian] after Anacletus had been bishop of Rome twelve years, he was succeeded by Clement, who, the apostle in his epistle to the Philippians shows, had been his fellow laborer, in these words: 'With Clement and the rest of my fellow laborers, whose names are in the book of life.'" Eusebius, *Eccles. Hist.* III. 15. Modern scholars very generally doubt this identification of the Clement in question with the one here mentioned by Paul. It is immaterial to our purpose whether he is the same or not.

[75] "Owing, dear brethren, to the sudden and calamitous events which have happened to ourselves, we feel that we have been somewhat tardy in turning our attention to the points respecting which you consulted us; and especially to that shameful and detestable sedition which a few rash and self-confident persons have kindled to such a pitch of frenzy, that your venerable and illustrious name, worthy to be universally loved, has suffered grievous injury." *Epistle of Clement*, c. I.

[76] Charteris, *Canonicity, Int.* x., xi.; but see Donaldson, *Hist. Chris. Lit. and Doc.* I., 105–110; Westcott, *Canon of N. T.*, 22, 23.

large church like that in Rome, he had probably lived through all the period of the apostolic writings. The earliest of these, 1 Thessalonians, was written AD 52, just 41 years before Clement's appointment to office. He had means, therefore, of knowing what writings had come from the pens of Apostles up to the date of his own Epistle, and all the books that he quotes belong unquestionably to the apostolic age, seeing that his epistle was written before the death of John.

He makes no express quotation except one from the First Epistle to the Corinthians. In rebuking the Corinthians for a sedition existing among them, he says: "Take up the Epistle of the blessed Apostle Paul. What did he write to you in the beginning of the gospel? Truly, under the inspiration of the Spirit he wrote to you concerning himself and Cephas and Apollos, because even then parties had been formed among you."[77] Now Clement could not have written thus to these brethren unless he and they both knew that Paul had written to them such an Epistle.

Though Clement makes no other quotations of the first class from the New Testament, he makes many of the third class. In one passage he combines texts from Matthew and Luke.[78] In another he combines peculiar expressions from Ephesians, Romans, Matthew, and Mark or Luke.[79] Of Paul's other epistles he quotes

---

[77] Epistle, c. xlvii. He proceeds: "But that inclination for one above another entailed less guilt upon you, inasmuch as your partialities were then showed toward apostles already of high reputation, and towards a man whom they had approved. But now reflect who those are that have perverted you, and lessened the renown of your far-famed brotherly love. It is disgraceful, beloved, yea, highly disgraceful, and unworthy of your Christian profession, that such a thing should be heard of, as that the most steadfast and ancient church of the Corinthians should, on account of one or two persons, engage in sedition against its presbyters. And this rumor has reached not only us, but those also who are unconnected with us; so that, through your infatuation the name of the Lord is blasphemed while danger is also brought upon yourselves."

[78] "Being specially mindful of the words of the Lord Jesus which he spoke, teaching us meekness and long suffering. For thus he spoke: Be ye merciful that ye may obtain mercy (Matt 5.7); forgive that it may be forgiven you (Luke 6.37); as ye do, so shall it be done to you, as ye judge, so shall ye be judged (Matt 7.2); as ye are kind, so shall kindness be shown to you; with what measure ye mete, with the same it shall be measured to you. (Luke 6.38) *Epistle*, c. xiii.

[79] "Have we not all one God and one Christ? Is there not one spirit of grace poured out upon us? And have we not one calling in Christ? (Eph 4.4–6). Why do we divide and

Titus[80] and Hebrews.[81] He has undoubted quotations from 1 Peter, and in two passages he seems to quote 2 Peter.[82] We may say, then, that he makes use in his epistle, of the first three Gospels, five of Paul's epistles, and the First and probably the Second Epistle of Peter. He has nothing from the writings of John, for none of these had gone into circulation, unless Revelation is an exception, and perhaps none of them had been written at the date of Clement's epistle.

We have now presented the evidence from quotations, omitting some writers because of the small number of quotations which they make, and others because the genuineness or the antiquity of their writings is in dispute.[83]

By this source of evidence we have traced every book of the New Testament back to the apostolic age, except Philemon, the Second and Third Epistles of John, Jude, James, and possibly 2 Peter. From the last we have found three probable quotations (those by Irenaeus, Justin and Clement); from 2 John one (that by

---

tear in pieces the members of Christ, and raise up strife against our own body, and have reached such a height of madness as to forget that we are members of one another? (Rom 12.5). Remember the words of our Lord Jesus Christ, how he said: 'Woe to that man by whom offenses come' (Matt 18.7). It were better for him that he had never been born (Matt 26.24) than that he should cast a stumbling-block before one of my elect. Yea, it were better for him that a millstone should be hung about his neck, and that he should be sunk in the depths of the sea, than that he should cast a stumbling-block before one of my little ones" (Mark 9.42, or Luke 17.2). *Epistle,* c. xlvi.

[80] "Ye never grudged any act of kindness, being ready to every good work." *Epistle,* c. ii., *comp.* Titus 3.1.

[81] By Him the Lord has willed that we should taste of immortal knowledge, who, being the brightness of His majesty, is by so much greater than the angels, as He hath by inheritance obtained a more excellent name than they." *Epistle,* c. xxxvi., comp. Hebrews 1.3–4.

[82] "Let us look steadfastly to the blood of Christ, and see how precious that blood is to God (1 Pet 1.19) which, having been shed for our salvation, has set the grace of repentance before the whole world. Let us turn to every age that has passed, and learn that, from generation to generation, the Lord has granted a place of repentance (Heb 12.17) to all such as would be converted unto Him. Noah preached repentance (2 Pet 2.5) and as many as listened to him were saved (1 Pet 3.20)." *Epistle,* c. vii. "Noah being found faithful, preached regeneration (2 Pet 2.8) to the world through his ministry." *Epistle,* c. ix. It should be observed, that nowhere in the Bible is Noah represented as a preacher, except in 2 Peter 2.5, the passage from which Clement is supposed to have derived this idea.

[83] We have especial reference here to the writings of Ignatius and the letter to Diognetus. The early date of the latter is too uncertain to give it very great value in this discussion, and the genuineness of the former is yet a warmly contested question among Christian scholars.

Irenaeus); but from Philemon, Jude and 3 John, no quotations at all. We have traced the first three Gospels all the way to Clement, and the fourth to Papias. We have traced Acts and all of Paul's epistles except Philemon back to Polycarp, and five of the latter back to Clement. We have traced Peter's first epistle to Clement, and his second by evidence not so conclusive to the same period. That of James is quoted by none as early as Irenaeus. Finally, we have traced John's first epistle back to Polycarp, and the Apocalypse to Papias. Thus all these books, with the exceptions named, are found to have been in actual use among the Disciples at a period too early for them to have originated and come into use after the close of the apostolic age.

The absence of quotations from the three short personal epistles, Philemon, Jude and 3 John; and the absence of any earlier than the time of Irenaeus from James and 2 John, can not be fairly construed as proof that they were not known to those early writers: for first, the extant writings of all these authors beyond Irenaeus are very brief, the whole of them covering less than four hundred octavo pages, and it is not surprising that the quotations which they had occasion to make failed to take the whole range of the New Testament books; second, these epistles, with the exception of James, are the very books of the New Testament which, from that clay to this, have been most rarely quoted by Christian writers. While the evidence from quotations, then, can not be arrayed in favor of these books in this early period, the want of it can not be held as evidence against them.

The force and value of the evidence from quotations can be more properly appreciated if we compare the evidence from the same source for some of the most noted classical writings of antiquity. The writings of Herodotus, the most famous of Greek historians, are quoted by only one author (Ctesias) in the first century after they were written, by only one (Aristotle) in the second, by none in the third, and by only two in the fourth. Thucydides, second among Greek historians, is not quoted at all during the first two centuries after he wrote; Livy, the early Roman historian, is quoted by only one writer in the first hundred years, and the first to quote Tacitus is Tertullian, who wrote about 100 years later.[84] If, then, our task had been to trace back to their authors the works of these celebrated writers, works the genuineness of which is never called in question, the case which we could make for them would be weakness itself compared with that which we have made for the writings of the New Testament.

---

[84] The facts have been collected by the learned and painstaking (George Rawlinson, one of the greatest masters of ancient history, in his work entitled *Historical Evidences of Christianity. Lecture* vi. *n.* 9.

FOUR

Internal Evidence

The claim of authorship which a book sets forth on its own pages has a presumption in its favor. It is the same presumption which attaches in law to a will or a deed when written and signed in due form. It is not proof, but in the absence of proof to the contrary it stands good. The evidence necessary to set it aside or to confirm it, may be external, or internal, or both. External evidence is that derived from other sources than the book itself. It is that with respect to the New Testament, which we have already considered. Internal evidence is that found in the contents of the book. If events are mentioned in it, or alluded to as having transpired, which really took place; after the supposed author's death, or which, for any other cause, could not have been known to him; or it words are employed which did not come into use until after his death, the claim is disproved. If no such evidence is found, and if, on the contrary, evidence in support of the claim is found, the presumption is turned into proof. From the nature of the case, however, internal evidence is much more effective, and much more commonly employed in disproving the claims of spurious books, than in establishing those of the genuine: for it is extremely difficult for one writer to personate another, and especially another belonging to a different country and a different age, without betraying himself in unguarded moments, and even failing in the prominent features of the imitation.

The proper method of procedure in this inquiry is to first presume that the book is genuine, and then search its pages for evidence *pro* and *con.*, allowing the preponderance of evidence to decide the question. But the decision thus reached is not final until the internal evidence is considered in connection with the external. A slight preponderance of evidence from either source may be overbalanced by weightier evidence from the other; or both sources may unite in support of one conclusion.

We now proceed to collect out of the several books of the New Testament the internal evidence of their genuineness, and we shall see whether or not this supports the external evidence which we have already considered. In doing so we shall not attempt to be exhaustive, but, as in the former case, we shall present only those prominent evidences on which the decision chiefly depends.

The Gospel of Matthew. This book contains no express statement of its date or its authorship; and the same is true of all the historical books of the New Testament. It is true likewise of the same class of books in the Old Testament, and of ancient historical works in general. As regards its date, however, the book of Matthew confines itself within very narrow limits and it contains some confirmation of the external evidences as to its authorship. It incidentally claims to have been written before the destruction of Jerusalem, which occurred AD 70, by giving as unfulfilled prophecy the prediction of Jesus concerning that event. (24.1–28) Had this prophecy been fulfilled when the book was written, the author could not have failed to mention the fact, because it would have been a strong confirmation of his own testimony in favor of Jesus. Moreover, he included in the prophecy, and most probably he himself inserted it, a parenthetical note of warning, by which the Jewish disciples of Jesus might be prepared to escape from the city on the eve of its destruction. It is quite certain from these considerations that, unless the author was guilty of a fraudulent pretense, the book was written before the year 70. On the other hand, there is conclusive evidence that it was written a number of years after the death of Jesus. The author says concerning the spot where Judas hung himself, "That field was called the field of blood, unto this day"; and concerning the assertion of the guards at the sepulchre, that the disciples of Jesus came by night and stole his body away, he says, "This saying was spread abroad among the Jews until this day." These passages show that the book was written a sufficient length of time after its closing events to make it worthy of remark that the story of the guards was still in circulation, and that the name "field of blood" was still in use. This implies the expiration of a large portion of the thirty-four years that intervened between the death of Jesus and the final siege of Jerusalem, and it throws the date of Matthew's Gospel into the latter half of this period. We know nothing more definite as to the date.

In confirmation of the reputed authorship, we find in the book a few peculiarities which can scarcely be accounted for on any other hypothesis. For example, while the other writers, in their lists of the Apostles, give Matthew's name without the opprobrious epithet, "the publican," an omission quite proper under the circumstances, this writer, with a humility equally proper, if Matthew is he, gives it, "Matthew the publican."[1] Again, in speaking of the feast which Matthew gave after his call to follow Jesus, Mark and Luke both speak of it as "in his house," while this writer, as is natural with the owner of the house, says, "in the house."[2] These circumstances, from their very minuteness, tend strongly to confirm the preceding evidence that Matthew was the author.

The Gospel of Mark. This Gospel treats the Saviour's predictions concerning the destruction of Jerusalem in the same way as does Matthew's, and by the same process of reasoning it is proved to have been written before that event. It was also written after the general dispersion abroad of the Apostles in the execution of their commission; for it closes with the statement that "They went forth and preached everywhere, the Lord working with them and confirming the word by the signs that

---

[1] Mark 3.18; Luke 6.15; Acts 1.13, *comp.* Matthew 10.2.

[2] Mark 2.15–16; Luke 5.29, *comp.* Matthew 9.9–10.

followed." Its date therefore was earlyenough for its reputed authorship, and it was not far from that of Matthew's Gospel.

The external evidence that it was written by Mark for the purpose of presenting the story of Jesus as it was habitually preached by Peter, is confirmed by the fact that in it Peter is made much less conspicuous than in the other Gospels. While it does not fail to relate those incidents which are discreditable to Peter, even the denial of his Lord, it omits nearly all of those that are creditable to him, such as the high commendation of him by Jesus after his celebrated confession, the promise to him of the keys of the kingdom, the catching of the fish with money in its mouth, and the fact that Peter was the first Apostle to see the risen Lord. It also omits his name in describing his courageous attack upon the band who came to arrest Jesus in the garden, saving only that "a certain one of them" did this.[3]

The Gospel of Luke. The evidence that this Gospel was written before the destruction of Jerusalem is the same us in the case of Matthew and Mark, except that in the report of the prediction of that event, he omits the warning, "Let him that readeth understand."[4] It was written before the book of Acts by the same author, and there is internal evidence that the latter was written in the year 63.[5] It was written early enough for the author to have consulted the original witnesses of the events which it records; for he claims these witnesses as his sources of information.[6] It was written, then, early enough for Luke, the companion of Paul, to have been its author, as the external evidence declares.

The Gospel of John. This Gospel claims to have been written by one of the twelve Apostles, "the disciple whom Jesus loved." Near the close its says: "This is the disciple who bears witness of these things and wrote these things"; and the reference is to the disciple just before mentioned as the one whom Jesus loved,

---

[3] Matthew 16.l6-19; 17.24–27; Luke 24.12, 34; Mark 14.47.

[4] Luke 21.20, *comp.* Matthew 24.15; Mark 13.14.

[5] Acts of Apostles 1.1; and see our remarks on the date of this book, page 117.

[6] Luke 1.1–4.

and who leaned on his breast at the last supper.[7] Now there are only three of the twelve whom Jesus received into such intimacy that one of them could be known as the disciple whom he loved. These were Peter, James and John, the three who alone were permitted to witness the transfiguration, whom alone he took with him into the garden of Gethsemane, and whom he especially honored on other occasions.[8] But the one whom he loved can not have been Peter, seeing that he is especially distinguished from Peter in the statement that "Peter, turning about, seeth the disciple whom Jesus loved following," etc.[9] Neither can James have been the one thus designated, for he was beheaded by Herod long previous to the earliest date that can be assigned to this Gospel.[10] Furthermore, while all the other writers in speaking of John the Baptist, give him his title to distinguish him from John the Apostle, the writer of this Gospel alone refers to him simply as John, a circumstance to be accounted for only by the fact that this writer was the other John.

This method of designating himself contains very strong evidence of the author's sincerity: for a spurious writer of a later period could scarcely conceive of such a method, but, lest the reader should fail to recognize him as the Apostle John, he would have written openly under that name, after the manner of the spurious Gospels of the second century.[11]

The principal internal evidence as to the date of this Gospel is found in the fact that it differs so widely in its subject matter from the other three, thus indicating that its author knew the contents of the others, and that it was written after these had become so widely circulated as to make it superfluous to reiterate what they had made known. This wide divergence from the other

---

[7] John 21.24; *comp.* 20–23; 13.23–25; 20.2–9; 19.26.

[8] Matthew 17.1; 26.30, 37; Mark 5.37.

[9] John 21.20.

[10] Acts 12.1. This event, soon followed by the death of Herod, is known by the statements of Josephus to have occurred in the year 44, only ten years after the death of Jesus. *Antiquities*, XIX., viii. 2.

[11] This line of evidence is presented clearly and strongly by Prof. Geo. P. Fisher. *Supernatural Origin of Christianity*, 84–86.

three Gospels is proof not only of a later date than theirs, but also of a date too early and of an authorship too authoritative for a spurious document: for if the three previous Gospels had alone gone down to a late period as the accepted record of the career of Jesus, no man in attempting to write a Gospel in the name of John would have ventured to depart so widely from them, or if he had, his book would have been rejected at once as a forgery. Its very divergence from the other Gospels is no mean proof, under the circumstances, of its apostolic authorship.[12]

Acts of Apostles. This book claims to have been written by the same author as the third Gospel, and it incidentally, by the use of the pronouns "we" and "us," represents its author as being an actor in many of the scenes which it describes.[13] The external evidence that its author was Luke is confirmed by the fact obtained from two of Paul's epistles, that he was a companion of Paul as the narrative represents, during its closing scenes.[14] The date of composition could not have been earlier than the last event mentioned in the book, Paul's two years imprisonment, which terminated AD 63. Neither could it well have been later than this: for the last four chapters of it are occupied with a very interesting account of proceedings and journeys consequent upon Paul's appeal to Caesar from the rulings of Festus; and after dwelling so long upon this subject it would have been a most unnatural termination of the narrative to have omitted the final decision, had it been rendered when the book left the author's hands. It would have been like the sudden close of a drama or of a novel just previous to the winding up of the plot; or the close of the history of some celebrated jury trial without giving the verdict of the jury. The internal evidence therefore fixes the date at the end of the second year of Paul's Roman imprisonment, which was the spring of the year 63.[15] An-

---

[12] For a full and forcible statement of this evidence, see the work last cited, 97, 98.

[13] Acts 1.1–2; 16.10, 17; 20.5–6, 13; 21.1, 7, 15; 27.1; 28.1, 11, 16.

[14] Colossians 4.15; Philemon 24. These epistles were both written while Paul was a prisoner (Col 4.3, 10; Phlm 23), and the evidence is conclusive that it was during the imprisonment spoken of in the closing sentences of Acts.

[15] The accession of Festus occurred in the year 60. In the autumn of the same year Paul was sent to Rome (Acts 27.9); he passed the winter of 60–61 in Melita, reaching Rome

other internal evidence of the early date of Acts, is the manner in which the author speaks of members of the Herod family. Nothing is more puzzling to the modern reader who is not familiar with the secular history of that period, than the way in which these men are spoken of in the Gospels and Acts. For example, the author of Acts and of the third Gospel has "Herod the King" reigning before the birth of John the Baptist; then he has "Herod the tetrarch" imprisoning and killing John; then Jesus is sent by Pilate to "Herod"; then the Apostle James is slain by "Herod the King"; and finally Paul is brought before "King Agrippa"; yet there is not a line of description to distinguish these Herods from one another, or to show their relationship. A writer of his carefulness in other matters could not have written thus unless he was writing when these princes were still well known, and therefore in the very generation to which the majority of them belonged.

Paul's Thirteen Epistles. All of the epistles usually ascribed to Paul, with the exception of that to the Hebrews, contain the name of Paul as the writer, not subscribed at the close, after the modern custom, but according to the ancient custom embodied in the opening salutation. They contain also many allusions to the author's personal experiences agreeing with what is known of Paul through other sources, and thus they bear all the internal marks by which the genuineness of epistolary documents of a past age is tested.[16] Their several dates are fixed with a good degree of accuracy between the years 52 and 68.

The Epistle to the Hebrews. Unlike all the other epistles ascribed to Paul, this one is anonymous. It is not addressed formally

---

in the spring of 61 (28.11–14); and he remained there in prison two whole years (28.30) which extended to the spring of 63.

[16] There is evidence furnished by some of the epistles, that Paul usually dictated to an amanuensis, but that, in order to certify the genuineness of his epistles by his handwriting, he wrote with his own hand the closing salutations. In the Epistle to the Romans the name of the amanuensis is given (16.22), and that he employed one habitually, yet always wrote with his own hand the salutation appears from 2 Thessalonians 3.17: "The salutation of me Paul with mine own hand, which is the token in every epistle: so I write." In Galatians he makes the remark, "See with how large letters I have written to you with mine own hand," which probably refers to the whole epistle, making this an exception to his rule. This evidence is lost to us in the loss of the autographs.

to any individual or community, and it is known to have been intended for Hebrew readers only by its arguments. Notwithstanding these peculiarities, it has enough of the characteristics of an epistle to be properly so called. It was written before the destruction of Jerusalem, as appears from its frequent references to the temple service as being still in existence;[17] and from the consideration, that had the city been destroyed and the temple worship thus abolished, the author could not have failed, in his elaborate argument on the temporary nature of that service and of the Jewish priesthood (ch 7–10) to make use of the fact.

As to its author, the external evidence, as we have seen in Chapter Third, is divided, but the preponderance is in favor of Paul,[18] and the internal evidence points in the same direction. It was written by one who sustained very intimate relations with Timothy, as appears from the statement (13.23). "Know ye that our brother Timothy hath been set at liberty, with whom, if he come shortly, I will see you"; and the writer himself had been in some trouble from which he was not yet entirely freed, as appears from his request, "Pray for us ... that I may be restored to you the sooner" (13.18–19) These allusions point to Paul as the author, and they show that the Epistle was written before the death of Timothy. On the other hand, it contains some allusions which point to a date as late as the preceding facts can well allow. First, the writer rebukes his readers because they needed to be taught the first principles of the oracles of God, though "by reason of time" they ought to be teachers (5.12). Second, he asks them to remember the former days in which, after they were enlightened, they endured a great conflict of sufferings (10.32–34.). Third, he

---

[17] See Hebrews 8.4; 9.6–9; 10.11–12; 13.10–11.

[18] The sum of the external evidence on this point already given in Chapter Third is as follows: The Council of Carthage ascribes it to Paul (p. 60); Eusebius does the same, but says that the church at Rome did not (p. 64, and n. **3)**; Origen ascribes the matter to Paul, but the composition to some other person, and says that it had been credited by some to Clement of Rome, and by others to Luke (p. 67); Clement of Alexandria says that it was written by Paul but translated into Greek by Luke. Paul's name being suppressed to make it more acceptable to Jewish readers (p. 70); Tertullian ascribes it to Barnabas (p. 72); and Irenaeus is represented on doubtful authority as denying that it was written by Paul. Page 87, n. 2.

exhorts them to remember their deceased spiritual rulers, and to imitate their faith (13.7). All of these allusions agree very well with the supposition that Paul was the writer, and they suggest no other person. They also indicate the close of his two years imprisonment in Rome, AD 63, as the probable date of the composition.

The Epistle of James. This document claims to have been written by "James a bond-servant of God and of the Lord Jesus Christ, to the twelve tribes who are of the Dispersion" (1.1). The high authority with which he speaks throughout the Epistle, identifies him either with James the Apostle, son of Alphaeus (Luke 6.15), or with the James who so long presided over the Church in Jerusalem (Acts 12.17; 21.18; Gal 2.12) and was called by Paul "the Lord's brother" (Gal 1.19; 2.9.). It is still an unsettled question whether these two are the same or different persons;[19] but it is generally agreed that if they are different the latter is the author of the Epistle. He suffered martyrdom in Jerusalem AD 63,[20] and consequently the Epistle must have been written previous to this date. That it was written in Palestine, where James resided, is evident from its local allusions. For instance, in his comparison of a rich man to a flower of the field, he says: "The sun ariseth with the scorching wind and withereth the grass; and the flower thereof filleth, and the grace of the fashion of it perisheth" (1.11.). This is an allusion to the green grass and the profusion of wild flowers that cover the surface of Palestine in the early spring, but wither and perish as the hot sun and desert winds come upon them soon after the close of the rainy season. Again, when he demands, "Can a fig tree yield olives, or a vine figs" (3.12), he derives his figures from the three most abundant fruits of Palestine; and when he speaks of the husbandman being patient until he receives "the early and the latter rain" (4.7), he alludes to the early rain of autumn which in Palestine is necessary to early sowing, and the latter rain of spring without which the dry season sets in too soon for the grain to mature.

---

[19] For the arguments on the affirmative of this question, see the article on James in Smith's Bible Dictionary; and for those on the negative, see an essay appended to Lightfoot's Commentary on Galatians.

[20] Josephus, *Ant.,* XX., ix. 1; Farrar, *Early Days,* 302.

The Two Epistles of Peter. The first of these two Epistles is written in the name of "Peter an Apostle of Jesus Christ" (1.1); and in it the author speaks of himself as "a witness of the sufferings of Christ" (5.1). Its date is indicated proximately by three considerations: First, it was addressed to the disciples in Pontus, Galatia, Cappadocia, Asia and Bithynia (1.1), regions which were evangelized by Paul and his associates; and consequently it must have been written after those churches had been established, and after their condition had become known to Peter. Paul closed his labors there on leaving Ephesus in the spring of AD 57. Second, it was written after Peter had read Paul's Epistles to the Romans and the Ephesians; for the author adopts many of the peculiar expressions of Paul from these two Epistles.[21] Third, as Ephesians was written AD 62, and Peter's death occurred in 68, the Epistle must have been written between these dates. It was written from Babylon (5.13); but whether from the real Babylon, or from Rome figuratively called Babylon, is a question of long-continued controversy and still unsettled.

The Second Epistle is also written in the name of Peter, the author styling himself "Simon Peter, a servant and apostle of Jesus Christ"; and besides the formal salutation in Peter's name, the author alludes to the Saviour's prediction concerning the manner of his death (1.14, *comp.* John 21.18); to his presence at the transfiguration of Jesus (1.18); and to his having written the previous epistle to the same disciples (3.1). Confirmation of these

---

[21] The reader can see the full force of this evidence by comparing the following passages in 1 Peter with those set opposite to them in Romans and Ephesians: 1 Peter 1.1, *comp.* Ephesians 1.4–7.

1 Peter 1.3, *comp.* Ephesians 1.3.
1 Peter 1.14, *comp.* Ephesians 2. 8, Romans 12.2.
1 Peter 2.6–10, *comp.* Romans 9.25–32.
1 Peter 2.1, *comp.* Romans 7.23.
1 Peter 2.13, *comp.* Romans 8.1–4.
1 Peter 2.18, *comp.* Ephesians 6.5.
1 Peter 3.1, *comp.* Ephesians 5.22.
1 Peter 3.9, *comp.* Romans 16.17.
1 Peter 3.22, *comp.* Ephesians 1.20, Romans 8.34.
1 Peter 4.1, Romans 6.6.
1 Peter 4.10, Romans 12.6.
1 Peter 5.1, *comp.* Romans 13.18.
1 Peter 5.5, *comp.* Ephesians 5.21.

formal indications of authorship is found in the fact that the Second Epistle contains many of the characteristic expressions of the First, and of Peter's speeches recorded in Acts of Apostles.[22]

As the First was written in the year 62 and Peter died in 68, the date of the Second can not be much later than that of the First: but there is nothing to indicate the exact year.

The Epistle of Jude. This brief document claims as its author "Judas the brother of James." There is some doubt as to whether he was Judas the Apostle (Luke 6.16; John 14.22) or the Judas who was one of the Lord's brothers (Mark 6.3). If the correct rendering of Luke 6.16 were "Judas *brother* of James," this would identify him as the Apostle; for here he gives himself this title. But the general usage of the Greek language is against that rendering (the Greek words are Ἰού<dan Ἰαχω<bou) and in favor of the rendering "Judas *son* of James." Again, it has been held by some that the James whose brother he was, is James the Apostle, son of Alphaeus; but this is highly improbable. The preponderance of opinion is that he was brother of the James called the Lord's brother, and consequently himself a brother of the Lord, and that he designates himself by the former title rather than by the latter, because it was more modest in view of the fact that the Lord had long ago ascended to heaven.[23] It is confirmatory of this view, that he omits to style himself an Apostle, and that he rather distinguishes himself from the Apostles by speaking of the latter in the third person, saying, "Remember the words which have been spoken before by the Apostles of our Lord Jesus Christ."

This Epistle bears no internal evidence of date except that it was written after the church had become infested by a large number of desperately wicked men (4–12). Its striking similarity to the second chapter of 2 Peter shows that one of the two writers had seen the other's Epistle and made much use of its material. If it

---

[22] The list of references is too long for insertion here. It may be found complete in the Introduction to 2 Peter by Prof. Lumby, in the Bible Commentary.

[23] The arguments on this question are more fully stated by Farrar in the chapter on this epistle in his *Early Days of Christianity;* and by Prof. Lumby, *Intro. to Jude, Bible Com.* The whole subject of The Brothers of the Lord is discussed with great ability and clearness by Lightfoot in an essay appended to his Commentary on Galatians.

could be determined with certainty which is the older of the two, this would help to fix the date of Jude; but the question, though long debated, is still unsettled.[24]

The Three Epistles of John. These three Epistles, like the Gospel ascribed to the same author, are written without a name, but the first paragraph of the First Epistle clearly implies that it was written by an Apostle, while identity of style and diction indicates that all three came from the same writer, and from the writer of the Gospel.[25] They were all three written late in the life of their author, and at a period in the history of the church which implies a long life on his part. See 1 John 2.6–18; 4.1; 2 John 1, 5, 6; 3 John 1, 4.

Revelation. This book claims John as its author (1.1, 4, 9; 22.8); and claims to have been written in the Island of Patmos, whither John had been sent on account of his testimony for Jesus (1.9, 11, 19; 10.4; 14.13; 19.9; 21.5). It is addressed to "the seven churches of Asia" (1.4–11), and as he styles himself "a partaker with them in the tribulation, and kingdom, and patience in Jesus" (1.9), he must already have lived among them before the book was written. These churches had been established by Paul, and though several of his epistles (Ephesians, Colossians, 1 Timothy and 2 Timothy) had been sent into their midst, the last just previous to his death, in all these there is no allusion to John, from which it is inferred that his residence there did not begin until after or about the time of Paul's death. As Paul was beheaded in the year 68, this is about the earliest date which can be assigned to John's residence in Asia, and to the composition of this book. This is the date actually assigned to the book by recent skeptical writers in general, and also by many others.[26] Their opinion is supported by

---

[24] Canon Farrar (*Early Days of Christianity*), presents the full force of the evidences for the priority of Jude, while Prof. Lumby in the Introductions to 2 Peter and Jude in the Bible Commentary, does the same in favor of the priority of 2 Peter.

[25] For the specification necessary to the proof of the statement made on this point we refer the reader to the Introduction to I. John in the Bible Commentary, and to the many works on this epistle. To set them forth fully would require more space than we can here appropriate.

[26] "We might fix the date of the Vision in the summer or autumn of AD 68. This is, indeed, the all but certain date of the book." Farrar, *Early Days of Christianity*, 413. "The Apocalypse is after the close of St. Paul's work. . . . On the other hand, it is before the destruction

many ingenious arguments, of which the following are the most forcible: First, that the continued existence of the city and temple are implied in what is said of them in 11.1–2. Second, that there is such a difference in style between the Apocalypse and the other writings of John, as can be accounted for only on the supposition that he wrote the former when he was but little acquainted with the Greek language, having just removed from Judea, and the latter after a long residence among the Greek-speaking inhabitants of Ephesus and its vicinity. Third, the interpretation of the book adopted by these writers, which makes the Emperor Nero its Anti-christ, requires this date.[27] All who contend for this date, set aside the positive statement of Irenaeus, which we cited in a former chapter (page 89), as a mistake based on misinformation. On the other hand, the great mass of the older critics, and some of the most recent, contend for the correctness of the statement of Irenaeus, that the book was written near the close of the reign of Domitian, who died in 96. They interpret the words in 11.1–2 concerning Jerusalem and the temple in a symbolical sense; they contend that the differences in style between the two books are less than is asserted, and that they can be accounted for by the difference in subject matter; and they give to the book a totally different interpretation.[28] Strong internal evidence of the latter opinion is found in the condition of some of the churches addressed. The church at Ephesus had endured "toil and patience" worthy of praise, and had encountered and exposed some who falsely claimed to be Apostles; but she had left her first love and was exhorted to repent and do her first works (2.2–5). The church at Pergamos had passed through a severe persecution in which at least one martyr had been slain (2.13), while in at least three of these churches corrupt parties called Nicolaitans, followers of Balaam, and imitators of Jezebel, had become common pests (2.6,

of Jerusalem." Westcott, *Introduction to Gospel of John*, p. lxxxvi. "The Apocalypse was written shortly after the death of Nero, and shortly before the destruction of Jerusalem." Fisher, *Sup. Origin of Christianity*, 125. Nero died in June, 68, and Jerusalem fell in August, 70.

[27] These reasons are set forth elaborately in Farrar's *Early Days of Christianity*, c. xxv.

[28] A very able and elaborate presentation of this side of the question is furnished by Archdeacon Lee, in his Introduction to Revelation in the Bible Commentary.

14–15, 20). In none of Paul's Epistles sent to these communities are any of these parties or incidents alluded to, although his last (2 Tim) was written the year of his death, and there is every reason to believe that he would have rebuked them had they existed. So great changes could not well have taken place until quite a number of years after his death, and if they did not the earlier date must be rejected. But the genuineness of the book is not affected by the decision of this question; for this is conceded by both parties to the controversy.

We have now considered the internal evidence of the genuineness of all the New Testament books, and we find that it unites with the external evidence in supporting the claim that they were written by Apostles and "apostolic men." Objections to this line of evidence will be stated and discussed in the following Chapter.

FIVE

Positions Taken by Unbelievers

Unbelievers as a class deny the genuineness of all but a few of the New Testament books, and assign to them dates too late for apostolic authorship. The most learned and ingenious of the class are the German writers of the Tübingen school, so called from the University of Tübingen, in which the founder of the school, Ferdinand Christian Baur,[1] and several of its later writers were Professors. In this chapter we shall confine our remarks in the main to the positions and arguments of these writers, because, in so doing we shall be able to thoroughly test the conclusions reached in our former chapters on this subject, and because a refutation of their arguments will involve *a fortiori* the refutation of all that have been advanced on the negative side of the question.

Their scheme of dates and authorship according to Schwegler, one of the most advanced thinkers of the school, is as follows:[2]

1 They recognize as genuine, the Apocalypse, and four of Paul's Epistles, viz.: Romans, 1 and 2 Corinthians, and Galatians.

---

[1] Baur's principal works are a Life of the Apostle Paul and a History of Christianity in the first Three Centuries. In these all the essential features of his theory are set forth. He attempts to reconstruct the early history of the church with all that is miraculous and all that tends to the proof of miracles, carefully eliminated. He is regarded as the greatest of modern German rationalists. He died in 1860.

[2] This scheme is condensed from Westcott (*Canon of New Testament*, 6, n. 2). He says, at the conclusion of his note, "Schwegler's theory has been variously modified by later writers of the Tübingen school, but it still remains the most complete embodiment of the spirit of the school in which relation alone we have to deal with it." The last remark is equally applicable to the use which we make of it in this volume.

2. They assign the Gospel of Luke, Acts of Apostles, and Hebrews, to about the year 100, and Colossians and Ephesians to a little later date.

3 All the other books they place between 115 and 150 AD, except 2 Peter, which they date about the year 200.

From this it appears that in reference to the five books in the first class there is no dispute; that in reference to the five in the second class the question of date is narrowed down to a period of about forty years, the time between the year 100 and the received dates; and that in reference to the rest no date later than AD 150 is assigned to any except 2 Peter. The evidences then, by which we have traced this last epistle back from the year 200, and the others back from the dates just mentioned to the period in which their reputed authors were living, are all that are called in question. We will now proceed to examine in detail the principal objections urged against these evidences.

The evidence of catalogues is unassailed, except that drawn from the Canon of Muratori,[3] the early date of which is called in question. That it was written as early as the year 170, is evinced by the following remark in the document itself: "Hermas wrote The Shepherd very recently in our own time in the city of Rome, while his brother Pius was occupying the bishop's chair in the church at Rome." As Pius held office from 142 to 157, the author could scarcely speak of that period as being very recent, and "in our own time," if he were writing much later than the year 170. But the author of Supernatural Religion, the best representative in England of the Tübingen school of rationalists, claims that this expression may have been used by a writer living in "an advanced period of the third century,"[4]—with how much reason we leave the reader to judge. In view, however, of the admission that all of the books except 2 Peter came into existence before the year 150, and of the

---

[3] See Chapter I., p. 74.

[4] "It is unsafe upon the mere interpretation of a phrase which would be applicable even a century later, to date this anonymous fragment regarding which we know nothing, earlier than the very end of the second or beginning of the third century, and it is still more probable that it was not written until an advanced period of the third century." *Supernatural Religion*, ii. 244.

fact that this Epistle is not found in the Canon in question, the objector has nothing to gain on the main question by establishing, were it possible, a later date for this document. We may therefore regard the evidence which we have presented from catalogues as being virtually unassailed.

The same may be said of the evidence from translations presented in Chapter II; for although a later date than that which we have assigned to the four versions from which this evidence is drawn has been contended for, yet the admission by the objectors that all the books contained in the Peshito Syriac and the Old Latin were in existence before the date assigned to these (AD 150), and that all the other books were in existence at the date which we have assigned to the Coptic versions (AD 200), renders nugatory, as respects this question, the attempt to bring these versions down to later dates.

The only parts of the preceding evidence which are seriously contested, are those in Chapters III and IV, the evidence from quotations, and the internal evidence. In regard to the former, the contest begins with the quotations cited from Justin Martyr, all the evidence which we derived from Irenaeus being admitted, except that referring to 2 Peter, which we have defended in Chapter III. Moreover, the concession already mentioned, that all the books except this short Epistle were written before Irenaeus wrote, would render superfluous any contest over his quotations.

The dispute concerning the evidence from Justin turn chiefly upon what he says about the Gospels. It is denied, of course, that he quoted 2 Peter, and on this point we have presented our own reasonings in Chapter III. As to the other books which we have represented him as quoting, the genuineness of First Corinthians, Romans, and Revelation, is admitted, while Colossians and Hebrews are assigned to the year 100 or a little later, farther back than the memory of Justin reached. But the Gospels are the books on which the proof of the divine origin of Christianity chiefly depends, and the admission that Justin made use of these would throw their origin back so far as to break up entirely the scheme of dates adopted by the school whose views we are representing: consequently they have contested very hotly the evidence on this point.

The contest concerns wholly the question, whether the Memoirs which Justin so freely quotes and describes, are our four Gospels, or some previously existing documents. The infidel position is, that they were not our Gospels, but apocryphal documents which alone were used up to Justin's time, and that our Gospels were written afterward and substituted for these older narratives. The principal arguments in favor of this position, and the answers to them, we shall now state.

1. Justin does not name the author or authors of his Memoirs. This is held as proof that he did not know the names, and that therefore the Memoirs were not our Gospels. The argument is supposed to be strengthened by the fact that in a large majority of his quotations from the Old Testament he does name the books or authors quoted; and by the fact that in citing the Apocalypse he names John as its author. It is especially argued from this last circumstance, that he could not have known a Gospel by John, or he would likewise have mentioned his name in connection with it.[5] That this argument is without force is seen from the following considerations. First, in arguing with the heathen Emperor and the unbelieving Jew, after stating that the facts he gives were attested by writings of Apostles and their followers, nothing would

---

[5] "That Justin does not mention the name of the author of the Memoirs would in any case render any argument as to their identity with our canonical gospels incomplete; but the total omission to do so is the more remarkable from the circumstance that the names of Old Testament writers constantly occur in his writings. Semisch counts 197 quotations from the Old Testament, in which Justin refers to the author by name, or to the book, and only 117 in which he omits to do so, and the latter number might be reduced by considering the nature of the passages cited, and the inutility of repeating the reference.... The fact is that the only writing of the New Testament to which Justin refers by name is, as we have already mentioned, the Apocalypse, which he attributes to 'a certain man whose name was John, one of the apostles of Christ, who prophesied by a revelation made to him,' etc. The manner in which John is here mentioned, after the Memoirs had been so constantly indefinitely referred to clearly shows that Justin did not possess any gospel also attributed to John. That he does name John, however, as the author of the Apocalypse and so frequently refers to Old Testament writers by name, yet never identifies the author of the Memoirs is quite irreconcilable with the idea that they were the canonical gospels." *Supernatural Religion*, i., 297, 298.

have been gained by giving the writers' names. It was their relation to the facts recorded that gave them credence, and not their names. Second, it was the custom of early Christian writers, even of those who, according to the admission of modern skeptics, certainly used our Gospels, to quote them anonymously, and it would have been strange if Justin had done otherwise.[6] Even since the introduction of printed books, with chapters and verses, it is quite customary to cite the Scriptures in the same way; for the only value of special references is that it enables the reader to more readily find the passages quoted. Third, Justin's quotations from the Old Testament were almost exclusively the predictions that had been fulfilled in Christ, and in arguing on this subject with the Jew Trypho, it was necessary for him to be explicit. It is precisely in this way that he was led to name John as the author of the Apocalypse, for he was quoting from him a prediction concerning the millennium.[7] Justin's failure, then, to give the names of his authors, has no bearing on the question at issue.

2. On comparing Justin's quotations from the Memoirs with the corresponding passages in the Gospels, it is found that there are many verbal differences, and from this it is argued that the Memoirs and the Gospels can not have been the same books.[8]

---

[6] Westcott gives the names of twelve writers extending from Tatian of the second century to Eusebius of the fourth, who in their works addressed to unbelievers almost uniformly quote the gospels anonymously, and he closes his remarks on the subject with the statement that Justin "is not less but more explicit than later Apologists as to the writings from which he derives his accounts of the Lord's life and teaching." *Canon of New Testament,* 116–119.

[7] "Moreover also among us a man named John, one of the apostles of Christ, prophesied in a revelation made to him, that those who have believed on our Christ shall spend a thousand years in Jerusalem." *Dialogue, c.* 81. This is of course only Justin's interpretation of Revelation 20.1–7.

[8] The most striking of these differences are the following: In Justin's quotation of the words spoken to Mary by the angel (Luke 1.31) after the words "shall call his name Jesus," he appends the additional words used by the angel in speaking to Joseph (Matt 1.21), "for he shall save his people from their sins." *Apology,* i. 33. In his account of the census ordered at the time of Joseph's removal to Bethlehem, he represents the census as being taken in Judea, whereas Luke has it, "all the world"; and he speaks of Quirinius, as Procurator (ἐπίτροπος) of Judea, whereas he was according to Luke Governor (ἡγεμών) of Syria. *Apol. i.,* 34; *Dial,* c., 78. In his account of the voice that came from heaven at the baptism of Jesus, he adds to the words in the Gospels the words, "Thou art my Son, this day have I begotten thee." *Dial. c.,* 88.

These differences consist partly in slight alterations and transpositions of words, and partly, as in the instances cited below in the last note, in the commingling of passages from different writers. Whether they furnish any evidence of having been taken from some other source than our Gospels, depends upon Justin's habit in making quotations—whether or not he was in the habit of quoting with verbal accuracy. We are at no loss to ascertain his habit in this respect, for it is exhibited in his numerous quotations from the Old Testament. He quotes Old Testament writers with similar verbal variations, and he commingles passages from different authors as if he were quoting but one.[9] This refutes the argument. His evident purpose in making these variations, when he does it intentionally, is to bring out what he supposed to be the meaning, or to indicate some application of the text by a modification of its words.[10] But much the greater number of his variations is unquestionably due to quoting from memory. This appears from the fact that in a large majority of the instances in which the same passage is quoted twice or three times its phraseology is more or

---

[9] Westcott (*Canon of N. T.* 120–123) quotes a number of passages illustrative of this habit, of which the following is the most striking, and it is sufficient for our purpose. "What then the people of the Jews will say and do when they see Christ's advent in glory, has been thus told in prophecy by Zechariah: 'I will charge the four winds to gather my children who have been scattered. I will charge the north wind to bring and the south wind not to hinder, (Zech 2.6; Isa 43.6). 'And then shall there be in Jerusalem a great lamentation, not a lamentation of mouths and lips, but a lamentation of heart' (Zech 12.11), 'and they shall not rend their garments, but their minds' (Joel 2.13). 'They shall lament tribe to tribe" (Zech 12.12–14); 'and then shall they look on him whom they pierced (12.10) and say: Why, O Lord, did'st thou make us to err from thy way?' (Isa 43.17). 'The glory which our fathers blessed is turned to our reproach' (Isa 44.11, *Sept. Version*)."

[10] The following are remarkable instances illustrative of both of these purposes. He quotes a well-known passage from Ezekiel (3.17–19) in this form: "I have placed thee as a watchman to the house of Judah. Should the sinner sin, and thou not testify to him, he indeed shall perish for his sin, but from thee I will require his blood; but if thou testify to him thou shalt be blameless." *Dial.* c. lxxxii. "In the writings of Moses it is recorded that at the point of time when the Israelites came out of Egypt, and were in the wilderness, venomous beasts encountered them, vipers and asps and serpents of all kinds, which killed the people; and that by inspiration and impulse of God Moses took brass and made an image of a cross, and set this on the holy tabernacle, and said to the people: Should you look on this image and believe in it, you shall be saved. And he has recorded that when this was done the serpents died, and so the people escaped death." *Apol.* i. 60, *comp.* Numbers 21.6–9. By parity of reasoning the skeptic should say of these quotations that they certainly must have been taken from some spurious Ezekiel and Numbers, and not from the books known to us by these titles.

less varied every time.[11] In the time of manuscript books it was far more inconvenient to open to a passage and copy it verbatim, than it is now with our printed books divided into chapters and verses, yet the number of free quotations to be found in print is even now very large. We conclude, then, that Justin's verbal variations from our Gospels furnish no evidence that he did not quote them.

3. A ground of argument at first sight more serious than the preceding, is the fact that Justin quotes utterances of Jesus and of others connected with him, that are not found in our Gospels in any form; from which it is inferred that his Memoirs were not our Gospels.[12] We give the three most conspicuous examples. He represents Jesus as predicting, in his warnings to the disciples (Matt 24.24), the coming of "false apostles," as well as false Christs and false prophets; in his account of the mockings around the cross, he quotes among the other taunts of the people, "Let him come down and walk," the word walk not occurring in our Gospels; and he cites from Jesus the saying, "In whatsoever I find you, in this will I also judge you."

The last of these is not found in our Gospels at all, and Justin must have derived it from some other written source, or from tradition. He does not say that he found it in his Memoirs, and consequently it can not be used as proof that the Memoirs contained it. Moreover, it is the only entire sentence which he quotes from Jesus that is not in the Gospels, and it is not at all remarkable that, living as he did, when sayings of Jesus orally transmitted may still have been in circulation in large numbers, he quotes one of them. Paul makes a quotation of this kind derived from a similar source (Acts 20.35).

The other two variations from the gospel text are accounted for by Justin's habit of expanding the text while quoting it. As false apostles had appeared (2 Cor 11.13; Rev 2.2), it was but a slight departure from the letter of the prediction and none from the

---

[11] Westcott has collected in a brief table all the quotations which Justin makes more than once, and it shows that while there are twenty-three instances of agreement, there are thirty-five instances of difference. *Canon of N. T.* 173, 174.

[12] *Sup. Rel.* ii. 286, 333, 412–16. *et at.*

meaning, to represent them as included among the false teachers against whom the warning was uttered. And in quoting the words of those who mocked Jesus on the cross, he was but expressing more fully their meaning when, to their saying, "Let him come down," he added the words, "and walk." They did not mean that he should come down to sit, or to lie down, but to walk about and show that he had recovered from the maiming of the crucifixion. Surely these additions to the text can not be regarded by a serious mind as proof that the Memoirs were not our Gospels.

4. In the fourth place, it is alleged that Justin mentions facts derived from his Memoirs that are not found in the Gospels and that are contradictory to them.[13] Three specifications are sufficient to test this allegation as a source of argument. First, it is said that Justin, contrary to the Gospels, derives the genealogy of Jesus from David through Mary.[14] This Justin does, but it is not contradictory to the Gospels. The genealogy given by Luke has been understood by the majority of scholars from the earliest times as doing the same, and it is but fair to suppose that Justin so understood it. Moreover, the words of the angel quoted by Luke as addressed to Maryimply the same thing. Speaking to her of her own son who was to be born without an earthly father, he says to her: "The Lord God shall give to him the throne of his father David." The use of the word father here would have been unintelligible to her had she not been a descendant of David. Second, Justin states that when Jesus descended to the water to be baptized, "a fire was kindled in the Jordan," and that among the words addressed to him from heaven were these: "Thou art my Son, this day have I begotten thee."[15] But these words actually existed in some early MSS. of Luke, and they are still found in one Greek MS., and in the Old Latin version.[16] He may therefore have quoted them from his copy of Luke. As for the fire on the river, he

---

[13] "Facts in the life of Jesus and circumstances of Christian history derived from the same source, not only are not in our Gospels, but are in contradiction with them." *Ib.* 286.

[14] *Ib.* 300–302.

[15] *Ib.* 316–319.

[16] Westcott on the Can., 158 and *n.* 4.

does not claim to have learned this from the Memoirs, but he uses language that implies the reverse. He says: "When Jesus came to the Jordan where John was baptising, when He descended to the water both a fire was kindled in the Jordan, and the apostles of our Christ himself recorded that the Holy Spirit as a dove lighted upon him."[17] This careful citation of the apostles for the latter fact alone implies that for the former he had not their authority. The incident was legendary, and it was quite widely circulated in the second century.[18] Third, in referring to the arrest of Jesus by the Jews, Justin says, "There was not even a single man to run to his help as a guiltless person"; and this is held to be a contradiction of what is said in the Gospels about the attempt of Peter to defend his Lord.[19] But Justin evidently refers to help from without, and not to the fruitless attempt of Peter. The expression, "run to his help," shows that he refers to persons at a distance, and not to those who were standing by his side.

5. It is alleged in confirmation of the preceding arguments, that Justin's quotations agree in their variations from the Gospels with certain apocryphal gospels, and with quotations made by persons who are known to have used them.[20] This is true in a few instances, but it proves nothing more than that Justin and the authors of these works had some common source of information whence these variations were derived. It can not be proved that any of the apocryphal gospels were credited to "followers of the apostles," as were a portion of the Memoirs cited by Justin.

In answer to the very decisive fact that Justin speaks of his Memoirs as being "called Gospels," showing that this was the name by which they were more commonly known, and furnishing strong evidence that they are those which still bear the same title,[21] it is answered, that this expression is probably an interpola-

---

[17] *Dialogue,* c. 88.

[18] Westcott on the Canon, 159, *n.* 1.

[19] *Sup. Rel. 2* 329.

[20] *Ib.* 303–332.

[21] See chap. III. p. 94.

tion in Justin's works.[22] But no evidence of interpolation has been found, and therefore the answer amounts to nothing.

A very complete and altogether sufficient refutation of the theory that Justin's Memoirs were other than our Gospels, is, found in the fact admitted on all hands, that in the days of Irenaeus and of the author of the Muratorian Canon, only about twenty years after Justin's works appeared, our Gospels were in universal use as apostolic documents. This fact, in order to be reconciled with the theory, requires the supposition that Justin's Memoirs were the recognized apostolic Gospels up to the year 150, and that ere the year 170 four other Gospels materially different and bearing the names of different authors, come to be substituted for them without a word of remonstrance or comment by any writer of the day. Mr. Westcott demanded of the author of Supernatural Religion an explanation of this anomaly, and his reply was, that it was "totally unnecessary" for him to account for it—a tacit confession of inability.[23]

The evidence from the writings of Papias, who stands next in our list of authors, is contested as vigorously as that from Justin. It is contended that the Matthew and Mark mentioned by him were

---

[22] "A single passage has been pointed out in which the Memoirs are said to have been called Gospels in the plural: 'For the Apostles in the Memoirs composed by them, which are called Gospels,' etc. The last expression, 'which are called Gospels,' as many scholars have declared, is probably an interpolation." *Sup. Rel.* ii. 292.

[23] "Is it then possible to suppose that within twenty or thirty years after his [Justin's] death, these Gospels should have been replaced by others similar and yet distinct? That he should speak of one set of books as if they were permanently incorporated into the Christian services, and that those who might have been his scholars should speak in exactly the same terms of another collection as if they had had no rivals in the orthodox pale? That the substitution should have been effected in such a manner that no record of it has been preserved, while similar analogous reforms have been duly chronicled? The complication of historical difficulties in such an hypothesis is overwhelming; and the alternative is that which has already been justified on critical grounds, the belief that Justin in speaking of Apostolic Memoirs or Gospels, meant the Gospels which were enumerated in the early anonymous Canon of Muratori, and whose mutual relations were eloquently expounded by Irenaeus." *Canon of New Testament,* 165. "The last of these general objections to which I need now refer, is the statement that the difficulty with regard to the gospels commences precisely where my examination ends, and that I am bound to explain how, if no trace of this existence is previously discoverable, the four gospels are suddenly found in circulation at the end of the second century, and quoted as authoritative by such writers as Irenaeus. My reply is that it is totally unnecessary for me to account for this. *Sup. Rel.* ix.

not our two Gospels under those names, but older documents, and of quite a different character. In regard to Matthew the following positions are taken:

First, it is affirmed, that the term by which Papias designates the subject matter of Matthew's work, "The Oracles," shows that it was not a history like our present Matthew, but a collection of the sayings of Jesus.[24] It is admitted that the term refers to the sayings of Jesus regarded as divine oracles, but the inference that the book thus designated can be no more than a collection of these sayings is denied. In giving titles to books it is common to name them after some subject which is conspicuous in them, even when it occupies but a small part of the space. The title Gospel is itself an instance of this, as are also the titles Genesis, Exodus, Numbers and others in the Old Testament. Now the "Oracles" of Jesus occupy much the greater part of Matthew's book, for besides his shorter sayings and conversations, it contains nineteen formal speeches from his lips covering more than half the pages of the book. Mark, on the other hand, devotes to formal speeches only 28 percent of his space. To distinguish Matthew, then, as having composed "the Oracles," is a correct representation of his work as we have it, and it is a more appropriate expression than the word Gospel. Neither Papias nor Justin was pleased with the latter title.

Furthermore, the Apostle Paul uses this term for the Old Testament Scriptures in general, saying of the Jews, "They were entrusted with the Oracles of God" (Rom 3.2.). The term Oracles, then, is an appropriate expression for the subject matter of Matthew's Gospel, and Papias showed good sense in using it.

Second, it is argued that the work of Matthew, which Papias mentions, can not be our Matthew, because that was written in

---

[24] "There can be no doubt that the direct meaning of the word λόγια (oracles) anciently and at the time of Papias, was simply words or oracles of a sacred character; and however much the signification became afterwards extended, that it was not then at all applied to doings as well as sayings. There are many instances of this original and limited signification in the New Testament; and there is no linguistic precedent for straining the expression used at that period to mean anything beyond a mere collection of sayings of Jesus which were estimated as oracular or divine, nor is there any reason for thinking that λόγια (the oracles) was here used in any other sense." Ib. I. 464.

Hebrew and this in Greek.[25] The question turns upon the meaning of Papias. If he means that the only composition by Matthew known to him was composed in Hebrew, then the conclusion, so far as his testimony is concerned, is logical. But that it is unfair to construe his language thus is evident from the fact, that later writers who are known to have had our Greek Matthew, and to have believed that it came from Matthew's pen, speak in the same way of the original composition. So speak Irenaeus, Origen, Eusebius, and others.[26] That they do so, proves clearly that the use of such language is not inconsistent with a knowledge of the Greek Gospel of Matthew, nor with the belief that Matthew himself composed the latter. Papias, then, like them, may have had the Greek Gospel and may have believed that it came from Matthew, notwithstanding the assertion in question. The only rational way in which these authors could have held this double position, was by believing that Matthew wrote his Gospel first in Hebrew and then in Greek. It is a fact, however, not to be overlooked in this connection, that not one of the writers referred to, including Papias himself, claims to have seen the Hebrew Gospel.[27] Its use had necessarily been confined to Jewish Christians; and it had gone out of use with the disappearance from the church of its Hebrew element.

Third, it is argued that Papias could not have known the Gospels of Luke and John, or he would have mentioned them also; and Eusebius, through whom alone we have knowledge of what he wrote, would have recorded the fact: for, it is said, "Eusebius never fails to state what the Fathers say about the books of the New Testament."[28] This argument contains two assumptions:

[25] "If it be denied that Matthew wrote in Hebrew, it can not be asserted that he wrote at all. It is therefore perfectly certain from this testimony that Matthew can not be declared the direct author of the Greek Canonical Gospel bearing his name." *Ib.* 476.

[26] The author of Supernatural Religion himself quotes to this effect the words of these and other authors (ii. 471–474) without seeming to know that he thereby furnishes evidence to refute his own argument.

[27] This fact is emphasized by Alford (Prolegomena to Greek New Testament c. 2 § 2) who shows that an apparent exception in the case of Jerome is not a real one.

[28] "Eusebius, who never fails to state what the Fathers say about the books of the New Testament, does not mention that Papias knew either the third or fourth gospel. Is

First, that Papias would certainly have mentioned these two Gospels, had he known them; and second, that had he mentioned them Eusebius would have noted the fact. That the last is a false assumption appears from the plan which Eusebius followed in writing of such matters. After mentioning the books of the New Testament which had been disputed, and those which had been undisputed, he declared it his plan to name the previous writers who had made use of any of the former, and to quote what had been related by them concerning the latter.[29] In carrying out this plan, he fails to mention many express quotations from the undisputed books made by writers whose works have come down to us, although he uses these works frequently for other purposes. Had these works been lost, like those of Papias, this argument would have been applied to them also, and how falsely we can easily see.[30] It should also be carefully observed that the citation which he does make from Papias is in perfect keeping with his plan. It is not a quotation made by Papias from Matthew or Mark, but a piece of information which he gives concerning the origin of these two books. In regard to Luke and John, Papias had no occasion to record such information, because Luke tells his readers plainly the origin of his book (1.1–4), and that of John was well known in the region in which Papias lived, for there John had published it after many then living were born. The absurdity of the argument that Papias knew nothing of the Gospels of Luke and John because he mentions them not, and that if he had known them and mentioned them Eusebius would certainly have

---

it possible to suppose that if Papias had been acquainted with those gospels he would not have asked information about them from the Presbyters, or that Eusebius would not have recorded it as he did that regarding the works ascribed to Matthew and Mark?" *Sup. Rel.* 2 484.

[29] "But as my history proceeds I will take care along with the successions (of the bishops), to indicate what church writers from time to time have made use of any of the disputed books, and what has been said by them concerning the Canonical and acknowledged Scriptures, and anything that (they have said) concerning those which do not belong to this class." *Eccles. Hist.* iii. 3, Dr. Lightfoot's translation.

[30] Dr. Lightfoot, in an elaborate article on this question published in the Contemporary Review for January, 1875, presents this answer with great force, and shows conclusively that Eusebius thus dealt with the writings of Clement of Rome, Ignatius, Polycarp, Justin Martyr, Theophilus of Antioch, and Irenaeus.

said so, is strikingly exposed by Dr. Lightfoot as follows: "Not only is it maintained that A knows nothing of B, because he says nothing of B, but it is further assumed that A knows nothing of B, because C does not say that A knows anything of B."[31]

Fourth, it is urged that even if Papias knew some of the New Testament books, he regarded them as of little importance, seeing that he preferred oral tradition as a source of information.[32] This argument misrepresents the reason which he gives for preferring the living voice to books, and it falsely assumes that the books referred to are his Gospels. The facts of the case are these: He writes a work in five books under the title, "Exposition of Oracles of our Lord." The oracles which he expounds are contained in sacred books, among which Matthew and Mark are expressly mentioned. In his preface to this Exposition, he speaks of the aids which he employed, saying: "But I shall not regret to subjoin to my interpretations also for your benefit, whatsoever I have at any time accurately ascertained and treasured up in my memory, as I have received it from the elders, and have recorded it in order to give additional confirmation to the truth by my testimony"; and in this connection he adds: "For I do not think that I derived so much benefit from books as from the living voice of those that are still surviving."[33] The benefit referred to is in the way of confirming his interpretations; and his comparison is not that of the living voice with the books on which he was commenting, but that of the former with books which were used as helps in his Exposition. In brief, he was commenting on the Gospels, and he derived more help in this task from conversing with men who had seen the Apostles, than from reading the books of uninspired men. If a commentator on the Gospels could enjoy the same privilege today, he would probably prize it as highly.

---

[31] Contemporary Review, January, 1875, p. 170.

[32] "Whatever books Papias knew, however, it is certain, from his own express declaration, that he ascribed little importance to them, and preferred tradition as a more beneficial source of information regarding evangelical history. 'For I held that what was to be derived from books,' he says, 'did not so profit me as that from the living and abiding voice.'" *Sup. Rel. 2* 486.

[33] *Eccles. Hist.* iii. 39.

Fifth, it is urged as a special objection in reference to what Papias says of Peter's connection with the book of Mark, that this can not refer to our Mark because in this Peter is less conspicuous than he must have been in that, and less so than he is in the other Gospels.[34] That Peter is far less conspicuous in Mark's Gospel than in the other three is true; for nearly all of the incidents which reflect credit on Peter are omitted by Mark.[35] This, however, instead of proving that the statement of Papias can not have reference to our second Gospel, bears in the opposite direction; for unless Peter was a vainglorious man, of which there is not the slightest indication, a narrative derived from his oral teaching would make him less conspicuous than one derived from other sources. Mark's Gospel, then, is in this particular precisely what we should expect if the representation of Papias is true.

Sixth and last, it is argued that our Mark can not be the one of which Papias speaks, because the latter says that Mark "did not arrange in order the things which were either said or done by Jesus," whereas our Mark has "the most evident character of orderly arrangement."[36] It is true that Mark's Gospel has an orderly arrangement, but its order is quite different from that of the other gospels, and notably from Matthew's which in some other respects it most resembles. Such is the difference that should one form a conception of the order of events from reading Matthew, as Papias probably did, and as many beginners in Gospel study now do, he could but be struck, on reading Mark, with the very thought expressed by Papias, that Mark has not arranged in order (that is, in the order of time) the things done and said. Not until he had made a careful study of the two gospels with reference to chronological order, would he think otherwise. The remark of Papias, then, is precisely the remark that he would naturally make if, in preparing his work on the Oracles of the Lord, he had been

---

[34] *Sup. Rel. 2* 452–455.

[35] For the specifications, see p. 115.

[36] "Now it is impossible in the work of Mark here described [by Papias] to recognize our present second Gospel, which does not depart in any important degree from the order of the other two synoptics, and which, throughout, has the most evident character of orderly arrangement." *Sup. Rel. 2* 456.

chiefly absorbed in the study of Matthew where these Oracles are so abundantly found.

In regard to the testimony of the still earlier writers whom we have cited, Polycarp, Barnabas and Clement of Rome, the only position taken by infidel writers worthy of serious consideration, is this: that the quotations which are cited from them were derived not from our New Testament books, but from other documents older than these and from oral tradition.[37] The express quotations are not, of course, disposed of in this way, because they can not be; and these have forced the admission that the Epistle to the Romans, the two to the Corinthians, and that to the Galatians, together with the book of Revelation are genuine. There is no doubt that in those early times many sayings of Jesus not recorded in our Gospels were current among the disciples, and it is altogether probable that some of them were adopted by these writers, as at least one was at a later period by Justin; but that the mass of those found in these writers and also found in our New Testament books were derived from other sources, is an assumption supported by no proof and in itself it is wholly improbable. It could be adopted only by one who had previously and from other considerations reached the conclusion that these writers wrote at an earlier period than the New Testament writers. The argument is illogical, because it assumes the very thing in dispute. If it be said that though it may not be certain that these passages were derived from such other sources, they certainly may have been, and that this throws doubt upon the evidence; the answer is, that the number of these quotations is too great, and their correspondence with what is written in the New Testament too close, to allow the probability of such a supposition. The position, therefore, while it is ingenious, and the only one on which a skeptic in regard to the genuineness of our books can stand, must be set aside as arbitrary and illogical.

---

[37] The author of Supernatural Religion, after discussing separately the quotations from the authors named, makes the following remark as applicable to all: "Now we must repeat that all such sayings of Jesus were the common property of early Christians, were no doubt orally current amongst them, and still more certainly were recorded by many of the numerous gospels then in circulation, as they are by several of our own." 2 279.

We shall now consider briefly the objections of rationalists to the internal evidence which we have adduced.

Those writers who deny the reality of miracles unite in denying the genuineness of all the gospels in preference to admitting it and charging their writers with deliberate falsehood. This denial is based, not on internal evidence, but on the ground of opinions formed independently of these narratives; and its discussion belongs to the question of the authenticity of the gospels and not to that of their genuineness. If the miraculous accounts are false, the falsehoods may have been written by Matthew, Mark, Luke and John as well as by other Christian writers.

No internal evidence against the genuineness of the first three gospels has been adduced, except such as springs from the theories of the various objectors as to what would have been their characteristics had they been genuine. It is not claimed that any facts mentioned in them or alluded to, were beyond the reach of their reputed authors, or that any of the words employed may not have been known to them. But it is assumed that had they been genuine they would have been more definite in their statements of time, and of the connection of events; and that they would have harmonized more completely with one another in regard to historical details.[38]

---

[38] Meyer's objection to the genuineness of the gospel of Matthew may be cited as a fair specimen of the mode of reasoning applied by Rationalists to all of the first three gospels, except that, unlike the Rationalists in general, he admits the genuineness of John and uses it to discredit Matthew. He says: "In the form in which the gospels now exist it can not have originally proceeded from the hands of the apostle Matthew. The evidence in favor of this view consists not merely of the many statements of time, place and other things which are irreconcilable with the living recollection of an apostolic eye-witness and a participator in the events, even upon the assumption of a plan of arrangement carried out mainly in accordance with the subject matter; not merely in a partial want of clearness and directness, which is a prominent feature in many of the historical portions (even in 9.9ff included), and not seldom makes itself felt to such a degree that we must in this respect allow the preference to the accounts of Mark and Luke; not merely in the want of historical *connection* in the citation and introduction of a *substantial* portion of the didactic discourses of Jesus, by which the fact is disclosed that they were not interwoven in a living connection with the above; decisive, the reception of narratives the unhistorical character of which must certainly have been known to an apostle (such as, even in the history of the Passion, that of the watchers by the grave, and of the resurrection of many dead bodies); the reception of the preliminary history with its legendary enlargements, which far oversteps the original beginning of the gospel announcement (Mark 1.1, *comp.* John 1.19)

These assumptions are based, like the one in regard to miracles, on purely dogmatic grounds; and the questions which they raise pertain not so much to the genuineness of the gospels as to their authenticity. We defer the consideration of them to Part Third of our inquiry.

In regard to the gospel ascribed to John the case is quite different. Although it was never classed among the disputed books in ancient times, its genuineness has recently become a subject of heated controversy, and chiefly on the ground of internal evidence.[39] The discussion has taken a wide range, and has extended to many minute and collateral questions which have but little bearing on the main issue. We will state and consider only those objections which have sufficient plausibility to deserve attention.

1. It is argued from internal evidence that the author of this gospel was not a Jew, as was the apostle John. The evidence in support of this objection lies chiefly in the fact obvious to every careful reader of the gospel, that the author habitually speaks of the Jews in the third person, as if he were not one of them, and that he distinguishes them constantly from Jesus and his disciples who were also Jews.[40] In answer to this objection we remark: *First,*

---

and its original contents (Acts 10.37ff; Papias in Eusebius H. E., iii. 39; the things which were spoken or done by Christ), and which already presents a later historical formation, added to the original gospel history; the reception of the enlarged narrative of the temptation, the non-developed form of which in Mark is certainly older; but most strikingly of all, the many, and in part, every essential correction which our Matthew must receive from the fourth gospel, and several of which (especially those relating to the last supper of the risen Saviour) are of such a kind that the variations in question certainly exclude apostolic testimony on one side, and this, considering the genuineness of John which we must decidedly assume, can only affect the credibility of Matthew. To this, moreover, is to be added the relation of dependence which we must assume of our Matthew upon Mark, which is incompatible with the composition of the former by an apostle." *Introduction to Com. on Matthew, Sec. 2*

[39] The controversy was opened by Bretschneider in a work published in 1820, under the title *Probabilia de Evangelio et Epistolis Joannis Apostoli.*

[40] "He writes at all times as one who not only is not a Jew himself, but has nothing to do with their laws and customs. He speaks everywhere of the feasts of 'the Jews,' 'the passover of the Jews,' 'the manner of the purifying of the Jews,' 'the Jews feast of tabernacles,' 'as the manner of the Jews is to bury,' 'the Jews preparation day,' and so on. Moreover, the Jews are represented as continually in virulent opposition to Jesus, and seeking to kill him; and the word 'Jew' is the unfailing indication of the enemies of the truth, and the persecutors of the Christ." *Sup. Rel.,* ii. 414.

that this was the most natural way for the author, whether Jew or Gentile, to express himself; for he wrote long after the disciples had become a distinct community, separated from both Jews and Gentiles, and how could he speak so intelligibly of the bulk of the Jewish people who had stood opposed to Christ and his disciples as by calling them the Jews? *Second*, the apostle Paul, himself a "Hebrew of the Hebrews," had already, long before this gospel was written, made free use of the same phraseology in such expressions as these: "To the Jews I became as a Jew, that I might gain the Jews"; "Give no occasion of stumbling, either to Jews, or to Greeks, or to the Church of God."[41] The argument in question, if valid, would prove that Paul's epistles were not written by a Jew. *Third*, both Matthew and Mark, who were confessedly Jews, have left one instance each of the same use of the word, while Luke has left but two, though he is a Gentile and in his writings we would expect, according to this argument, to find it most frequently of all.[42] These considerations show that the argument is without force; and not only so, but that the phraseology on which it is based is what we should expect to find.

2. It is said that the difference between the author as represented by himself and the John of the Synoptics, is proof that the author was not John.[43] The specifications chiefly relied on to support this assertion, are the following: *First*—The author represents himself as being known to the high priest (xviii. 15), and it is held that this could not have been true of the young fisherman of Galilee.[44] But the absurdity of this inference is seen in the

---

[41] 1 Corinthians 9.20; 10.32. See the following: "The Jews require a sign" (1 Cor 1.22); "Of the Jews five times I received forty stripes save one" (2 Cor 11.24); "And the rest of the Jews dissembled likewise with him" (Gal 2.13); "Ye also suffered the same things of your own countrymen, even as they did of the Jews" (1 Thess 2.14).

[42] "This saying was spread abroad among the Jews" (Matt 28.15); "For the Pharisees and all the Jews, except they wash," etc. (Mark 7.3); "He sent unto him the elders of the Jews" (Luke 7.3); "Arimathea, a city of the Jews" (23.51).

[43] "Without pausing to consider the slightness of this evidence [the evidence that John is the author], it is obvious that supposing the disciple indicated to be John the son of Zebedee, the fourth gospel gives a representation of him quite different from the Synoptics and other writings." *Sup. Rel.*, ii. 425.

[44] *Ib.* 427, 428.

fact that it is one of the most common things in life for men in high positions to have acquaintance with others in the humblest callings. *Second*—The author represents himself as "the disciple whom Jesus loved," whereas, neither in the other Gospels, nor in Paul's Epistles, nor elsewhere except in this Gospel, is John represented as if he occupied such a position; on the contrary, the preeminence is uniformly given to Peter.[45] It is true that the preeminence in activity and leadership is elsewhere given to Peter, and it is tacitly conceded to him even in this Gospel"[46]; but the distinction claimed by the author for himself is that of sympathetic affection such as appears in his leaning on the Master's breast at the supper. The two representations are not inconsistent. It is true also that such a relation between John and the Master is nowhere else alluded to; but this is no ground for denying its existence. That it was credited as a fact by the contemporaries of the author is evident from the consideration, that in the absence of such a belief he could not hope to be understood when designating himself as "the disciple whom Jesus loved." But the belief can not be satisfactorily accounted for unless it had came down to the time at which the Gospel was written as an authentic tradition. Moreover, the evident sincerity of the author forbids the supposition that he falsely represented himself as John by styling himself "the disciple whom Jesus loved." *Third*—It is claimed that the author represents himself as not an eye-witness of what he records, by appealing for confirmation of his word to some one who was. The alleged appeal is in the following passages: "And he that hath seen hath borne witness, and his witness is true; and he knoweth that he said true, that ye also may believe" (19.35). "This is the disciple who beareth witness of these things, and wrote these things; and we know that his witness is true" (21.24).[47] In regard to the first of these passages we

---

[45] *Ib.* 429–433.

[46] See the incidents recorded in 1.42; 6.68; 13.6; 18.10; 21.3, 7, 11.

[47] "That the apostle himself could have written of himself the words in 19.35 is impossible. After having stated so much that is much more surprising and contradictory to all experience without reference to any witness, it would indeed have been strange had he here appealed to himself as a separate individual." *Sup. Rel.,* ii. 440. "Such a passage, received in

remark, that inasmuch as the author uniformly refers to himself in the third person, the fact that he uses the third person here can not justify the inference that he refers to another. No one who reads the passage without a foregone conclusion can fail to realize that it is but a strong reiteration of the author's own testimony. It is somewhat surprising that he should employ such reiteration in regard to the circumstance to which it is applied, the issuing of blood and water from the side of Jesus, but he may have been led to it by some special doubts on this point prevalent when the Gospel was written. It must be admitted, too, that this appeal to one's certain knowledge of the fact, is an unusual way of supporting one's testimony; but though unusual it is not unprecedented. Paul does the same when he says, "I say the truth in Christ, I lie not, my conscience bearing witness with me in the Holy Spirit," etc. (Rom 9.1). That John should appeal to the certainty of his knowledge in support of his own testimony is no more singular than that Paul should call up the testimony of his own conscience to support his. In regard to the second passage cited above we remark, that the last clause of it was certainly written by some persons unknown to us, and it is scarcely possible that they could have written this clause without writing the whole sentence. Their purpose was to identify the author of the Gospel with the beloved disciple just mentioned before, and to certify the reliability of his testimony. The form of their statement was evidently suggested by that of the author in 19.35. If it be thought strange that such endorsement of the testimony of an Apostle would be made by any other persons, we should remember that these persons, though unknown to us, were known to those who first received this Gospel, and that they may have been men whose testimony would add some weight to that of John—they may have been, like him, eye-witnesses of many events in the life of Jesus, and full of the Holy Spirit. To argue as if they were not is to argue from our ignorance.

---

any natural sense, or interpreted in any way which can be supported by evidence, shows that the writer of the gospel was not an eye-witness of the events recorded, but appeals to the testimony of others." *Ib*. 445.

3. Another ground of objection is the striking difference between the matter of this Gospel and that of the Synoptics. That this difference is very great, leaving but little matter in common, is known to every student of these narratives; but that the difference does not amount to a contradiction, as all rationalists assert,[48] is equally well known by all who have carefully compared them. It grows exclusively out of the plan of the author, which evidently contemplated the presentation of certain events and certain phases of the teaching of Jesus not found in the first three Gospels, and not commonly recited in the oral teaching of the early preachers. The details are so numerous that we can not specify them here; nor is it important that we should, seeing that they are made familiar by any ordinary course of instruction in sacred history. We shall notice only one specification. It is affirmed that the Synoptics limit the teaching of Jesus to one year, and confine his labors to Galilee except the closing scenes at Jerusalem, while the fourth Gospel extends the time to more than three years, and mentions several visits to Jerusalem previous to the last.[49] This representation of the fourth Gospel is correct; but it is not true that the other Gospels limit the teaching of Jesus to one year. They date the beginning of his ministry after the imprisonment of John the Baptist, and his death in Jerusalem at the beginning of a Passover; but they contain not a word that indicates the length of the interval, or that points to one year rather than three. The sole ground for the assumption is the fact that the only Passover which they mention is the one at which Jesus suffered; but this merely shows that they are silent in regard to other Passovers, not

---

[48] "The difference between the fourth gospel and the Synoptics, not only as regards the teachings of Jesus, but also the facts of the narrative, is so great that it is impossible to harmonize them, and no one who seriously considers the matter can fail to see that both can not be accepted as correct." *Sup. Rel.*, ii. 451. This author proceeds through a number of pages to give specifications, all of which are familiar to the ordinary student of sacred history, and none of which are really difficult of reconciliation with the synoptic narratives.

[49] "The Synoptics clearly represent the ministry of Jesus as having been limited to a single year, and his preaching is confined to Galilee and Jerusalem, where his career culminates at the fatal Passover. The fourth gospel distributes the teaching of Jesus between Galilee, Samaria and Jerusalem, makes it extend at least over three years, and refers to three Passovers spent by Jesus at Jerusalem." *Sup. Rel.*, ii. 453.

that others had not transpired. Neither is it true that they confine the labors of Jesus, except the closing scenes, to Galilee; for while they describe no visit to Jerusalem till the last, two of them show a knowledge that he had been there often. They do so by quoting the words of Jesus addressed to Jerusalem: "How often would I have gathered thy children together, even as a hen gathereth her chickens under her wings, and ye would not"; and Luke still further shows his knowledge of it, by describing a visit of Jesus to the home of Martha and Mary at Bethany, two miles from Jerusalem, previous to his last journey.[50] This is a fair specimen of the specifications under this objection; they are all based on false or groundless assumptions.

4. The fourth objection which we shall mention is based on the striking difference between the speeches of Jesus found in the fourth Gospel, and those in the other three. It is held, that if the portraiture of Jesus thus given in the first three is correct, that given in the fourth is so thoroughly different that it must be false, and can not have been the work of an Apostle.[51] The principal points of difference on which the objection is based

---

[50] Matthew 23.37; Luke 13.34; 10.38–42. The force of the evidence from the words of Jesus quoted above was so apparent to Strauss that he could evade it only by denying that Jesus uttered them. He says: "This expression can Jesus least of all have used where Luke puts it, on his journey to Jerusalem, and before he had once during his public activity seen that city. But even in Jerusalem itself, after a single stay there of only a few days, he can not have pointed out how *often* he had attempted in vain to draw its inhabitants to himself. Here all shifts are futile, and it must be confessed if these are really the words of Christ he must have labored in Jerusalem oftener and longer than would appear from the synoptical reports." *Life of Jesus*, 249. The author of *Supernatural Religion* evades the issue, and says only this: "Apologists discover indications of a three years' ministry in Matthew 23.37, Luke 13.34; 'How often,' etc.; and also in Luke 13.32f.: 'To-day, to-morrow and the third day.'" ii. 453.

[51] "The teaching of the one is totally different from that of the others, in spirit, form and terminology; and although there are undoubtedly fine sayings throughout the work, in the prolix discourses of the fourth gospel there is not a single characteristic of the simple eloquence of the Sermon on the Mount." *Sup. Rel.*, ii. 464. "It is impossible that Jesus can have two such diametrically opposed systems of teaching—one purely moral, the other wholly dogmatic; one expressed in wonderfully terse, clear, brief sayings and parables, the other in long, involved and diffuse discourses; one clothed in the great language of humanity, the other concealed in obscure, philosophic terminology; and that these should have been kept so distinct as they are in the Synoptics on the one hand, and the fourth gospel on the other." *Ib*. 470.

are those in style; in the representation made of Jesus himself; and in the doctrine of salvation which he teaches. His style in the Synoptics is much simpler, and his speeches in the main are much shorter. In them he appears chiefly as the Jewish Messiah; in John, as the Son of God. In them he insists chiefly on deeds of obedience and benevolence as the ground of salvation; in John, on faith in himself.

That these distinctions exist is admitted; but the inference drawn from them is denied. To deny that Jesus could have spoken on different occasions and to different persons in style as different as that to which we refer, is not only to deny the supernatural powers which the Scriptures ascribe to him, but also to deny that versatility of genius which is ascribed to him by all intelligent unbelievers: and that the occasions and persons are different can be seen by a glance at these in the several Gospels. As to his representation of himself, his divinity is not less explicitly asserted in the Synoptics than in John, it is only asserted less frequently and discussed less elaborately.[52] That this should be the case can appear strange only to those who deny his divinity, as the objectors do. As to the terms of salvation, while faith is made more conspicuous in the speeches recorded by John, its necessity is constantly implied in the obedience emphasized in the Synoptics. The final test submitted at the close of the Sermon on the Mount, "He that heareth these sayings of mine and doeth them," "He that heareth these sayings of mine and doeth them not," turns upon the faith or the unbelief on which the two courses of action depend; the supreme blessing pronounced on Peter was for a confession of his faith; faith is made explicitly a condition of salvation in the apostolic commission as preserved by Mark, and by implication in that preserved by Matthew; and, in a word, all the matter of the three Gospels is evidently intended to lead men to faith in Christ as a necessary condition of salvation. He who has learned the simple fundamental lesson of the New Testament, that faith and obedi-

---

[52] His divine authority and sonship are affirmed in the following passages: Matthew 7.22; 10.1; 11.27; 13.41; 16.16, 17, 27; 18.20; 22.42–45; 25.31–34; 28.20; Mark 2.5–10; Luke 24.49.

ence are both necessary to the final salvation of accountable beings, can find no difficulty in the fact that now one of these conditions and then the other receives especial emphasis.

5. The style of the speeches of Jesus is made the ground of another objection to the genuineness of the fourth Gospel. The style
of the speeches is the same in its general features, with that of
the narrative, and from this it is inferred that they can not be the
real speeches of Jesus as they would be recalled by an Apostle; but
that they are fictitious speeches composed by the author and put
into the lips of Jesus.[53] I answer to this we remark, that while the
last supposition, if true, would account for the sameness of style,
it can as readily be accounted for on a different hypothesis. If we
suppose, as the genuineness of the Gospel would require, that
Jesus actually spoke in the style represented, the similarity of style
is at once accounted for by the natural inclination of an admiring
disciple to adopt the style of his teacher. It is certain that, whether
John wrote this Gospel or not, his whole mental and moral nature
was deeply impressed by Jesus while living, and that during the
half century and more in which he had preached and meditated
upon the sayings of Jesus previous to the supposed date of this
book, this impression was made still deeper; why then should it
be thought strange that in speaking on the same subject with his
adored Lord, he should have learned to employ the same vocabulary, and to frame his sentences in the same style? Again, it should
be remembered that in writing his Gospel, John was translating
into Greek both the speeches of Jesus, which had been uttered in

---

[53] "We have already pointed out the evident traces of artificial construction in the
discourses and dialogues of the fourth gospel, and the more closely these are examined the
more clear does it become that they are not genuine reports of the teachings of Jesus, but
mere ideal compositions by the author of the fourth gospel. The speeches of John the Baptist, the discourses of Jesus, and the reflections of the evangelist himself, are marked by the
same peculiarity of style, and proceed from the same mind." *Sup. Rel.,* ii. 471. As regards
this assertion concerning John the Baptist, we may remark that the speeches quoted from
him in the fourth gospel are necessarily different from those in the Synoptics; for whereas
the latter were all spoken before the baptism of Jesus, the former were all uttered after
that event and after the temptation; yet it is also true that the latter speeches are closely
connected in matter with the former, and they follow the same train of thought respecting
Jesus.

the current Hebrew, and his own thoughts, which were conceived in the same tongue. It is the style of this translation which we are considering, and not the original style of either John or Jesus. But the style in which a writer translates his own thoughts into a foreign language and that in which he translates the speeches of another must necessarily be the same so far as fidelity to the original will allow.

6. The last objection which we shall notice is based on the style of the Apostle John. It is claimed by recent skeptics in general, that John was certainly the author of the Apocalypse, and that the radical difference in style between that book and the fourth Gospel forbids the supposition that he also wrote the latter.[54] It is claimed, and it is admitted, that while the latter composition is written in purer Greek than any other book of the New Testament, the Apocalypse is remarkable for its Hebraisms, and other defects in style. This difference was observed by the Greek writers of the early church; and it is one of the causes which led many in that period to deny the genuineness of the Apocalypse; for then no doubt existed as to the genuineness of the Gospel.[55] It

---

[54] "It is impossible to assume that the author of the gospel was one and the same person with the author of the Apocalypse, but it is equally impossible to ignore the fact that the evangelist conceived himself in place of the Apocalyptic writer, and meant to use the weight of John's name for the purposes of his gospel," etc. Baur, *Church History*, i. 154. "Whilst a strong family likeness exists between the epistles [of John] and the gospel, and they exhibit close analogies both in thought and language, the Apocalypse, on the contrary, is so different from them in language, in style, in religious views and terminology, that it is almost impossible to believe that the writer of the one could be the author of the other." *Sup. Rel.*, ii. 386. "We think it must be apparent to every unprejudiced person that the Apocalypse singularly corresponds in every respect—language, construction and thought—with what we are told of the character of the apostle John by the synoptic gospels and by tradition, and that the internal evidence, therefore, accords with the external in attributing the composition of the Apocalypse to that apostle." *Ib.* 406.

[55] Dionysius of Alexandria, who wrote about the middle of the third century, is quoted by Eusebius as closing a discussion of this question with the following remarks: "We may also notice how the phraseology of the Gospel and the Epistle differs from the Apocalypse. For the former are written not only irreprehensibly as it regards the Greek language, but are most elegant in diction, and in the whole structure of the style. It would require much to discover any barbarism or solecism, or any odd peculiarity of expression at all in them. For, as is to be presumed, he was endued with all the requisites for his discourse, the Lord having granted him both that of knowledge and that of expression and style. That the latter, however, saw a revelation, and received knowledge and prophecy, I do not deny. But I perceive that his dialect and language is not very accurate Greek; but that he uses

is one of the singular revolutions which characterize skeptical thought, that in the hands of modern unbelievers the scales have turned, and the shafts of doubt are hurled in the opposite direction. In reply to this it is urged by those who believe in the early date of the Apocalypse, that time sufficient elapsed between that date (AD 68) and the date of the Gospel (95–97) to allow a marked improvement in the author's use of the Greek language, especially as he spent this period of his life among a cultivated people whose native tongue was Greek.[56] By those who assign to the Apocalypse the later date (96) and allow no great difference of time between it and John's other writings, it is answered, that the Hebraisms of the former are to be accounted for by the fact that the book is to a large extent a reproduction of the imagery of the Old Testament prophets, and that it therefore of necessity assumed much of their style.[57] Either answer suffices to show that the objection furnishes no adequate reason for denying the genuineness of the Gospel.

Modern skeptics admit that the author of Acts and of the third Gospel was the same person,[58] but they are divided among themselves on the question whether that author was Luke. Some

barbarous idioms, and in some places solecisms which it is now unnecessary to select; for neither would I have any one suppose that I am saying these things by way of derision, but only with the view to point out the great difference between the writings of these men." *Eccles. Hist.*, vii. 25. Dionysius makes other remarks on the general question which are echoed by modern disputants.

[56] "Nor is it difficult to see that in any case intercourse with a Greek-speaking people would in a short time naturally reduce the style of the author of the Apocalypse to that of the author of the Gospel." Westcott, *Introduction to John*, lxxxvi.

[57] "The language of the Apocalypse, in fact, is more akin to the Hebrew than to the Greek, and while the fourth gospel proceeds in propositions of the usual historical and narrative character, the Apocalypse is occupied with visions and imagery corresponding to the Hebrew diction of the Old Testament, especially to its prophetic and sacred forms of speech." Prof. Lee, *Introduction to Revelation, Bible Commentary*, 455.

[58] "It is generally admitted, although not altogether without exception, that the author of the third synoptic Gospel likewise composed the Acts of the Apostles. The linguistic and other peculiarities which distinguished the Gospel, are equally prominent in the Acts." *Sup. Rel.* iii. 32. "There can be no doubt that the Acts of the Apostles were written by the author of the third Gospel, and form a continuation of that work. It is not necessary to stop and prove this proposition, which has never been seriously contested. The preface which is at the beginning of each work, the dedication of both to Theophilus, and the perfect resemblance of style and ideas, are abundant demonstration of the fact." Renan, *Apostles* 13, 14.

scholars of the Tübingen school deny that Luke had any connection with the authorship; but Baur himself, while denying that he composed the narrative as we have it, supposed that he left memoranda which were used in the final composition. Renan, on the contrary, though he unites with the rest in denying that the book is true to history, contends that Luke is certainly the author of the whole book.[59] The only ground on which its genuineness is denied, is its alleged untruthfulness. It is held that it was written for the purpose of covering up an unreconciled hostility between Paul and the other Apostles, and that to this end many facts were distorted and some invented. The merits of this allegation will be considered in Part Third of this book; but even if it is true, it has no material bearing on the question of the genuineness of the book; for on the rationalistic hypothesis which denies inspiration, Luke may as well be charged with the fraud, as a later Christian writer. Whether the charge is true or false, then, it affords no ground for doubting the genuineness of Acts. The genuineness of the Epistles to the Galatians and Romans, and of both of those to the Corinthians is conceded, as we have already stated, by all modern skeptics.[60] There is no internal evidence in conflict with that which we have presented in Chapter IV., not even in the es-

---

[59] "A careful study of the contents of the Acts can not, we think, leave any doubt that the work could not have been written by any companion or intimate friend of the Apostle Paul. * * * It is unreasonable to suppose that a friend or companion could have written so unhistoric and defective a history of the Apostle's life and teaching. The Pauline epistles are nowhere directly referred to, but where we can compare the narrative and representations of Acts with the statements of the Apostle, they are strikingly contradictory." *Sup. Rel.* iii. 51. "It may not be impossible that sketches, collections, narratives, chronicles, especially those concerning the last journey of the Apostle, from the hand of Luke, may have formed the foundation of the Acts. * * * In such passages the author is very willing to be considered as one person with Luke; but he did not venture to declare himself in the character of Luke as the writer of the Acts of the Apostles, for he was well aware of the difference in dates, and could not so completely escape from his own identity." Baur, *Life of Paul*, i. 12, 13. Renan, after affirming and arguing that the author of the third Gospel must be the author of Acts, closes the discussion of the question by saying: "We believe, then, that the author of the third Gospel was really Luke, the disciple of Paul." *Apostles*, 19.

[60] "There has never been the slightest suspicion of un-authenticity cast on these four epistles, and they bear so incontestably the character of Pauline originality, that there is no conceivable ground for the assertion of critical doubts in their case." Baur, *Life of Paul*, i. 246. "Epistles unquestioned and unquestionable; namely, the epistle to the Galatians, the two epistles to the Corinthians, and the epistle to the Romans." Renan, *Life of Paul*, 10.

timation of the most destructive critics of the present age, except with reference to the last two chapters of Romans which are held in doubt by some of them.[61]

The genuineness of first and second Thessalonians, the earliest of Paul's writings, and probably the earliest writings of the New Testament, was never questioned until recent times, and that of the first Epistle was not assailed until the publication of Baur's *Life of Paul*.[62] This author bases his rejection of the first Epistle chiefly on the following grounds: First, that a large part of it contains nothing that the Thessalonians did not already know, being an extended account of their conversion; second, that it contains "reminiscences" of other Epistles known to have been written at a later date than is claimed for this; third, that it contains different and later views of the second coming of Christ (4.14–18) than are expressed in 1 Corinthians. In regard to the second Epistle, he holds that it borrows its idea of Anti-Christ (2.1–8) from the Apocalypse, and must therefore be later than that book; and that the caution about testing the genuineness of any epistle purporting to come from him by the salutation being written in his own hand (2.2; 3.17) implies that it was written after many other of his epistles instead of being among his first.[63]

---

[61] Baur, *Life of Paul*, i. 352–365; *Sup. Rel.* iii. 330–336.

[62] "The second of the Epistles has already been attacked by criticism, but the first has as yet excited no suspicions." i. 85.

[63] "The chief part of the epistle is nothing but a lengthy version of history of the conversion of the Thessalonians, as we know it from Acts. It contains nothing that the Thessalonians would not already know, and the author may have taken his account of the transaction either from the Acts or from some other source." *Life of Paul*, i. 85. "In addition to all this, we find in the narrative reminiscences more or less distinct, of other Pauline epistles, particularly of those to the Corinthians." *Ib.* 86. "It is scarcely probable that an author who expresses his views of the last things with such caution and reserve, as in 1 Corinthians 15, should, in a writing of earlier date, have entered into the question so fully and given evidence of a belief entirely preoccupied with Rabbinical opinions." *Ib.* 91. "There can be no doubt, when we consider it, that the key to the chief passage of the epistle, and therefore to the aim and character of the whole writing, is to be found in the Apocalypse. The Apocalypse is the earliest writing in which we find the concrete representation of a personal Anti-Christ." *Ib.* 324. In reference to the autograph salutation, he says: "Are we to suppose that, at the time when the Apostle had written hardly any epistles at all, pretended Pauline ones had already made their appearance, which called for caution in discriminating, such as is here given (2.2), or could he foresee so distinctly, even so early as this, that he would have a large correspondence afterward?" *Ib.* 95.

In regard to the first of these objections it is sufficient to say, that it is common with Paul, as with all other teachers, to remind persons of what they know when giving them encouragement and exhortation. In regard to the second, it is obviously a mere assumption to say that the ideas and words common to this and other epistles are reminiscences by a later writer, when they may have been, as they purport to be, but repetitions characteristic of the same writer; and that while the account of the second coming of Christ, given in 1 Thessalonians is certainly different from that in 1 Corinthians, there is no ground for the assertion that it is of later origin. As to the conception of Anti-Christ, it is begging the question to say that it originated in the Apocalypse; for it certainly may have originated with Paul. As to the autograph salutation, it seems that one or more letters purporting to have come from Paul had actually been received in Thessalonica (2.2), and there could be no better occasion than this for giving the sign by which all of his genuine letters could be known. Renan says of all these objections that they are "without value"; and of the Anti-Christ, that this idea did not originate with the Apocalypse, for it was current at a much earlier period.[64] Thus we have the judgment of one learned Rationalist against that of another in regard to these objections, while the objections are in themselves so trivial as to scarcely deserve serious attention.

The three Epistles, Ephesians, Colossians and Philemon, may be considered together, both because they all purport to have been written at one time, and to have been carried to their destination

---

[64] "Not the slightest doubt has been raised by serious criticism against the authenticity of the epistle to the Galatians, the two epistles to the Corinthians, or the epistle to the Romans; while the arguments on which are founded the attacks on the two epistles to the Thessalonians and that to the Philippians are without value." *Apostles*, 35. "The only serious difficulty which has been raised against the epistles to the Thessalonians results from the theory of the Anti-Christ expounded in the second chapter of the second epistle, a theory apparently identical with that of the Apocalypse, and which would consequently lead us to suppose that Nero was already dead when the piece was written. But this objection permits itself to be overcome, as we shall see in the present volume. The author of the Apocalypse did nothing more than apply to his day a collection of ideas, one part of which dated back to the very sources of the Christian belief, while the other was introduced toward the time of Caligula." *Paul*, 11. The reign of Caligula began AD 37.

by two messengers traveling together;[65] and because the former two are assailed on common grounds. The principal ground on which Baur rejects these two is, that they appear to him to contain the doctrine of Gnosticism, a heresy which came into existence after the death of Paul.[66] Renan rinds echoes of the same doctrine in them, yet he admits the genuineness of Colossians.[67] The charge of Gnosticism is based upon statements concerning the divinity of Christ, and the ranks and orders of angelic beings, which these epistles contain (Eph 1.20–23; 3.8–12; 6.11–12; Col 1.15–18). But these conceptions can be regarded as unapostolic only by men who deny the divinity of Christ and reject the revelations in Scripture concerning the spirit world. To a mind not thus prepossessed the objection has no force. A special objection to Ephesians is based on its similarity to Colossians.[68] These writers are not willing to admit that Paul could write two epistles near the same time so nearly alike; and yet Renan suggests that Ephesians may have been written by one of Paul's companions while his mind was preoccupied with the words and thoughts of Colossians. If one of these might do it, why not Paul himself? It is a common experience of letter writers, when writing several let-

---

[65] Tychicus bore the epistles to the Ephesians and Colossians (Eph 6.21–22; Col 4.7–8); Onesimus accompanied him (Col 4.9), bearing the note to Philemon (Phlm 11–12); and all were written while the writer was in prison (Eph 3.1; 4.1; Col 4.10, 18; Phlm 1).

[66] "The numerous echoes of Gnosticism and its peculiar doctrines which are to be found in the three epistles to the Ephesians, Colossians and Philippians, are sufficient, had we no other ground to go upon, to fix the position of these works in the post-apostolic age." *Church History,* i. 127. See also ii. 6–31.

[67] "The epistle to the Colossians has been subjected to the test of much graver objections. Certain it is that expressions made use of in this epistle to designate the role of Jesus in the bosom of the Divinity, as Creator and prototype of all creation (1.15), show very plainly alongside the language of certain epistles, and appear to favor the style of the writings attributed to John. In reading such passages we imagine ourselves in complete Gnosticism. * * * Nothing in all this, however, is decisive. If the epistle to the Colossians is the work of Paul (as we believe it to be), it was written in the latter part of the Apostle's life, at a period in which his biography is very obscure." *Paul,* 11, 12.

[68] "As soon as we admit the epistle to the Colossians to be a work of Paul's, the question puts itself as follows: How could Paul pass his time in disfiguring one of his works, in repeating himself, in making a common letter out of a topical and particular one? This is not exactly impossible; but it is quite improbable." *Paul,* 17. These words of Renan are almost a copy from Baur's Life of Paul, ii. 2. De Wette, a German scholar who died 1849, was the first to deny the genuineness of this Epistle.

ters to different persons at one sitting, to use in all of them much of the same matter; and why may not Paul have done the same, especially as these two churches were located in the same country and were exposed to similar dangers?[69] Another objection to the genuineness of Ephesians is based upon the fact that the persons addressed were strangers to the writer, and their faith a matter of hearsay; whereas Paul planted the church in Ephesus and lived three years in the midst of it. If it were certain that the epistle was addressed to the church at Ephesus, this objection would have more force than either of the preceding (Eph 1.15; 4.20–21); yet even in that case it would appear very strange that a forger, at a later date, should represent the Apostle as being a stranger to that church. But although this objection is urged with vehemence by Rationalists, they admit, what is well known, that the words "at Ephesus" in the salutation of the epistle are of doubtful genuineness, and that many scholars both ancient and modern have held that the Epistle was addressed to no particular church, or if to any, to that at Laodicea.[70] *Comp.* Colossians 4.16.

---

[69] "The resemblance of this general epistle [Ephesians] to the Colossians might have resulted either from the fact of one man's writing several letters in a few days, and through preoccupation with a certain number of fixed ideas unconsciously falling into the same expressions; or from the circumstance of Paul's directing Timothy or Tychicus to compose the circular letter after the model of the epistle to the Colossians, but with the rejection of everything of a topical nature." *Ib.* 18.

[70] "In addition to these considerations regarding the external form of the epistle, we have further to consider that if it was actually addressed to the Ephesians, it can not possibly have been written by Paul. They were a church in the midst of which he had lived for a considerable time, and with which he was intimately acquainted; and how could he write to them as to a church that was strange to him, and speak of their faith as a thing he had learned about through others." *Comp.* i. 15. The title and address which are found in the text (1.1) are doubtful; but even in the case that the epistle was not an epistle to the Ephesians, even though the local address were wanting altogether, or ran thus: "To the Laodiceans," this indistinctness and uncertainty of the destination (which even in the last case is not removed) would of themselves afford a presumption against the Pauline origin of the epistle." Baur, *Paul,* ii. 5, 6. The presumption last spoken of in the extract is not apparent; for certainly Paul may have written an epistle intended as a kind of circular address to several churches and without a local address.

Renan, while denying the genuineness of the Epistle has this to say about its destination: "The perusal of the so-called epistle to the Ephesians will therefore be sufficient to lead us to suspect that the writing in question was not addressed to the church of Ephesus. The testimony of the MSS. transforms these suspicions into certainty." *Paul,* 14, 15. For the testimony of the MSS. and other ancient documents, see the notes of Tischendorf,

Of the epistle to Philemon, Renan remarks, "Paul alone, as far as it appears, was able to write this little masterpiece."[71] Yet Baur rejects it on the singular ground that the story of Onesimus involved in its allusions, has the air of a romance.[72] The story is certainly an interesting one, but none of its incidents are at all improbable, unless a selfish age like ours should so regard the wonderful generosity manifested in the case by Paul.

Baur claims the credit of being the first author to raise a doubt concerning the genuineness of the epistle to the Philippians.[73] He bases his doubt, first, on the Gnostic ideas and expressions which he claims to find in it; especially in 2.6; second, on the want of a motive or occasion for writing it; and third, on the assumed incredibility of its assertions concerning the effects of Paul's preaching on the Praetorian guard and on Caesar's household.[74] Philippians

Tregelles, or Westcott and Hort *in loco*.

[71] Life of Paul, 13.

[72] After stating the facts which make up the story of Onesimus, Baur says: "This is a very remarkable concurrence of chances, such as rarely indeed takes place." And again he says: "Thus it can not be called either an impossible or an improbable construction of this Epistle, if we regard it as a Christian romance serving to convey a genuine Christian idea." *Life of Paul,* ii. 82, 84. So acute a writer could scarcely feel satisfied with such an effort, and he betrays his anticipation of what the learned world would think of it by the following reflections: "In the case of this Epistle, more than any other, if criticism should inquire for evidence in favor of its apostolic name, it seems liable to the reproach of hypercriticism, of exaggerated suspicion and restless doubt, from the attacks of which nothing is safe. What has criticism to do with this short, attractive, graceful and friendly letter, inspired as it is by the noblest Christian feeling, and which has never yet been touched by the breath of suspicion?" *Ib.* 80.

[73] "The critic who first ventured to cast doubt on the genuineness of the Epistle to the Ephesians, [De Wette] has lately asserted of the Epistle to the Philippians that its genuineness is above all question. It is true that no sufficient reasons have been alleged as yet for doubting its apostolic origin; yet I think there are such reasons, and I deem it necessary to state shortly for the further consideration of criticism, what they are." *Ib.* ii. 45.

[74] "This Epistle, like the two we have just discussed, is occupied with Gnostic ideas and expressions, and that not in the way of controversy with Gnostics, but employing them, with the necessary modifications, for its own purposes. The passage 2.6, one of great importance for dogmatics, and of as great difficulty, can scarcely be explained save on the supposition that the writer's mind was filled with certain Gnostic ideas current at the time." (*Ib.* 45, 46). "Connected with this there is another consideration which must count as an important element in judging of the Epistle, *viz.,* that we find no motive nor occasion for it, no distinct indication of any purpose, or of any leading idea." (*Ib.* 52). "We have still to consider what is said in 1.12, both about the progress of the gospel in Rome, and of the deep impression which the captivity of the Apostle and his preaching of the Gospel are said to have produced in the whole Praeto-

1.12; 4.22. The first of these objections has been answered in answering the same when arrayed against Ephesians and Colossians (page 158); the second is contradicted by the epistle itself, for an occasion is indicated in 2.19–28, and a motive in the exhortations with which it abounds; and the third evinces a most unreasonable incredulity; for Paul was guarded night and day for two whole years by different soldiers of that guard who heard all that he said to his many visitors, and it would be strange indeed if he failed to leaven them and through them their comrades, and even some of the multitudinous attendants on the Emperor's palace, with the doctrine which he was incessantly preaching. Even Renan places this epistle among those that are "certain"[75]; and Farrar expresses the common judgment of critics when he says, "This epistle is genuine beyond the faintest suspicion or shadow of doubt."[76]

The epistles to Timothy and Titus remained undisputed until the present century, and now their genuineness is impugned only on internal grounds. It is said: First, that they are tinged with Gnosticism, which originated after Paul's death; second, that they indicate a stage of progress in the organization of the church which was not attained during Paul's life; and third, that there is no place in Paul's career for the journeys and incidents to which

---

rium and throughout the city. This statement stands quite alone and unsupported; it is not corroborated either by the Epistles which profess to have been written from the Apostle's captivity in Rome, or from any other quarter. Yet the fact is not in itself incredible, and no one would have thought of calling it in question had not the author himself taken up into his Epistle another fact which gives us no clear an insight into his plot, that it is impossible for us to take his assertions as simple history. The attention which the Gospel commanded in the whole Praetorium, and in Rome generally, is supposed, as we see from 4.22, to have had for one of its consequences that there were believers even in the imperial household." *Ib.* 59.

[75] In his classification of the Epistles credited to Paul with reference to their genuineness, he has the following: "*Second.* Certain Epistles, to which, however, objections have been raised, namely, the two to the Thessalonians and the Epistle to the Philippians." *Life of Paul*, 10.

[76] Farrar. Life and Work of Paul c. xlvi. In the same connection this author very justly satirizes the critics of the Tübingen school in the following terms: "With these critics, if an Epistle touches on points which make it accord with the narrative of the Acts, it was forged to suit them; if it seems to disagree with them, the discrepancy shows that it was spurious. If the diction is Pauline, it stands forth as a proved imitation: if it is un-Pauline, it could not have proceeded from the Apostle."

they allude.[77] Other objections of less importance are urged, but by these three the question is to be settled.

It is admitted that the false teachings against which Timothy and Titus were warned (1 Tim 1.1–7; 6.20–21; Titus 1.13–16; 3.9–11) were in part of the same nature as Gnosticism, but it is a baseless assumption to affirm that no such teaching was introduced before the death of Paul. The heretical ideas had not been systematized as they were afterward, but such ideas always exist in a nebulous form before they are reduced to a system. That they are noticed in these epistles, and alluded to in the earlier epistles to the Ephesians, the Colossians and the Philippians, instead of throwing doubt on the genuineness of these documents, simply proves that these ideas were propagated at this early date.

That a more advanced organization of the church is indicated in these epistles than existed before Paul's death, is another baseless assumption, and one that can be made only by those who deny the credibility of Acts of Apostles: for the organization of churches by the appointment of elders or bishops, and deacons, the only organization alluded to in these epistles, had existed in Judea before the beginning of Paul's missionary tours, and Paul himself thus organized the churches which he planted among the Gentiles.[78]

The third objection is the only One of the three which has any real force, and should it be decided that Paul's life terminated with his first Roman imprisonment described at the close of Acts, its force would be almost if not altogether irresistible. The follow-

---

[77] "I was the first to assert, and to give evidence for the assertion, that in these heretics [those combated in the Epistles] we recognize throughout the familiar features of Gnosticism: and nothing of importance has since been urged against this view." Baur, *Life of Paul,* ii. 99. "A second point in the criticism of the Pastoral Epistles, and one of no less importance than that, just spoken of, is the reference they contain to the government and the external institutions of the church. This second point is intimately connected with the first. The Gnostics, as the first heretics properly so called, gave the first occasion for the Episcopal constitution of the church." *Ib.* 102. "A further point in the criticism of the Pastoral Epistles is that it is impossible to find a suitable place for the composition of them in the Apostle's history as we know it." *Ib.* 103. Renan employs the same arguments, and dwells with especial earnestness upon the last. *Life of Paul,* 12–32.

[78] Acts 6.1–6; 11.30; 14.23; 20.17, 28; 21.18; Philippians 1.1.

ing journeys and incidents can find no place in his previous life, though many ingenious scholars have sought one, viz: his departure from Ephesus for Macedonia, leaving Timothy behind him (1 Tim 1.3); his labors in Crete where he left Titus (Titus 1.5); his wintering in Nicopolis where he desired Titus to join him (3.12); and his journeying through Miletus where Trophimus was left sick, and through Corinth where he left Erastus (2 Tim 4.20).[79] But this argument has force against the genuineness of these Epistles only on the supposition that Paul was not released from his first imprisonment in Rome. This supposition is adopted by those who reject the Epistles as if it were a settled fact; whereas there is positive and uncontradicted testimony that he was released, that he performed other labors during the interval of freedom, and that he was imprisoned a second time before his death. Clement of Rome declares that after he had been seven times in bonds, he reached in his preaching "the boundary of the West,"[80] an expression then used for the western boundary of Spain. If Clement uses it in this sense, and not, as some suppose, for Rome (a very unnatural meaning for one living in Rome), we have in his statement the testimony of a competent witness implying Paul's release and the fulfillment of a cherished purpose to visit Spain.[81] The Muratorian Canon, written about AD 170, also speaks of

---

[79] The various schemes suggested by German writers to find a place for these events within the period covered by Acts are mentioned by Renan in the course of his successful refutation of them. *Life of Paul,* 22–30. Farrar can scarcely be said to be too emphatic when he says: "If, indeed, St. Paul was never liberated from his first Roman imprisonment, then the Pastoral Epistles must be forgeries; for the attempts of Wieseler and others to prove that they might have been written during any part of the period covered by the narrative of Acts — during the three years' stay at Ephesus, for instance, or the stay of eighteen months at Corinth — sink to the ground not only under the weight of their own arbitrary hypotheses, but even more from the state both of the church and of the mind and circumstances of the Apostle which these letters so definitely manifest." *Life of Paul,* c. lv.

[80] "By reason of jealousy and strife, Paul, by his example, pointed out the prize of patient endurance. After that he had been seven times in bonds, had been driven into exile, had been stoned, had preached in the East and in the West, he won the noble renown which was the reward of his faith, having taught righteousness to the whole world, and having reached the boundary of the West; and when he had borne his testimony before the rulers, so he departed from the world and went into the holy place, having been found a notable pattern of patient endurance." *Epistle of Clement,* c. v. *Lightfoot's Translation.*

[81] Romans 15.28.

Paul's departure from the city into Spain as a well known fact;[82] and Eusebius, who had searched carefully into the early history of the church, says that his martyrdom did not take place at the time of his first imprisonment, but that he was released, went again upon his ministry, and at a second visit to the city was put to death.[83] While the first of these testimonies is indecisive, and while it is possible that in the second there may be a mistake as to the country to which Paul departed, it is scarcely possible that they should all be in error as to the fact of his release. By the side of this testimony we have that of these three epistles, all well attested by external evidence, and all implying journeys and incidents of a later date than the first imprisonment. The conclusion, then, instead of being adverse to the genuineness of the epistles, is in favor of the supposition that the events implied in them occurred after the author's first imprisonment. Were it Christopher Columbus instead of Paul, the date of whose death is in dispute, and should we find well authenticated letters purporting to be his, alluding to journeys and labors which can not have transpired before the supposed date of his death, who would hesitate to decide that the date which has been received is erroneous, and that in these letters we have an additional chapter of his life? This is the conclusion in the present instance that has been reached by many of the ablest critics of the present age, not including those of the Rationalistic school.[84] There is only one seeming difficulty in the

---

[82] The passage concerning Acts is defective in the MS., but the words on which the evidence turns are not. The original document may be found in Westcott on the Canon, appendix C. It is thus translated by Dean Howson, Life and Epistles of Paul, 438. "Luke relates to Theophilus events of which he was an eye-witness, as also, in a separate place he evidently declares the martyrdom of Peter, but [omits] the journey of Paul from Rome to Spain." Westcott would insert the word "omits" before the words "martyrdom of Peter." *Canon of New Testament*, 214.

[83] "And here Luke, who wrote the Acts of the Apostles, after showing that Paul passed two whole years at Rome as a prisoner at large, and that he preached the Gospel without restraint, brings his history to a close. After pleading his cause, he is said to have been sent again upon the ministry of preaching, and after a second visit to the city, he finished his life with martyrdom. * * * Thus much we have said, to show that the martyrdom of the Apostle did not take place at that period of his stay at Rome, when Luke wrote his history." *Eccles. Hist.* c. xxii.

[84] Among these we may mention Alford, Howson and Farrar, and the writers on these Epistles in Lange's Commentary and in the Bible Commentary.

way of this conclusion, and this is the conflict which it involves between the return of Paul to Ephesus (1 Tim 1.3) and the saying of Paul to the Ephesian elders, "I know that ye all, among whom I went about preaching the kingdom, shall see my face no more" (Acts 20.25). But the context shows that whatever positive knowledge of his own future he enjoyed at that time was through the prophetic foresight of others, not his own—and indeed neither he nor any of the apostles claimed to know their own future by their prophetic powers. This remark, therefore, can be regarded only as a strong statement of his conviction based on the predicted bonds and afflictions awaiting him at Jerusalem. Neither is this conclusion an afterthought, as is charged by Renan,[85] gotten up to meet the objection; for although it was doubtless the objection which led to the investigation, the result reached is self-consistent and commends itself to acceptance independently of the objection. It adds a most thrillingly interesting[86] chapter to the biography of Paul, one that throws a halo of intenser glory over the sunset of a glorious life.

The question of the genuineness of Hebrews refers not so much to its Pauline authorship as to its authorship by some apostolic man: for, as we have before stated (p. 119), its authorship has been in dispute from a very early period even among those who have accepted it as genuine Scripture. The arguments from internal evidence which have been arrayed against its Pauline origin are more numerous than forcible. They are based partly on the style, which is said to be materially different from that of Paul's undisputed epistles, and partly on statements which it is said Paul could not have made. In regard to the former, the specifications of which are too numerous and minute for discussion here, it is

---

[85] "All this, it must be confessed, resembles an artificial defence on the part of a criminal, who, in order to meet objections is forced to imagine an *ensemble* of facts which have no connection with anything known. These isolated hypotheses, defenceless and disconnected from all precedents, are, in the law, a sign of guilt, in criticism the sign of apocryphal." *Paul* 31. Contrary to his usual custom M. Renan here indulges in strong words while his arguments are proportionately weak.

[86] The crowning act of this inimitable story is set forth by Farrar (Life of Paul, c. 55) with an eloquence which has seldom been equaled.

sufficient to say that the departures from Paul's usual style which are found in the epistle are not more numerous than are the words and forms of expression which are peculiar to Paul, so that the latter serve as an offset to the former, and take away the force of the objection.[87] As to statements which Paul could not have made, the one which is urged with the greatest confidence is his statement that the great salvation which was at first spoken through the Lord, "was confirmed unto us by them that heard" (Heb 2.3). Of this it is said, "The author was not an Apostle, for he classes himself with those who had been taught by the Apostles."[88] True, he classes himself with those who had been taught by the original Apostles concerning the words that had been spoken by Jesus, and this was certainly true of Paul; for although he was an Apostle, and although he received by direct revelation, as he affirms (Gal 1.12) a knowledge of the gospel, yet it is true that his knowledge of the personal ministry of Jesus was derived from the older

---

[87] The reader will find the arguments on this ground in the Introduction to this Epistle in Lange's Commentary, and those on the opposite side in the corresponding place in the Bible Commentary. The question is also discussed in Davidson's Introduction to the New Testament and in Farrar's Early Days, c. xvii. Farrar enumerates ten facts by which to identify the author; but all of them except the one mentioned above, so far as they are facts and not inferences, agree fully as well with the supposition of a Pauline authorship as of any other. They are these: "1. The writer was a Jew, for he writes as though heathendom were practically non-existent. 2. He was a Hellenist, for he exclusively quotes the Septuagint version, even where it diverges from the original Hebrew. 3. He had been subjected to Alexandrian training; for he shows a deep impress of Alexandrian thought, and quotes from Alexandrian MSS. of the Septuagint without pausing to question the accuracy of the renderings. 4. He was a man of great eloquence, of marked originality, of wide knowledge of the Scriptures, and of remarkable gifts in the application of Scripture arguments. 5. He was a friend of Timotheus, for he proposes to visit the Jewish churches in his company. 6. He was known to his readers, and writes to them in a tone of authority. 7. He was not an apostle, for he classes himself with those who had been taught by the apostles. 8. The apostle by whom he had been taught was St. Paul, for he largely though independently adopts his phraseology, and makes a special use of the Epistle to the Romans. 9. He wrote before the destruction of Jerusalem, and while the temple services were still continuing. 10. It is doubtful whether he had ever been at Jerusalem, for his references to the temple and its ritual seem to apply, not indeed to the temple of Onios at Leontopolis, but mainly to the tabernacle as described in the Septuagint version of the Pentateuch."

[88] Among those who have doubted the Pauline authorship, the majority in former times ascribed it to Luke; but in recent years the opinion first advanced by Martin Luther that Apollos is the author, has been revived, and it has been adopted by a number of eminent scholars. The arguments in favor of this opinion are forcibly presented by Farrar in the chapter last cited from his Early Days of Christianity.

Apostles, partly before his own conversion and partly after it. The very warfare which he waged against the name of Jesus before his conversion implies a knowledge, though imperfect, of the life and teaching of Jesus. All this he obtained, directly or indirectly, from the older apostles, and it is to this that the remark under discussion has reference. Moreover, in his speech at Antioch in Pisidia Paul refers his hearers for evidence concerning the career of Jesus and his resurrection from the dead, not to his own testimony, but to that of those who came with Jesus from Galilee, "Who," he says, "are now his witnesses to the people" (Acts 13.26–31). The statement in question, then, could have been made by Paul, because it harmonizes both with the facts of the case and with his habit on other occasions. We conclude that there is no sufficient ground to abandon the generally received opinion that Paul wrote the epistle; and none at all to doubt that it came from the midst of the apostolic age.

The only internal evidence that has been urged against the Epistle of James by believers, was based on the opinion held by a few, that its doctrine of justification is contradictory to that of Paul;[89] but, as is now universally conceded, there is no such contradiction, and the objection has been abandoned. By Rationalists its genuineness has been questioned on the ground of a supposed allusion to the Epistle to the Hebrews in the use made of the history of Rahab. As Hebrews was written at too late a date for James to have seen it, an allusion to that epistle could not have been made by him.[90] But the fact of an allusion is imaginary; for the incident in which Rahab figured has ever been familiar to readers of the Old Testament, and any Jewish writer might have referred to it independently of others.

---

[89] The alleged contradiction lies between James 2.24 and Romans 3.28, but the context in the latter epistle shows that Paul speaks of the work of a perfectly righteous life, and in the former James speaks of those works of special divine command by which faith is tested and on which for this reason justification is dependent. Luther once urged this objection, but he afterward withdrew it.

[90] This objection is adopted by Baur from De Wette, and the former adds the remark that 'Every unprejudiced person must see that an epistle which contains references to that to the Hebrews must be post-Pauline." *Life of Paul,* ii. 308, *n,* 1.

The Rationalists of the Tübingen school deny the genuineness of the First Epistle of Peter solely on the ground of their favorite theory that there was an antagonism between Paul and Peter to the end of their days, and that this Epistle, in common with some others and the Book of Acts, was written for the purpose of making it appear that this antagonism did not exist. But the theory is based on a false assumption and the inferences drawn from it must therefore be groundless. There is in fact nothing within the Epistle to furnish the slightest ground for doubt that it was written by Peter; its genuineness has never been doubted except by a very few persons;[91] and even Renan remarks that "The First Epistle of Peter is one of the writings of the New Testament which are the most anciently and most unanimously cited as authentic."[92]

With the Second Epistle it is far different. Although the material evidence in its favor is very positive and explicit (see p. 121), yet many believers have in the earliest as well as in the latest times, doubted its genuineness, while unbelievers have rejected it both for the reasons which have led believers to doubt it, and for reasons growing out of their own unbelief in miracles and in prophecy, both of which are attested in the Epistle. The specifications on which these doubts are based may all be grouped under three heads; first, differences of style between this and the First Epistle; second, remarks and expressions which it is thought that Peter would not have used; and third, a supposed copying from the Epistle of Jude to which it is thought that Peter would not have resorted.

1. That a striking difference of style exists between the two Epistles is admitted by all competent scholars, yet the striking similarity which we have mentioned before (p. 122), neutralizes the force of this difference. Even Farrar, who insists with great earnestness upon the force of the argument on the former ground,

---

[91] "The first epistle of Peter has always retained its high position in the estimation of the church; nor was there any question as to its authenticity until within the last few years, when rationalism, guided by the sure instinct of antipathy, has assailed it in common with all documents which attest the faith and unity of the primitive church." F. C. Cook, *Introduction to I. Peter, Bible Com.,* § 1.

[92] *The Antichrist,* p. vi.

presents the latter as a reason why he can not regard the Epistle as "certainly spurious."[93] When, in addition to this consideration, we reflect upon the variations which a man's style may undergo under change of circumstances, of feelings, and of the subject matter on which he writes; and when we remember that these two short Epistles and the few short speeches of Peter recorded in Acts, are our only sources of information as to what Peter's real style was; it must seem hazardous, if not reckless, to set aside on such ground the solemn assertions of the Epistle itself as to its authorship (see p. 122). From such a conclusion the better instinct of scholars has withheld even those who have attached the greatest weight to this objection, infidel scholars, of course, being excepted.[94]

2. Of the remarks and expressions which it is thought that Peter would not have employed the specifications are numerous, but with a single exception they are void of force. Many of them are such as would excite no surprise if found in an unquestioned Epistle of Peter, and the others are such that Peter is as likely to have employed them as any man writing in his name. It would require space disproportionate to their value to discuss them individually.[95] The one specification which we think worthy of notice here is the remark made concerning Paul's Epistles in 2 Peter 3.14–16. It has been said by some that the words "all of his

---

[93] *Early Days,* c. ix, p. 113. The specifications which prove similarity of style and diction are presented by Prof. Lumby, in his Introduction to I. Peter, in the Bible Commentary.

[94] Dean Alford, than whom our age has produced no better Greek scholar, says: "The diversity of style in the two epistles has been frequently alleged. But on going through all that has been said, I own I can not regard it, considerable as it undoubtedly is, as any more than can well be accounted for by the total diversity of subject and mood in the two epistles, and by the interweaving into this second one of copious reminiscences from another epistle." *Greek New Testament.* Vol. IV., *Prolegomena,* IV., § 4. And Dr. Davidson, though he takes the same view of the argument from style and diction with Canon Farrar, makes the following remarks: "Too much caution can not be used in drawing a conclusion from style and diction, favorable or unfavorable to the authenticity of an epistle. There are many modifying circumstances. A writer appears differently on different occasions. In the present instance we can hardly tell precisely what the peculiar style of Peter was; for the First Epistle is of small compass, and it may have been colored by familiarity with the productions of Paul." *Introduction to New Testament,* iii. 435.

[95] Many of the specifications here referred to were first advanced by Farrar (*Early Days,* c. ix), nineteen in number. I have answered arguments on all of them *seriatim* in an article on the Genuineness of Second Peter, published in the July number of the *Christian Quarterly Review* for 1884.

Epistles" means all of the Epistles now ascribed to Paul, which implies a later date than the death of Peter. But the writer obviously alluded only to those that were known to himself, whether many or few. There is positive evidence in Peter's First Epistle, as we have stated (p. 121), that he had read the Epistles to the Romans and the Ephesians; and if he had seen Ephesians, he may have seen 1 and 2 Thessalonians, 1 and 2 Corinthians, Galatians and Colossians; for all these had been written before the date of Ephesians except the last which was written at the same date. It has also been said, that the words in the passage under discussion, "as also in all his epistles, speaking in them of these things," can not apply to all the Epistles already written by Paul, because the things referred to are not mentioned in them all. The truth of this depends upon what is meant by "these things." The second coming of Christ is the chief theme of the chapter, but the more immediate context (14–15) limits the thought to preparation for that event—such preparation that we "may be found of him in peace, without spot and blameless in his sight." Now this topic is discussed in every one of the Epistles written by Paul before this date, and in six out of the eight the second coming of Christ is itself a conspicuous topic.[96] The allegation then is not true. A third objection based on this passage is, that the designation of Paul's Epistles as Scripture belongs to a date later than the death of Peter, this term being applied in the apostolic age to the Old Testament exclusively. But this is a begging of the question; for if Peter wrote this Epistle, then at least one Apostle did apply the term Scripture to the Epistles of another. The main question must be settled in the negative before this affirmation can be sustained.

3. The objection that Peter would not have adopted from the Epistle of Jude so many thoughts and expressions as are found in common in that Epistle and the second chapter of 2 Peter, depends for its relevancy upon the assumption that the latter Epistle is the later of the two, a proposition which is combated

---

[96] See 1 Thessalonians 4.13–5.11; 2 Thessalonians 1.3–2.12; 1 Corinthians 15.35–58; 2 Corinthians 4.16–5.11; Romans 2.1–16; 8.12–25; Galatians 5.16–24; 6.6–10; Ephesians 5.25–27; Colossians 3.3–4.

with great plausibility by some eminent scholars.[97] But waiving this question, and granting the position assumed in the objection as probable, it would appear not more surprising that Peter should himself make use of material previously used by Jude, than that some later writer professing to be Peter should have done so in his name. Nor should it be thought at all incredible that Peter, wishing to emphasize by his own endorsement Jude's earnest exhortation to "contend earnestly for the faith once for all delivered to the saints," may have composed the second chapter of this Epistle just as we find it for this very good purpose. A similar, and even a more remarkable, coincidence of both words and thoughts is found in the Old Testament between Isaiah and Micah; and these prophets, like Peter and Jude, were contemporaries. (See Isaiah 2.2–3; Micah 4.1–2).

In conclusion, we may safely remark, that the objections which we have just considered can certainly furnish no justification for setting aside as false the solemn assertions of the writer in which he assumes to be the Apostle Peter, and for pronouncing the author of this most edifying and eloquent document an impostor.

The only internal evidence worthy of notice that has been alleged against the genuineness of the Epistle of Jude, is the fact that the author makes a quotation from an apocryphal work called the Book of Enoch,[98] and ascribes the words quoted to "Enoch the seventh from Adam" (14). It is thought that neither an Apostle, nor one so nearly related to the Apostles as was the brother of James, would have done this. In answer to this, it may be said, first, that the quotation from an apocryphal book of certain words

---

[97] See Prof. Lumby's Introduction to 2 Pet. in the Bible Commentary.

[98] The Book of Enoch has been preserved from ancient times only in an Ethiopic translation. Three manuscript copies of it were brought to England from Abyssinia by the explorer Bruce, in 1773. Since then translations of it have been made into German and English. In the judgment of a majority of the critics who have examined it, it was written before the Christian era, but how long before is quite uncertain. It is also uncertain whether it was written in Greek or in Hebrew, but the Ethiopic version was made from the Greek. It contains a series of revelations said to have been made by Enoch and Noah. A full account of it is given by Westcott in Smith's Bible Dictionary.

ascribed in that book to a previous author, is not an endorsement of the book as a whole, but only of the part quoted. Second, it is by no means incredible that among the many written documents in possession of the ancient Jews a genuine prophecy of Enoch may have been preserved, and if so, it would very naturally be copied into any work pretending to give an account of Enoch. Third, it is by no means certain that Jude quoted from the apocryphal book in question, because he may have obtained the prediction from the same source whence it was obtained by the author of this book, that is, from some older document and one that was authentic. From these considerations it appears that the objection is altogether insufficient to set aside as false the writer's assertion that he was the brother of James.

The attempts that have been made to find internal evidence against the genuineness of the First Epistle of John, are so vague and intangible that Dr. Davidson, with allusion to Pharaoh's lean kine, styles them "ill-favored and lean observations."[99] Against the other two epistles it has been urged that as the author styles himself not the Apostle, but the Elder, in the opening sentence of each, he must have been some other than John the Apostle. It has even been argued that he was a certain "John the Elder" mentioned by Papias as having given the latter some items of information which he had gathered from the lips of Apostles.[100] But this last conjecture is baseless; and upon a close examination of the language of Papias it appears highly probable that by "John the Elder," he means the Apostle John himself.[101] That John should

---

[99] Having stated and briefly noticed Zeller's objections on internal grounds, he says: "The preceding observations will show the flimsy arguments which hyper-criticism is not ashamed to adduce. Indeed, there is no proper reasoning in such ill-favored and lean observations advanced against the epistle's authenticity. *Introduction to New Testament,* iii. 456.

[100] Papias says: "But if at any time any one came who had been acquainted with the elders, I used to inquire about the discourses of the elders—what Peter or what Andrew said, or what Thomas or James, or what John or Matthew, or any one of the disciples of the Lord; and what Aristion and John the Elder, the disciples of the Lord say. For I thought that the information derived from books would not be so profitable to us as that derived from a living and abiding utterance." Quoted from Eusebius and translated by Farrar, *Early Days,* 619.

[101] That such is the meaning of Papias is argued with great force by Farrar in the appendix to his Early Days of Christianity, *Excursus* xiv.

call himself "the Elder" appears quite natural when we remember that if he did write these epistles he was at the time a very old man and the only Apostle still lingering on the earth. Moreover, he was writing briefly to private persons much younger than himself, and there was no occasion to assert his apostolic authority by styling himself an Apostle. The objection, if not as lean and ill-favored as as those brought against the first Epistle, is far-fetched and has the appearance of being the result of preconception rather than of candid investigation.

Against the genuineness of the Apocalypse no internal evidence is adduced, except by a very few critics who regard the Gospel and Epistles of John as genuine, but doubt the genuineness of this book on account of its marked difference from the others in style. As we have stated before (p. 127) the most radical of the rationalistic critics regard it as unquestionably a work of the Apostle John, and they are led to this conclusion not so much by the external as by the internal evidence.

CONCLUSION

Having completed our inquiry into the genuineness of the New Testament books, we now restate the conclusions to which it has conducted us.

1. By the evidence of manuscript copies yet in existence, we have traced all the books to the first half of the fourth century.

2. By the evidence of catalogues we have traced them all to the second half of the second century.

3. By the evidence of translations we have traced all the books except the Second Epistle of Peter to the first half of the second century.

These three conclusions are derived from evidence so indisputable that in regard to them there is no controversy. See page 127.

4. By the evidence of quotations we have traced all the books to the age of the Apostles, with the exception of Philemon, James, Second and Third John, Jude, and possibly Second Peter. These last we have traced by the same evidence so near to the Apostles as to render their spuriousness in the highest degree improbable, and we have found that the absence of quotations from them at the very earliest period this side of the Apostles, is no evidence against their genuineness. See page 110.

5. Should we be compelled, for want of evidence, to set aside the six Epistles last mentioned as not genuine, and thus to reject them from the New Testament, the result would not in the slightest degree affect the genuineness of the other books, and the loss

to the New Testament would be, not all the contents of these books, but only that portion of their contents not found in a different form in other books. The loss as respects matters of faith and practice would be inconsiderable.

6. By internal evidence we have traced every book to its reputed date and its reputed author; and we have found that for four out of the six whose external evidence is comparatively weak, that is, for Philemon, James, Second Peter and Jude, the internal evidence is positive and explicit.

This last conclusion is supported by evidence so forcible that it is conceded by the most radical of the rationalistic writers as regards four of the most important Epistles (page 127); and although in reference to the others it is denied, the grounds of the denial have been found to be totally insufficient to support even a rational doubt, and to consist mainly in foregone conclusions derived from theories unsupported by facts.

That all of these books were written by the authors whom they claim for themselves, so far as such a claim is made; and that the others were written by the authors to whom they have been ascribed by believers in the ages past, is the final and only conclusion which the evidence seems to justify.

APPENDIX

Chapters From the Epistle of Polycarp to the Philippians

Chapter 2 Wherefore, girding up your loins (Eph 6.14; 1 Pet 1.13) serve the Lord in fear and truth, as those who have forsaken the vain, empty talk and error of the multitude, and believed in Him who raised up our Lord Jesus Christ from the dead and gave Him glory (1 Pet 1.21) and a throne at his right hand. To Him all things in heaven and on earth are subject (Phil 2.10; 1 Pet 3.22). Him every spirit serves. He comes as the judge of the living and the dead (Acts 10.42). His blood will God require of those who do not believe in him. But He who raised Him up from the dead will raise up us also (2 Cor 4.14) if we do his will, and walk in his commandments, and love what he loved, keeping ourselves from all unrighteousness, covetousness, love of money, evil-speaking, false-witness; not rendering evil for evil or railing for railing (1 Pet 3.9) or blow for blow, or cursing for cursing, but being mindful of what he said in his teaching; judge not that ye be not judged (Matt 7.1); forgive and it shall be forgiven you (Matt 6.12, 14); be merciful that ye may obtain mercy (Luke 6.36); with what measure ye mete it shall be measured to you again (Matt 7.2; Luke 6.38); and once more, blessed are the poor, and those that are persecuted for righteousness' sake, for theirs is the Kingdom of God (Luke 6.20; Matt 10.10).

Chapter IV. But the love of money is the root of all evils (1 Tim 6.10). Knowing, therefore, that as we brought nothing into the world, so we can carry nothing out (1 Tim 6.7), let us arm ourselves with the armor of righteousness (Eph 6.11), and let us teach first of all ourselves to walk in the commandments of the Lord. Next, your wives in the faith given to them, and in love and purity tenderly loving their own husbands in all truth, and loving all equally in all chastity, and to train up their children in the knowledge and fear of God. Teach the widows to be discreet as respects the faith of the Lord, praying continually (1 Thes 5.17) for all, being far from all slandering, evil-speaking, false-witness-ing, love of money, and every kind of evil; knowing that they are the altars of God, that He clearly perceives all things, and that nothing is hid from Him, neither reasonings, nor reflections, nor any one of the secret things of the heart.

Chapter VII. For whosoever does not confess that Jesus Christ has come in the flesh, is anti-Christ (1 John 4.3), and whosoever does not confess the testimony of the cross, is of the devil; and whosoever perverts the oracles of the Lord to his own lusts, and says there is neither a resurrection nor a judgment, he is the first-born of Satan. Wherefore, forsaking the vanity of many, and their false doctrines, let us return to the word which has been handed down to us from the beginning, watching unto prayer (1 Pet 4.7); and persevering in fasting, beseeching in our supplication the all-seeing God not to lead us into temptation (Matt 6.13) as the Lord said: "The spirit truly is willing, but the flesh is weak" (Matt 26.41; Mark 14.38).

PREFACE

Five years have passed by since the volume containing the first two Parts of this work on Evidences was published. Those two Parts, treating of the Integrity of the New Testament Text, and the Genuineness of the New Testament Books, met with such a reception from the public as to encourage the author to continue the work, and he had progressed so far with it as to have written a large portion of Part Third, when a fire, which laid his dwelling in ruins, consumed his manuscript together with all the notes and references which he had accumulated. This caused an unexpected delay in the preparation of the present volume.

The reader is reminded, as was stated in the preface to the former volume, that this work is intended, not for those already proficient in the knowledge of Evidences, but for those who have given the subject little or no attention. It does not, therefore, attempt to exhaust the subject, but only to present so much of it as can be mastered in a course of instruction in high schools and colleges. It is prepared with an especial reference to class-room instruction.

It would argue inexcusable ignorance of the state of public opinion in our generation if the author should expect all of the positions taken and defended in this volume to meet with universal approval even among the friends of the Bible. Especially is this true of what he has written concerning Inspiration. On no other subject are the minds of believers so unsettled and bewildered. On this, as on all the other topics discussed in the volume,

I have done what I could to arrive at the truth, and to present my conclusions in an intelligible form. I humbly trust that my feeble effort may be blessed of God in helping to settle in the truth some minds that are now unsettled, and to guard some of the youth of our country from the doubts and perplexity which have harassed many of their seniors.

Whether I shall live to carry out my undertaking, so as to extend the inquiries which I have now completed as regards the New Testament, to the books of the Old, is of course known only to Him in whose hands are "life and breath and all things." To Him and to his people I trustfully commit the destiny of this present work.

PART III

Credibility Of
The New Testament Books

ONE

Canons of Historical Criticism

Having reached the conclusion in Part Second, that the New Testament books were written by the authors to whom they are commonly ascribed, we now inquire whether they are credible writings. By this inquiry is meant, not whether they are infallibly accurate, but whether they possess that degree of reliability which belongs to historical works of the better class. The question of their infallibility will be considered farther on.

It is obvious that this inquiry has reference chiefly to the historical books of the New Testament, but it does not refer to them exclusively. The Epistles and the Apocalypse contain some historical matter, and to this extent the question of credibility applies to them equally with the books formally historical. In other words, it applies to all the statements of fact found in all the books. These statements are distributable into four classes: those of ordinary history; those concerning miraculous events; the reports of speeches written long after they were delivered; and the revelations which the writers claim to have received from God. We are to inquire, first, whether the events here mentioned, which belong to the ordinary course of human history, actually took place; second, whether those of a miraculous character really occurred; third, whether the reports of speeches delivered by Jesus and certain others, not one of which was written at the time of delivery, but some of which were written almost a life-time after delivery, can be relied on as correct; and, fourth, whether the direct communications of God's will on various subjects pertaining both to the present and the future, which some of these writers claim to have received, should be accepted as such.

The subject of this inquiry is a branch of the modern science of Historical Criticism.[1] The province of this science is to distinguish the true from the false in historical documents. It differs from Textual Criticism, in that it deals with facts, while the latter deals with words. It has acquired the title, Higher Criticism, because of the greater importance attached to facts than to the exact words in which they are described, and because of the greater learning necessary to its application. By the application of its rules of evidence the secular history of the ancient world has been revolutionized, and a new ancient history constructed. So complete is this revolution, that such works as Rollin's Ancient History, which was a standard in the early part of our century, is now obsolete, and the same fate has befallen many other works once regarded as authentic.[2] In the later development of the science an attempt has been made to revolutionize in a similar manner the history contained in the Bible. So zealous have been the efforts of some scholars in this direction, that the science itself has become associated in the popular mind with unbelief in the Scriptures, and has thus come into disrepute. This result is by no means legitimate; for by a proper application of the rules of historical criticism the authenticity of all histories, sacred as well as profane, must be determined.

---

[1] "The last century has seen the birth and growth of a new science of Historical Criticism. Beginning in France with the labors of Pouilly and Beaufort, it advanced with rapid strides in Germany under the guidance of Niebuhr, Otfried, Muller and Bockh, and finally has been introduced and naturalized among ourselves by means of the writings of our best living historians." (George Rawlinson, *Historical Evidences*, 28).

[2] "The whole world of profane history has been revolutionized. By a searching and critical investigation of the mass of materials on which that history rested, and by the application to it of canons embodying the judgments of a sound discretion upon the value of different sorts of evidence, the views of the ancient world formerly entertained have been in ten thousand points either modified or reversed; a new antiquity has been raised up out of the old, while much that was unreal in the picture of past times which men had formed to themselves has disappeared, . . and a firm and strong fabric has arisen out of the shattered debris of the fallen system." (*Ib.*)

The Canons of historical criticism were first formulated by George Rawlinson in his Bampton Lectures of 1859 (Lecture First), and published in his work entitled Historical Evidences. Abbreviated and otherwise modified, they are as follows:

Canon I. The writings of a contemporary, who is credible, and who has had opportunity for personal knowledge of the facts recorded, have the highest degree of credibility. Under this head must be included public records, monuments and inscriptions, made by persons who are contemporary with the events.[3]

Canon II. Those of a writer who may be reasonably supposed to have obtained his information from eye-witnesses possess the second degree of credibility.

Canon III. Those of a writer who lived in an age later than the events, and whose source of information was oral tradition, have the third and least degree of credibility. But if, in this case, the events are of public notoriety, and of such importance as to have affected national life, or to have been commemorated by some public observance, their credibility is greatly enhanced by these considerations.

Canon IV. When the traditions of one people are corroborated by those of another, especially by those of a distant and hostile people, this greatly increases the probability of the events. The value of such evidence depends on the improbability of accidental agreement, and the impossibility of collusion.

Canon V. The concurrent testimony of independent writers greatly increases the probability of an event; and their agreement has the greater force when it is incidental, as when one only alludes to an event which the other narrates, or mentions a circumstance incidentally explained by another. The probability in this case is increased in a geometrical ratio to the number of witnesses. That is, the testimony of two is not twice as strong, but four times as strong as that of one.[4]

---

[3] "The most important documents for history are those which possess in the least degree the historic form. The authority of chronicles must give place to medals, maps, or authentic letters." (Renan, *Apostles*, 27).

[4] *Butler's Analogy*, Part 2, ch. vii.

If we make a general application of these Canons to the writers of the New Testament, we find them arranged as follows: Of the four Gospels, Matthew and John come under Canon I., seeing that these writers were eye-witnesses of nearly all the events which they record. The same is true of Luke as respects those portions of Acts in which he speaks in the first person; and of the apostles Paul, Peter, James, Jude and John in their epistles, so far as they mention events which transpired under their own observation. The two Gospels of Mark and Luke, together with those parts of Acts in which Luke does not use the first person, come under Canon II, seeing that these writers were not eye-witnesses, but wrote what had been narrated to them. Thus we see that of the eight writers of the New Testament, six possess the highest degree of historical credibility so far as opportunities to know are concerned, and only two have the second degree. Not one of them belongs to an age later than that of the events, or was dependent for his information on uncertain oral tradition.

As to the credibility of these writers, we may say in general terms, in advance of a more critical inquiry, that their high character, indicated by the unvarying purity of the sentiments found in their writings, lifts them above the suspicion of being untrustworthy, and secures to them a credibility at least equal to that of the best secular historians. This consideration unites with the preceding to place them among the most credible of writers, and to render any event which they record, concerning which there is no special ground of doubt, as probable as any of the facts that make up history. This much is conceded by all, even among unbelievers, whose opinions are respected by intelligent men; and it is conceded on the ground which we have stated.

TWO

Evidence from Agreement with Other Writings

One very satisfactory method of testing the credibility of a writer, is to compare his statements with those of other writers with similar opportunities for information. When the writers compared are independent, that is, when neither obtained his information from the other, an agreement on any fact imparts to that fact the degree of probability referred to in Canon V. When they disagree, this raises a question as to the relative credibility of the two writers. Unfortunately, the writers who were contemporary with those of the New Testament, and whose writings have come down to us, are very few, especially those whose subjects led them to speak of the same events, or who possessed the information necessary to speaking of them with any degree of accuracy. Among Jewish writers there is only one, and among Roman writers, three or four.[1] Their statements are few, but valuable.

1. Josephus, the most noted of all uninspired Jewish writers, was born in Jerusalem in the first year of the reign of Caius Caesar, AD 37. This was the third year after the founding of the church in Jerusalem, and the next year after its dispersion under

---

[1] Why the latter are so few is satisfactorily explained by Renan, as follows: "As to the Greek and Latin writers, it is not surprising that they paid little attention to a movement which they could not comprehend, and which was going on within a narrow space foreign to them. Christianity was lost to their vision upon the dark background of Judaism. It was only a family quarrel among the subjects of a degraded nation; why trouble themselves about it?" (*Apostles*, 227).

the persecution which arose about Stephen. The death of the elder James, AD 44, occurred in the same city when Josephus was seven years old. At the age of nineteen he joined the sect of the Pharisees, who were then extremely hostile to the church, and especially to the apostle Paul and others who preached among the Gentiles. When he was twenty-six years old (AD 63), he visited Rome for the purpose of interceding for certain priests whom Felix had sent thither in bonds to defend themselves before Caesar. He suffered shipwreck on the voyage, as Paul had done three years previous, and this visit was made in the year in which Paul was released from his two years' imprisonment in that city. The year previous to this voyage, James, the Lord's brother, was slain in Jerusalem, and Josephus must have been cognizant of the fact. At the beginning of the Jewish war against the Romans, which resulted in the downfall of the Jewish nation, he was in command of the native forces in Galilee, which was then thickly set with Christian churches. He was overpowered and taken prisoner by the Romans, and was a prisoner in the camp of Titus during the last siege of Jerusalem. He spent the rest of his life in Rome, and was for some years the guest of the emperor Vespasian. His principal works are The Antiquities of the Jews, a History of the War with the Romans, and an Autobiography. From the last we have gleaned the facts in his career mentioned above, from which it appears that he lived in the very midst of the times and places in which the Apostles figured, and that he must have had personal knowledge of many of the events mentioned in Acts and the Epistles as having transpired in Jerusalem, Judea and Galilee. He died about the year 100.

As Josephus gives a detailed history of his country covering all the period of New Testament History, we might reasonably expect of him an account of the career of Jesus, and of the stirring events in the early history of the Jewish Church. In this we are disappointed; and the omission is doubtless to be accounted for by his connection with the Pharisees. He could have given no truthful account of Jesus or of the Church, which would not have been a story of shame for the sect to which he belonged; and as his chief purpose in writing was to elevate his people in the minds of Greeks and Romans who despised them, national pride and religious bigotry alike demanded silence on this theme. Still, he did not altogether avoid the subject, and we shall now take notice of some of his statements.

a. In stating the cause of a war between Herod the Tetrarch and Aretas, king of Arabia Petrea, he gives a minute account of the intrigue by which the former induced his brother Philip's wife to leave her lawful husband and come to live with him.[2] These details are all omitted by the New Testament writers; but Matthew, Mark and Luke all mention the fact of the incestuous marriage, and they all mention it incidentally, as does Josephus. This is a clear case of undesigned agreement between totally independent writers.

b. In his account of the war just mentioned above, Josephus says that Herod's army was destroyed; and that some of the Jews regarded this disaster as a punishment for the murder of "John who was called the Baptist." He then speaks of John as a "good man," as one who "commanded the Jews to exercise virtue, both as to righteousness towards one another, and piety toward God, and so to come to baptism." He gives a false interpretation of John's baptism, but one about as near the truth as might be expected from a Pharisee, and then says that Herod, fearing lest John might raise a rebellion, sent him as a prisoner to the castle of Machaerus, and there beheaded him.[3] Here the agreement in matters of fact with well known passages in our first three Gospels is complete, while the omissions, and the motive ascribed to Herod, show that the account given by Josephus is totally independent of the other three.

c. Josephus gives the only account which has come down from the first century of the death of James, the Lord's brother; and in the course of it he calls him "the brother of Jesus who was called

---

[2] *Ant.*, xviii. 5, 1.

[3] Ant., xvii. 5, 2.

Christ, whose name was James."⁴ The introduction of these two names in this informal way shows clearly that he regarded them as well known to his readers; and as the readers for whom he wrote were the Greeks and Romans of his day, it shows that these two persons, and especially Jesus, were then well known in the heathen world, just as the Scriptures represent them.

d. There is another passage in Josephus, the genuineness of which has been so much disputed, and the spuriousness of which has been conceded by so many eminent defenders of the faith, that we may not base a confident argument on it, and yet it should be known to those who make any study of Evidences. We copy it as follows:

"Now there was about this time Jesus, a wise man, if it be lawful to call him a man; for he was a doer of wonderful works, a teacher of such men as receive the truth with pleasure. He drew over to him both many of the Jews and many of the Gentiles. He was Christ. And when Pilate, at the suggestion of the principal men among us, had condemned him to the cross, those who had loved him at the first did not forsake him; for he appeared to them alive again the third day; as the divine prophets had foretold these and ten thousand other wonderful things concerning him. And the tribe of Christians, so named from him, are not extinct at this day."⁵ As the plan of this work forbids the use of doubtful evidences, we pass by this passage, and refer those who may wish to study the arguments for and against its genuineness, to Lardner's Credibility for those against it, and to Horne's Introduction for those in favor of it.

2. The first Roman writer whom we cite in this connection is Tacitus. He was born about the middle of the first century; was chosen praetor of Rome in the year 88, and consul in 97. He was author of a Description of Germany; a Life of Agricola (his father-in-law); a History of Rome from Galba to Domitian; and Annals of Rome, from Tiberius to Nero. He is one of the most

---

⁴ *Ib.,* xx. 9, 1.

⁵ *Ant.,* xviii. 3, 3.

famous and most reliable of Roman writers, and such is the superiority of his style that the first two of his works are used as text-books of Latin in our best colleges. He closed his career as an author about the year 100.

In giving an account of a fire that consumed about one-third of Rome in the reign of Nero, coupled with the belief among the people that it was started and kept up by Nero himself, Tacitus says that Nero sought to turn this suspicion away from himself to the Christians in the city, whom he accused and tortured as if they were guilty. In describing the Christians, he states the following facts: first, that there were Christians in Judea before the death of Christ, and that they derived their name from his; second, that Christ suffered death under Pontius Pilate; third, that belief in him was checked for a time by his death, but that it soon broke out again; fourth, that it spread over Judea, and thence to Rome; fifth, that there was a vast multitude of Christians in Rome at the time of the fire (AD 64); sixth, that Nero accused the Christians of causing the fire, and punished them most cruelly; seventh, that their sufferings, believed to be unjust, awakened the sympathy of the people for them.[6] These statements would be credited if we had no other evidence to support them. In other words, had the New Testament failed to come down to our age, these statements alone would have furnished an account of the origin, progress and

---

[6] Tacitus says, speaking of the fire that consumed Rome in Nero's time, and of the general belief that he had caused it: "In order, therefore, to put a stop to the report, he laid the guilt and inflicted the severest punishments upon a set of people who were held in abhorrence for their crimes, and called by the vulgar Christians. The founder of that name was Christ, who suffered death in the reign of Tiberius, under his procurator, Pontius Pilate. This pernicious superstition, thus checked for a while, broke out again; and spread not only over Judea, where the evil originated, but through Rome also, whither all things horrible and shameful find their way and are practised. Accordingly the first who were apprehended confessed, and then on their information a vast multitude were convicted, not so much of the crime of setting Rome on fire, as of hatred to mankind. And when they were put to death, mockery was added to their sufferings; for they were either disguised in the skins of wild beasts and worried to death by dogs, or they were clothed in some inflammable covering, and when the day closed were burned as lights to illumine the night. Nero lent his own gardens for this exhibition, and also held the shows of the circus, mingling with the people in the dress of a charioteer, or observing the spectacle from his chariot. Wherefore, although those who suffered were guilty, and deserving of some extraordinary punishment, yet they came to be pitied, as victims not so much to the public good, as to the cruelty of one man." (*Annals*, xv. 44.)

sufferings of the church, in a general outline, substantially as we have them in our New Testament. This information comes to us through a hostile witness, as appears from his bitter words concerning the Christians, saying that they were "held in abhorrence for their crimes"; calling their faith a "pernicious superstition," and classing it among things "horrible and shameful"; and charging them with "hatred to mankind." He even says that "those who suffered were guilty, and deserving of some extraordinary punishment." These opprobrious expressions also show that as respects the facts in Christian history which he relates, he was an independent witness; for if he had obtained his information, even in part, from the New Testament writers, he could not have entertained the opinions which he expresses. So far, then, as he supports the statements of the New Testament, he furnishes independent and hostile testimony, which, according to Canon V., very greatly enhances the probability of the facts themselves.

It may be well to remark in passing, that this passage in Tacitus convicts Joseph us of suppressing information concerning Jesus and the Church; for if this heathen writer, living in Rome, and having no personal knowledge of Jewish affairs, was so well informed, Josephus, who lived in Judea, and was surrounded on every side by Christian churches during the first thirty years of his life, must have been still better informed, and must have suppressed much the greater part of what he knew, even if the disputed passage in his writings is genuine. In doing so he suppressed the most important part of the history of his own generation. This is accounted for by his position as a Pharisee, and his consequent hostility to the cause of Christ.

3. The next Roman writer whom we quote is Pliny, called "the younger" to distinguish him from an uncle who bore the same name, and who was also a man of note. He was born at Como, near Milan in Italy, AD 61 or 62. He was one of the most elegant of Roman writers, but he devoted his literary efforts chiefly to epistolary writing. He witnessed the eruption of Mount Vesuvius, which in the year 79 overwhelmed the cities of Herculaneum and

Pompeii, and in which his uncle perished. He wrote in two letters to Tacitus, who was his friend and correspondent, a very graphic account of that tragic event, and the only one that has come down to posterity. He was a consul of Rome in the year 100, and was proconsul of Bythinia under Trajan in the years 106108.

When he entered on the administration of Bythinia, he found a fierce persecution by government authority in progress, and for a time he continued it; but finally he wrote a letter to the emperor which furnishes the following points of information: first, a vast number of Christians were then in Bythinia, of every age and rank, of both sexes, and in all parts of the country; second, such was the influence of their teaching, that the heathen temples were almost deserted, and the victims for heathen sacrifices could hardly find a purchaser; third, Pliny was constrained, on account of the vast number of victims of the persecution, to suspend it and write to the emperor for further instruction; fourth, after the most searching inquiry, including the torture of certain Christians to force confessions from them, he had found no vices among them; fifth, they had suffered for the name of being Christians, without the charge of any crime—a procedure of which Pliny doubted the propriety; sixth, those who were Roman citizens were sent to Rome; seventh, on a stated day they were accustomed to hold two meetings, one for singing "in concert" hymns to Christ, and for making vows to live righteously; and the other for eating a "harmless meal."[7]

---

[7] Pliny's Letter to Trajan: "It is my custom, sir, to refer to you all things about which I am in doubt. For who is more capable of directing my hesitancy, or instructing my ignorance? I have never been present at any trials of the Christians; consequently I do not know what is the nature of their crimes, or the usual strictness of their examination, or the severity of their punishment. I have, moreover, hesitated not a little whether any distinction was to be made in respect to age, or whether those of tender years were to be treated the same as adults; whether repentance entitles them to pardon, or whether it shall avail nothing for him who has once been a Christian, to renounce his error; whether the name itself, even without any crime, should subject them to punishment, or only the crimes connected with the name. "In the mean time I have pursued this course toward those who have been brought before me as Christians. I have asked them whether they were Christians; if they confessed, I repeated the question a second and a third time, adding threats of punishment. If they still persevered, I ordered them to be led away to punishment; for I could not doubt, whatever the nature of their profession might be, that a stubborn and unyielding obstinacy certainly deserved to be punished.

These details, though descriptive of scenes that transpired after the close of the New Testament canon, are strikingly confirmatory of the representations in that book. The character of Christians set forth in the two documents, their stated meetings "for a harmless meal" (the Lord's supper), and for the worship of Christ, their rapid increase where the gospel was preached, and their causeless persecution, are the same. The sending of those who were Roman citizens to Rome for trial, is parallel with this experience of the apostle Paul; and as to other particulars, we learn from the apostle Peter that there were Christians in Bythinia in his day, and that they suffered "for the name of

---

There were others also under the like infatuation; but as they were Roman citizens, I directed them to be sent to the capital. But the crime spread, as is wont to happen, even while the persecutions were going on, and numerous instances presented themselves. An information was presented to me without any name subscribed, accusing a large number of persons, who denied that they were Christians, or had ever been. They repeated after me an invocation to the gods, and made offerings with frankincense and wine before your statue, which I had ordered to be brought for this purpose, together with the images of the gods; and moreover they reviled Christ; whereas those who are truly Christians, it is said, can not be forced to any of these things. I thought, therefore, that they ought to be discharged. Others, who were accused by witnesses confessed that they were Christians, but afterwards denied it. Some owned that they had been Christians, but said they had renounced their error, some three years before, others more, and a few even as long ago as twenty years. They all did homage to your statue and the images of the gods, and at the same time reviled the name of Christ. They declared that the whole of their guilt or error was that they were accustomed to meet on a stated day before it was light, and to sing in concert a hymn of praise to Christ as God, and to bind themselves by an oath, not for the perpetration of any wickedness, but that they would not commit any theft, robbery, or adultery, nor violate their word, nor refuse when called upon to restore anything committed to their trust. After this they were accustomed to separate and then to re-assemble to eat in common a harmless meal. Even this, however, they ceased to do, after my edict, in which, agreeably to your commands, I forbade the meeting of secret assemblies. After hearing this I thought it the more necessary to find out the truth, by putting to the torture two females slaves, who were called deaconesses. But I could discover nothing but a perverse and extravagant superstition; and therefore I deferred all further proceedings until I could consult with you. For the matter appears to me worthy of such consultation, especially on account of the number of those who are involved in peril. For many of every age, of every rank, and of either sex, are exposed, and will be exposed to danger. Nor has the contagion of this superstition been confined to the cities only, but it has extended to the villages, and even to the country. Nevertheless, it still seems possible to arrest the evil, and to apply a remedy. At least it is very evident that the temples, which had already been almost deserted, begin to be frequented, and the sacred solemnities, so long interrupted, are again revived; and the victims, which could hardly find a purchaser, are now everywhere in demand. From this it is easy to imagine what a multitude of men might be reclaimed, if pardon should be offered to those who repent." (*Epistles of Pliny, x.* 97).

Christ"—they suffered "as Christians," even when they were charged with no crime (1 Pet 4.12–19).

These testimonies from independent and hostile writers not only confirm the facts attested by them in common with the New Testament writers, so as to place them beyond all doubt, but they go farther: they give good ground to believe that if the details mentioned by these secular writers had been more numerous, the points of agreement would have extended proportionately; in other words, by showing that our New Testament writers are accurate so far as we are able thus to test them, they justify the inference that they are accurate throughout their narratives. It should be noted, however, that had we found some discrepancies between these two classes of writers, the preference would belong of right to those of the New Testament, seeing that they were the better informed on the main subject.

THREE

Evidence from Incidental Agreement with Other Writings

In Chapter 2 we considered the evidential force of certain points of agreement between the New Testament writers and others, when both were making formal statements; now we consider points of incidental agreement, in which formal statements are made by the one class of writers, and only allusions to the same things by the other. In the instances to be cited the formal information is furnished by secular writers, and the allusions are made by the writers of the New Testament.

I. The period covered by New Testament history was characterized by frequent and complicated changes in the political affairs of Judea and the countries connected with it. None of these are formally described in the New Testament, though it contains many allusions to them of an incidental and isolated kind, while they are all described in detail by Josephus. Here, then, is an excellent opportunity to test the accuracy of the former writers; for perfect agreement here is attainable only through perfect accuracy of information and of statement on both sides.

This test is the more severe from the fact the New Testament allusions to these affairs are so brief, and so void of explanation, as to leave the reader who has no other source of information in great confusion concerning them. The history opens, in both Matthew and Luke, under "Herod the king." In the second chapter of Matthew, Herod the king dies; yet in the fourteenth chapter Herod appears again, and is called both "the king" and "the tetrarch"; and in the twelfth chapter of Acts, "Herod the king" beheads the apostle James. All this is said without a word of explanation. Again, at the close of the second chapter of Matthew Archelaus is king of Judea; in the twenty-seventh chapter Pilate is *governor* of the same; in the twelfth of Acts, Herod is king of the same; and in the twenty-third, Felix is its *governor*. Not a word of explanation. Yet again, Augustus Caesar issues a decree just previous to the birth of Jesus, that all the world shall be enrolled; when John the Baptist begins his ministry it is the fifteenth year of *Tiberius* Caesar; yet Paul many years afterward makes an appeal from Festus to *Augustus*. (Luke 2.1–7; 3.1–2; Acts 24.21). Here, in reference to kings, governors, and emperors, there is both confusion and apparent contradiction. It is impossible for one who has not made a special study of the political history of the times, to get through this tangled network of allusions understandingly; but when we consult the formal history furnished by the unbelieving Jewish historian, we find every one of them strictly correct. As to the Herods, we find that the one under whom John and Jesus were born, and who soon afterward died, was succeeded by his son Herod as ruler of part of his father's dominions, with the titles, king and tetrarch; and that the Herod who beheaded James was a grandson of the first, made king by Claudius Caesar. As to the rulers of Judea, we learn that Archelaus who succeeded his father Herod as king of that part of the ancestral dominion, was deposed by the Romans when he had reigned only ten years, and governors, or more properly procurators, were appointed to rule over Judea. Pilate was the fifth of these in succession. Afterward the Herod who appears as king at the time of the death of James was made king as a personal favor by Claudius Caesar; but at the death of Herod the country was again placed under procurators, of whom Felix was one. As to the Augustus Caesar who appears in the narratives of Luke as if he was dead and yet alive again, we learn that the emperor called Augustus in the second instance was Nero, who bore the title Caesar Augustus Nero, and that his flatterers frequently styled him Augustus.

In the writings of Luke and John we find another allusion, partly of a political and partly of a religious character, which furnishes similar evidence. It is the allusion to the high priesthood of Annas and Caiaphas. Luke (3.2) represents the two as being high priests at the same time, although the law of Moses allowed only one man at a time to occupy the office. He also, in another place, mentions the two together, calling Annas the high priest, and omitting the title from the name of Caiaphas (Acts 5.6). John indirectly recognizes Annas in the same light by representing the band that arrested Jesus as taking him to Annas first, and adding the remark that Caiaphas, the son-in-law of Annas, was "high priest that year," as if the high priest was appointed annually (18.13. See also 11.49). Inasmuch as the high priest was appointed for life, and there could be but one at a time, these two writers appear to have fallen into two mistakes in these allusions, and the charge that they have done so has been used as proof that these three books were written by men so ignorant of Jewish affairs as to suppose that there might be two high priests at one time, and that the office was filled annually. But it so happens that Josephus, in his elaborate account of Jewish affairs, furnishes facts which explain these apparently incorrect allusions, and show them to be strictly accurate. From him we learn that Annas was the rightful high priest by inheritance in the direct line from Aaron, but that he had been unlawfully deposed by Valerius Gratus, Pilate's predecessor, who appointed first one and then another in his place; and of these Joseph Caiaphas was the fourth (Ant. xviii.2,2). Under these circumstances there were two high priests, one holding the office by right of succession, a right which could not be disregarded by those who feared God, and the other exercising the functions of the office by virtue of military interference. The representations of Luke and John are therefore in perfect harmony with the facts. As to the remark that Caiaphas was high priest "that year," it is justified by statements of Josephus, that Valerius Gratus, after appointing his first successor to Annas deprived him of the office "in a little time," and that his next two appointments were made at intervals of one year each. It was this rapid and unlawful succession of appointments to the office which both suggested and justified the remark.

To this uniform accuracy of allusions to political affairs there are two apparent exceptions, which have been set forth by unbelievers as historical blunders. The first is the statement of Luke concerning an enrollment ordered by Augustus Caesar just previous to the birth of Jesus, and the consequent journey of Joseph and Mary to Bethlehem (Luke 2.1–5). Three points of objection have been urged which are worthy of consideration:

First, it is said that there is no evidence other than Luke's statement, that Augustus issued such a decree. This objection is without force; for it consists in nothing more than an array of the silence of other writers against the positive statement of Luke, and this, too, when the silence is accounted for by the consideration that other writers had no such occasion for mentioning it, and no occasion at all that we know of. Second, Luke represents the enrollment as having been made when Quirinius was governor of Syria, whereas it appears from Josephus that he was not governor of Syria till after the deposition of Archelaus, which occurred not less than ten years subsequent to the birth of Jesus.[1] It is here alleged that in connecting it with the birth of Jesus he has made a chronological mistake. But a careful inspection of Luke's language shows that he connects only the issuing of the decree, and the beginning of its enforcement in Judea, with the birth of Jesus; and that only the making of the enrollment as a whole is connected with the governorship of Quirinius. Moreover, the statement, "This first enrollment was made when Quirinius was governing Syria," is parenthetical, and it indicates a distinction in time between the issuing of the decree and the making of the enrollment. Now, if Luke's contemporaries knew that there

---

[1] *Antiquities*, xvii. 13, 2; xviii. 1,1.

was an interval of ten years between the issuing of this decree and its general execution in the empire, but that it was partially executed, at least in Judea, at the time it was issued, no thought of a chronological mistake could have occurred to them on reading this passage; and as it so happens that we are in possession of this knowledge given by Luke, no such thought should occur to us.[2] Third, it is urged that the execution of the decree could not have required Joseph and other Jews, as stated by Luke to go every man to his own ancestral city. Probably this is true as respects the letter of the decree itself; but certainly such a procedure was not forbidden in the decree; and if the Jewish polity required it, it is most unreasonable to pronounce it incredible. That the Mosaic law of inheritance, coupled with the restoration of lands which had been sold, at the end of every fifty years, to the heirs of the original owners, required a registry to be kept in every town of the land-owners in the vicinity, is a well known fact; and this together with the fondness of the Jews from other considerations for keeping their genealogies, is sufficient to account for the circumstance, without supposing that there was anything said about it in the decree. The fact that Joseph took Mary with him in her present condition, may be accounted for, either because he wanted her under his immediate care in the trial through which she was about to pass, or because, being an heiress with a prospective interest in the ancestral inheritance, it was needful that her name be enrolled as well as his. There is certainly nothing so strange in this circumstance as to justify a doubt of its credibility.

The second of the two allusions which are held to be mistakes, is that in the speech of Gamaliel (Acts 5.36–37) to the careers of Theudas and Judas of Galilee. In this passage Theudas is represented as preceding Judas of Galilee, whereas Josephus describes a Theudas whose career was quite similar, but who figured much later than Judas.[3] It is charged that the author of Acts put this speech into the lips of Gamaliel, Theudas not having yet figured

---

[2] For a more elaborate discussion of this question, *pro* and *con*, see Strauss, *New Life*, ii. 22–26; and F. C. Cook, *Speaker's Commentary, in loco,* and authors there referred to.

[3] *Antiquities*, xviii 1, 1.; xx. 5, 1.

when the speech is said to have been made; and that in doing so he betrays the fraud by his chronological blunder. But this charge depends altogether on the identity of the Theudas mentioned by Luke with the one mentioned by Josephus. If there may have been an earlier Theudas, answering to the account given by Gamaliel, then Luke may be accurate both in his facts and his chronology. Now it so happens that Josephus, though he mentions no other Theudas as heading an insurrection, does mention a number of insurrections occurring at the right period to suit the remark of Gamaliel, without mentioning their leaders. He says of the period just preceding the deposition of Archelaus: "Now at that time there were ten thousand other disorders in Judea, which were like tumults, because a great number put themselves in a warlike posture, either out of hopes of gain to themselves, or out of enmity to the Jews"; and more directly to the point, he says: "And now Judea was full of robberies; and as the several companies of the seditious lighted upon any one to lead them, he was created a king immediately, in order to do mischief to the public."[4] That one of these leaders may have been named Theudas is not at all improbable in itself; and when we have the statement of a veracious writer that he was, it is a most unjust procedure, in the absence of all conflicting evidence, to charge him with error. No ordinarily veracious writer, not a Bible writer, would be so charged.

This unfailing accuracy, often appearing in the midst of what at first seems to be confusion and contradiction, not only evinces the historical reliability of the New Testament writers, but it shows, by the absence of explanation where explanation to us of a later age seems needed, that they were conscious of telling a story which would be recognized as true by the people of their own generation—a story which needed no bolstering up in order to sustain itself. If they had written, as has been alleged, in a later generation, they would have felt the necessity of many explanations which they have omitted, and by this very circumstance they would have betrayed themselves; but, writing as they did in the

---

[4] Ant., xvii. 10, 4, 8.

midst of the generation wherein all these political changes took place, the known intelligence of their readers forbade the introduction of explanations, or rather precluded the thought of them.

II. Under the Greek and Roman dominions, the former beginning about BC 333, and the latter about BC 60, Jewish coins went out of use in Palestine, and those of these two nations took their place, both sets being in circulation at the same time. There is no account of this change in the New Testament, but there are many allusions in it to the coins in current use, and as such a mixture of coins is necessarily a source of confusion, incidental references to them furnish a very good test of a writer's accuracy.

1. The shekel, the coin in most common use among the early Jews, and the one most frequently mentioned in the Old Testament, is not mentioned at all in the New Testament. This is just as it must have been if these writers were well posted in the affairs of Palestine at the time of which they write; but if they were pretenders, writing at a later age, and after the Jewish nation had been dispersed, they could not have been thoroughly familiar with such matters, and they would naturally have adopted the phraseology of the Old Testament. This they never do.

2. Where, according to the supposition just mentioned, the Jewish half-shekel would have been mentioned, that is, in connection with the poll tax for the expenses of the temple (Ex 30.15), the collector of this tax, in asking Jesus for it, calls it the didrachma, a Greek coin of nearly but not exactly the same value; and when Jesus, in order to procure the money to pay for Peter and himself, sends the latter to catch a fish and find the money in its mouth, he tells him he will find a *stater*, another Greek coin twice the value of the didrachma, and nearly the value of the shekel. (Matt 17.24–27).

3. The two coins which the poor widow cast into the treasury, called mites in our version, were pieces of the smallest Greek copper coin, called the *lepton*, a coin in use at the present day in Greece; and Mark, lest his readers might not know the value of Greek coins, tells them that the two were equal to the Roman

quadrans (12.42). How could this little matter have been so accurately represented, if Mark had not been both a well informed
and a very careful writer?

4. In stating the value of two sparrows, Matthew resorts to Roman coinage to get the exact amount, and says that they sold for
an *assarius,* the piece next in value above the *quadrans.* Here, that
we may see the extreme care for accuracy, we should observe that
the quadrans was worth about half a cent of our money, and the
assarius about a cent and a half. (Matt 10.29).

5. As the Romans had dominion in Palestine in the New Testament period, their coins must have been in more general circulation than those of the Greeks; and we should therefore expect to
see them more frequently mentioned if our writers are accurate.
This is just what we find; for the Roman *denarius,* about sixteen
cents of our money, was the most common silver coin in use in all
the Roman empire, and it is the one most frequently mentioned
in the New Testament. It is mentioned fourteen times, and in the
following passages: Matthew 18.28; 20.2,9,13; 22.19; Mark 6.37;
12.15; 14.5; Luke 7.41; 10.35; 20.24; John 6.7; 12.5; Revelation 6.6.

Such accuracy as this, an accuracy that never fails, is under the
circumstances proof of perfect familiarity with the subject, such
familiarity as is acquired only by personal contact with it, and also
of such care in writing as is known only among historians of the
first class.

III. In the account of the Jewish people given by Josephus,
their sentiments on various subjects, and the views of the various
parties among them, are fully stated. The New Testament writers do not attempt such an account, but they have occasion now
and then to allude to these matters, and these allusions furnish
another test of their accuracy. We make a few specifications.

1. We first specify their allusions to the Jewish expectation
of a Messiah. It is assumed throughout the Gospels and Acts
that the Jews were looking for a Messiah, called in Greek the
Christ, in fulfillment of prophecies contained in the Old Testament; and in many places the unbelieving Jews are represented

as giving utterance to this expectation. They had fixed upon the place of his birth (Matt 2.4–6); they expected him to be a son of David (22.41–43); they thought that he would settle all difficult questions (John 4.25); that he would restore the kingdom of David (Acts 1.6); and that he would abide forever (John 12.32–34). Now the existence of this expectation among the Jews, thus tacitly assumed by the New Testament writers, is formally asserted by at least three secular writers of that period. Josephus says that one reason why the Jews were bold enough to undertake a war with the Romans, was that there was an oracle found in their sacred writings to the effect that about that time one from their country would become ruler of the habitable earth. He claims that the oracle was fulfilled in Vespasian, who was called from the command of the Roman army in Judea to be emperor of Rome; but this is an evidence at once of his unbelief in Jesus, and of his willingness to flatter the emperor who had bestowed on him many signal favors.[5] Suetonius says: "An ancient and settled opinion had prevailed throughout the whole East, that fate had decreed that at that time persons proceeding from Judea should become masters of the world. This was foretold, as the event afterward proved, of the Roman emperor; but the Jews applied it to themselves, and this was the cause of their rebellion."[6] Tacitus says: "The greater number believed that it was written in the ancient books of the priests, that at that very time the East should become very powerful, and that persons proceeding from Judea should become masters of the world."[7] His language is so nearly

---

[5] "But now what did most elevate them in undertaking this war was an ambiguous oracle that was also found in their sacred writings, how, about that time, one from their country should become governor of the habitable earth. The Jews took this prediction to belong to themselves in particular, and many of the wise men were thereby deceived in their determination. Now this oracle certainly denoted the government of Vespasian, who was appointed emperor in Judea." (*Wars*, vi. 5, 4).

"When we were come to Rome, I had great care taken of me by Vespasian; for he gave me an apartment in his own house which he lived in before he came to the empire. He also honored me with the privilege of a Roman citizen, and gave me an annual pension, and continued to respect me to the end of his life. . . . I also received from Vespasian no small quantity of land, as a free gift, in Judea." (*Life of Josephus*, Sec. 76).

[6] *Life of Vespasian*, Sec. 4.

[7] *History*, v. 13.

identical with that of Suetonius as to suggest that they obtained their information from a common source, (probably from Josephus), but this does not render their statements any less credible. Certain it is that if we had no information on this subject at all in the New Testament, we would believe on the testimony of these three writers that such an expectation as they mention in common did prevail at that time, and this is all that is necessary to prove the truthfulness of the New Testament writers in assuming the same thing.

2. There is similar evidence in the allusions to the state of feeling between the Jews and the Samaritans. John represents a Samaritan woman as being surprised that Jesus asked her for a drink of water, and explains her surprise by saying that the Jews and the Samaritans have no dealings (4.9); and he represents the Jews when reproaching Jesus as saying, "Say we not well that thou art a Samaritan and hast a demon?" (8.48). Luke says that on one occasion Jesus and his disciples were going towards Jerusalem, and wishing to lodge in a Samaritan village by the way, "they did not receive him because his face was as though he were going to Jerusalem" (9.51–56). These statements are made in an incidental way while giving accounts of other matters, and they are given without a word of explanation as to the cause or causes of this animosity. On examining the formal history of the Jews by their countryman Josephus, we find the same state of feeling. He gives a full account of an incident very similar to that mentioned by Luke, which resulted in a great deal of bloodshed. He says that it was the custom of the Galileans, when they went to Jerusalem to the festivals, to pass through the country of the Samaritans; and that on one occasion certain persons belonging to the border town of Ginea came out against a company of the Galileans thus journeying, and killed a great many of them. This led to retaliation on the part of the Jews, and to contentions before the Roman commanders, which finally culminated in a settlement of the contest by an appeal to the emperor.[8]

---

[8] *Antiquities*, xx. 6.

3. In all of the five historical books of the New Testament the sect of the Pharisees plays a conspicuous part, and the Sadducees are occasionally mentioned; but in not one of them is there a formal account of either of these sects, stating whence they originated, or what in full were their peculiarities. The writers allude to them constantly as if they were well known to their readers, and such doctrines or practices as characterized them are referred to in the same incidental way. Josephus, on the other hand, mentions them quite frequently with formal statements of their doctrines and practices, and as he was himself a Pharisee, his statement must be regarded as authentic, except where they can be suspected of party bias. A comparison of his formal statements with the informal allusions of the New Testament writers, is a very good test of the accuracy of the latter. Matthew represents Jesus as alluding to the reputation of the Pharisees for righteousness of a high order, by saying to his disciples that unless their righteousness shall excel that of the scribes and Pharisees, they shall not enter into the kingdom of heaven (5.20). On this point Josephus says that the Pharisees "are a certain sect of the Jews who appear more religious than others, and seem to interpret the laws more accurately" (*Wars*, i. 5, 2). Matthew in another place represents them as reproaching Jesus for transgressing the tradition of the elders; and Mark, in speaking of the same incident, says that they held the tradition of the elders; but neither tells what the tradition of the elders is; and to this day commentators and critics are dependent on the statements of Josephus for a definition. He confirms what these writers say, and at the same time explains it by saying, "The Pharisees have delivered to the people a great many observances by succession from their fathers, which are not written in the laws of Moses; and for that reason it is that the Sadducees reject them and say that we are to esteem the observances to be obligatory which are in the written word, but not to observe what are derived from the tradition of our forefathers. And concerning these things it is that great disputes and differences have arisen among them, while the Sadducees are able to persuade none but the rich,

and have not the populace obsequious to them, but the Pharisees have the multitude on their side" (*Ant.*, xiii.10.6). The popular influence of the Pharisees here alluded to by Josephus is repeatedly affirmed by him, and it constitutes another point of coincidence. He says that the Pharisees have so great power over the multitude, that when they say anything against the king, or against the high priest, they are presently believed" (xiii.10.5). He says again, that "on account of their doctrines they are able to greatly persuade the body of the people; and that whatsoever the latter do about divine worship, prayers, and sacrifices, they perform according to their directions" (xviii.1.3). This is precisely the kind of influence that is ascribed to them in the New Testament. Jesus devoted the whole speech recorded in the twenty-third chapter of Matthew to an effort to break down their influence; while John says they had agreed to exclude from the synagogues in Jerusalem every one who should confess that Jesus was the Christ, and that at one time many of the rulers believed on Jesus, but because of the Pharisees they did not confess him lest they should be put out of the synagogue (9.13,22; 12.42). As to the more prominent differences between the parties, concerning angels, spirits and the resurrection of the dead, the joint testimony of the two sets of writers is equally explicit.[9]

IV. One of the greatest difficulties in the way of historical composition, is the maintenance of geographical and topographical accuracy. This is strikingly true when a writer attempts to describe events which transpired in a country with which he is not thoroughly familiar. When the Encyclopedia Brittanica, for example, was first published, although its articles were written by experts in the several departments, it contained so many blunders of this kind in regard to places in America, that the publishers of its rival, the New American Cyclopedia, issued a pamphlet of considerable size, containing a list of these blunders. A more notable instance is found in the Germania of Tacitus. So many and so serious are his mistakes in the geography of Germany, that some scholars

---

[9] Matthew 22.23; Acts 23.8; cf. *Ant.* xviii. 1. 3, 4.

have doubted whether a work so erroneous could have been written by an author of his known reliability.[10] Josephus, though a native of Palestine, and familiar from his early days with every part of it, especially with Jerusalem and Galilee, makes some prodigious misstatements in regard to both of these localities. He says, for instance, of the outer wall of the temple, that "the lowest part of it was erected to the height of three hundred cubits, and in some places more"; whereas it is known by the observations of modern explorers that the highest part of it could never have been half that high. He also says, with greater exaggeration, that such was the height of the battlement on the southern end of this wall, that if one standing on top looked down into the valley "his sight could not reach to such an immense depth." Again, he says of Galilee, that "the cities in it lie very thick, and that its villages are everywhere so full of people, that the very least of them contains above fifteen thousand inhabitants."[11]

But the most remarkable of these classes of mistakes are those yet to be mentioned—those of writers who have visited Palestine for the express purpose of describing its localities for the instructions of others. It is notorious that a considerable part of the task of every writer who visits that country consists in correcting the topographical mistakes of his predecessors. And even the guide books written by scholars with the most minute attention to details, with a view to enabling the tourist to find his way to every spot without the aid of a living guide, are more or less characterized by similar errors. The author used in his tour of Palestine the very best of these, and its accuracy was a constant source of gratification; but in a few instances it was found at fault, especially in the points of the compass, and the relative order of the location of villages.

In the New Testament no such mistakes are found. Whether its writers speak of their own or of foreign lands, they always speak with faultless accuracy, so that their argus-eyed critics for

---

[10] Encyclopedia Brittanica, Art. *Tacitus.*

[11] *Wars,* v. 5. 1; *Ant.* xv. 11. 5; *Wars,* iii. 3. 2.

two thousand years have not been able to detect them in an error.[12] This accuracy extends not only to the relative location of places, and to the points of the compass, but to the most minute details, even to the relative elevations of places mentioned in the narratives. One of the most difficult things in the experience of a traveler is to remember, as he passes from one place to another, whether he has come up or down. Indeed, there are few persons who can say of places not far from their own homes, whether it is up or down to them, unless there is a very striking difference in the level. But in this particular the New Testament writers, and the same may be said of the Old Testament writers, are never at fault. The man who fell among robbers was going "*down* to Jericho" (Luke 10.30); everybody went "*up* to Jerusalem" (Matt 20.17–18; Luke 19.28–29; Acts 11.2, 15.2; Gal 1.17); they went "*down* to Gaza" (Acts 8.26); "*down* to Caesarea" (9.30); "*down* to Lydda" (9.32); "*down* to Antioch" (11.27); and so with equal accuracy of every other place. How impossible it would be for writers who were not very familiar with the country to do this, can at once be realized if the reader will imagine himself describing the movements of men from place to place in Palestine, and noting when they go up and when they go down.

These facts not only establish for the New Testament writers a character for accuracy and closeness of observation above that of other men, but they suggest the question, How were they able to maintain an accuracy so unprecedented? If the fact does not prove that they enjoyed supernatural guidance, it points, at least, in that direction.

---

[12] The author of "Supernatural Religion" attempts to break the force of this evidence by asserting that there are several geographical errors in the Gospel of John; but he makes only two specifications, both of which are errors on his own part. He charges that the writer of this Gospel, in speaking of a Bethany beyond Jordan where John was baptizing, either referred to the Bethany near Jerusalem and mistook its position, or invented a second Bethany, and thus displayed an ignorance improbable in a Jew. But this is assuming without proof that there was no Bethany beyond the Jordan; an assumption which claims knowledge where the author possesses none. Again, he asserts incorrectly that John locates Ænon near to Salem in Judea; and because the place was quite unknown in the third century, he thinks that there is here another blunder. But the place has been recently identified by Capt. Conder, as all persons know who are acquainted with Palestine exploration literature, and thus another false charge is refuted. (See *Sup. Rel,* ii. 417, 418).

FOUR

Alleged Contradictions Between John and the Synoptists

The severest test to which writers, concerned like those of the New Testament with a common series of events, can be subjected, is a careful comparison of their statements one with another. Contradictions between them are certain to be found, unless all are thoroughly informed in regard to all particulars and unfailingly accurate in detailing them. So difficult is it to avoid such contradictions, that when they occur in reference to minor details they are not considered inconsistent with the degree of authenticity which belongs to firstclass writers. When, however, the contradictions between two or more writers are numerous, and when they affect the more important events of which they speak, this is demonstrative proof that one or more of them is unreliable. On the other hand, when a number of such writers are proved to have written independently of one another, and are found to be free from contradictions, the facts which they state in common possess the highest degree of credibility. If, in addition to this, there are found numerous incidental agreements between them, the evidence of authenticity is the most conclusive known to human testimony.

Strong as this kind of evidence is when it assumes the form last mentioned, it is nevertheless more frequently and effectively employed in exposing the claims of inauthentic documents than in establishing the claims of those that are authentic. For this reason it has always been the choice weapon of the enemies of the New Testament. So many and so serious are the charges of contradiction which have been preferred against the various writers of this book, that we think it proper to consider these before we take up the evidence from this source which is in their favor. As regards the evidence set forth in the preceding chapters of this Part, there is no serious controversy between believers and unbelievers; but that which we are about to consider has been, and still is, very warmly contested, and it demands very careful attention. It is not practicable in this volume, nor is it needful for the purpose of settling the question, that we consider all the specifications which are made under this head. It is only necessary to consider those on which unbelief chiefly relies; for by these the controversy is to be settled. The alleged contradictions may be classified as follows:

I. Those between the Gospel of John and the other three, called the Synoptic Gospels;

II. Those between the several Synoptic Gospels;

III. Those between Acts of Apostles and other Books.

Before we take up these allegations for special consideration, it is necessary that we state very clearly what is meant by a contradiction. Two statements are contradictory not when they differ, but when they can not both be true. If, on any rational hypothesis, we may suppose them both to be true, we can not rightfully pronounce them contradictory. We are not bound to show the truth of the given hypothesis; but only that it may be true. If it is all possible, then it is possible that no contradiction exists; if it is probable, then it is probable that no contradiction exists; and the degree of the latter probability is measured by that of the former. This being true, it follows that an omission by one writer of a fact which in a full account would have been mentioned, and is mentioned by another, is not a contradiction. It shows that the writer who makes the omission does not give a full account; but throws no suspicion on the anther by whom the fact is mentioned.[1] It

[1] "The omission by a contemporary author to notice a fact which *we*, from whatever reason, may consider of the greatest moment, is a case by no means unusual. The younger Pliny,

follows, also, that when there is an appearance of contradiction between two writers, common justice requires that before we pronounce one or both of them false we should exhaust our ingenuity in searching for some probable supposition on the ground of which they may both be true. The better the general reputation of the writers, the more imperative is this obligation, lest we condemn as false those who are entitled to respectful consideration. With these rules of common justice to guide us, we now take up for separate examination the three classes of alleged contradictious which we have named.

I. In Part 2 we have already considered two or the alleged inconsistencies between John and the Synoptic Gospels (pages 148–151), and we stated that all the others were based on false assumptions. We are now to see whether this statement can be made good. In testing it we shall omit for the present all that pertains to the resurrection and ascension of Jesus, reserving these for separate consideration.

There are two very prominent events mentioned in John's Gospel which are discredited because they are not mentioned by any other writer. These are the healing of the man born blind, and the raising of Lazarus. They are discredited, not merely because they are omitted by other writers, but because it is alleged that they are so much more convincing than the wonders mentioned by the Synoptists, that the latter would certainly have used them if they had heard of them and believed them.[2] It is a sufficient answer to this to remark that the other writers adopted plans for their narratives which involved the omission from them of the visits to Jerusalem with which those two miracles are connected, and which limited their accounts of the miracles of Jesus almost exclusively to those wrought in Galilee. The mention of these two would have required a reconstruction of their plans. Furthermore,

---

although giving a circumstantial detail of so many physical facts, and describing the great eruption of Vesuvius, the earthquake, and the showers of ashes that issued from the volcanoe, makes no allusion whatever to the sudden overwhelming of two large and populous cities, Herculaneum and Pompeii." (Lee, *Inspiration*, 255).

[2] *Sup. Rel,* ii. 461–464; Strauss, *New Life*, ii. 223; Francis Newman, *Phases of Faith*, 117.

one of the reasons for which they adopted such plans may have been that these two miracles were so well known by those whom they looked to as their first readers that they thought it well to omit these and record others less familiar. Certainly the miracles wrought in Jerusalem and made subjects of public discussion there, were more familiar to the first converts of the Apostles than those wrought in the remote districts of Galilee. As the omission, then, can be accounted for by the great notoriety of these two miracles, as well as by the plans of the writers, it certainly affords no ground for suspicion that they were not known at all.

Another event mentioned by John, not so suspicious, and not miraculous, is treated in the same way. It is the arraignment of Jesus before Annas, who is said to have sent him to Caiaphas (John 18.13,24), and, as alleged, the location of Peter's denial in the court of Annas.[3] As to the former, its mere omission from the other narratives is no evidence against its reality; it is only an additional piece of information furnished by John which is perfectly harmonious with that furnished by the other writers. As to the latter, it is not true that John represents the denial as taking place before Annas. A careful reading of the passage will show that John describes no proceedings at all in the "court of Annas." He says, at verse 13, that the officers led Jesus to Annas first, and that the latter was father-in-law to "Caiaphas, who was high priest that year." He distinctly calls Caiaphas the high priest, and does not give that title to Annas. He next represents himself as being known to the high priest, meaning Caiaphas, and as being emboldened by that circumstance both to enter the court and to ask the portress to admit Peter. He was then in the court of Caiaphas, and it appears to have been in that very court that the officers had led Jesus to Annas. Annas, being father-in-law to Caiaphas, may very naturally have been found in the court of the latter that morning, especially as Caiaphas had some business on hand in which his father-in-law was as deeply interested as himself. Furthermore, the very next step in the proceedings

---

[3] Strauss, *New Life*, ii. 346, 347.

mentioned by John, the interrogation of Jesus about his disciples and his teaching, was conducted by "the high priest," the title which John applies exclusively to Caiaphas. To show that by "the high priest" all through this account he meant Caiaphas, he says "Annas therefore sent him bound unto Caiaphas *the high priest.*" There is, then, not the slightest discrepancy between the writers; and the only difference between them is that John introduces the comparatively unimportant circumstance that when Jesus was led into the palace of Caiaphas he was presented before Annas first. This was done by the officers for the very natural purpose of showing respect to the one who was their rightful high priest, but who had been unlawfully deprived of his office by military power.

While an attempt has been made to thus discredit these three incidents in John's narrative on account of their absence from the other Gospels, on the other hand some facts recorded in the latter have been discredited because not mentioned by John. The most conspicuous of these, which must stand as representatives of all, are the Temptation of Jesus (Strauss, ii.111,112); his Transfiguration (Sup. Rel., ii. 461); his Agony in the Garden (Strauss, ii.333); the darkness attending the Crucifixion (Sup. Rel., iii.422–424); the other miracles connected with the Crucifixion mentioned by Matthew alone (*ib.*, 425); and the expulsion of demons by Jesus (*ib.*, ii.461; Strauss, ii.191). In order to see how groundless is this objection, we have only to consider the peculiar plan of John's Gospel.

First we notice its peculiarity as respects chronology. While John's is the only Gospel that is chronological throughout, the incidents which it records are confined to a very small number of days, with wide gaps between them. Its first group of events, extending to the eleventh verse of the second chapter, occurred in the space of four days. The next group, extending to 3.21, occupied a few days in Capernaum without incident, and a Passover week in Jerusalem. During the next twelve months, if the feast mentioned in v. 1 is a passover, there is nothing recorded except his baptizing in Judea (3.22), his journey to Galilee (4.3–43), with two days in Sychar, and one day, a sabbath, in Jerusalem

(5.10). We next find a perfect blank of twelve months (5.1–6.4), and this is followed by the incidents of two consecutive days in Galilee (6.5, 22). Next there is another total blank of six months, followed by three days at the feast of tabernacles, ending on a sabbath (6.4, comp. 7.2, 14, 37; 8.59; 9.14). Then there is still another blank of three months followed by one day at the feast of dedication (10.22, 39). In the next three months, from the feast of dedication to the passover, nothing is recorded except the retirement of Jesus beyond the Jordan (10.40–42); the four days connected with the raising of Lazarus (11.6, 17); and the retirement to Ephraim (11.54). See 10.22–11.55; 12.1. Glancing back over these figures and summing them up, we find that the whole number of days occupied with recorded incidents up to the last week of the life of Jesus is only twenty-five. This result must prove a surprise to every reader of the Gospel who has not taken pains to make the count. Who would have supposed that in giving an account of a career which ran through more than three years, with the whole of which the writer was familiar, he would limit himself to the incidents of less than thirty days, and these so selected as to leave gaps between them varying from a few days to three months, and even to whole years? Yet this is what we find. Now, to argue from a narrative thus constructed, that incidents recorded by the other writers are discredited by his silence in regard to them, is to argue without the slightest regard to facts; it is to array nothing against something.

But, second, the absurdity of this mode of reasoning appears yet more glaring when we observe the peculiar character of John's selections and omissions. He selects for insertion what the Synoptists have omitted, and makes his gaps where they have spoken, in such a manner as to demonstrate a fixed intention to do so. All three of the Synoptists advance from their respective starting points to the temptation of Jesus; but he, without mentioning that event, or anything that preceded it, begins his narrative immediately after it. Next after the temptation they all unite in following Jesus into Galilee; but he fills a gap left by them, with the reappearance of Jesus at the Jordan; his visit with five disciples gained there to Cana and Capernaum; his attendance at the next passover; and his baptizing in Judea while John was at Enon (1.19–4.3). Moreover, instead of merely mentioning the fact that Jesus went into Galilee, as the Synoptists do, he describes the journey in his fourth chapter. On reaching Galilee, they remain there, each filling the larger part of his whole narrative with incidents which transpired there, while John gives just one miracle wrought there which is omitted by them (4.46–54), and then returns immediately to Jerusalem, to describe a visit to that city which they omit (5.1–47). Leaving then a whole year blank, a year rich with incidents in the other narratives, he returns to Galilee, and mentions the first miracle which he has in common with them, the feeding of the five thousand; but he mentions it only for the purpose of introducing a long conversation which grew out of it next day, and which they all three omit (6.1–4; 22–71). The remainder of their Galilean record he omits entirely, but he touches the thread of their story at the point where Jesus finally departs from Galilee, and gives a conversation omitted by them in which Jesus discusses with his brothers the propriety of his going up to the feast of tabernacles just at hand (7.1–10, comp. Matt 19.1; Mark 10.1; Luke 9.51). Skipping now all the incidents recorded by them between the passages last cited and the public entry into Jerusalem, John records incidents which they omit in that interval, the visit to the feast of tabernacles, to that of dedication, the journey beyond the Jordan, the return to Bethany to raise Lazarus, and the retirement to Ephraim, thus again filling large gaps left by the other writers while making many in his own. Finally, on reaching Jerusalem and touching their thread a second time in the feast at Bethany and the public entry, he continues throughout the closing scenes in Jerusalem to skip what they record, and to fill gaps left by them, except that he mentions in common with them the paschal supper, the betrayal, the trial, the crucifixion and the burial. In his treatment, however, of these common incidents, he deals almost exclusively in details not given by the Synoptists.

We think it impossible to fairly consider this remarkable feature of John's Gospel without concluding either that its author was familiar with the other Gospels, and wrote with the purpose of avoiding a repetition of their accounts, or that he was supernaturally guided to write as he did. Should we see on the freshly fallen snow three tracks along the highway made by pedestrians, sometimes close together, then far apart, then crossing one another, occasionally identical for a few steps, and then parting; and should we also observe the track of a fourth pedestrian, usually wide apart from the others, and winding about as if to avoid them, sometimes making a long leap to cross over without touching them, and when from necessity it does touch them, touching toe to heel or heel to toe, who could make us believe that the fourth man did not see the tracks of the other three as he made his own? Even should it be proved that he made the walk in a dark night, we would be constrained to believe that he carried a lantern in his hand. Not less manifest is it that the author of our fourth Gospel must have known the other three Gospels, or that he was guided by supernatural intelligence. How idle, then, and how preposterous it is to argue that incidents found in the other Gospels which he omits are rendered doubtful by the omission.

Let it not be inferred from what we have now said of John's Gospel that we regard it as a fragmentary document, or as a mere supplement to the other narratives. While it deals with fragments of the life of Jesus, it is not alone in this, for all the others do the same; and while it furnishes information in almost every sentence not supplied by the others, and is to this extent supplementary, it fails at last, according to its own confession, to give a tithe of the incidents in that life which are omitted by them. See the statement with which it closes (21.25). Instead of being either fragmentary or supplemental as its chief characteristic, it contains a unique and well sustained portraiture of Christ, distinctly conceived at the outset, and consistently filled out to the close; and the marvel is that it could be drawn while so carefully avoiding the colors employed by the other painters, and taking its lights and shades from so small a number of the days in the life which it portrays.

A third class of alleged discrepancies between John and the Synoptists consists in the omission of details by one or the other while the principal event is mentioned in common. A few examples must stand for all.

1. It is alleged that the first three Evangelists represent the multitude that welcomed Jesus into Jerusalem with hosannas as having come with him, while John represents them as being from the city itself, and as being moved to do so by the raising of Lazarus. The truth of this matter is that the three Synoptists omit to say whence the multitude came (Matt 21.1–11; Mark 11.1–10; Luke 19.29–40). John alone gives us this information, and while he intimates, without saying it, that they went out from the city, he explicitly says that they were "a great multitude that had come to the feast" (John 12.12–18). Some of them had doubtless come with Jesus; for there was a multitude with him when he left Jericho (Matt 20.29; Mark 10.46; Luke 19.1–4); and it is highly probable that most of these followed him to Jerusalem; but the Synoptists do not affirm this, much less do they affirm that all the multitude who welcomed him thus came with him. There is here, then, no difference except that John says plainly who composed the multitude, and what chiefly moved them to act as they did, while the other Evangelists omit these details.

2. It is alleged that in the account of the arrest of Jesus the Synoptists, by representing Judas as pointing out Jesus to the guard by a kiss, are contradicted by John, who represents Jesus as being well known to the guards, and as coming forward to address them while Judas was still standing with them. Here the appearance of inconsistency grows entirely out of omissions, as is clearly seen by the fact that if the details are put together as parts of one story they are harmonious. Supposing all to be true, Judas did draw near to Jesus to kiss him, when Jesus said to him, "Judas, betrayest thou the Son of man with a kiss?" (Luke 22.47–48). He did kiss him, and Jesus said to him, "Friend, do that for which thou

art come." Jesus then stepped forward toward the officers, and demanded, "Whom seek ye?" They answered, "Jesus of Nazareth." Judas had by this time stepped back and was standing with them. Jesus says, "I am he"; and when he said this they "went backward and fell to the ground." He again demands of them whom they are seeking; receives the same response; tells them; "If ye seek me, let these go their way." Peter smites one of them and is rebuked for it; the wounded ear is healed; and then the officers, having recovered their courage, rush forward and seize him. (John 18.4–12; Luke 22.50–51). These are the statements of the several writers, and the fact that they weave together and form a consistent story shows that there is no inconsistency between them. Only when isolated details of a transaction derived from different sources are all true, are they likely, when thus brought together, to prove consistent with one another.

Before dismissing this incident, it may be worth the space to observe that while Luke and John make the sword-stroke of Peter come before the arrest of Jesus, Matthew and Mark mention it next after the arrest, and this has been treated as another contradiction. By turning to the passage in Matthew and Mark the reader can readily see that neither of them makes a note of sequence to indicate that he is following the order of time; so that this difference, like the others of the class, grows out of an omission to state precisely when the stroke was made.

3. It is alleged that John is contradicted by Mark and Luke in respect to the removal of the body of Jesus from the cross. John states that the Jews requested Pilate to have the legs of the bodies broken, and the bodies taken away; while Mark says that Joseph asked Pilate for the body of Jesus; that Pilate wondered if he were already dead; inquired of the centurion if it were so; and then granted the body to Joseph. It is argued that this hesitation on Pilate's part is impossible if he had already ordered the bones to be broken and the bodies to be removed (Strauss, ii.394; *Sup. Rel.*, iii.436).

The impossibility is not apparent. The affirmation of it is based on the assumption that when Pilate gave the order to break the legs of the bodies and remove them, he knew that Jesus was dead; but the text does not so affirm, neither is such knowledge implied in the order. The breaking of the legs was evidently intended to extinguish what life might yet remain in the bodies, and the order for it rather implies that none of them was supposed to be yet dead. When, therefore, Joseph came in, and asked for the dead body of Jesus, there is no ground of surprise that Pilate inquired whether he was dead, before granting the request. His hesitation evidently grew out of the fact that it was a friend of Jesus who preferred the request, and it was important to keep that body out of such hands until its life was certainly extinct. It is only the circumstance that Mark omits the request of the Jews for the removal of the bodies which furnishes apparent room for this fallacious argument. The proximity of the place of crucifixion to the palace of Pilate made it quite possible for Joseph's interposition to take place between the death of Jesus and the time at which the soldiers would have taken the body from the cross, especially if the centurion had chosen to leave that task to him after learning that he had applied for the privilege.

4. Perhaps the most remarkable of the class of alleged discrepancies now under consideration is that respecting the several accounts of the embalming of the body of Jesus. It is stated by the author of "Supernatural Religion" in the following words: "According to the first Gospel, there is no embalmment at all; according to the second and third Gospels, the embalmment is undertaken by the women, and not by Joseph and Nicodemus, but is never carried out; according to the fourth Gospel, the embalmment is completed on Friday evening by Joseph and Nicodemus, and not by the women. According to the first Gospel, the burial is completed on Friday evening; according to the second and third, it is only provisional; and according to the fourth, the embalmment is final, but it is doubtful whether the entombment is final or provisional; several critics consider it to have been only provisional. In Mark, the women buy the spices when the sabbath was past; in Luke, before it has begun; and in Matthew and John they

do not buy them at all. In the first and fourth Gospels the women come after the Sabbath to behold the sepulcher, and in the second and third they bring apices to complete the burial (iii.439)." If we accept without qualification this series of statements we should conclude that the Gospels are involved in the utmost confusion and contradiction on this point; but that the apparent contradictions are only cases of omission by one writer of details mentioned by another, can be made to appear by merely quoting this passage again with the addition of such words as will point out the real state of the case. To be a truthful representation, it should read as follows: In the first Gospel, the embalmment is not mentioned; in the second and third Gospels, the embalmment undertaken by the women, but not carried out because they found the tomb empty, is mentioned, but that by Joseph and Nicodemus is omitted; according to the fourth Gospel, the embalmment is completed so far as Joseph and Nicodemus were concerned, but that by the women is not mentioned. According to the first Gospel, the burial is completed on Friday evening; according to the second and third, it is also completed, though the embalmment is not; according to the fourth, the embalmment is final so far as was intended by Joseph and Nicodemus; there is no hint that the entombment is temporary, and the only critics who think it was are unbelievers like the author of Supernatural Religion. In Mark, the women buy not "*the* spices," but spices, when the sabbath is past; in Luke, they buy some before it has begun; and in Matthew and John, the purchase of spices by the women is omitted. In the first and fourth Gospels, the women come after the sabbath to behold the sepulcher, not "*merely* to behold it," and in the second and third, they come bringing spices to complete, not "the burial," but the embalming. Thus all of the points of alleged discrepancy in this portion of the history are only cases of omission, which can not without the grossest injustice be charged as contradictions.

In regard to the embalmment of the body, it may be well to remark, before leaving the subject, that it was not the process which bore this name in Egypt. It was not intended as a means of preserving the flesh; and it could have no other design than to provide an absorbent for the humors and gases that would exude from the body in the process of decomposition. The greater the quantity of the drugs employed, the more complete the absorption; and this accounts both for the hundred pounds weight provided by Nicodemus, and for the two purchases made by the women, one on Friday evening, and the other on Sunday morning.

As a fourth class of the discrepancies in question, we mention a few that do not depend on omissions, but have more the appearance of contradictions.

1. Mark represents the crucifixion as taking place at the third hour, or the hour, according to Jewish count, from eight to nine A. M. (15.25); while John represents Pilate's final sentence against Jesus as being pronounced at the sixth hour (19.14.) If the two writers use the same method of reckoning the hours of the day, there is here a contradiction in point of time; for the sentence that Jesus should be crucified is placed by John three hours later than the crucifixion itself is placed by Mark. An attempt has been made by some acute scholars to show that the modern usage among western nations, of counting the hours from midnight, had already been introduced into the Province of Asia, where John wrote, and that he follows this usage not only here, but in other passages of his Gospel where hours of the day are mentioned (1.39; 4.6, 52); but we are constrained to regard this attempt as a failure, notwithstanding its defense by some of the most eminent scholars of the present day.[4] As the text now stands, we think there is a contradiction. But the discussion should not end here. Knowing, as all scholars now do, that errors of transcription crept into the Greek text at a period antecedent to all of our extant manuscripts and versions, and that numerals were especially liable to alteration from this source, it is an obvious dictate of justice, before pronouncing against an author on such a point, to consider the probability of a clerical corruption. If John wrote here "the sixth hour," he seems to have committed an error; for he contradicts not

---

[4] See Alford on John, xix. 14, and also Westcott, Com. on John, *Speaker's Commentary.*

Mark alone, but Matthew and Luke as well, seeing that though the latter do not say at what hour Jesus was crucified, they do say that the darkness which came over the earth while he was on the cross commenced at the sixth hour, the very hour at which, according to this reading of John, Pilate pronounced the sentence of crucifixion. It is impossible that John was thus mistaken; and if some one of a later age, assuming to be John, is the real writer of this Gospel, it is in the highest degree improbable that he wantonly contradicted all of the other Evangelists on a point like this. We think that these considerations render it morally certain that there is here an error of transcription, the Greek numeral for "sixth" having accidentally supplanted the one written by John.

2. The Synoptic Gospels represent the women who were witnesses to the crucifixion as standing "afar off," while John says they were standing "by the cross of Jesus." This is held to be a contradiction, and so it would be if the several writers were speaking of the same moment of time; but if they are speaking of different moments of time, the contradiction disappears. That they do speak of different moments appears in the text. The remark about the women in all three of the Synoptics occurs at the close of the description, and it has reference to the closing scenes. If the women had arrived on the ground only a few minutes before the death of Jesus, all that they say would be strictly true. John, on the other hand, speaks of the beginning, or near the beginning, as appears from a little reflection. When Jesus said to his mother, "Woman, behold thy son"; and to the disciple, "Behold thy mother no one could have known to whom he spoke unless he accompanied his words by some sign to point the persons out. The natural sign would have been a movement of the hand toward the persons addressed; but his hands were pinioned to the cross, and this was impossible. The only sign left to him was the direction of his eye, and the inclination of his head as he addressed the one and the other. But this could not have been after the darkness set in, and consequently this incident must be located within the first three hours, and while the group of friends were near

enough to the cross to distinguish the direction of his eye. Now, was there anything in the circumstances to make them retire to a greater distance as the dreadful hours passed on? We have but to place ourselves in the midst of the scene, and enter as best we can into the feelings of this group, in order to see that there was. The angry and blasphemous taunts of the raging mob around the cross, growing more defiant as it appeared more certain that the sufferer would not come down, made it painful and dangerous for friends to stand near by, and naturally caused them to shrink farther away from the awful spectacle. It is a most true and natural representation, then, that they were standing "afar off" when the agony ended.[5]

3. In nothing are unbelievers more confident than in the assertion that there is a contradiction between John and the Synoptists in regard to the night of the last supper. Mark and Luke are explicit in stating that the day previous to the supper was the day in which the paschal lamb was sacrificed (Mark 14.12; Luke 22.7). In common with Matthew (26.17), Mark calls it "the first day of unleavened bread," by which they can only mean consistently the day in which, according to the law, the leaven must be put out of the houses preparatory to eating unleavened bread the next seven days (Ex 12.15, 18). All three unite also in representing the paschal supper as being eaten, and the Lord's supper as being instituted, on the following night, the night, according to the law just cited, after the fourteenth day of the first month. It is claimed that, in contradiction to this, John represents the supper which Jesus ate as being eaten *before* the passover (13.1); while the fact that the remark of Jesus to Judas at the supper, "That thou doest, do quickly," was construed by the disciples as an order to

---

[5] The author of "Supernatural Religion" (iii. 419), in attempting to correct others on this point, fell upon the truth without recognizing its force. He says: "Olshausen, Lucke and others suggest that they subsequently came from a distance up to the cross, but the statement of the Synoptists is made at the close, and after this scene is supposed to have taken place. The opposite conjecture, that from standing close to the cross they removed to a distance, has little to recommend it." The conjecture of which he can say nothing worse than that it has little to recommend it, is the very one supported by adequate evidence, as we have shown above.

buy something for the feast (13.29), and the refusal of the Jews on the next morning to go into Pilate's praetorium, because it would prevent them from eating the passover (18.28), are held as proof that the passover was yet in the future even on the day of the crucifixion. It is said that "we have here a contradiction as entire as a contradiction ever was, and in which one side must be wrong."[6] This allegation we are now to test.

We begin by observing that the Synoptists not only unite, as we have just remarked, in styling the day previous to the last supper "the day of unleavened bread," but they also unite in styling the day of the crucifixion "the preparation." Matthew does so by styling the day following "the day after the preparation" (27.62). Luke calls it "the day of the preparation" (13.54); while Mark, appending an explanation, calls it "the day of preparation, that is, the day before the sabbath" (15.42). Undoubtedly they all use the term in the sense here defined by Mark, meaning by it the day of preparation for the sabbath; and by the sabbath they mean, not the first day of the feast, as some have supposed, but the weekly sabbath of the passover week. Of this we may be sure from the fact that neither the first day nor the last day of the feast, though each was a day of holy convocation and of rest from servile labor, is ever in the Scripture called a sabbath.[7] If it be asked why this sabbath was preceded by a preparation day, we answer that, like the limitation of a sabbath day's journey to seven furlongs, it was a custom of the Jews unauthorized by the law. That such a custom did exist, we have further evidence from Josephus. He copies a decree of Augustus Caesar intended for the protection of the Jews, in which occurs the provision, "that they be not obliged

---

[6] Strauss. *New Life*, ii. 307, 308; Baur, *Ch. Hist.*, i. 174.

[7] It is surprising that so careful a scholar as Westcott should be mistaken, here, and should make the following remark and citations: "This day, the first day of unleavened bread, was a sabbath, on which the sabbath law of rest was especially binding (Ex 12.16; Lev 13.7)." It is not called a sabbath in either of the passages cited. The same author further says: "To those familiar by experience with Jewish usages, as all the Evangelists must have been, the whole narrative of the crucifixion, crowded with incidents of work, would set aside the notion that the day was the fifteenth." (*Introduction to Gospels*, 338). He overlooks the fact, as do all others who agree with him about the day, that the "incidents of work" alluded to were all wrought by the Gentile soldiers of Pilate, and not by the Jews.

to go before any judge on the sabbath day, nor on the day of the preparation to it, after the ninth hour" (*Ant.* xvi.6,2). There is a parallel to this custom in the preparation day observed by some of the modern sects for their observance of the Lord's supper. Now John, instead of contradicting the Synoptists on this point, uses the same phraseology with the same meaning. He too calls the day of the crucifixion "the preparation," and "the preparation of the passover"; and he indicates that he means the preparation for the sabbath, and not for the feast, by saying: "The Jews, therefore, because it was the preparation, that the bodies might not remain on the cross upon the sabbath (for the day of that sabbath was a high day), asked of Pilate that their legs might be broken, and that they might be taken away" (19.14, 31). Thus far, then, there is perfect agreement between John and the other writers.

We next consider the three statements of John which are held to be contradictory to the other writers. First, his statement that those who led Jesus to Pilate entered not into the praetorium, "that they might not be defiled, but might eat the passover" (18.28). It is only by forgetting a provision of the law which no Jew could ever forget that this remark can be understood of eating the paschal supper. This provision is that a person unclean from any other source than a dead body or leprosy could be cleansed by sunset the same day, by washing his clothes and bathing his flesh, and remaining unclean until the evening. (Lev 15.1–24; 16.26, 28; 17.15–16). In reality, entering the house of a Gentile did not render one unclean according to the law; it was only tradition which made it so; and it could not deprive one of eating the paschal supper on the following night, because the prescribed process of purification was completed before sunset. Unquestionably, then, the eating here referred to by John was some other than that of the paschal lamb, and it was to occur before sunset that day.[8] What

---

[8] When Westcott says (*Int. to Gospels*, 337), "Nothing but the determination to adapt these words to a theory could suggest the idea that 'eating the passover' applies to anything but the great paschal meal," we are tempted to reply, that nothing but ignorance of the law of purification could allow a man to think that it applies to the paschal meal at all. To the argument made above, as advanced by Wieseler, Ebrard replies: "to have entered the house of a Gentile would certainly have rendered a Jew unclean, so as to disqualify him for the

eating is really meant we may not be able to discover; but this can not alter the fact that it was not the eating of the paschal lamb. If the remark had reference to the priests, and this may be its reference, seeing that John uses the indefinite "they" and the chief priests were certainly the persons who dealt with Pilate (28, 35), the law itself furnishes a probable explanation. It provides that on this first day of the feast the priests should offer ten burnt offerings, each accompanied by its proper meal offering, amounting in all to an ephah and a half, or about a bushel and a half of fine flour made up into bread, all of which was to be eaten by the priests. In addition to this, one he goat was offered as a sin offering, all of the flesh of which must also be eaten (Num 28.16– 23). It is probable that it became customary to call this consumption of holy food, which was peculiar to the passover feast, "eating the passover." It would be easily distinguished from eating the paschal lamb, by observing the day of the feast to which reference is made. If this is not the eating referred to in the passage before us, we are left to the only alternative, that it was some eating invented by the Pharisees, and called eating the passover. This passage then, furnishes no ground at all for a charge of difference between John and the Synoptists.

Second, John's statement that when Jesus said to Judas at the supper, "That thou doest, do quickly." the disciples thought that he meant "Buy what things we have need of for the feast" (13.26– 29). It is held that by "the feast" is meant the paschal supper; and that therefore when the supper described by John was eaten the paschal supper was yet in the future. The correctness of this inference depends on the question whether the word feast can be properly referred to anything else than the paschal supper. When we remember that the passover feast lasted seven days, and that Jesus and his twelve disciples were in the city on expense for that length of time, it must appear very arbitrary to confine the term feast, and the wants of twelve during this feast, to a single meal;

slaughter of the lambs in the temple, which occurred towards the close of the afternoon." (*Gospel History,* 398). But the question is not about slaughtering the lambs; it is about eating them; and it was not necessary that the same persons should do both.

yet such is the arbitrary assumption which lies at the basis of this objection. But this is not all. Judas went out at a late hour of the night, but not as late as midnight. If this had been any other night of the week than one preceding a day of rest, they could scarcely have thought that Judas went out to buy supplies for the company, seeing that he could easily wait till morning. But if the following day was a holy day, as was the first day of the feast, though not a sabbath, it might be difficult to make the purchases after the day set in,[9] and thus there would be a reason for going out at night. This consideration affords no mean evidence that the supper described by John was, as the Synoptists represent it, the paschal supper, for this supper preceded the first day of the feast in which there must be a holy convocation and no servile work. Here, then, instead of a contradiction, we find in John's language concerning the feast perfect agreement with the Synoptists, and, in addition to this, independent evidence that he fixes the supper on the same night with them.

Third, John's statement which is said to explicitly locate the last supper on a night preceding the first day of the Passover. His words are these: "Now before the feast of the passover, Jesus knowing that his hour was come that he should depart out of this world to the Father, having loved his own who were in the world, he loved them to the end. And during supper, the devil having already put into the heart of Judas Iscariot, Simon's son, to betray him," etc. It is claimed that the words, "before the feast of the passover," modify the whole of the narration following, and that they consequently fix the time of the supper here mentioned *before* the feast of the passover. We can not see that this is true.

---

[9] Westcott says (*Int.* 338): "On the fifteenth such purchases would have been equally illegal and impossible"; and Ebrard says (*Gospel History,* 399): "It was forbidden by the law either to work, or to buy, or to sell after that time"; that is, after sunset, the 14th. But these writers forget that the law was this: "In the first day there shall be to you a holy convocation, and in the seventh day a holy convocation; no manner of work shall be done in *them, save that which every man must eat,* that only may be done by you" (Ex 12.16). Now this exception concerning that which every man may eat carries with it all such buying and selling of food as could not well be avoided. Still, buying and selling of food must have been very limited under the strict interpretations of the Pharisees, and Judas might well take the precaution to buy during the previous night.

On the contrary, the first sentence is complete in itself, although the connection of its clauses is a little obscure. The obscurity is at once removed if we arrange the clauses in the order of their dependence, as follows: "Now Jesus, knowing that his hour was come that he should depart out of this world to the Father, having loved his own who were in the world before the passover, he loved them unto the end." The clause, "having loved his own," etc., is the only one that admits of modification by the words, "before the passover." The clause about knowing his hour was come points to the time of the feast; and the clause, "he loved them to the end," points to the continuance of his love from the time of the feast onward. The whole sentence is prefatory to the narrative of the feet-washing and the tender discourse which follows, all of which was a remarkable exhibition of that love that continued to the end. An advance in the narration sets in with mention of the supper; but it was anticipated in the expression, "the feast of the passover," which was itself a supper. The words, "and during supper," beginning the sentence next after the mention of the feast of the passover, can refer only to the paschal supper. It is as if one should speak of the feast of Christmas, or of Thanksgiving, and should add, And during dinner so and so occurred; or as if, after mentioning a wedding, he should add, And during supper so and so occurred. No one could think, in these cases, of any other dinner than the Christmas or the Thanksgiving dinner; of any other supper than the wedding supper. So, in the present instance, no one would think of any other than the paschal supper, from the mere reading of the passage itself. The thought of another is read into the passage; it is not suggested by it. On the contrary, the passage represents the events following as occurring at the paschal supper, and the account is in perfect harmony, as respects time, with Synoptic accounts of the same supper.[10]

---

[10] For opposite views of the time of the Last Supper, and the authorities on the subject, ancient and modern, see Ebrard, *Gospel History*, Sec. 92; Westcott's *Introduction*, 335–341; Alford's Commentary *in loco*.

FIVE

Alleged Contradictions Between the Synoptic Gospels

Having discussed the specifications of contradiction between John's Gospel and the Synoptics, we now take up those in which the latter are said to contradict one another.

1. From the days of Celsus, the first infidel writer, till the present day, the genealogies of our Lord given by Matthew and Luke have furnished material for objections to the Gospel narratives. It was acknowledged even then that they present some difficulties of interpretation, but the ever varying objections of unbelief have from that day to this been successfully answered.[1] We shall state and answer briefly those most commonly urged in modern times; and though not in the direct line of the present chapter, some that are directed against Matthew alone.

It is said, first, that Matthew deliberately leaves out the names of four kings between David and Jechoniah, which is true; second,

---

[1] "In finding fault with our Lord's genealogy, there are certain points which occasion some difficulty even to Christians, and which, owing to the discrepancies between the genealogies, are advanced by some as arguments against their correctness, but which Celsus has not even mentioned. For Celsus, who is truly a braggart, and who professes to be acquainted with all matters relating to Christianity, does not know how to raise doubts in a skillful manner against the credibility of Scripture. But he asserts that the framers of the genealogies, from a feeling of pride, made Jesus to be descended from the first man, and from the kings of the Jews. And he thinks that he makes a notable charge when he adds, that the carpenter's wife could not be ignorant of the fact, had she been of such illustrious descent." (*Origen against Celsus*, b. ii., c. xxxii.).

that inasmuch as the period between Jechoniah and Jesus is about six hundred years, and in that period he gives only thirteen names, he must have left out several names here; and this is true; third, that although he has left out names in two divisions of his list, he says that all the names in each are fourteen; and this is also true.[2] But while this last statement is true, it is not inconsistent with the other two; for it is of Matthew's own list that the remark is made, and not of those from which he copied. Of his list it is true that it contains three divisions of fourteen each, if we count as he does by repeating the name of Jechoniah at the beginning of the last. And what of his having out names? If it were necessary to give all the names in order to make good the purpose for which he quoted any, the omission would invalidate his argument; but his purpose in this part, as all admit, is merely to show that Jesus was descended from David; and this is done, no matter how many names are omitted, provided those which he gives are certainly in the line of descent. That they are, down to Jechoniah, is known to us by the books of Kings and Chronicles; and whether they are from Jechoniah to Joseph, could have been known in Matthew's day by any one who would take the trouble to consult the sources which he used. If we were called to say why Matthew made these omissions, we might, or we might not give a satisfactory reason; but whether there is a good reason or not, the facts in the case do not invalidate in the slightest degree the evidence which he gives of the ancestry of Joseph and of Jesus.[3]

But the chief objection urged against the genealogy is the alleged contradiction between Matthew and Luke as to the father of Joseph. It is demanded, "How can Joseph have been at the same time a son of Jacob and of Heli?" The answer is easy to any one acquainted with Jewish usage as to genealogical terms. There are four ways in which one man could be son of another in Jewish

---

[2] Strauss, *New Life*, ii. 11, 15; Francis Newman, *Phases of Faith*, 65, 66.

[3] A probable reason is, that the list was divided into three divisions of fourteen names each, to aid the memory of the early preachers among the Jews, who would be constantly called on to prove the descent of Jesus from David, and who, not always having the book at hand, would need to have the names memorized.

usage: when he was son in our sense of the word; when he was a grandson; when he was son by a levirate marriage; and when he was a son-inlaw. Of the second, there are many examples in the Old Testament. Of the third, we have one unquestionable example in this very genealogy as given by both Matthew and Luke, and we have a law providing for it. The law is, that if a man take a wife and die childless, his brother, which means in this instance his nearest kinsman, shall take the widow and raise up seed to his brother (Deut 25.5–10). The example is that of Obed, son of Boaz. The latter took Ruth, the childless widow of his kinsman Mahlon, son of Elimelech, "to raise up the name of the dead upon his inheritance," and begat Obed. In compliance with the law, Obed was the levirate son and heir of the deceased Mahlon, and inherited the land of Elimelech, his grandfather on that side (Ruth 1.1–5; 2.1; 3.12–13; 4.1–6, 9–11, 13, 17). While his ancestry by the blood line goes back through Boaz to Judah, as it is traced by Matthew and by Luke (Matt 1. 3–5; Luke 3.32–33), if any one had seen fit to trace the line by which he inherited the lands of Elimelech, he would have written, Obed son of Mahlon, son of Elimelech, and so on back to Judah.[4] In other words, Obed had two fathers, just as Joseph had; and two lines of genealogy meeting in Judah, just as Joseph had two lines meeting in David. This shows one way, then, in which Joseph might have been son of Jacob and also son of Heli. He might have been real son of one and levirate son of the other, or he might have been real son of one and grandson of the other. As respects the question of contradiction, it matters not which of these is the true relationship; for the appearance of contradiction is removed in either case, and the question of contradiction is the only one with which we are now concerned.

The fourth sense of the word son mentioned above has not so much Scripture evidence in its favor, yet it has some; for king Saul repeatedly called David his son, though he was his son-in-law.[5]

---

[4] As Elimelech was of Bethlehem-Judah, and was the owner of lands there, he must have been a lineal descendant of Judah.

[5] 1 Samuel 24.16; 26.17, 21, 25.

As the Hebrew has no distinctive word for son-in-law, but uses for this and similar relationships a word which means a kinsman by marriage, the term son might well be employed in this way; and Saul's use of it shows that at least it was not unauthorized. Joseph, then, might have been son-in-law of Heli, and son of Jacob; and thus in another way the appearance of contradiction is removed. In this case, too, Jesus would inherit the blood of David through his mother; and to set forth this fact would be an adequate motive for the insertion of Luke's genealogy.

Against all three of these explanations, any one of which being accepted, the charge of contradiction must be abandoned, the objection has been persistently urged, that they all involve the use of the term son in two or more different senses in the same connection. This is true as to our own usage, but not as to the Jewish usage; for in Jewish usage the term has, as we have seen, a range of meaning which covers all these relationships, and one has to determine by the context, or by what is known in each instance from other sources, which one of these it designates. We have a parallel to it in the word begat as used in Matthew's genealogy. When he says that David begat Solomon, he employs the word in the sense which we attach to it; but when he says in the same sentence that Uzziah begat Jotham, where three intervening generations are omitted, he uses the word in a different sense from ours, but in the same Hebrew sense; for in Hebrew it means nothing more than that one is the progenitor of another, as son means that one is the descendant of another.

It has been urged, as a still further objection to the preceding explanations, that the same difficulty which attaches to the parentage of Joseph attaches also to that of Shealtiel, who is called son of Jechoniah, and also son of Neri (Matt 1.12; Luke 3.27); and that this involves the supposition of two levirate marriages, or something of the kind, in the same genealogy. This is true; but what of it? As we have just seen, there is still another instance higher up in the list where a levirate marriage certainly took place, and why should it be thought strange that such should be the case in a family whose genealogy is traced through two thousand years? Indeed, there would have been still another of the kind in this very list, if Judah had complied with his promise to Tamar in regard to his son Shelah; for in that case her son Perez would have been begotten in a levirate marriage by Shelah, instead of being begotten by Judah himself.[6]

We now see that while there has been from almost the beginning a difference of opinion as to the exact sense in which Joseph was the son of Jacob and also of Heli, and this because of the ambiguous use of the word son by Hebrew writers, this very ambiguity precludes the charge of contradiction, and lifts these genealogies above the reach of the weapons of unbelief.

2. Luke represents Joseph and Mary as residing before the birth of Jesus in Nazareth, and as returning to this their home after the birth in Bethlehem (1.26–27; 2.4, 39). Matthew says nothing of this previous residence in Nazareth, and it is claimed that, in contradiction to Luke, he represents them as having resided permanently in Bethlehem until after the flight into Egypt, when they resorted to Nazareth through fear of Archelaus.[7] It is true that Matthew represents them as being in Bethlehem when the child was born, and as at first purposing to live there after the return from Egypt; and from this we might, if we had no Gospel but Matthew's, infer that Bethlehem had been their home; just as, if we had no narrative but Mark's, we would not know that they had been in Bethlehem at all; but the inference would only be an assumption grounded on the silence of the writer; for Matthew says absolutely nothing as to the place of residence before the birth (1.18–25). The argument then is this: Luke says that the residence of the couple was Nazareth; Matthew does not say where it was; therefore Matthew contradicts Luke! If we wished to extend the line of argument, we might add: Matthew and Luke say the child was born in Bethlehem; Mark does not say where he was born; therefore Mark contradicts both Luke and Matthew.

---

[6] See the account of Judah's family, Genesis 38.6–15; 25–29; and compare Luke 3.33; Matthew 1.3.

[7] Strauss, *New Life*, ii. 21.

3. The next alleged contradiction, taken in order of time, is that between Matthew and Luke about the movements of Joseph soon after the birth of Jesus. Luke represents him as taking the child, at the end of forty days, to Jerusalem for presentation in the temple; and he says that "when they had accomplished all things that were according to the commandment of the Lord, they returned into Galilee, to their own city Nazareth" (2.22–39, comp. Lev 12.1–4). It is claimed that if this preceded the flight into Egypt (the only tenable supposition), the latter incident, and the coming of the wise men which led to it, are contradicted by Luke's assertion that from the temple they went immediately back to Nazareth.[8] But unfortunately for this assertion, Luke does not say that they went "immediately" back to Nazareth. He uses no adverb of time, and no expression of any kind to indicate how soon the return to Nazareth took place. The interval, whether long or short, is passed over in silence, and it may therefore have been either a long one or a short one. There is nothing to prevent the interval from being long enough for the arrival of the magi, the flight into Egypt, and the return therefrom. The accounts do "admit of being incorporate into one another," and therefore there is no contradiction between them.

4. In the accounts by Matthew and Luke of the healing of the centurion's servant there are two apparent discrepancies which have been habitually treated by unfriendly critics as contradictions. First, Matthew says that the centurion "came to him, beseeching him, and saying, Lord, my servant lieth in the house sick of the palsy, grievously tormented"; while Luke says that he sent unto Jesus "elders of the Jews, asking him that he would come and save his servant." Second, Matthew says that when Jesus proposed to go to the house and heal the servant, the centurion said, "Lord, I am not worthy that thou shouldst come under my roof"; while Luke says that when Jesus was now not far from the house, the centurion "sent friends to him, saying to him, Lord, trouble not thy self: for I am not worthy that thou shouldst

---

[8] Strauss, *New Life*, ii. 92; Newman, *Phases of Faith*, 79.

come under my roof." This should never have occasioned the least trouble to any one inclined to do justice to the two writers. It is one of the most common features of condensed narration to represent a man as saying what he says through another who speaks in his name. This is what Matthew does in his condensed account of this cure; while Luke, wishing to bring out in the boldest relief the great faith of the centurion, and in connection with it two traits of his character left out of view by Matthew, his generosity and his liberality, names the messengers through whom he prefers his request, and quotes from their lips the statement, "He is worthy that thou shouldst do this for him: for he loveth our nation, and himself built us our synagogue." His faith is brought out fully by the fact that he in the first place thought himself unworthy to come in person to speak to Jesus, and in the second place thought himself unworthy that Jesus should come under his roof. The latter he did not think of till Jesus was already near his house, when he began to realize what was about to take place, and shrank from it. This appearance of discrepancy, then, like so many others, grows entirely out of the more elaborate account given by one of the writers, in carrying out the different purpose for which he mentions the incident.

5. There are several instances in which Matthew speaks of two persons or things in a transaction, while Luke and Mark in describing the same speak of only one; and these have been treated even by eminent critics as grave discrepancies. For example, Matthew says there were two demoniacs healed in the land of the Gadarenes (8.28); two blind men healed at Jericho (20.30); and two asses brought to Jesus for his ride into Jerusalem (21.7); while Mark and Luke mention only one in each instance. It is obvious at a glance that there is no contradiction here, and that the difference lies only in this, that Mark and Luke mention the more fierce of the two demoniacs, saying nothing of the other; that they mention by name the blind man who was well known (Mark 10.46), saying nothing of the one who was not; and that they mention the ass which Jesus rode, saying nothing of the one

which he did not ride. It is a difference characteristic of these two writers as distinguished from Matthew. The latter, for instance, uses the plural number of seeds in the parable of the sower (13.4–7), and of the servants sent for fruits in the parable of the wicked husbandmen (21.34–37), while Mark and Luke in each instance use the singular (Mark 4.3–7; Luke 8.5–7); and in case of the cures in Decapolis, Matthew speaks of a multitude being healed (15.29–31), while Mark selects a single one of the number and describes the process of his cure (7.31–8.3). Instead of being contradictions, they are examples of the more specific style of delineation employed by Mark and Luke.

6. Another alleged contradiction, as trivial, and yet as gravely set forth as the preceding, is found in the remarks ascribed to Jairus concerning his little daughter when he asked Jesus to heal her. In Matthew he says, "My daughter is even now dead"; in Mark, "My little daughter is at the point of death." This case is a fair representative of several others in which remarks apparently inconsistent are ascribed to the same person. In all such cases fair dealing requires us to allow both remarks to have been made if we fairly can; and surely we can in this instance; for the child was so nearly dead that she died before the father, accompanied by Jesus, returned to the house; and how natural it would be for the father, knowing the extremity she was in, to say in the vehemence of his entreaty, "My daughter is at the point of death; she is even now dead; but come and lay thy hands on her, and she shall live."

7. The place of curing the blind man at Jericho, whether as Jesus entered the city, apparently stated by Luke, or as he went out, expressly stated by Matthew and Mark, has long been held up as a palpable contradiction; but on examination we shall find that, instead of being such, the incident furnishes no mean evidence of the extreme exactness of these writers. If we examine Luke's account closely, we find that he does not, as would appear at first glance, locate this cure at the entrance into the city; on the contrary, his representation implies that it was effected elsewhere. Notice, first, that as Jesus drew nigh to the city, the

man was sitting by the wayside begging. Second, he ascertained by hearing, his only way to learn it, that a multitude was passing by. This he could know only by the noise they were making, or by the fact that many had passed by and still they were passing. But they were not making a noise, as appears from the fact that when he began to make a noise they rebuked him and insisted that he should hold his peace. They were evidently intent, at least those near Jesus, on hearing the Master's words. He knew that it was a multitude, then, by the number that had already passed, while others were still passing; and he asked what it meant. When he learned that Jesus was passing by, he cried out for mercy, and it was "they that went before" who rebuked him, and told him to hold his peace. How could this be, when they who went before had already gone far past the man before he began to cry out? It could only be by a change of relative position, in which the blind man had got before the multitude, so that he cried out as they approached him again, and was rebuked by those in the front of the moving column. Luke, in giving compactness to his recital, has passed in silence over this change of position, leaving it as an unimportant detail, to be discovered or not by inference from his description. And as to the place of healing, he leaves this in the dark, but the accounts of Matthew and Mark step in, and in the most incidental way supply the missing link by saying that it was as he went out of the city. This not only fills out Luke's account, but it furnishes time and opportunity for the change of relative place which Luke's account implies; for it gives the man time to get around to the gate of exit while Jesus and his large following were passing through the city. Furthermore, the next paragraph in Luke, in which he resumes the march of Jesus and his company where he had ceased to trace it when he began the account of the blind man, shows that while passing through Jericho he stopped, apparently for a meal, at the house of Zacchaeus, thus giving ample time for the blind man's movement. The fact now apparent, that the two narratives of Matthew and Mark thus supply a missing link in that of Luke, so that the three combine to complete the story where they appeared to be inconsistent, furnishes striking evidence that all three are strictly accurate. The different parts of a broken story fit one another only when the story is true.

8. The Lord's prediction of Peter's denial is made to represent two contradictions, one as to the time of it, and one as to the terms of it. It is said that while Luke and John unequivocally represent it as being uttered at the supper, Matthew and Mark say it was uttered on the way to the mount of Olives.[9] The former part of this statement is true (Luke 22.31–34, 39; John 13.36–38; 14.31); but the latter is not. Matthew and Mark both follow the account of the Lord's supper with the statement in identical words: "And when they had sung a hymn, they went out unto the mount of Olives"; but then, as if they had forgotten an item and returned to it, they mention the prediction, and, returning the thread of the narrative where it was broken, they say, "Then cometh Jesus with them to a place called Gethsemane," which place, as we know by the topography, was the first point at which they touched the mount of Olives. Really, then, the prediction, according to their accounts, took place within the room of the supper. (Matt 26.30–36; Mark 14.26–32.)

As regards the terms of this prediction, all have it that the three denials should occur before the cock should crow, except Mark, who has it, "Before the cock crow twice, thou shalt deny me thrice." Now no two of the writers quote the words exactly alike; and this shows that at least three of them quote them freely, not giving the exact words. In such cases the most precise form, if any, is likely to be the exact one. In this instance, Mark's being the most precise, we may presume that he quotes the very words of Jesus, and that the others quote the idea without aiming at exactness. The idea expressed in all is that the denial should take place about the time of cock-crowing. Now it is well known by every one who has often listened to this morning music, that almost invariably an early cock crows, but is not answered for a while by others. After an interval another crows, then another, and finally there is a chorus

---

[9] Strauss, *New Life*, ii. 323, 324.

from all the cocks in the neighborhood. Jesus located the three denials between the first two crowings and the general chorus; Mark reports him literally, while the others give the substance, but all indicate the same time. There is no contradiction, then, but only free quotations without change of the thought.

9. No two of the Gospels quote the inscription on the cross in precisely the same words, and here it is claimed that we have another contradiction. In order to see the exact amount of difference between the several quotations, we place them side by side.

Matthew:	This is Jesus	the King of the Jews.
Mark:		The King of the Jews.
Luke:	This is	the King of the Jews.
John:	Jesus the Nazarene,	the King of the Jews.

At a glance it is seen that the essential part, that which constituted the accusation, that he claimed to be "the King of the Jews," is the same, word for word and letter for letter, in all four, the difference being only in the way of designating the person who made the claim. In this there are three variations not differing at all in meaning, and two of them agreeing in all but the use and non-use of the name Jesus. In meaning, then, there is no difference whatever; and the slight difference in form may be accounted for either by supposing that all but one aimed only at quoting the substance of the part designating the person, or that this part was variously written by Pilate himself. Latin was doubtless his native tongue, and the Hebrew and Greek forms of the inscription were translations. At least two of the variations may have been made by him or his scribe in translating, and another may have been made by one of the Evangelists in translating from his translation. Seeing, then, that the essential part is perfectly preserved by all, that the unessential part is preserved without change of meaning by all, and that there are three ways of accounting for the slight verbal variations in the latter part without charging either ignorance or inaccuracy on the writers, all appearance of contradiction passes away.

10. Much more plausible than the last is the charge of contradiction between Matthew and Luke respecting the conduct towards Jesus of the robbers who were crucified with him. Matthew and Mark both say, in almost identical terms, that "the robbers that were crucified with him cast upon him the same reproach" (Matt 27.44; Mark 15.32). Luke says that "one of the malefactors that were hanged railed on him," but that the other rebuked him, and called on Jesus to remember him when he came into his kingdom. It is held that there is here a contradiction, and that the conduct ascribed to the penitent robber is incredible. Now if, as is very commonly affirmed, Luke's statement had been that *only* one robber railed at him,[10] the contradiction would be real; but he does not so assert. He merely asserts that one of them did so, and was rebuked by his fellow; and this is not inconsistent with the supposition that both had done so at an earlier moment. It can not be denied that Matthew and Mark may speak of what took place at the beginning, and Luke of what occurred at a later hour of the time spent on the cross. This being so, both of the robbers may have joined in the railing at first, and one may have continued it to the end, while the other may have ceased, and toward the close have rebuked his fellow. As this is possible, we must give the writers the benefit of it before we pronounce them contradictory. But this is not only possible, it is even probable; for we can readily discover motives which were likely to lead to this result on the part of the one who repented. In the first agonies of crucifixion, the consideration that it was the execution of Jesus which led to their being crucified that day, most naturally excited the wrath of both against him, and caused them to echo the outcries of the mob. It was quite unnatural that one of them should continue these outcries persistently; but it was most natural that, as the weary moments wore away, and unavoidable reflections about death and eternity came over them, in connection with the remembrance of

---

[10] "According to the first and second Gospels, the robbers joined with the chief priests and scribes and elders and those who passed by in mocking and reviling Jesus. This is directly contradicted by the third Synoptist, who states that only one of the malefactors did so." (*Sup. Rel.,* iii. 416).

their past criminality, they should cease to reproach their fellow-sufferer, and turn their thoughts to God. Luke's representation as to one of them is just what we should expect of both; and instead of being surprised at the change which come over one, we should rather be surprised that it did not come over the other also. Indeed this is the very feeling expressed by the penitent robber himself: "Dost thou not even fear God, seeing thou art in the same condemnation? and we indeed justly, for we receive the due reward of our deeds; but this man has done nothing amiss." Reflection upon their own wickedness in contrast with the innocence of Jesus, and indignation at the continued obduracy of his fellow, are the two thoughts of this rebuke. Seeing, then, that this is a most rational hypothesis, suggested by the circumstances of the persons, the accounts are relieved of all ground for the charge of inconsistency, and the alleged conduct of the penitent robber is thus far freed from all improbability. As to the appeal which he made to Jesus, "Jesus, remember me when thou comest in thy kingdom," it is a much worthier ground for surprise than that he should have railed at Jesus at first and afterward repented. It implies belief that Jesus was yet to come in his kingdom, though now he was in the agonies of death, and the petitioner believed that he would soon be dead. This belief, as has been truly remarked, transcended that of the apostles themselves.[11] Is it incredible? If not, how had the robber acquired it? It is not incumbent on us to trace the process by which he had acquired it; it is only necessary to show that it is possible for him to have done so. His remark to his fellow robber, "This man has done nothing amiss," implies much previous knowledge of Jesus; for he could not have learned it by the events of that day, even had he been a free man. He must have learned it before his imprisonment. Even while he was carrying on his nefarious business of highway robbery, he may have

---

[11] "This exemplary robber speaks like an Apostle, and in praying Jesus as the Messiah to remember him when he came into his kingdom, he shows much more than apostolic appreciation of the claims and character of Jesus." (*Sup. Rel.,* iii. 416). "Here then we have a criminal, who undoubtedly came now for the first time into contact with Jesus, understanding without preliminary instruction the doctrine of a suffering and dying Messiah." (Strauss, *N. L.,* ii. 375).

mingled very often in the crowds which gathered about Jesus, and by this means become well instructed in his teaching. He may, indeed, have believed on him as many wicked men now believe; and it is not going farther than facts often witnessed at the present day, to suppose that he had, under the influence of that faith, abandoned his course of crime before he was arrested and condemned for it. Such opportunities may certainly have been within his reach, and although they would scarcely enable him to understand the doctrine of the kingdom fully, they may have enabled him to form the conception of it expressed in his dying petition. It is not necessary to suppose that this conception was altogether correct. It probably was about this: that the kingdom which Jesus had failed to establish on earth he would, by some means and in some undefined way, establish in the spirit world into which he was about to enter. The thief may have had a very vague idea as to the nature of that kingdom, and yet, from the strong evidences which Jesus had given of his power and goodness, have believed that something called a kingdom would yet be established, and that, whatever it was, and wherever it was to be, there would be life and peace within it. In the greatest act of Abraham's faith, his conception was a mistaken one; for he believed that God would raise up Isaac from the dead, whereas God did not intend that Isaac should die; yet the faith of Abraham was the more highly commended on this very account. So, whatever may have been the dying robber's conception of the kingdom, he believed that Jesus, notwithstanding his death, would establish one, and this procured for him the blessing. After all, then, the repentance and faith of the penitent robber is not so wonderful as the obduracy of the one who continued to rail at the Son of God in the very agonies of his own death.

We have now considered all of the alleged contradictions between our four Gospels which we think worthy of attention in this work, except those in the accounts of the resurrection. There are no others, I believe, that can not be disposed of an easily as we have disposed of these, and as satisfactorily; there are none which a thoughtful young person, after studying these, can not dispose of without assistance: we shall therefore turn next to some which are said to exist between the Gospels and Acts of Apostles, and between the latter book and some of Paul's Epistles.

SIX

Alleged Contradictions Between Acts and Other Books

There is no writer in the New Testament the credibility of whose statements has been so fiercely assailed by recent unfriendly critics as have those of the author of Acts. We desire to give the charges of his enemies fair consideration, and to form an intelligent conclusion as to their merits.

Christian Baur, followed by later rationalists in general, asserts that the design of the author was not to write a truthful history, but to defend the Apostle Paul against the attacks and accusations of the Judaizing party, at the head of which they place the Apostle Peter; and that in carrying out this purpose he did not hesitate to falsify history when it suited him to do so.[1] They seek to sustain the charge of falsifying history by maintaining that he frequently contradicts both himself and other writers, especially the Apostle Paul. Whether the credibility of the book can be maintained depends on the reality of these alleged contradictions, and we shall now proceed to consider those which are relied on most implicitly.

I. Contradictions of Matthew and of Himself

1. We first notice an alleged contradiction between Acts and Matthew in regard to the death of Judas. An appearance of contra-

---

[1] Baur, *Life and Works of Paul,* i. 6, 10; Renan. *Apostles,* 26, 27; *Sup. Rel.,* iii. 62, 64.

diction is apparent to every reader of the two accounts; for while Matthew represents Judas as hanging himself (27.5), it is said in Acts that he fell headlong, and burst asunder in the midst, and that all his bowels gushed out (Acts 1.18). But instead of being a contradiction, the latter statement is only a supplement to the former. Falling headlong would not cause a man to burst asunder, unless something had previously occurred to weaken the wall of his bowels, or unless the fall was from a great elevation. But both of these conditions are supplied by Matthew's account: for if he hung himself, this would elevate him some feet above the ground; and if he remained hanging a day or two, which would be very probable, this would weaken the walls of his abdomen, so that a fall, whether effected by the breaking of the cord, or the limb, or the parting of his neck, would cause the result in question. The two accounts are therefore harmonious, and not only so, but the horrible result stated in the one is accounted for by the fact mentioned in the other.

But the two accounts differ also in reference to the purchase of the potter's field, and the origin of its name, Akeldama, the Field of Blood. Matthew says that it was bought by the chief priests with the money which Judas returned to them, and that for this reason it was called the field of blood; while in Acts it is said that Judas bought it "with the reward of iniquity" (the same money), and that this, together with his falling there, caused it to receive the name (Matt 27.6–9; Acts 1.18–19). But here there is no contradiction; for if Matthew's account of the purchase is true, that in Acts is also true, with this only difference, that Judas bought the field indirectly, it being bought with his money, and in consequence of his vain attempt to return the money to the priests; and as for the name, the account in Acts only furnishes an additional and very good reason for calling the loathsome spot Akeldama. It must be admitted that the account in Acts would be misleading to persons not acquainted with that in Matthew; but Luke's first readers were not thus uninformed, and his present readers have Matthew's account before them and can combine the two if they will.[2]

---

[2] As a curious illustration of the confusion into which men of genius fall when they attempt to resolve these simple narratives of the Scriptures into legends, and thus rob

It should be observed that while the account in Acts which we have been considering is printed in the midst of a speech made by the Apostle Peter, the words concerning Judas are an interpolation in the speech by the author of Acts. This is proved by the fact that Akeldama is translated into Greek, and this could not have been done by Peter, who was speaking to Hebrews; but Luke, writing to a Greek, would be constrained to translate this Hebrew word. It suits the purpose of skeptical writers to deny this, and to maintain that the author of Acts here puts into Peter's mouth a speech which he could not have made.[3] But this assumption is equivalent to charging the author with a blunder which the most stupid writer could scarcely commit—the blunder of making Peter speak to Jews in their own tongue, and translate one of their familiar words into a foreign tongue to enable them to understand it; and in doing so to speak of the Hebrew language, which was the native tongue both of himself and his hearers, as "*their* language." Whether this author was Luke or some one else, if he had ordinary common sense he could not have been guilty of a blunder so gross.

2. It is alleged that the author of Acts contradicts himself in regard to the time of the ascension.[4] In Acts he certainly represents the ascension as taking place forty days after the resurrection (1.3–9), and it is affirmed that in the Gospel he represents it as occurring on the same day as the resurrection. This is another instance in which the charge involves the grossest stupidity on

---

them of historical verity, it is well to notice the following passage in Renan: "As to the wretched Judas of Kerioth, there were terrible traditions of his death. It is said that with the price of his perfidy he bought a field in the environs of Jerusalem. There was indeed to the south of Mount Sion a place called Hakeldama (the field of blood). It was supposed that this was the property purchased by the traitor. According to one tradition he killed himself. According to another, he had a fall in his field, in consequence of which his bowels gushed out. According to others, he died of a species of dropsy, accompanied by disgusting circumstances, which were regarded as a chastisement of heaven. The desire to show in the case of Judas the accomplishment of the threats which the Psalmist pronounced against the perfidious friend, may have originated these legends. It may be that Judas retired upon his property at Hakeldama, led a peaceful and obscure life, while his former friends were conquering the world and spreading the report of his infamy." (*Life of Jesus,* 359, 360).

[3] *Sup. Rel.,* iii. 100, 106.

[4] Renan, *Apostles,* 20.

Luke's part, if it is true; for both narratives are addressed to the same person, Theophilus, and the matter of the ascension is made conspicuous in both. The truth of the matter is, that in the Gospel he does not say how long the interval was, but he passes from the account of the first meeting with the Eleven to that which ended with the ascension without noting that there was an interval, reserving to his later account a statement of the details. If, when Theophilus read the first account, he had concluded that the ascension took place on the day of the resurrection, when he received the second he could but conclude that he had misunderstood the first on account of its brevity. He could not have concluded that the writer was telling two contradictory stories; for this could but discredit all that he narrated; and he certainly wrote with the hope of being believed.

3. It is claimed that Luke contradicts himself in the three accounts of Paul's conversion, it being assumed that the two which are represented as given by Paul himself were really composed by the author of the book. The specifications are these: one account has it that those who journeyed with Paul "stood speechless"; the other, "that all fell to the earth"; one, that these companions heard the voice, but saw no man; the other, that they heard not the voice (9.7; 12.9; 26.14).[5] As to the latter point of difference, nothing in speech is much more common than to use the word hear in two slightly different senses, one for hearing the mere sound of a voice, and the other for so hearing it as to know what is said. We hear a person speak to us, and we answer, "I did not hear you." No one accuses us of a false answer, because such is the usage of the word hear. So, in the present instance, the companions of Paul heard in the sense of catching the sound of the voice, but they heard not in the sense of distinguishing what was said. No one disposed to deal fairly with an author would think of construing this as a contradiction. As to the other point, it is easy to see that Paul's companions could have fallen to the ground at the beginning, and have stood speechless afterward; and the fact that they

---

[5] Baur, *Paul*, i. 60–62.

did not understand what was said to Paul is accounted for by this consideration. When all fell, and the companions found that they were not addressed by the person who spoke, they most naturally sprang to their feet as soon as they could use their limbs, and ran to a safe distance, where they stood speechless, still hearing the voice, and yet not hearing it.

It must be conceded that if Luke actually wrote all three of these accounts himself, it is difficult to say why he gave the details thus differently. But if, as the narrative asserts, two of them were given by Paul in two different speeches, the difference in narration is at once accounted for, and this furnishes a very good reason for rejecting the hypothesis, baseless in itself, that Luke wrote the speeches and put them into Paul's mouth.

II. Contradictions of Paul in Galatians

The most serious of the alleged contradictions in Acts, and those which are made the most of in argument by the rationalists, are those between it and the Epistle to the Galatians. We will notice them in the order of their occurrence.

1. Paul says that after his conversion he did not go up to Jerusalem until "after three years"; but that he went into Arabia, and returned to Damascus before going up to Jerusalem (Gal 1.15–18). Luke omits his going into Arabia, and says that "he was certain days with the disciples in Damascus," and then, when "many days were fulfilled," he went up to Jerusalem. This is treated as a contradiction, the objectors claiming that "many days" can not cover a period of three years.[6] But the objection is captious: for surely when a writer intentionally uses indefinite terms it is folly to put a close restriction on his meaning. As well say that when Joshua remarks to the Israelites, "Ye dwelt in the wilderness a long season," while Moses says they were there forty years, that there is here a contradiction, because a long season is not so long as forty years. Or, taking the opposite expression, as well say of Job's remark, "Man is of few days, and full of trouble," that according to this, men in Job's time lived only *a few days*. But the Old Testament

---

[6] Baur, *Paul*, i. 107.

furnishes another example still more in point, in the case of Shimei, who, when spared by Solomon on condition that he should not depart from Jerusalem, "dwelt in Jerusalem many days," and yet, as the context shows, he went out of the city "at the end of three years" (1 Kings 2.36–46).

2. It is claimed, also, that in describing Paul's first visit to Jerusalem after his conversion Luke contradicts Paul in several particulars, and manufactures some incidents which did not occur. (1) It must be false, because incredible, that the disciples in Jerusalem, as asserted by Luke, had not heard of Paul's conversion.[7] But Luke does not say they had not heard of Paul's conversion. He says, "They were all afraid of him, not believing that he was a disciple" (9.26). They might have heard of his conversion forty times, and they might have been told all of the details of the story, without believing it; for they might have thought that the story was made up for the purpose of enabling Paul to gain their confidence, and thus to more effectually persecute them. So sudden a conversion of such a persecutor would be next to incredible in any age of the church's history. (2) It is held to be incredible that Barnabas, as Luke affirms, took Paul and brought him into the confidence of the Apostles.[8] But surely this is most natural: for under the circumstances some one had to be the first to acquire confidence in him, and to influence the others, and why not Barnabas as well as any one else? (3) It is affirmed in Acts that Paul was with the disciples, going in and out, and preaching boldly in the name of the Lord; that he spoke and disputed against the Hellenists, and that they went about to kill him (9.28–29); while Paul says that he was there only fifteen days (Gal 1.18); and it is claimed that fifteen days are not enough for all that Luke relates.[9] But why not? If it was his custom to preach and dispute only on Sundays as is the custom of many rationalistic critics, there would be plausibility in the objection; but the apostles, like their Master, disputed daily in the temple, and even a single week of such disputations would be

---

[7] Baur, *Paul,* i. 107.

[8] *Ib.,* 110, 111.

[9] *Ib.*; Renan, *Apostles,* 194.

enough to stir up all the strife which Luke mentions. It would be enough in some places even at the present day. (4) It is claimed that this amount of preaching in Jerusalem is inconsistent with Paul's statement, "I was still unknown by face to the churches in Judea which were in Christ" (Gal 1.22).[10] But while such preaching and disputation necessarily made him known to the brethren in Jerusalem, he might still say that he was unknown by face to the churches in Judea, meaning, as he certainly docs, the churches in general in that country. (5) It is again charged that this want of acquaintance with the churches in Judea is contradicted by Luke in Acts 26.20, where he represents Paul as saying that he preached "throughout all the country of Judea" next after preaching in Jerusalem.[11] But while this preaching is mentioned next after that in Jerusalem, it is not said that it *came* next. No adverb of time, or any other indication of sequence is given. The words are: "I was not disobedient to the heavenly vision; but declared both to them of Damascus first, and at Jerusalem, and throughout all the country of Judea, and also to the Gentiles, that they should repent and turn to God." As there is no note of time except in placing Damascus first, it is but a fair construction to suppose that Judea is mentioned next after Jerusalem because of its contiguity, and to avoid a backward movement in thought after mentioning the Gentiles. (6) It is affirmed that the cause assigned in Acts for cutting short this visit to Jerusalem, the determination of the Hellenists to kill him, and his consequent removal by the brethren to Caesarea and thence to Tarsus, is contradicted in the twenty-second chapter, where Paul is represented as saying that he was ordered away by the Lord himself in a vision (ix. 29, 30, cf. 22.18–20).[12] But the two causes of his departure are not inconsistent. The latter passage shows clearly that Paul was very unwilling to leave Jerusalem, by showing that when the Lord first told him to go he attempted to remonstrate against the order. This is enough to prove that the brethren could not have sent him away had he not also been commanded by the Lord.

---

[10] Renan, *ib.*

[11] Baur, *ib.*, iii.

[12] *Ib.*

3. Another alleged contradiction is found in the numbering of Paul's visits to Jerusalem. His second visit mentioned in Acts is the one made in company with Barnabas, when they were sent with alms from Antioch "to the brethren who dwelt in Judea." This mission led them to Jerusalem as one of many places to which they were sent, and it seems to have been the last point in Judea which they visited; for it is said that they "returned from Jerusalem when they had fulfilled their ministration" (11.30; 12.25). In Paul's account this visit is omitted, for he says "Then after the space of fourteen years I went up to Jerusalem again with Barnabas," and the incidents which are mentioned show that this visit is the third mentioned in Acts (Gal 2.1, cf. Acts 15.1–5). But while this is the second visit mentioned by Paul, he does not say, nor does his language imply, that it was the second in reality. Furthermore, in Galatians the aim of the apostle is to show how little opportunity he had enjoyed for learning the gospel from the older apostles; and the second visit mentioned in Acts gave him no such opportunity, seeing that under the persecution then raging the elder James had been beheaded, and Peter had fled from the city (12.1–3, 16–17). The third visit in the order of time, then, was the second in the order of Paul's discussion; that is, the second in which he saw any of the older apostles; and he had no occasion at all to mention the second one of Acts.[13] In the face of these obvious considerations, it is a matter of surprise that unfriendly critics insist that there is here a contradiction.

4. Alleged contradictions in the accounts of Paul's visit to Jerusalem during the controversy about circumcision are next in order, and on these are based some of the most serious charges which rationalists prefer against the book of Acts. The statements in

---

[13] Baur, the leader in opposing the view here stated, unwittingly confirms it by saying: "The apostle could not, considering his argument, in the passage, have passed over the journey mentioned in Acts 11. His object required that no communication which occurred between Galatians 1.18 and 2.1 should be omitted, else the proof of his teaching being independent of the tuition of the rest of the apostles would be defective" (*Paul* i. 114). But the very consideration urged here justified him in passing over the visit of 11, seeing that on that visit he had no opportunity, as we have shown above, for instruction by the other apostles.

Acts on the subject are briefly these: first, that Barnabas and Paul were sent to Jerusalem by the disciples in Antioch; second, that on their arrival they were received in a public meeting by the church with the apostles and elders, in which meeting they rehearsed all that God had done with them, and in which there arose certain believing Pharisees, who said that it was needful to circumcise the Gentile converts, and charge them to keep the law of Moses; third, that the apostles and elders came together to consider this matter, that after much questioning Peter made a speech in opposition to the Pharisees, that Barnabas and Paul then rehearsed what signs and wonders God had wrought among the Gentiles by them, that James followed with a speech in support of the same views, and that finally a letter to the brethren in Antioch, Syria and Cilicia was drawn up with the approval of the whole church, enforcing the views set forth in the speeches (15.1–29). The statements of Paul on the same subject are these: first, that he went up to Jerusalem on this occasion "by revelation"; second, that he took Titus with him; third, in his own words, "I laid before them the gospel which I preached among the Gentiles, but privately before them who were of repute"; fourth, that Titus, being a Greek, was not compelled to be circumcised, though an effort to this effect was made by certain false brethren; fifth, that the other Apostles present, James, Peter and John, imparted nothing to him, but that on the contrary they gave to him and Barnabas the right hand of fellowship, that the latter should go to the Gentiles, and the former to the circumcision (Gal 2.1–10). At almost every point these two accounts are charged with contradiction. It is held that Paul speaks the truth, but that every one of Luke's statements is false. We shall now state the specifications of this charge, and examine the evidence by which they are supported.

(1) Because Paul says that he went up by revelation, it is charged that Luke is false in saying that he and Barnabas were sent by the brethren in Antioch.[14] But why should the two be considered inconsistent? Paul was an apostle, possessing equal inspiration and

---

[14] *Sup. Rel.,* iii. 227.

authority with any other apostle, and on this he insisted again and again when it was called in question; why then should he not have hesitated to go to the Apostles and elders at Jerusalem for a decision as to whether he had taught the truth, and have required a revelation directing him to go before he would comply with the wishes of the brethren? This is precisely what is implied in the two accounts when considered together; and to the suggestion, that if Paul had been sent by the brethren he certainly would have said so, it is an adequate reply that after stating the main cause of his going and the one which gave divine sanction to the proceeding, it was altogether needless to state the inferior cause which in itself would have been insufficient. Moreover, his aim in Galatians is to show his independence as an apostle, and the fact that he had been sent by the brethren in Antioch, although true, and not inconsistent with his argument, could not strengthen it, and it was therefore very properly omitted.

(2) Paul's silence in reference to the public meetings is held as proof that no such meetings took place: for, it is demanded, how could he, in showing the results, fail to mention the large meeting "which alone could decide the question at issue"? But the very author who is the leader in making this demand himself furnishes the answer, when, on another page of his work, he says: "The Apostles had to be considered in this as the chief personages, whose attention to any matter rendered further transactions superfluous."[15] It was in reality the decision of the three Apostles whom Paul mentions that settled the question on its merits; and this alone rendered a reference to any other transactions superfluous with Paul's readers: it was therefore with the utmost propriety that he omitted the public meeting, and his doing so furnishes not the slightest ground for doubting that it took place. The real purpose of the second meeting was to give the apostles an opportunity to silence the Pharisees and bring the whole church to unanimity.

(3) It is asserted, with a boldness and confidence proportionate to the want of evidence, that Paul's opponents in this visit were

---

[15] Baur, *Paul*, i. 117, 118.

not "Pharisees who believed," as they are called in Acts; nor "false brethren privily brought in," as Paul styles them; but the older Apostles themselves.[16] It is admitted that the representation in Acts is the reverse of this, but it is held that on this point Acts is contradicted by Galatians. On reading the passage in Galatians, we find that the "false brethren privily brought in, who came in to spy out our liberty which we have in Christ Jesus," are spoken of as adversaries, while of the Apostles it is said: "They who were of repute imparted nothing to me: but contrariwise, when they saw that I had been intrusted with the gospel of the uncircumcision, even as Peter with the gospel of the circumcision, they gave to me and Barnabas the right hands of fellowship, that we should go to the Gentiles and they to circumcision." There is in this not the slightest indication of a conflict, but the most positive declaration of agreement. The agreement, too, is the result not of a protracted discussion, or of any debate at all; but of a simple rehearsal by Paul of the Gospel which he had preached. "I laid before them the gospel which I preached among the Gentiles, but privately before them who were of repute, lest by any means I should be running, or had run in vain." This last remark is accounted for by the consideration that, had the older Apostles been found in opposition to Paul, their influence in the church would have broken his down, and he would have run in vain. The whole value of the statement which he makes on the subject depends on the fact brought out, that there was no such opposition. In support of the charge under discussion, the only argument advanced which has the semblance of force is found in the demand, How could Peter have acted as he did so soon afterward in Antioch, that is, in refusing to longer eat with the Gentiles, so that Paul rebuked him before all (Gal 2.11–14), if he had so perfectly agreed with Paul in Jerusalem?[17] It may as well be asked, How could this same Peter have denied his Lord, as he is said to lave done, so soon after declaring, "Even if I must die with thee, yet will I not deny thee" (Matt 26.35)? The

---

[16] Baur, *Paul,* i. 119, 121, 124.

[17] Baur, *Paul,* i. 129.

very rebuke which Paul administers to him implies that he had previously agreed with Paul; for he says, personating Peter, "If I build up again those things which I have destroyed, I prove myself a transgressor." This remark depends for its relevancy on the fact that Peter was now acting in opposition to his previous course, and it sustains the representation made in Acts and Galatians, that he had agreed with Paul in Jerusalem.

(4) The decree said in Acts to have been issued on this occasion by the apostles and elders is pronounced a forgery. This is argued, first, on the ground that if it had been issued Paul could not have failed to refer to it in his subsequent controversy with the Judaizers who continued to insist on the circumcision of the Gentile converts.[18] This omission on Paul's part certainly does appear singular; but his course of argument is precisely what we should expect if all that is stated in Acts were already known to his readers in Galatia and disregarded by them. If this decree had been carried to them by Paul and Silas, as its application to Gentile Christians in general renders quite probable, and if the teachers who had supplanted Paul in their confidence (Gal 1.6–7) had persuaded them to disregard its teaching, as they certainly had, any appeal to it by Paul would have been useless. His only recourse was to do just what he has done in this epistle, supply them with the additional information herein contained. This not only takes away the force of the argument, but it supplies a good reason for the omission.

The same proposition is argued in the second place, from Paul's failure to cite the decree when arguing with the Corinthians against eating meats offered to idols; and this, too, when they had written to him for information on this very subject. It is argued that if this decree had been issued at all it would have been known to the Corinthians, and consequently they could not have written to Paul for information on the subject; that Paul could not, as he does in his reply to them, treat it as a matter of indifference in it-

---

[18] *Ib.,* 134; Renan, *Apostles,* 32; *Sup. Rel.,* iii. 269.

self.[19] It must be admitted that if the decree was in existence Paul had almost certainly made the Corinthians acquainted with it, inasmuch as they were especially liable to do what it forbids. From this it follows that they could not write to Paul for information as to the matters expressly declared in the decree; and if this is what they did write for, the argument would seem to be good. But Paul's answer shows that this was not the purport of their question. His argument meets an objection—the objection that as an idol is known to be nothing, it could not defile a man's conscience to eat flesh which had been offered to one. Paul, without admitting the correctness of the conclusion, takes the objector on his own ground, and shows that inasmuch as this knowledge is not possessed by all men, there would still be sin in the act, because it would embolden some whose consciences were weak to eat as an act of homage, and thus it would cause them to perish (1 Cor 8.1–13). This shows that the question raised and discussed had the nature of an objection to the doctrine of the decree, and that the answer called for was not a statement of what was taught in the decree, but a reason why it should be observed even by those who thought they could violate it without injury to themselves. Let it not be forgotten, also, that while Paul waived the question whether those who were enlightened about idols could eat the offerings without sin, farther on in the Epistle he forbade it absolutely (10.20–21). It was only the eating of flesh thus offered without knowing that it was an idol offering which be allowed as innocent (10.25–29)

(5) We have now sufficiently accounted for the fact that Paul fails to mention the public meeting described in Acts, but it is still insisted that, as Luke was certainly acquainted with the Epistle to the Galatians, be must have had some sinister design in failing to mention the private meeting between the apostles.[20] It is a sufficient answer to say that when he wrote Acts, the Epistle to the Galatians was already in circulation, and he supplies

---

[19] Baur, *Paul,* i. 135; Renan, *Apostles,* 32, 33; *Sup. Rel,* iii. 270–273.

[20] *Sup. Rel.,* iii. 226.

precisely those details in these proceedings which the author of the Epistle had omitted, and avoids repeating those which the Epistle contained. This is just what any sensible writer would be apt to do, and the charge of a sinister design is preposterous. The same answer applies to another charge in this connection: that there is something wrong in omitting the rebuke of Peter by Paul, which occurred soon after this conference.[21] The account of it was already in the hands of the disciples, and it had been for more than five years when the book of Acts was written; and if Rationalists are right as to the date of Acts, it had been for more than forty years.[22]

One more incident connected with this visit to Jerusalem deserves some notice at our hands, not because it is treated as a contradiction between Acts and Galatians, but because it furnishes a striking instance of contradiction between the assailants of Acts. Renan says that Titus consented to be circumcised, but only through the representations of two intruding brethren;[23] while Baur says he was *not* circumcised; and with reference to an interpretation of Paul's words to the effect that Titus was not *compelled* to be circumcised, but submitted to it for the sake of peace, he says, "Nothing can be more absurd."[24]

III. We may next consider some alleged contradictions between Acts and other Epistles of Paul

1. It is claimed under this head that the perfect agreement between Paul and the other Apostles which is set forth in Acts is proved to be unreal by the sentiments of parties in the church of Corinth. Paul speaks of certain parties in that church whose watchwords were, respectively, "I am of Paul, I am of Apollos, I am of Cephas, I am of Christ" (1 Cor 1.12). It is claimed that the parties of Cephas and of Christ held strong Judaistic views, in opposition

---

[21] *Sup. Rel*; Baur, *Paul*, i. 129.

[22] Galatians was written not later than the beginning of the year 58, and Acts not earlier than 63; though according to the Tübingen School, the latter was not written till about the year 100.

[23] *Apostles* 31.

[24] *Paul*, i. 121, 122.

to Paul's; that its leaders had come from Jerusalem with letters of commendation from some of the older Apostles, and that they could not have claimed Cephas as their leader without knowing that he was in sympathy with their views. It is also argued that if this claim of theirs in reference to Peter had been false, Paul could have refuted it by saying so, which he never does.[25] From these assumptions and inferences it is concluded that there could not have been that agreement between Paul and Peter which is claimed in Acts, but that Peter was in open antagonism to Paul. This charge, and the whole theory on which it is based, involves the assumption that the question at issue between these parties was the one about circumcision and keeping the law, and of this there is not the slightest evidence. This subject does not come into view in the Epistle at all; and therefore the antagonism assumed has no appearance of an existence. The only question which comes into view in the Epistle with respect to Paul and the twelve is the one whether Paul was really an Apostle in the sense in which they were. The rebellious parties in the church at Corinth sought to break down the influence of Paul, not by arraying the teaching of the twelve against that of Paul, for there is no intimation of any such antagonism being claimed by them, but by claiming that Paul was not possessed of apostolic authority, such as he was presuming to exercise. They took the name of Peter in this discussion, if Peter's was the real name they took (see 1 Cor 4.6), because he was certainly an Apostle, and the chief of the original twelve. As to the false teachers who headed the party, to assume that they brought their letters of commendation from Jerusalem is to assume what can not be known to be true; and if it were true, it would prove nothing as to the relation between Paul and those by whom the letters were written. Unfortunately, it was, and is, no uncommon thing for men with letters of commendation from good men to make use of them for wicked purposes.

2. The most extreme and inexcusable of all these allegations against the author of Acts is the assertion that, in contradiction

---

[25] Baur, *Paul,* i., 281; *Sup. Rel,* iii. 307–309; 2 Corinthians 3.1.

to his representation of agreement between the older Apostles and Paul, Paul is the very person denounced in unmeasured terms by John in the Epistles to the seven churches of Asia. It is asked, Who but Paul and his followers can be referred to as those who were tried by the church at Ephesus for claiming to be Apostles, and found liars; by those who held the doctrine of Baalam, and taught men to eat things offered to idols; and by the woman Jezebel, who taught the disciples to commit fornication, and to eat things offered to idols?26 The obvious answer is that they were men and women whose teaching and practice were condemned by the teaching of Paul in most emphatic terms— as emphatic as those employed by John. It should also be said that, according to the admission of the very men who make this charge, John had given Paul the right hand of fellowship many years previous at Jerusalem; and it is a reflection on his honor to assume that he here denounces him whom he had acknowledged as a fellow Apostle. Indeed, this charge carries a false theory to the extreme of villification and abuse, and it is unworthy of men who profess to be seeking the truth of history.

3. While Paul in the Epistle to the Romans represents the church in Rome as one of world-wide fame (1.8; 16.16), it is claimed that Acts represents it as being so obscure as not to be known to the Jews who dwelt in Jerusalem—so obscure that the Jews there could speak of Christianity itself "as a thing about which they had still to learn; with which they had not yet come in contact; which was known to them only by hearsay."27 This allegation would be scarcely worthy of notice were it not for the fact that so eminent a commentator as Olshausen understands the representation in Acts in the same way.28 It is shown to be a false representation by a mere glance at the passage in Acts which is referred to (28.17–22). In response to Paul's statement about himself, the Jews are represented as saying: "We neither received letters from Judea concerning thee, nor did any of the brethren

---

26 *Sup. Rel.,* iii. 314; *Rev.,* ii. 2, 14, 20.

27 Baur, *Paul,* i. 326.

28 *Ib.,* 324–326, *n.*

come hither and report or speak any harm of thee. But we desire to hear of thee what thou thinkest: for as concerning this sect, it is known to us that it is everywhere spoken against." Now these words, instead of showing that the Jews were ignorant of Christianity, so ignorant that it was a thing about which they had still to learn, shows the very opposite. It shows that it was known to them, and known as a sect which was everywhere spoken against. It was Paul of whom they had not heard, and their remark does not show that they had heard nothing of him, but only that they had not heard "any harm" of him.

We have now discussed all of the principal charges of contradiction brought against the author of Acts, and the reader must judge whether any of them can be sustained. We shall hereafter institute quite a different comparison between this book and others, by which it will appear from undesigned coincidences that it is surprisingly correct in even the minutest details of its narration.

SEVEN

Undesigned Coincidences Between the Gospels

Having now applied to the Gospels and Acts the principles of Canon V. (page 4), with reference to the alleged contradictions between their narrations, we next propose to apply the same Canon with reference to incidental agreements of the former with one another, and of the last with the Gospels and Paul's Epistles. As we have stated (page 30), this evidence, when the points of incidental agreement are numerous and striking, is the strongest possible evidence of the accuracy of a set of writers dealing with a common series of events. As in the ease of alleged contradictions, we shall not attempt to exhaust this source of evidence, but we shall consider only the more important and striking of the coincidences, and we shall take them up in the order of their occurrence.

1. John the Baptist is represented as making the following speech concerning Jesus: "I have beheld the Spirit descending as a dove out of heaven; and it abode upon him. And I knew him not; but he that sent me to baptize in water, he said to me, Upon whomsoever thou shalt see the Spirit descending and abiding on him, the same is he that baptizeth in the Holy Spirit. And I have seen, and have borne witness that this is the Son of God" (1.32–34). Now it is very clear, from what John says he had seen, that he could testify that Jesus was he who was to baptize in the Holy Spirit; but how could he from this testify that he was the Son of

God? There is nothing in the previous narrative from which this inference could be drawn. But this inference, or rather this positive assertion, is accounted for when we turn to the other Gospels, and find that every one of them asserts that when the Spirit descended as a dove a voice was heard in heaven, saying, "This is my beloved Son, in whom I am well pleased." The latter statement accounts for and explains the former, and therefore they mutually throw credit on each other.

2. The accounts given by Matthew and Luke of the call of the four fishermen appear to be contradictory, so different are the details which they give, and it has been treated as a real contradiction by skeptics.[1] But the accounts touch each other at such points as to incidentally explain each the other. Matthew says that when Jesus was walking by the lake shore he saw Peter and Andrew "casting a net into the sea"; and that when he came to James and John, they were in the boat, mending their nets" (4.18,21). Now both of these incidents are accounted for by Luke's statement, that they had been fishing all the preceding night (v 5). A whole night's fishing would naturally necessitate mending some of the nets in the morning; and if it was early in the morning, it would be very natural that the two men whose nets were not broken should not yet have desisted from their toil, especially as they had caught nothing through the night. Again, Matthew represents the four as following Jesus at his word, leaving their business in order to do so, when, so far as his narrative informs us, they had neither seen nor heard of him before that hour. Had we Matthew's Gospel alone, it would be impossible to account for this action on their part, without the conjecture, which rationalists would not have allowed, that in some way unexplained they had formed a previous acquaintance with him. But all is explained without conjecture, when we learn from Luke's independent narrative that when Jesus approached the lake, Peter and Andrew drew their boat ashore, went out of it to wash their nets, allowed Jesus to sit in the boat while he taught the people, and then, thrusting out

---

[1] Strauss, *New Life*, ii. 129, 130.

into the deep water again at his bidding, took a draught of fishes which appeared to them to be miraculous (5.1–8).

3. Mark represents Jesus as going from the synagogue meeting into the house of Simon and Andrew, and there healing the former's mother-in-law of a fever. This occurred, as we judge from the fact that the synagogue had just been dismissed, not long after noon. Mark then represents the whole town as being excited by the cure, and bringing all their sick to Jesus to be healed, but not till evening when the "sun had set" (1.29–33). He gives us no reason for this delay; but leaves us to what would be endless and unsatisfactory conjecture and doubt on the point, if we had no narrative but his. But on reading Luke's account of the incident, we learn that it occurred on the sabbath (4.31); and on reading the Gospel of John, we learn in an entirely different connection that the Jews held it to be unlawful to bear a burden on the sabbath (5.10); and thus is explained the strange delay of the people in bringing their sick. Now it is impossible to believe either that Luke said it was on the sabbath to confirm what Mark says about the delay, or that John mentions the rebuke of the man who carried his bed on the sabbath to confirm what either Mark or Luke says about the people of Capernaum; yet the confirmation is complete, and the evidence is the stronger from the search which we have had to find it.

4. Matthew's statement that John the Baptist heard in his prison of the works of Jesus, and sent a message to him by his disciples, assumes that his friends had easy access to him in his prison, contrary to what we would naturally suppose from the facts connected with his arrest by Herod, and his subsequent cruel execution. This circumstance is not accounted for until we read in Mark that, notwithstanding the imprisonment, "Herod feared John, knowing that he was a righteous man and holy, and kept him safe. And when he heard him he was much perplexed, and he heard him gladly" (6.20). Thus the writer who says nothing about John's message from the prison furnishes an item, in a totally different connection of thought, which accounts for his ability to send it.

5. Matthew says that when Herod heard of Jesus he "said to his servants, This is John the Baptist" (14.1–2). It is very natural that he should have made the remark to his servants, that is, to his officers; but the question naturally arises, how did Matthew, or any of the disciples, who seem to have been far removed from connection with Herod's household, learn that he did so? To the answer Matthew nowhere gives us the slightest clew; but in a purely incidental way we obtain a natural answer from Luke. The latter writer mentions, among the women who ministered to Jesus out of their substance, Joanna, the wife of Chuza, Herod's steward (8. 2–3). How certainly would Chuza tell his wife what Herod said about him whom she so admired, and how certainly would she tell it to Jesus and the disciples! Furthermore, the same writer tells us that Manaen, afterward a noted teacher and prophet in the church at Antioch, was Herod's foster-brother; and thus, without having Matthew's account in his mind, he gives his readers another clew to the source of Matthew's knowledge of the private conversation of Herod.

6. Mark informs us that on a certain occasion, when the apostles returned to Jesus from a tour of preaching and healing, there were so many persons about them coming and going that they had no leisure so much as to eat bread; and that on this account Jesus ordered them into a boat that they might cross the lake and rest awhile in a desert place (6.30–32). So eager and pressing a crowd is not mentioned on any other occasion, and we naturally wonder what could have been the cause of it; but on this point Mark leaves us completely in the dark. Here again we might have employed conjecture, but we could never have reached any certainty had not Matthew, who says not a word about the pressure of the crowd, informed us that just at that time some disciples of John had arrived, and brought to Jesus and the people the exciting news that John had been beheaded by Herod (14.12–14). Furthermore, these two circumstances combined help to explain a strange act of the people on that very day, which is mentioned only by John, and for which John gives no adequate cause. It is the

circumstance that the multitude, after being fed with the loaves and fishes, were about to take Jesus by force and make him a king (6.15). The miracle of feeding is not a sufficient cause for this, yet it is all that is mentioned by John; but when we consider what is said by Matthew about the fresh and exasperating news of the cruel death of John, who had hitherto been the leader of the people, and the excitement which had preceded the crossing of the lake, all is most naturally explained. And how perfectly obvious it is that none of these coincidences could have been the work of design! How certain that they result only from the fact that each of the three writers tells the exact truth so far as he speaks at all!

7. In describing the preceding event, the feeding of the five thousand, Mark says that Jesus commanded the multitude to sit down "on the green grass" (6.39). John says that there was much grass in the place, but he says nothing about its being green. He says, however, that this feeding occurred when the feast of the Passover was at hand, and we know that this feast occurred at the next full moon after the vernal equinox, the very time in Palestine when grass is abundant and green. A few weeks before this it is not abundant, and a few weeks later it is dry. This combination of coincidences connected with the account of feeding the five thousand not only shows that the writers are very accurate in their accounts, but that they were aiming to tell the exact truth in the whole story.

8. Luke represents Jesus as preaching in Nazareth before he began his labors in Capernaum (4.16, 31–38); yet he quotes him as saying to the people in Nazareth, "Doubtless ye will say unto me this parable, Physician, heal thyself; whatsoever we have heard done at Capernaum, do also here in thine own country." With Luke's narrative alone before us, it would be impossible to account for this language. Not only so, but the course of his narrative implies that Jesus had not been in Capernaum since his return into Galilee. When we turn to John, however, we find that on his first arrival in Galilee, while he was yet at Cana and had not yet gone to Nazareth, he healed a nobleman's son in Capernaum,

the cure being effected without his being in Capernaum at all. This, then, accounts for the demand which the people of Nazareth were disposed to make; and the very fact that he had done this in Capernaum while in Cana, which was twenty miles distant, gave more force to the demand that he should do something similar in Nazareth where he was present. This very striking coincidence, let it be observed, is drawn from a portion of John's Gospel which it has suited the purpose of rationalists to particularly discredit.

9. John gives no account of the birth of Jesus; neither does he tell us the place of his birth; but he represents people in Jerusalem as contending that he could not be the Christ, because, instead of coming from Bethlehem as the Christ should, he had come from Galilee. Even the chief priests themselves thus argued (7.41–42, 52). Had we John's Gospel alone, we would not be able to determine whether the objection was well taken or not. He evidently takes it for granted that his readers would know that it was not well taken, but he does not himself furnish us the means of so knowing. It is only when we turn to Matthew and Luke that we find the information that he was actually born in Bethlehem. Thus the information which we find in two of the Gospels is assumed in the third as if it were already in our possession, and the tacit assumption proves to be correct.

10. Mark gives the following very singular account of the feelings of the disciples when Jesus started on his last direct journey to Jerusalem: "And they were in the way going up to Jerusalem; and Jesus was going before them; and they were amazed; and they that followed him were afraid." He then goes on to state that Jesus, as if he were desirous of increasing this fear and amazement, took the twelve aside and told them that he would be betrayed in Jerusalem and killed (10.32–34). There is nothing in his preceding narrative to account for the beginning of this fear and amazement; and there is nothing in the preceding parts of Matthew or Luke. Had we none but these three gospels, it would be impossible, except by conjecture, which rationalists would seriously object to, to assign a cause for these feelings. Should that conjecture be that

Jesus had been in Jerusalem before this, and had met with such treatment that his disciples were amazed that he should return thither, we would be charged with imagining facts to explain an incredible statement. But this is the exact state of the case as we learn from John's Gospel, which informs us of five previous visits to Jerusalem, at the close of the last four of which the Jews had sought to kill Jesus (John 2.13; 5.1, 18; 7.10; 8.59; 10.22–23, 31, 39; 11.7–9, 53). We find, too, that when about to go on the last of these five visits, the disciples even that early expressed their astonishment, saving, "Rabbi, the Jews were but now seeking to stone thee; and goest thou thither again?" And when he would go, one of them said, "Let us also go, that we may die with him" (John 11.8, 16). When, after all this, he starts thither again, there is no longer any wonder that, as Mark says, they were amazed and followed him with fear. Thus we see that not only do John's statements account for and explain that of Mark, but they are really necessary to this end; they make Mark's statement most credible, and his remark reflects credit back on them. Let it be noted, too, that these very visits to Jerusalem are a part of the Gospel of John which have been blindly treated by rationalists as inconsistent with the narratives of the Synoptists.[2]

11. The minute circumstance as to where the ass was procured on which Jesus rode into Jerusalem, will furnish our next example. Matthew says that it was procured at Bethphage; and he says nothing of any other village (21.1–2). Mark and Luke both say that Jesus and his company had arrived near Bethphage and Bethany, and that in ordering two disciples to go for the ass Jesus said, "Go your way into the village over against you "—leaving it uncertain which of the villages he meant (Mark 11.1; Luke 19.29–30). John simply says that they "found an ass," without saying where, though he says that they spent the previous night in Bethany, and the village over against them must have been Bethphage. Here, then, are three accounts differing from Matthew's in omitting the particular which he mentions, while Matthew's

---

[2] *Sup. Rel.*, ii. 453.

differs from all of them by omitting nearly all of the details which they mention; yet even in a matter so minute as this there is perfect agreement, and the ambiguity of Mark and Luke is cleared up by the briefer statement of Matthew. How could this be if all were not speaking the exact truth so far as they spoke at all?

12. While John mentions five visits of Jesus to Jerusalem or its vicinity, between his baptism and his last visit, the other writers mention not one. This is held by some unbelievers as proof that the latter knew of no such visits; by some as proof that the author of John misrepresented the facts; and by all as a contradiction. But we find in both Matthew and Luke incidental proof that John is right, and that the others were not ignorant of these visits. They both quote the apostrophe to Jerusalem in which Jesus says, "How often would I have gathered thy children together as a hen gathers her brood under her wings, and ye would not" (Matt 23.30–39; Luke 13.34). He could not have made this attempt often without being often in the city; and the quotation of his language implies the knowledge that these visits had taken place. This agreement, appearing in the midst of apparent contradiction, and being discoverable only after a careful search, affords the stronger evidence from these two considerations.

13. Our next example is a coincidence of a topographical kind. In Mark's account of the withering of the barren fig tree, the disciples are represented as not seeing the tree until the next morning after the curse was pronounced on it, although they went out to Bethany the next afternoon, and we should suppose that they passed by it (11.14, 19–20). This appears quite strange, if not unaccountable, until we inspect the route of travel between Jerusalem and Bethany, and find that there are two different paths, by either of which a person may pass up the western side of the Mount of Olives from the one place to the other. One of the paths is very steep, while the other has a gradual slope. The steep path is the shorter of the two, and the one which a person would naturally take when coming down the mountain side toward the city, while the other would naturally be preferred by one going the other way.

Now Jesus was coming into the city when he cursed the tree, and this accounts for the failure of the disciples to see it as they went out, and also for their seeing it when they came in the next morning. A coincidence so minute as this, and so artless, can be the work of none but an accurate writer.

14. Matthew and Mark both state that when the Pharisees sent men to Jesus to tempt him with the question about paying tribute to Caesar, they sent to him, with the others, Herodians. The particular bearing of this circumstance is not apparent until Luke, who says nothing about the Herodians being sent, brings out in a totally different connection the fact that Herod was at that time in the city. This last circumstance accounts for the former, yet it is impossible to suppose that it was mentioned for this purpose.

15. John says that Jesus and his disciples arrived at Bethany on his last visit to the city "six days before the passover." Neither of the other Evangelists says how long it was, but Mark, without apparently aiming to count the time, incidentally mentions the days as they pass, and the count which we are able to make from his statements agrees with the statement of John. On the next day after the arrival at Bethany the public entry took place (John 12.1, 12), and of course this was five days from the passover. Now, following Mark, we find that, counting the day of the public entry as one, at the close of which they went out to Bethany, the next day on which the fig tree was cursed would be two (11.11– 12); the day following, on which they found the tree withered, is three (11.20); and when at the close of that day it is said, "Now after the two days was the feast of the passover" (14.1), we have the five days, and the count is even with that of John. This is unmistakably a case of agreement which could have resulted from nothing but strict accuracy of statement on the part of both writers.

16. The fact that when Jesus was about to be arrested one of his disciples, whom John alone designates as Peter, cut off the ear of the servant of the high priest, is attested by all four of our Evangelists. They all assert, too, that when Peter came into the house of the high priest he was accused of being one of the disciples of

Jesus; but strange to say, the servants and soldiers who make this accusation have nothing to say about the very serious offense of cutting off a man's ear in resistance to arrest. Stranger still, as we learn from John, who knew the servant and calls him Malchus, one of the persons who accused Peter was a kinsman of Malchus, and yet even he says nothing of cutting off the ear. This silence has been treated as proof that the ear was not cut off, and that all the Evangelists are here at fault; but the true explanation is found in a statement by Luke, evidently not made for the purpose of explanation, that when the ear was cut off Jesus healed it (Luke 22.51). Not even this would have saved Peter from censure, had it been possible to speak of the affair without giving evidence in favor of Jesus, whom Peter's accusers were seeking to condemn as an impostor. The incidental way in which this explanation is furnished goes far to establish also the reality of the miracle.

17. Matthew states that in mocking Jesus the servants of the high priest "smote him with the palms of their hands, saying, Prophesy to us, thou Christ; who is he that smote thee?" (26.68). Now this, were it not for a circumstance which we are about to notice, would undoubtedly be declared by unfriendly critics a piece of absurdity; for they would say, Why ask him to prophesy who smote him, when his assailant stood before his face? Believers would, of course, contend that something which Matthew omits would doubtless make the matter plain if we only knew a little more of the circumstances; but this would be ridiculed, as all other such suppositions are. But when we turn to Luke we find the very circumstance which Matthew omits, and the manner in which it is supplied shows clearly enough that it was not designed to explain Matthew's account. He says that they blindfolded Jesus (22.14). If Matthew had been making up his story he would probably have been on his guard against such omissions; but as he was conscious of writing only the truth, he left his statement to take care of itself.

18. All four of the Evangelists, in the account of Peter's denial of the Lord, state that it was a maid connected with the high

priest's household that first charged him with being one of the disciples. If we had only the first three, this would be difficult to account for, seeing that the men who had arrested him would be naturally much more likely to know Peter than the maid whose duties were confined within the house; and especially would this be so from the fact that Peter had used a sword in the garden. In this ease, as in the preceding, some hypothesis as to the omission of details would be necessary to preserve the credibility of the writers. But when we turn to John all is explained by the supply of the omitted circumstance. He tells us that Peter was at first standing at the door outside, until John asked the maid who kept the door to let him in. As John was known to be one of the disciples, his request that Peter might be admitted within the court naturally excited the maid's suspicion, and led her to be first in making the accusation.

19. The manner in which Mary Magdalene is spoken of in the Gospels affords another remarkable coincidence of the kind which we are considering. Matthew introduces her first at the time of the crucifixion, as one among "many women beholding from afar, who had followed Jesus from Galilee, ministering to him" (27.55–56). This shows that for some reason she had thus followed him and ministered to him, but it leaves us in the dark as to the particular motive which had actuated her. John introduces her also in the same group of women, without saying how she happened to be at the cross, but he indicates her great devotion to him by her visit to the tomb on the morning of the first day of the week; her extreme agitation when she found that the tomb was empty; and her weeping when she despaired of finding the body of Jesus (19.25; 20.1, 11). The reader would be utterly at a loss to conjecture the special cause of this devotion, and he might conjecture in vain but for a remark which is made incidentally by both Mark and Luke, that out of Mary Jesus had cast seven demons (Mark 16.9; Luke 8.2). While this explains perfectly her devotion, neither Mark nor Luke can be suspected of making the remark for this purpose, and it is therefore an undesigned coincidence.

Thus far we have considered coincidences between the several Gospels; and these, taken in connection with other evidences which have preceded them, appear sufficient to establish their authenticity as above that of any other writings to which the same tests can be applied. We now turn to Acts of Apostles, and we shall try it in the same way.

EIGHT

Undesigned Coincidences Between Acts and Paul's Epistles

We have seen that in assailing this book rationalists rely chiefly on its alleged inconsistency with certain statements in Paul's acknowledged Epistles, and especially with some in Galatians. We now propose to point out undesigned coincidences between these Epistles and Acts, and we shall see that the Epistles acknowledged by rationalists to be genuine confirm Acts in so many points as to make up a supplemental account of Paul's career.

1. Paul is first introduced in Acts as a persecutor of the church, giving consent to the death of Stephen, and afterward laying waste the church by entering into every house and seizing and dragging to prison both men and women. In these proceedings, though called a "young man," he is represented as a leader (7.58; 8.1–3). With this corresponds precisely his own statement in Galatians: "Ye have heard of my manner of life in time past in the Jews' religion, how that, beyond measure, I persecuted the church of God and made havoc of it; and I advanced in the Jews' religion beyond many of mine own age among my countrymen, being more exceedingly zealous for the traditions of my fathers" (1.13–14).

2. The next incident given in Acts is his journey to Damascus in pursuance of his persecuting policy, and his interview on the way with the Lord Jesus (9.1–9). In a later passage he is repre-

sented as receiving from the Lord on this occasion a commission to preach to the Gentiles and to the people of Israel (26.15–18). In the Epistle this interview is not described, but, like his career in the "Jews' religion," just previously mentioned, it is alluded to as being already known to the Galatians. He says: "But when it was the good pleasure of God, who separated me even from my mother's womb, and called me through his grace, to reveal his Son in me, that I might preach him among the Gentiles; immediately I conferred not with flesh and blood" (1.15–16). Now, whatever one may think of the miraculous incidents related at this point in Acts, there can be no doubt that in the remark just quoted from Paul he refers to the incident of his conversion to the faith of Christ. This, then, confirms the statement that his conversion occurred on this journey, and thus far it confirms the account in Acts. Furthermore, he speaks of this incident as a revelation: "When it was the good pleasure of God to *reveal* his Son." But a revelation is a miracle; and to this extent he confirms the representation that a miracle was wrought on the occasion. He uses the words, "to reveal his Son in me"; but he means by this not, as rationalists have asserted, to make an inward revelation, but to reveal his Son to the world as still living in heavenly glory, by using Paul's person as the instrument. In what way his person was made the instrument of this revelation we could not know from the Epistle, the process being already known to his readers, and therefore omitted from his statement; but the history conies to our aid as if written for the very purpose of giving us the desired information, though certainly having no such purpose in view. It shows that Christ was revealed in him by the fact that he was blinded by the sight, and remained so until the Jews in Damascus knew the fact, and until, on account of the new convictions which the incident had implanted in him, he was baptized. Thus by an allusion which, on account of its brevity, we could not have fully understood without the narrative in Acts, the latter narrative is confirmed and the obscure allusions of the Epistle are made intelligible. It is scarcely possible that two independent documents should more positively confirm each other.

3. The next item in Acts is Paul's successful preaching in Damascus, and the expressions of amazement by those who heard him at the change which had taken place in him (9.20–22). Nothing is said expressly in Galatians of this preaching, but it is implied in Paul's words, "Immediately I conferred not with flesh and blood" (1.15–16). This clause is evidently elliptical, the word "immediately" qualifying some word understood. This word must be supplied from the preceding clause, "that I might preach him among the Gentiles." The meaning is, I immediately preached him, and did not confer with flesh and blood before I did so. This, then, asserts an immediate beginning of his preaching, and of course a beginning in Damascus. The same ellipsis is to be supplied in the two clauses which follow about going into Arabia, and returning to Damascus, as if he had said, "I went away into Arabia to preach him, and again I returned unto Damascus to preach him." Thus while Acts speaks in general terms of his preaching in Damascus, Paul, by his allusions, brief as they are, shows that he preached there at two separate intervals, separated by a preaching tour in Arabia.[1]

4. The author of Acts next describes Paul's departure from Damascus. The items of the description are, first, a counsel of the Jews to kill him; second, their watching the gates day and night "that they might kill him"; third, his being let down by the disciples "through the wall" and "in a basket," by night (9.23–25). In

---

[1] The conjecture that Paul's excursion into Arabia was not for the purpose of preaching to the Jews in its town and villages, but for the purpose of meditating on his new relations to Christ, and preparing himself mentally for the work now before him, although it is adopted by such men as Alford, Lightfoot, and Farrar, appears to me so utterly at variance with the restless activity and burning zeal of the apostle as to be altogether incredible. The addition to this conjecture, that he went as far as Mount Sinai, more than four hundred miles from Damascus, where Elijah had retired before him, instead of confirming the original hypothesis, seems rather to weaken it; for Paul knew very well that when Elijah went thither he was rebuked by the Lord, who demanded, "Elijah, what doest thou here?" and that he was ordered back to his work. In the absence of all evidence for this conjecture, we should be governed in judging of the purpose of the excursion by what we know of Paul's habits during the remainder of his life; and by this standard we should judge that he was one of the last men on earth to waste any precious moments, not to speak of a year or two, in idle meditation in the desert, while the cause which he had espoused was now struggling for an existence. (Alford, *Com. Gal.,* i.18; Lightfoot, *Com. on Galatian's,* note, p. 87; Farrar, *Life of Paul,* chap. xi.)

Galatians nothing is said of this; Paul says only that after three years he went up to Jerusalem. But in 2 Corinthians, another admitted Epistle of Paul, we have this statement: "In Damascus the governor under Aretas the king guarded the city of Damascus, in order to take me: and through a window was I let down in a basket by the wall, and escaped his hands" (11.32– 33). This account is so different from the one in Acts as to make it quite certain that neither could have been taken from the other, and that neither could have been written to explain the other. Yet Paul's account does really explain some points in which the other would be very obscure but for the explanation. First, we would wonder how the Jews could dare, in a foreign city like Damascus, to watch the gates night and day to kill a man whom they hated; and our wonder would never cease, did we not know from Paul's account that the governor of the city was watching for the same purpose, and that therefore the Jews were acting in concert with him. Second, it would be a mystery how Paul could be let down *"through* the wall" in a basket, had we not his own more explicit statement, that it was "through a *window."* When, in addition to this, we visit Damascus at the present day, and observe that in one part of the city there are houses whose uppermost stories rest on the wall, with windows looking out over the wall, the accuracy of both writers is strikingly attested.

5. The next incident in Acts is Paul's arrival in Jerusalem, where the disciples, though they may have heard of his conversion, were doubtful whether he was a real disciple till they were reassured by Barnabas; and where he preached boldly until the Jews went about to kill him, when the brethren took him down to Caesarea and sent him away to Tarsus (9.26–30). This same journey to Jerusalem comes next in Paul's account of himself. He names the apostles whom he saw there, Cephas and James. Had he written not to tell the truth, but to confirm Acts, he would have named more of them to agree better with the plural of apostles used in Acts; but he gives the exact number, and it still confirms Acts. He says nothing about his preaching in Jerusalem, or about the plots

to kill him, or about his departure to Tarsus; but he next says, "Then I came into the regions of Syria and Cilicia," which agrees with the statement of Acts, that he was sent away to Tarsus, the capital of Cilicia.

6. Having sent Paul away to Tarsus, Acts leaves him there until Barnabas goes over to Tarsus to seek for Saul, finds him, and brings him to Antioch (11.25–26). The interval, as we gather from the received chronology of Acts, was from the year 39 to the year 43, about four years. Luke says nothing as to how Paul was engaged during this time, though we should readily infer, from his ceaseless activity at other times, that he was preaching; and this inference is confirmed by the very next statement which Paul makes of himself. He says: "I was still unknown by face to the churches of Judea which were in Christ: but they only heard say, He that once persecuted us now preaches the faith of which he once made havoc; and they glorified God in me" (Gal 1.22–24).

7. In Acts we next follow Paul on his first tour among the Gentiles, the incidents of which he has no occasion to mention in his Epistles; but even here, where the Epistles and the history stand most widely apart, they are not without coincidence. On this tour Paul was stoned at Lystra by Jews who had followed him from Antioch and Iconium, and left for dead. Many years afterward, when he was enumerating to the Corinthians his various sufferings for Christ, he says, "Once was I stoned" (2 Cor 11.25); and the reference is undoubtedly to the stoning mentioned in Acts.

8. After Paul's return from his first tour the controversy about circumcision arose in Antioch, an account of which is given in the fifteenth chapter of Acts, and another in the second chapter of Galatians, so different as to be declared contradictory. We have already considered the points of alleged contradiction, and these are sufficient proof that neither account was made up from the other. We now propose to point out the coincidences between them.

(1) The persons sent up to Jerusalem are differently represented, yet the representations are harmonious. In Acts they are Paul and

Barnabas and "certain others of them." In Galatians, Paul says: "I went up again to Jerusalem with Barnabas, taking Titus also with me." Now, if the record in Acts had been made up from the Epistle, it would naturally have specified Titus instead of including him in the vague expression, "certain others"; and if it had been made up at random without accurate knowledge, it could scarcely have hit upon this expression.

(2) The purpose of the mission is expressly stated in Acts; they were sent up to the apostles and elders about this question of circumcising the Gentile converts. In Galatians the same purpose is implied, though it is nowhere expressly stated. It is implied in the struggle over the attempted circumcision of Titus, and in the agreement entered into between Paul and the other three apostles as to their respective missions to the circumcision and the uncircumcision. But while this implication is obvious when the two accounts are read in connection, it is not sufficiently apparent in the Epistle, if read alone, to have suggested the account in the history.

(3) Acts represents the apostles Peter and James as expressing, in a meeting of the church, full approval of the position held on the mooted question by Barnabas and Paul; while the Epistle, without mentioning the public meeting, declares that the same apostles, in a private meeting not mentioned in Acts, expressed the same approval. The fact of this expression of approval is the same in both accounts, while the two combine to show that it was expressed first privately and afterward publicly. That the two accounts vary so widely in details, yet without contradiction, and agree so perfectly in the main result, can be explained only on the ground that each is accurate so far as it goes.

(4) In both accounts the persons in opposition to Paul, though represented in quite different terms, are the same. In Acts they are styled "certain of the sect of the Pharisees who believed"; in Galatians, "false brethren privily brought in, who came in privily to spy out our liberty which we have in Christ Jesus, that they might bring us into bondage." The two modes of describing them differ so widely as to show that neither description was

taken from the other, and the points of coincidence can be due to nothing but the truthfulness of both.

9. When Paul started on his second tour, he took Silas with him in place of Barnabas, who was his companion on the first tour; and Silas continued with him, according to Acts, until they were together in Corinth, when he disappears from the narrative and is seen in it no more (15.40; 18.5). In striking harmony with this we find that in the two Epistles to the Thessalonians, which were written during Paul's stay in Corinth, the name of Silas is joined with Paul's in the salutation. This shows that Acts is correct in its representation, and it affords no mean evidence of the authenticity of these two Epistles.

10. Among the first incidents that occurred on this second tour was the circumcision of Timothy (16.1–3). This act, occurring so soon after Paul's positive refusal to circumcise Titus, is a surprise; and when it is considered in connection with Paul's well known position that the law of Moses was no longer binding, it has the appearance of inconsistency, and it has been declared incredible.[2] But here it is said that he circumcised Timothy "because of the Jews who dwelt there; for they all knew that his father was a Greek"; that is, it was done to prevent that prejudice against Timothy, as an uncircumcised half Hebrew, which would have crippled his influence among the Jews. Now, this is the very motive by which Paul himself declares that he was governed in his dealings with the Jews. He says: "To the Jews I became as a Jew, that I might gain Jews; to them that are under the law, as under the law, not being myself under the law, that I might gain them that are under the law" (1 Cor 9.20). He could not have acted on this rule and refused the circumcision of men of Jewish blood like Timothy; and yet the rule did not bind him to the circumcision of Gentiles like Titus. So, then, Acts represents Paul as pursuing, in the case of Timothy, the line of conduct laid down in his Epistle. Instead of

---

[2] "That the same Paul who in Jerusalem resisted with all his might the proposal to circumcise Titus for the sake of the Jews and Jewish Christians, should soon after himself have caused Timothy to be circumcised from regard to the same persons, belongs undoubtedly to the simply incredible side of the Acts of the Apostles." (Baur, *Paul*, i. 129, note).

the act being incredible, therefore, and reflecting discredit on Acts, it has an important bearing in the opposite direction.

11. After the circumcision of Timothy at Lystra, Paul and his company are represented as passing through various districts of Asia Minor until they came to Troas, whence they went over into Macedonia, and preached at Philippi. During the stay here Paul and Silas are represented as being scourged and east into prison, whence they were released by proclaiming their Roman citizenship. To the church which he established there Paul afterward addressed an Epistle, and in it occurs the following passage: "To you it has been granted in the behalf of Christ, not only to believe on him, but also to suffer on his behalf: having the same conflict which ye saw in me, and now hear to be in me" (Phil 1.29–30). Here is an evident allusion to suffering which they had seen him endure, and it corresponds to the suffering mentioned in Acts; but the reference is too vague to be the work of an impostor, yet it is sufficiently definite to show that he did suffer somewhat as is represented in Acts. He makes another and similar allusion to the same suffering in writing to the church in Thessalonica, to which city he went directly from Philippi. He says: "Having suffered before, and been shamefully entreated, as you know, in Philippi, we waxed bold in our God to speak to you the gospel of God in much affliction" (1 Thess 2.2). There can be no doubt that this is another allusion to the same incident, yet it is made in a manner so incidental as to prove that it was not intended to support the statement of Acts. Thus these two Epistles unite to sustain the reliability of the narrative in Acts, while it in turn reflects credit on them as genuine productions of Paul's pen.

12. In the Epistle to the Thessalonians, Paul says: "For ye, brethren, became imitators of the churches of God which are in Judea in Christ Jesus: for ye also suffered the same things of your own countrymen, even as they did of the Jews" (1 Thess 2.14). Now this at first glance seems to be inconsistent with the account in Acts; for there the Jews are represented as the instigators of the persecution in Thessalonica, and they might be fairly represented

as the authors of it. But on closer inspection we see that they "took to them certain vile fellows of the rabble, and gathering a crowd, set the city on an uproar; and assaulting the house of Jason, they sought to bring them forth to the people" (17.5). Thus a fact obscurely brought out in the history is mentioned as a well known circumstance in the Epistle—well known, that is, to the victims of the persecution.

13. The coincidences between First Corinthians, the first in order of time of Paul's admitted Epistles, and Acts, are numerous and striking. We shall mention a few of them briefly. According to Acts, he came to Ephesus, whence the Epistle was written (1 Cor 16.8–9), from Galatia and Phrygia (18.23; 19.1); and this is implied in the Epistle by the remark, "Now concerning the collection for the saints, as I gave order to the churches in Galatia, so also do ye" (16.1). According to Acts, Priscilla and Aquila had gone to Ephesus with Paul (18.18–19); and in the Epistle written from Ephesus, he sends to the Corinthians their salutation (16.19). According to Acts, Apollos visited the church which Paul had planted in Corinth, and labored in it successfully (18.24–28); and in the Epistle Paul alludes to this by saying of the church, "I planted, Apollos watered, but God gave the increase" (3.6). According to Acts, Paul's success at Ephesus was at one time so great that "not a few of them who practised curious arts brought their books together and burned them before all: and they counted the price of them, and found it fifty thousand pieces of silver. So mightily grew the word of the Lord, and prevailed" (19.19–20); and in the Epistle he says: "I will tarry at Ephesus until Pentecost; for a great and effectual door is open to me, and there are many adversaries" (16.8–9). According to Acts, while Paul was preaching at Ephesus, as an indirect result of his preaching, "all they who dwelt in Asia heard the word of the Lord, both Jews and Greeks" (19.10); and in the Epistle he says to the Corinthians, "The churches of Asia salute you" (16.19).

14. In the second Epistle to the Corinthians we find a number of similar coincidences with Acts, and also a much larger number

with the first Epistle to the same church, with which our present argument is not concerned. In Acts we are told that under the leadership of Demetrius, a silversmith, a mob was raised to assault Paul, that they seized Gaius and Aristarchus, companions of Paul, and rushed into the theater; that Paul, evidently unwilling that these two friends should suffer in his stead, "was minded to enter in to the people," but that the disciples suffered him not, and that certain of the 'chief officers' of Asia also sent to him and besought him not to 'adventure himself into the theater'" (19.23–31). In the Epistle Paul says: "For we would not have you ignorant, brethren, concerning our affliction which befell us in Asia, that we were weighed down exceedingly beyond our power, insomuch that we despaired of life: yea, we ourselves have had the answer of death within ourselves, that we should not trust in ourselves, but in God who raiseth the dead; who delivered us out of so great a death, and will deliver" (1.8–10). On this coincidence Paley well says; "I can not believe that any forger whatever should fall upon an expedient so refined as to exhibit sentiments adapted to a situation, and leave his readers to find out that situation from the history; still less that the author of a history should go about to frame facts and circumstances fitted to supply the sentiments which he found in the letter."[3] In Acts it is said that after Paul left Athens and went to Corinth, Silas and Timothy came to him from Macedonia (18.1, 5); and in the Epistle Paul says to the Corinthians: "When I was present with you and was in want, I was not a burden on any man; for the brethren, when they came from Macedonia, supplied the measure of my want" (11.9). Here it is apparent that brethren came from Macedonia, and the way in which they are mentioned, "the brethren, when they came from Macedonia," shows that they were well known brethren; and the remark agrees perfectly with the fact that Silas and Timothy had come as stated in Acts, while it shows the additional circumstance for which it is chiefly introduced: that they brought means to supply Paul's personal wants. In the account of Paul's first visit to Corinth, it

---

[3] *Horae Paulinae, in loco.*

is evident that he went not beyond that city to evangelize more distant localities, but returned thence to Antioch whence he had started out (18.18–22); and in the Epistle he expresses the hope that, "as your faith groweth, we shall be magnified in you according to our province unto further abundance, so as to preach the gospel even to the parts beyond you" (10.15–16). It seems impossible that a coincidence such as this should be the result of contrivance or forgery.

15. We shall continue this line of evidence no farther than to include some coincidences found in the Epistle to the Romans, the only one of the Epistles of Paul acknowledged by skeptics to be genuine which we have not yet employed. Near the close of the Epistle the writer says: "But now I go to Jerusalem, ministering to the saints. For it hath been the good pleasure of Macedonia and Achaia to make a certain contribution for the poor among the saints who are at Jerusalem" (15.25–26). From this it appears that a journey to Jerusalem was about to be undertaken, and that the purpose of it was to minister to the poor saints in that city. Certain statements in the two Epistles to the Corinthians make it obvious that the journey in question is the one described in the twentieth and twenty-first chapters of Acts. In that description, however, though very minute in many particulars, not a word is said about the purpose of the journey or about any contribution; but strange as this omission is, both items are brought out in an incidental way in a later passage, and under peculiar circumstances. After Paul had reached Jerusalem and performed his task, had been cast into prison and sent to Caesarea to be tried by Felix the governor, in his defense before the latter he says: "Now, after many years I came to bring alms to my nation and offerings" (24.17). In Acts it is said of Paul, while he was yet in Ephesus, that he "purposed in the Spirit, when he had passed through Macedonia and Achaia, to go to Jerusalem, saying, After that I have been there, I must also see Rome" (19.21). When this Epistle was written he had accomplished so much of this purpose as to have passed through Macedonia and Achaia, and was now about to prosecute it further.

He says in the Epistle: "I would not have you ignorant, brethren, that oftentimes I purposed to come to you (and was hindered hitherto), that I might have some fruit among you even as among the rest of the Gentiles" (1.13), which confirms the statement in Acts that he had this purpose. Again in the Epistle, after speaking of his journey to Jerusalem, he says: "When, therefore, I have accomplished this, and have sealed to them this fruit, I will go on by you into Spain" (15.28). Here is the expression of the remainder of the purpose set forth in Acts, with the addition of a contemplated journey to Spain. That the complete agreement with Acts thus made out is purely incidental, and not a result of contrivance, is argued by Paley as follows: "If the passage in the Epistle was taken from that in Acts, why was *Spain* put in? If the passage in Acts was taken from that in the Epistle, why was Spain left out? If the two passages were unknown to each other, nothing can account for their conformity but truth."[4] In the Epistle Paul says: "From Jerusalem, and round about even unto Illyricum, I have fully preached the gospel of Christ" (15.19). In Acts, Illyricum is not mentioned among the regions in which he had preached; but it is said of his last visit to Macedonia, which was bordered on the west by Illyricum, that *"when he had gone through those parts* and had given them much exhortation, he came into Greece" (20.2–3). When he "had gone through those parts" which constitute Macedonia, he had gone as far as to Illyricum, but had not gone *into* it; and this is precisely what his words, "even unto Illyricum," mean. In Acts, Paul is represented, while on his journey to Jerusalem, as saying to the Ephesian elders: "I go bound in the spirit to Jerusalem, not knowing the things that shall befall me there, save that the Holy Spirit testifieth to me in every city, saying that bonds and afflictions abide me" (20.22–23). By "every city" he evidently means every city through which he had passed on his journey. In the Epistle we find, in strong confirmation of this, that when he was about to start on the journey he had the same apprehension; for he says: "Now I beseech you, brethren, by our Lord Je-

---

[4] *Horae Paulinae, in loco.*

sus Christ, and by the love of the Spirit, that ye strive together with me in your prayers to God for me, that I may be delivered from them that are disobedient in Judea, and that my ministration which I have for Jerusalem may be acceptable to the saints" (15.30– 31). It is quite certain from this instance, and it would be if we had no other, that neither of these two books was written for the purpose of conforming to the other; for if Acts had been written with such a purpose in view, the account of Paul's imprisonment, and the consequent failure of his prayer to be delivered from the disobedient in Judea, would have been omitted or greatly modified; and if, on the other hand, the Epistle had been forged after the event, it would not have contained a prayer which the writer knew to have been frustrated by the course of events. "This single consideration," says Paley, "convinces me that no concert or confederacy whatever subsisted between the Epistle and the Acts of the Apostles; and that whatever coincidences have been or can be pointed out between them are unsophisticated, and are the result of truth and reality."[5]

We here conclude our evidence from this source, though we have by no means exhausted it. For a fuller exhibition of it, and especially for specifications which prove the genuineness and authenticity of the Epistles ascribed to Paul, the student is referred to Paley's *Horae Paulinae*, a work from which a large part of the matter in this chapter is derived, and which, though it has been before the public since the year 1790, and has been regarded from the time of its first publication as a first class defense of Acts and Paul's Epistles, has never been replied to by an unbeliever. For a further statement of the coincidences between the Gospels, the reader is referred to Blunt's *Coincidences,* a work to which the present writer acknowledges much indebtedness.

Thus far in our discussion of the authenticity of the New Testament books we have prosecuted the inquiry without reference to the accounts of miracles; and having applied all the tests of

---

[5] *Ib., Epistle to the Romans,* No. 6.

historical criticism, we have found no error of fact, no discrepancy between these documents and other reliable histories, no inconsistency between the books themselves in regard to any of the multitudinous details into which their narratives run. On the contrary, we have found a very large number of those undesigned coincidences in detail between them and other books, and between these books individually, which are found only in such writings as are most minutely accurate in every particular. The same can not be said of the same number of books dealing with a common subject, and entering into so many details, in all human literature. It seems a perfectly legitimate conclusion from these premises that in the books of the New Testament the world has the most authentic historical documents, at least so far as ordinary facts of history are concerned, that have ever been written.

NINE

Positions of Unbelievers in Reference to Miracles

The conclusion which we have reached in the preceding chapters of this Part is conceded in a general way by the mass of modern unbelievers; that is, it is conceded that, in reference to all except their accounts of miracles, and a few details calculated to lend support to these accounts, the New Testament books are credible.[1]

It is the characteristic of all unbelievers to deny the reality of miracles. Those of them who affect scientific methods tacitly adopt, as a rule of historical criticism, that accounts of miracles must be summarily rejected as untrue.[2] This position is taken on various grounds, according to the varying theories of the parties.

1. By atheists, who deny that there is a God, and by Pantheists, who deny that there is a God apart from the forces of nature, miracles are held to be impossible; for, according to both of these positions, there can be nothing supernatural. Agnostics, who

---

[1] The position of Strauss is an exception to this remark. He says: "There is little of which we can say for certain that it took place, and of all to which the faith of the church especially attaches itself, the miraculous and supernatural matter in the facts and destinies of Jesus, it is far more certain that it did not take place." *New Life*, ii. 434.

[2] "Till we have new light, we shall maintain this principle of historical criticism, that a supernatural relation can not be accepted as such." (Renan, *Jesus*, 45). "The historian who approaches his subject imbued with the faith of the church finds himself confronted at the very outset with the most stupendous of miracles, the fact which lies at the root of Christianity being in his eyes that the only begotten Son of God descended from the eternal throne of the Godhead to the earth, and became man in the womb of the virgin. He who regards this as simply and absolutely a miracle, steps at once outside of all historical connection." (Baur, *Church Hist.*, i. 1).

claim that they can not decide whether there is a personal God or not, must be equally unable to decide whether or not miracles are possible, seeing that their possibility depends on the existence of a God to work them. The number of persons who are either Atheists, Pantheists or Agnostics is so small, and the tenets of these parties are so far apart from the convictions of the great mass of mankind, that we shall not dwell on their position farther than to state it.

2. A second class, who admit that there is a God, and that miracles are therefore possible, hold it to be impossible to prove that a miracle has been wrought.[3] Briefly stated, the argument is this: All human experience is against the occurrence of miracles, on the one hand, and it attests the very common occurrence of false testimony, on the other; consequently, in any case of alleged miracle, it is more probable that the testimony to it is deceptive than that the miracle actually transpired. This argument has been refuted in several ways, and so successfully refuted that many of the most acute infidels now reject it.[4] It is a sufficient answer to it to offset its universal affirmative by another, and say, Universal experience proves that miracles can be proved; for, as a matter of historical fact, men of all ages and kindreds have believed them, and to all these they have been proved. These include the immense majority of men, and of the most enlightened men. To say that it is impossible to prove that which has been actually proved to the satisfaction of nearly all men, is to speak falsely, or to use the words deceitfully.

3. A third class, and the only class of infidels with whose position it concerns us to deal, admit the possibility of miracles, and also the possibility of proving the occurrence of them should any occur; but they deny that the evidence within our reach is sufficient for the proof of any now on record.[5] This is the issue which

---

[3] The historian Hume has the credit of originating this argument. He elaborated it in his celebrated *Essay on Miracles*.

[4] "It is not, therefore, in the name of this or that philosophy, but in the name of constant experience, that we banish miracle from history. We do not say miracle is impossible; we say there has been hitherto no miracle proved." (Renan, *Jesus*, 44).

[5] *Ib.*

the experience of the world and common sense alike present as the one to be discussed. Forasmuch as there is a body of evidence on which a large majority of the men who have examined it base a belief in certain miracles, the task imposed on unbelief, and one which it can not avoid by any subterfuge, is to show that this body of evidence is insufficient; and especially is this true, when we consider that those who have accepted the miracles on this evidence will readily admit that no miracles can be proved if these can not.

Skeptics have felt it incumbent on themselves to take definite ground not only as to the reality of the New Testament miracles, but also as to the origin of the accounts of them with which the New Testament books abound. Some have held that they were false stories deliberately invented by the early disciples to deceive the people; more recently it has been asserted that they are myths, that is, stories invented to convey truths by analogy, but not propounded as actual occurrences; and yet again, they are regarded as legends, or stories which had their origin in natural events, but which, by natural exaggeration as they passed from mouth to mouth in early times, took upon them miraculous details, until they assumed their present form.[6] If the direct evidence for their reality should prove, after proper consideration, unconvincing, it might be worth while, as a mere matter of curiosity, to discuss the relative merits of these three theories; but in this case they would have lost all value as facts bearing on human destiny and duty; and, consequently, any inquiry into the real merits of these positions may be turned over to theorists who have the time to waste on them, while the earnest inquirer must devote himself to the question, Is the positive evidence of the reality of New Testament miracles sufficient to command our credence?

The most common and popular ground for the denial of the sufficiency of the evidence is this: that the miracles, having been wrought or supposed to have been wrought in an age fond of believing in such events, were received as real without the applica-

---

[6] Renan is an eminent advocate of the legendary theory; Strauss of the mythical.

tion of the tests by which their reality could be demonstrated. In other words, it is claimed that they were not wrought under scientific conditions.[7] The best way to test this assertion is to look into the record and see how the miracles were actually received, and what tests of their reality were actually applied.

First, we remark that, whatever may have been the habit of the age in which Jesus and the Apostles lived with respect to miracles in general, and those of these men in particular, there was certainly a large class of persons, including the most acute and intelligent of the Jews, who most persistently refused to credit them; and these men were sufficient in number and in influence to check any disposition on the part of the masses to receive them without question. Second, we have a detailed account of the way in which the miracles were tested by this class of men, and by a comparison of that with the methods which would be applied by scientific men of our own day, we can determine how much credence we should give to the assertion in question.

A notable case in point is found in the ninth chapter of the Gospel of John. It is the case of a man said to have been born blind, and to have been healed by Jesus. After the neighbors and former acquaintances of the man, who was a beggar, had satisfied themselves that a miracle had been wrought, as if to test their own judgment of the case they brought the man to certain Pharisees, the party most unwilling to admit the reality of the miracles, that they might see what those intelligent enemies of Jesus could say of the case. A formal investigation followed, and its method is clearly traced. They first asked the man how he received his sight, and he answered according to the facts (v 15). This shows that they knew he now had his sight, which could be known at once by his appearance. Then, after an irrelevant discussion about his doing such cures on the sabbath, and an equally irrelevant question as to what the man thought of Jesus, the Pharisees very properly demanded proof that the man had been born blind. They already had the testimony of the neighbors, who had brought

---

him to them as one who had been born blind, but with this they were not satisfied, and they called for his parents (16–18). When the parents appeared they were confronted with the threatening question, "Is this your son, who ye say was born blind? how then doth he now see?" Being alarmed, they answered: "We know that this is our son, and that he was born blind: but how he now seeth we know not: he is of age; he shall speak for himself" (19–21). The historian remarks, concerning the last part of this answer, that they gave it because they were afraid that they would he put out of the synagogue if they should say anything equivalent to confessing Jesus to be the Christ (22–23). The Pharisees then called again to the man, and said: "Give God the glory: we know that this man is a sinner," thus indirectly admitting that the miracle had been wrought, though unwilling to allow Jesus the credit of it. The process of the investigation, reduced to the simplest statement, was this: they first ascertained that the man could see; they next inquired what Jesus had done to him; and seeing that what he had done was only to put moistened clay on his eyes and require him to wash it off, they next inquired as to the certainty of his having been born blind, and they close this inquiry with the testimony of his parents.

Let us now suppose that, instead of the Pharisees who tested this miracle, it had been done by a "commission composed of physiologists, physicians, chemists and persons experienced in historical criticism," as is demanded by M. Renan. What advantage would they have had over the Pharisees in determining whether the man, when first brought before them, could sec? It is clear that no knowledge of physiology, or chemistry, or medicine, or historical criticism, could help them in this. The most stupid plantation negro could settle the question at once by striking with his hand toward the man's face and seeing whether he winked. When it was settled that the man could see, and the question was raised, What had Jesus done to give him sight? the commission would have an advantage over the Pharisees, in that they would know more certainly, on account of their scientific attainments, that merely putting clay on a blind man's eyes and washing it off could not give him sight. Uneducated and superstitious men might imagine that the clay had some mystic power; but scientific men would know better. On this point of inquiry, then, the advantage would be with the commission, but the advantage would be in favor of the miracle. As to the next question, whether the man said to have thus received sight was born blind, what more conclusive testimony could the commission obtain, or what more could they wish, than, first, that of the neighbors who had known the man as a blind beggar; and, secondly, that of his own father and mother? Who, indeed, could be so good witnesses that a child was born blind as the father and mother; for they always exhaust every possible means of testing the question before they yield to the sad conviction that their child is blind?

This comparison shows that in testing such a miracle there could be no use made of scientific knowledge; and the same is true of the miracles of Jesus in general. If, in the case just considered, the question had been, What defect in the organ of sight caused the man to be blind? or, What were the chemical constituents of the clay put on his eyes? a knowledge of physiology or of chemistry would have been needed for the investigation, and so in general; if the miracles had been such that to test their reality scientific knowledge would have been necessary, the evidence which we have would be incomplete; but the most unscientific men of common sense can know when a man is dead; when he is alive and active; when he has a high fever; is a cripple; is paralyzed, etc., as well as the greatest scientist. The cry, then, that the miracles of the New Testament were not wrought under "scientific conditions," is totally irrelevant, and can mislead none but those who do not pause to think.

Several other theoretical objections to miracles usually receive attention in this discussion, such as their assumed antecedent improbability, and the claim that they are discredited by the fact that many other accounts of miracles among the heathen, and among believers of the dark ages, are now rejected by intelligent

Christians; and it would be well for us to consider these, if we were aiming to exhaust the subject; but they amount to nothing at all if the direct evidence for miracles is conclusive. All antecedent improbability of any fact whatever vanishes in the presence of competent proof of the fact; and disbelief in all miracles but a single one could not discredit that one if the evidence for it were conclusive. On the other hand, it must be admitted that if the direct evidence for miracles is not conclusive in itself, no conclusions drawn from the discussion of these theories could establish their reality. On this account we omit the further consideration of these theories, and refer the student to works devoted to them.[8] The direct evidence shall be the subject of our next chapter.

---

[8] We especially commend to the student Mozley on Miracles, and Trench on Miracles—two works by master minds of the present century.

TEN

The Direct Evidence for the New Testament Miracles: The Resurrection of Jesus

The miracles of the New Testament are distributable into five classes: first, those wrought by Jesus; second, those wrought upon Jesus, such as his birth and his resurrection; third, those wrought by the Apostles; fourth, the inspiration of the Apostles; and fifth, the predictions which Jesus and the Apostles uttered. In considering the evidence of their reality, our task is simplified by the relation which all of them sustain to a single one. It Jesus arose from the dead, the other miracles will be admitted, as well as all else that is claimed for Jesus in the New Testament. This is freely granted by Strauss, who pronounces the resurrection "the crowning miracle—the touchstone, not only of Lives of Jesus, but of Christianity itself"; and who, when he reaches the formal consideration of it in his *New Life of Jesus*, says: "Here we stand on that decisive point where, in the presence of the accounts of the miraculous resurrection of Jesus, we either acknowledge the inadmissibility of the natural and historical view of the life of Jesus, and consequently retract all that precedes, and so give up our whole undertaking, or pledge ourselves to make out the possibility of the result of these accounts, *i. e.*, the origin of the belief in the resurrection of Jesus, without any corresponding miraculous fact" (i.41; 397). On the other hand, if the resurrection of Jesus was not a reality, all the other miracles would be valueless even if real, and all effort to establish their reality would be abandoned. This is admitted by the Apostle Paul, who says: "If Christ hath not been raised, then is our preaching vain, your faith also is vain. Yea, and we are found false witnesses of God; because we witnessed of God that he raised up Christ, whom he raised not up, if so be that the dead are not raised" (1 Cor 15.14–15). The reason given is conclusive; for if the Apostles are found false witnesses concerning the main fact of which they testify, we can not credit them as to anything else; and as all we know of Jesus comes to us through them, it must all be laid aside as untrustworthy.

From these concessions, and their obvious propriety, it appears that in discussing the question of New Testament miracles it is necessary to discuss the reality of only one of them. This simplifies the inquiry, and it should lead to a concentration of the whole discussion on this single point. The conflict between belief and unbelief is thus reduced to an issue like that presented by the challenge of Goliath: "Choose you a man for you, and let him come down to me. If he be able to fight with me and kill me, then we will be your servants; but if I prevail against him, and kill him, then shall ye be our servants." Let us settle all by settling the question, Did Jesus rise from the dead? This inquiry is simplified by the admissions of unbelievers. By the leading skeptics it is now admitted, first, that Jesus actually died and was buried;[1] second, it is admitted that on or before the third morning his body disappeared from the tomb; third, that the disciples came to believe firmly that he arose from the dead.[2] The exact issue has reference to the last two facts, and may be stated by the two questions, Did the body disappear by a resurrection, or in some other

---

[1] The hypothesis was advanced by Herder, and afterward supported by Paulus and Schleiermacher, that Jesus was not actually dead when he was placed in the tomb, and that he revived and disappeared; but it has been thoroughly refuted by Strauss himself, as well as by believing writers. (See *New Life of Jesus*, i. §§ *3*, 4, 5.)

[2] "In any case it is only through the consciousness of the disciples that we have any knowledge of that which was the object of their faith; and thus we can not go farther than to say that by whatever means this result was brought about, the resurrection of Jesus became a fact of their consciousness, and was as real to them as any historical event." (Baur, *Church History*, i. 43.)

way? and Did the belief of the disciples originate from the fact of the resurrection, or from some other cause? In seeking to answer these questions, infidels have adopted as their line of argument, first, an attack on the credibility of the witnesses; and second, the propounding of adverse theories as to the disappearance of the body, and of the origin of the belief in the resurrection. We shall state and consider the chief points in this line of argument before we present the body of the direct evidence.

Before considering the attack on the witnesses, it is necessary that we distinctly understand who the witnesses are and where their testimony is to be found. To us the witnesses are a group of women, not less than five in number; the twelve older Apostles; and the Apostle Paul. The testimony of the women and of the twelve is recorded in the four Gospels, in Acts, in the Epistles of Peter and John, and in Revelation. That of Paul is found in Acts and his Epistles. Of these documents none are admitted by infidels in general to be genuine, except Revelation and four of Paul's Epistles, viz.: Romans, Galatians, and 1 and 2 Corinthians. But while the genuineness of the other books is disputed, it is admitted that in these books the testimony originally given by the witnesses to the resurrection is preserved. We stand on common ground, then, with the unbeliever when we treat the testimony of the several witnesses which we find in these books as that by which the question must be settled.

The first charge against the witnesses which we shall consider is that, apart from the main fact of the resurrection, they assert some things which are incredible, and some which are impossible, and that they contradict one another, thus throwing discredit on their testimony to the main fact.

The most prominent specification of things incredible, and one which is urged by all recent infidels, is the account given by Matthew of the guard of Roman soldiers set to prevent the opening of the tomb. It is held to be incredible that the priests, as represented in this account, remembered the prediction by Jesus of his own resurrection on the third day, when the disciples did not; incredible that Pilate, at the request of the priests, would grant a guard; incredible that the soldiers reported to the priests rather than to Pilate, their commander; and incredible that, at the risk of their lives, they admitted for the sake of money that they had been asleep on guard.[3] In reply to all this it is sufficient to observe, first, that the soldiers took no risk at all in saying they had gone to sleep; when their statement came to the ears of Pilate, the priests had only to tell him privately that the soldiers had not been asleep at all, but had said this at their instigation, to prevent him from proceeding against them. Second, Pilate, according to the story told, had put the soldiers at the disposal of the priests, and to these it was their duty to report when the special service for which they had been detailed was accomplished. Third, Pilate was as much interested in preventing the circulation of a report that Jesus had arisen as were the priests; and therefore he would naturally be as ready to grant a guard as they to ask for it. Finally, there is a good and sufficient reason why the chief priests should remember the prediction of the resurrection, and speak of it after the death of Jesus; and why the disciples should not think of it at all. The reason is found in the totally different views of that prediction taken by the two parties when it was uttered. The disciples would not, and could not, believe that Jesus meant what he said when he spoke either of his death or of his resurrection. They construed his repeated remarks on the subject as a dark parable, the meaning of which they could not even conjecture.[4] When, therefore, he was put to death, they could not at first regard this as the fulfillment of the first part of the prediction, and consequently they could not look forward to a resurrection as the fulfillment of the second part. On the contrary, when the priests and elders heard that he had uttered this prediction they as naturally understood it literally, inasmuch as they not only expected him to die, but intended to kill him. They as naturally understood him to speak literally of his resurrection, and they expected to triumph over his disciples by his failure to rise. Thinking

---

[3] *Sup. Rel.*, iii. 444, 445.
[4] Mark 9.10.

now that this triumph was certainly within their reach, if only the body of Jesus could be kept secure till the three days should pass, they had every reason which shrewd and cunning men could have under such circumstances to proceed as they are said to have done.

It should also be observed, in reference to this matter of the guard, that in all the subsequent controversy between the Apostles and the chief priests the story of the guard was never denied, as it certainly would have been if it had been false; that, on the contrary, it was tacitly admitted in the very report which the priests caused to be spread abroad, that the disciples stole the body away while the soldiers were asleep. And if it should be assumed that neither this report nor the story of the guard had an existence until the publication of Matthew's Gospel, still the fact remains that it was published in the Gospel written especially for Jewish readers, and that after its publication the Jews made no such denial. Since it was not denied at the time when men knew the facts, it is too late to deny it now.[5]

As a second specification, it is held to be incredible that Mary did not at once recognize Jesus, if she saw him, instead of supposing him to be the gardener.[6] But it is answered, first, that her own statement, that she did not recognize him at first, is proof that her story was not made up; for surely she would not have made it up this way, but would have said, "As soon as I laid my eyes on him I knew him." Second, her failure to at once recognize him is naturally accounted for by the considerations that she thought he was still dead, that she was anxiously inquiring where his dead body could be found, and that her eyes were full of tears when she first turned toward the person who spoke to her.

---

[5] Strauss attempts to explain the origin of the story that a guard was placed over the sepulcher, in the following way: "In the dispute upon this point, a Jew may have said: No wonder that the sepulcher was found empty, for of course you had stolen the body away. 'We stolen it away,' said the Christian; 'how could we have done that, when you had certainly set a watch over it?' He believed this because he assumed it." (*New Life*, i. 207.) But it is certain that if such a conversation had occurred, it would not have stopped here. When the Christian said, "You had certainly set a watch over it," the Jew would have replied, "Now you are lying; and you know you are lying"; and thus the story would have been nipped in the bud.

[6] *Sup. Rel.*, iii, 457, 458.

Under the head of things impossible, it is said that Jesus could not have vanished as he is said to have done frequently, nor have entered a room through the boards of closed doors, if he had been in a real body. But these two things can be declared impossible only on the assumption that Jesus possessed no supernatural power; for if he had such power, neither was impossible. Both of the infidel writers cited in the footnote below unconsciously provide in their own words this answer to their objection. One of them says, if the incidents in question occurred, "there could be no question that the natural corporeality of the body and life of this human being was of a very peculiar, perfectly supernatural order"; while the other says of the entrance into the room, "It can scarcely be doubted that the intention of the writer is to represent a miraculous entry."[7] This charge is in reality based on the assumption that Jesus had not really risen from the dead; for if he had, he could certainly do all that is said of him; and the objection therefore contains a fallacious assumption of the very thing to be proved. In other words, it is an attempt to discredit the proof of the resurrection by assuming that the resurrection did not occur, and that therefore the witnesses must be mistaken. No fallacy could be more inexcusable. In reality, the sudden appearance of Jesus in a closed room, and his equally sudden disappearance without passing through the door, are no more wonderful than the omnipresence of God, or the fact that he sees in the darkness as well as in the light.

The second general charge against the witnesses is that they were incompetent. This charge is not made formally, but is involved, as will be seen, in certain specifications.

---

[7] "Now in this case, if the eating and the touching were historically true, it could not be doubtful that what appeared to the disciples was a human body, endowed with a natural life and a natural body; and if the showing and feeling of the marks of the wounds were so, there could be as little doubt that the human being was the Jesus who died on the cross; finally, if the entrance with closed doors were true, there could be no question that the natural corporeality and life of this human being was of a very peculiar, perfectly supernatural order." (Strauss, *New Life*, i. 407.) "If Jesus possessed his own body after his resurrection, and could eat and be handled, he could not vanish; if he vanished he could not have been thus corporeal. The aid of a miracle has to be invoked in order to reconcile the representations.... It can scarcely be doubted that the intention of the writer is to represent a miraculous entry." (*Sup. Rel.*, iii. 462, 466.)

First, it is insisted that not one of these witnesses actually saw Jesus come out of the tomb. By the author of Supernatural Religion the objection is stated in these words: "The remarkable fact is, therefore, absolutely undeniable, that there was not, and it is not pretended that there was, a single eye-witness of the actual resurrection."[8] There can be no reason for thus insisting on this fact, unless it be to show that the witnesses were incompetent for want of opportunity. But in this direction it has no bearing whatever; for if they saw him alive after his death, this is proof that he came to life. The fact that no one claims to have witnessed the actual resurrection is indeed a remarkable fact, remarkable as proof that the story of the resurrection was not made up by pretence; for if it had been, the witnesses, or at least some of them, would almost certainly have claimed to have seen him come out of the tomb, especially as some of them claim to have reached the tomb very nearly at the time of his departure from it.

A second specification is that the witnesses were demented, and therefore mentally incompetent. This objection is one of the oldest ever employed by unbelievers, and it has been more elaborately set forth in modern times than almost any other. It was urged by Celsus, the first known writer against the evidences of Christianity. He sneeringly remarks concerning the evidence of the resurrection, that the witnesses were "a half frantic woman," and some one else who "had either dreamed so, owing to a peculiar state of mind, or, under the influence of a wandering imagination, had formed to himself an appearance according to his wishes."[9] Echoing the sneer of the ancient Epicurean, modern infidels, notably Renan, say that Mary of Magdala, because seven demons had been cast out of her, was a woman of unsound mind, and that her vision of Jesus was a hallucination.[10] As to the other women, having heard Mary's story, they were seized

---

[8] *Ib.* iii. 449.

[9] *Origen Against Celsus,* b. ii. c. 55.

[10] "Divine power of love! sacred moments in which the passion of a hallucinated woman gives to the world a resurrected God!" (Renan, *Jesus,* 357). "If wisdom refuses to console this poor human race, betrayed by fate, let folly attempt the enterprise. Where is the sage who has given to the world as much joy as the possessed Mary of Magdala?" *(Ib., Apostles,* 61.)

with the hallucination that they had seen a young man in white who told them that Jesus had risen.[11] The two men at Emmaus fell into revery as a stranger who had journeyed with them was breaking bread at the supper table; the stranger walked away; they recovered from their revery, and concluded that the stranger was Jesus.[12] The twelve, shut up in a room, feel a light breath pass over them, or they hear a window creak, or a chance murmur, and they fancy that the feeble sound is the voice of Jesus. At once they conclude that Jesus is in their midst, and afterwards it was pretended that they had seen his wounds.[13] If we accept these statements, we must certainly conclude that the women and the Twelve were demented almost to idiocy.

One would suppose that Paul, with his sturdy common sense, would be excepted from this charge of hallucination; but it is boldly affirmed that at the time of his supposed conversation with Jesus a sunstroke or an attack of ophthalmia had thrown him into a delirious fever; a flash of lightning or a peal of thunder had blinded him, and for the time being he was demented.[14] It has also been affirmed that he was subject to epilepsy, with a view to making it appear possible that he had a fit at the time that he thought he saw Jesus.[15]

While this charge is as old as Celsus, those who prefer it have to this day made no attempt at proof that is worthy of the name. There are only two ways to prove that a man's testimony as to an object of sight is untrustworthy because of unsoundness of mind. If, in the first place, he gave evidence of insanity either before or after the event to which he testifies, his testimony may be ascribed to the workings of a disordered brain, provided there is in it anything highly improbable.

But in the case of these witnesses nothing of this kind is claimed except Mary's possession, which had long ago passed away, and

---

[11] *Ib.,* 62.

[12] *Ib.,* 66.

[13] *Ib.,* 67, 68.

[14] *Ib.,* 172, 173.

[15] Strauss, *New Life,* i. 417; *Sup. Rel.,* iii. 557–560.

the above mentioned charge against Paul, which is a mere fiction of the imagination. All that was done or said by any of the witnesses up to the moment of seeing Jesus, and all from that moment onward, is perfectly rational—it is that which any sane person under the same circumstances would do and say; and the only ground for charging them with insanity is the fact that they claim to have seen Jesus. But, in the second place, one may be pronounced a subject of hallucination without previous evidence of insanity if he sees something which is known by others present not to be a reality, or which is known for any reason to be impossible. For example, when a man sees snakes crawling on his bed, and feels them twining around his arms and his neck, while others standing at his bedside can see nothing of the kind, it is known that he is suffering from hallucination; or when he sees hobgoblins grinning at him through the ceiling and thrusting at him red-hot irons, he is known to be hallucinated because of the impossibility of what he sees. But in the cases of the witnesses to the resurrection neither of these conditions existed. When one of the women saw Jesus, all saw him who were present; and so with the Twelve. When Paul saw him, his companions saw the miraculous light in which he appeared, and they heard the voice speaking to Paul, though they heard not the words that were spoken. There is a total absence in every case of such circumstances as give evidence of hallucination, unless it be the assumed impossibility of what they saw; and this is not impossible if there is a God; for it is certainly not impossible that God should raise the dead, and especially such a dead man as Jesus. It appears, then, that the only ground for the charge of hallucination is the mere fact that these witnesses claim to have seen Jesus. If such a mode of reasoning were employed in the investigation of any other event, those who employ it, and not the witnesses to the event, would be pronounced of unsound mind.

The third and last charge against the witnesses which we shall consider is the charge that they contradict one another. If this were true, and the contradictions had a bearing on the main fact of the resurrection, some of the witnesses making statements inconsistent with this main fact, there would be force in the objection; and we would be left, as in other cases of conflicting testimony, to the necessity of deciding between the witnesses by the preponderance of evidence. But it is not claimed, nor is it true, that the alleged contradictions take this form. It is only subordinate and unessential details that are affected by them. Such contradictions could exist in large numbers, as they often do in the testimony of credible witnesses in courts of justice, without invalidating the evidence as to the main fact. Infidels themselves admit this in regard to the evidence of the crucifixion of Jesus; for while they claim that John contradicts the other Evangelists in respect to the hour of the crucifixion, yet not one of them on this account doubts the reality of the crucifixion itself. So it should be in respect to the resurrection; they should not allow similar contradictions about details to make them doubt the united and harmonious testimony as to the resurrection itself.

But is it true that the witnesses contradict one another? This can be determined only by examining closely the specifications under this charge, hearing in mind while we do so that a contradiction, as we have said before (page 31), can not be justly charged except when two statements are made which can not both be true; that if, on any rational hypothesis, they both can be supposed true, they both *may* be true, and no contradiction is made out. This rule is made necessary by the fact that writers and speakers often omit details, the absence of which give their statements the appearance of inconsistency, whereas their presence in the narrative would have prevented this appearance. It is unjust to refuse any writers the benefit of this rule; for in doing so we are liable to charge with falsehood the most truthful writers, and with incorrect information those best informed.

The first specification to be noticed under this head has reference to the time at which the women went to the sepulcher. Matthew says they came "as it began to dawn"; and John, "while it was yet dark," as it always is when it begins to dawn. In apparent conflict with this, Mark says they came "when the sun was risen."

Now if the word "came" (*erxomai*) used by all of these writers is employed here in the sense of arriving, which is its usual meaning, there is a contradiction of Matthew and John by Mark. But this word is sometimes used in reference to starting instead of arriving, and examples of this use are found elsewhere in the writings of both Matthew and John. A notable instance is the statement (Matt 14.12) that the disciples of John "came and took up the corpse and buried him; and they went and told Jesus"; where the word occurs twice, once rendered "came," and once "went," the former referring to their arrival where the corpse was, and the latter to their starting for Galilee to tell Jesus. In John (6.17) we find this instance: "They entered into a boat, and were going over the sea to Capernaum"; where the word in question is rendered "were going," with reference to their start and progress, and with no reference at all to their arrival. In the case in hand we have only to suppose that these two writers have their minds on the time when the women started to the sepulcher in order, according to their own usage elsewhere, to see that they do not contradict Mark; and at the same time it is not till we do this that we exactly understand their meaning. That Mark, on the other hand, refers to the arrival at the tomb is clear from the fact that in the preceding clause he mentions the purchase of spices by the women while on the way: "And when the sabbath was past, Mary Magdalene, and Mary the mother of James, and Salome, bought spices, that they might come and anoint him. And very early on the first day of the week they came to the tomb when the sun was risen."

Second, a contradiction is charged in reference to the names of these women. The most casual reader of the Gospels has observed that there is a difference on this point. Luke says that Mary Magdalene, Mary the mother of James, Joanna, and "other women" went; Mark, that Mary Magdalene, Mary the mother of James, and Salome went; Matthew, that Mary Magdalene, and Mary the mother of James and Joseph went; and John, that Mary Magdalene went. Now if either Mark, Matthew or John had said that only those whom he mentions went, they would all have contradicted

Luke; if Matthew had said that the two whom he mentions were all who went, he would have contradicted both Luke and Mark; and if John had said that the one whom he mentions was the only one who went, he would have contradicted all three of the other writers; but not one of them speaks thus. No exclusive term is used. If all these women went, then all these writers tell the truth. The only fair and just way, therefore, to deal with the several statements is to suppose that all of the women mentioned went, and that each writer, for reasons which we may or may not discover, chose to speak of them as he does. An omission is not a contradiction.

A third specification has reference to the number of angels said to have been seen by the women at the tomb.[16] Matthew mentions the one who rolled the stone away, and represents him as speaking to the women, while Luke says there were two angels, and John also says that two were seen by Mary Magdalene. This case is precisely like that of the number of women. Matthew having mentioned the one who rolled away the stone, and who was the speaker, sees fit to say nothing about the other; while Luke and John, not having mentioned the removal of the stone, see fit to speak of both the angels without distinguishing the one who did the speaking. It is an every day occurrence to speak of having met a friend and had a conversation with him, without mentioning another friend who was present at the time; and yet, in referring again to the same incident, to speak of having met both.

Fourth, a contradiction is charged in reference to the conduct of the women immediately after they left the tomb.

Matthew says that they were told by the angel to go and tell the male disciples that Jesus had arisen and would meet them in Galilee. Luke says that they delivered this message, while Mark says that "they fled from the tomb; for trembling and astonishment had come upon them; and they said nothing to any one, for they were

---

[16] Celsus stated this objection in these words: "It is related also that there came to the tomb of Jesus himself, according to some, two angels; according to others, one." Origen replies: "They who mention one say that it was he who rolled away the stone from the sepulcher; while they who mention two refer to those who appeared in shining raiment to the women who repaired to the sepulcher, or who were seen within sitting in white garments." (*Origen against Celsus,* book v. chap. 56.)

afraid." Whether this is a contradiction depends on the meaning of Mark. If he means that they said nothing even to the male disciples, there is a contradiction; but if he means that they said nothing to any except those to whom they were told to speak, there is none. The latter is the natural meaning of his words, for they stand in immediate connection with the angel's command to go and tell the disciples; and the fear which is mentioned as the cause of their not telling could not be a motive for not telling them, but only for not telling other men who might be enemies. In other words, their fear could not have been a motive for disobeying the angel; on the contrary, the greater their alarm, the greater their natural impulse to tell their brethren what they had seen and heard.

Fifth, it is charged that the writers contradict one another concerning the first appearance of Jesus to the male disciples. Matthew mentions first, that on a mountain in Galilee; Mark and John, that in Jerusalem on the night after the resurrection; Luke, that to Cleopas and his companion on their way to Emmaus; Paul, that to Peter alone (1 Cor 15.5); and this variation is the alleged contradiction.[17] These statements would be contradictory if the several writers had said that the appearance which they mention first was first in order of time; but not one of them makes such a statement, though Paul says that the appearance to Peter preceded that to the Twelve. The variation is fully accounted for if we suppose that all these appearances took place, and that each writer made his own selection of those which he chose to mention, and intentionally omitted the others. The omission is not readily accounted for, though there is a reason for it yet to be mentioned; but whether accounted for or not, it involves no inconsistency.

Sixth, it is alleged that Luke represents Jesus, at his first interview with the apostles, as commanding them to remain in Jerusalem, thus contradicting Matthew and John, who both represent him as meeting them in Galilee. The truth of this charge depends on the question whether the whole of the conversation in the last chapter of Luke (36–49), occurred at the first interview with the

---

[17] *Sup. Rel.,* iii. 451, 459, 489.

apostles. If it did, then the command (v 49) to tarry in Jerusalem was given, as is alleged, at this first interview. It must be admitted that, with Luke's Gospel alone before us, we would thus conclude; but this would not be a necessary conclusion, for it is the well known habit of the Gospel writers to often pass from one incident to another widely separated from it, without a note of time. For example, in the midst of his account of the last supper, Luke introduces, without a note of time, the statement, "And there arose also a contention among them, which of them is accounted to be the greatest"; whereas this contention had arisen among them several months previous, as we learn both from Luke himself and from Matthew.[18] Again, the conversation with certain of his disciples about following him is mentioned by Luke directly after that about the Samaritan village whose inhabitants would not receive him, and it is introduced by the words, "And as they went in the way"; yet it really occurred while they were yet in Galilee, and as they were about to take a boat for the eastern side of the lake.[19] With this knowledge of the writer's habit, one could not be sure that the conversation in question, beginning "and he said to them" (v 44), followed in point of time immediately upon the preceding; and consequently the charge of contradiction could not be made out, though it would have more plausibility in this instance than in any of the preceding. When, however, we turn to Luke's second narrative, and allow him to explain himself, as he did to Theophilus, his meaning is left without uncertainty, and the appearance of contradiction vanishes. In his introduction to Acts, as if for the very purpose of making clearer his condensed account in the close of his Gospel, he tells Theophilus that there was an interval of forty days between the first interview with the eleven and the one in which he gave them their last instruction and ascended to heaven (1.1–9).

The seventh and last specification which we shall consider under this charge is based on the passage in Acts last cited. It is

---

[18] Luke 22.24; cf. 9.46; Matthew 18.1.
[19] Luke 9.51–62; cf. Matthew 8.18–23.

charged that the statement about the interval of forty days is a contradiction of the preceding narrative, and that it is adopted in order to make room for the different appearances of Jesus.[20] It is difficult to have patience with critics who thus refuse to allow the later and fuller statements of a writer to modify and explain his earlier and more concise narrative, without the charge of fraudulent design. The author of these two narratives certainly had no thought that his friend Theophilus was in danger of seeing a contradiction between the two accounts, or he would have made some effort to guard against such a construction; and if he had the intention of deceiving, he would most certainly have made such an effort. The absence of the faintest trace of such an effort is proof sufficient that the need of it was not felt, but that, on the contrary, the writer was conscious of that candid truthfulness which casts aside all thought of guarding against suspicion. If a writer of the present day were to publish an account of having visited a certain friend at a certain date, and in connection with it were to repeat some conversation with that friend; and in a subsequent publication were to say that the visit lasted forty days, and that the conversation reported was separated by this interval, no sane man would think of charging him with contradicting himself; yet this is precisely the case before us.

We have now explained all the alleged contradictions in the several accounts of the resurrection which we consider worthy of notice, and we find that the charge is not sustained by a single specification. We may therefore safely dismiss the charge, and at the same time dismiss from our minds all thought of having to apologize, as some believers seem ready to do, for immaterial discrepancies. No discrepancies either material or immaterial have been discovered in these accounts after a search which began eighteen centuries ago, and has continued with little interruption to the present time.

---

[20] Strauss, *New Life*, i. 403; Renan, *Apostles*, 20.

ELEVEN

The Resurrection of Jesus: Adverse Theories Considered

When admitted facts are to be accounted for, there may be one of three cases: First, no adequate cause for the fact may be known: in this instance the fact remains unexplained as to its cause. Second, two or more causes may be known, either of which is adequate to account for the effect: in this instance there is a question of probability as to which of these is the real cause. Third, one, and only one, adequate cause may be known: in this instance the fact must be explained by that cause. In the inquiry concerning the resurrection of Jesus there are, as we have previously stated, two admitted facts having important bearing on the main question: first, that the dead body of Jesus disappeared from the tomb on or before the third morning; second, that the disciples came to believe that it disappeared by rising from the dead. These two facts are readily accounted for if Jesus actually arose; but if they can be accounted for on some other rational hypothesis, then the question is one of probability between that hypothesis and the resurrection. Again, if they can be accounted for on no other such hypothesis, we are logically shut up to the resurrection as the only adequate cause. Such hypotheses have been advanced by unbelievers, and we shall now give them careful consideration.

1. Very few infidel writers have seriously grappled with the question, how the body of Jesus disappeared. They have doubtless avoided it because they had no hypothesis on which they were willing to take a stand. Christian Baur, realizing his inability in this particular, sets the question aside by the following very remarkable statement: "The question as to the nature and reality of the resurrection lies outside the sphere of historical investigation."[1] This is remarkable, because it places outside the sphere of historical investigation the most momentous event in history, if it is an event; and it is the more remarkable in that it is made in a history of the Church. It leaves outside of church history an inquiry into the very fact on which the existence of the Church depends. It is like a history of the United States which leaves out of consideration the reality of the Declaration of Independence, or a treatise on the solar system which treats the reality of the sun's existence as an outside question. Baur could not have chosen a more emphatic method of declaring his dissatisfaction with the theories on this subject propounded by some of his fellow infidels.

Renan, more courageous than discreet, takes issue with Baur, and makes a bold attempt to account for the removal of the body. He formally raises the question, "In what place did the worms consume the lifeless corpse, which, on the Friday evening, had been deposited in the sepulcher?" He proceeds to answer as follows: "It is possible that the body was taken away by some of the disciples, and by them carried into Galilee. The others, remaining at Jerusalem, would not be cognizant of the fact. On the other hand, the disciples who carried the body into Galilee could not

---

[1] "The question as to the nature and the reality of the resurrection lies outside the sphere of historical inquiry. History must be content with the simple fact that in the faith of the disciples the resurrection of Jesus came to be regarded as a solid and unquestionable fact. It was in this faith that Christianity acquired a firm basis for its historical development. What history requires the necessary antecedent of all that is to follow is not so much the fact of the resurrection, as the belief that it was a fact." (Baur, *Church History*, i. 42). Strauss, dissatisfied with this strange position of his fellow unbeliever, makes the following comment: "But even Baur himself has vouchsafed to declare that the real nature of the resurrection of Jesus lies outside the limits of historical investigation, and has accordingly, at least in words, avoided the burning question." (*New Life*, i. 398.) Yet Strauss himself also avoids "the burning question," at least so far as not to attempt to say what became of the dead body.

have as yet become acquainted with the stories which were invented at Jerusalem, so that the belief in the resurrection would have been propounded in their absence, and would have surprised them accordingly. They could not have protested; and had they done so, nothing would have been disarranged." "It is also permissible to suppose that the disappearance of the body was the work of the Jews. Perhaps they thought that in this way they would prevent the scenes of tumult which might be enacted over the corpse of a man so popular as Jesus. Perhaps they wanted to prevent any noisy funeral ceremonies, or the erection of a monument to this just man." "Lastly, who knows that the disappearance of the body was not effected by the proprietor of the garden, or by the gardener? This proprietor, as it would seem from such evidence as we possess, was a stranger to the sect. They chose his cave because it was nearest to Golgotha, and because they were pressed for time. Perhaps he was dissatisfied with this mode of taking possession of his property, and caused the corpse to be removed."[2]

It will be observed that this ingenious author, although he suggests three ways in which he thinks it possible that the body may have been removed, does not make choice between them, nor does he state either with any confidence. He introduces one with the words, "It is possible"; another with "It is permissible to suppose"; and the third with "Who knows?" He also makes free use of the term "perhaps." All this shows conscious weakness and uncertainty; and when we come to consider the three suppositions, we shall see that he had good cause for so speaking.

The supposition that the disciples from Galilee carried the body with them is preposterous, for want of an adequate motive for so difficult an undertaking. The transportation of a dead body in the warm season of that warm climate to a distance of not less than sixty miles, with no facilities except a common bier borne on the shoulders of men, is an undertaking not to be thought of except under extreme necessity, and no such necessity existed. But if it had been thus transported it is still more absurd to assume

---

[2] Renan, *Apostles*, 78–80.

that the story of its resurrection would not have been contradicted by those who buried it in Galilee, or that a remonstrance from them would have had no effect. And even should both these suppositions be accepted as within the bounds of probability, still it would have been impossible for the disciples to carry the body through the country and bury it in Galilee without the cognizance of unbelieving Jews or Samaritans along the way, and they would have borne witness to the fact. The second supposition is not "permissible," for two reasons: first, the motive assigned could not have prompted the act, inasmuch as it would not have prevented either funeral ceremonies, if any had been desired, or the erection of a monument; second, if the Jews had disposed of the body they would certainly have produced it when the story of a resurrection became current; or, if the body had by this time been too much decomposed, they would have presented evidence that it had been disposed of in this way. This would have been a far more effective method of silencing the Apostles than to threaten them with death, and to scourge them, as was done afterward for "preaching, through Jesus, the resurrection of the dead."[3] The third hypothesis is equally unreasonable with the others; for if the garden did not really belong to Joseph, he certainly had the right of access through it to his own sepulcher; and if the gardener had removed the body he would have been very glad to give it up to

---

[3] See Acts of Apostles, 4.1–2, 21; 5.17, 40. Strauss, in attempting to reply to this argument, after saying that the Apostles kept quiet till Pentecost, about seven weeks, and that it is doubtful whether Jesus was actually laid in Joseph's tomb, proceeds to say: "But if Jesus was, as is probable, buried with the other condemned criminals in a dishonorable place, his disciples had not from the first the tempting opportunity of looking for his body. And if some time elapsed before they came forward proclaiming his resurrection, it must have been more difficult for their opponents also to produce his corpse in a condition still to be recognized or affording any proof. Moreover, when we remember the horror for dead bodies felt by the Jews it was far from being so obvious a thing to do as we may at this day imagine." (*New Life*, i. 432). The author of Supernatural Religion follows in a similar strain, but neither of them meets the point made above, that even if the body had been, too much decayed for identification, competent evidence as to what was done with it by the soldiers of Pilate would have been fatal to the preaching; and that such evidence was not even thought of by the chief priests. Moreover, both these writers, in common with all on their side, find it very convenient just here, as at other points in the discussion, to ignore the fact that the soldiers did give explicit testimony to the priests, which agreed with that of the apostles.

Mary when she was seeking for it. The dead body of a stranger, and especially that of a crucified criminal, is a piece of property of which men are very glad to be relieved. Finally, all three of these suppositions are proved to be absurd, from the fact that the sepulcher was guarded by Roman soldiers for the very purpose of preventing any such removal of the body. At this point we can see more clearly than before why unbelievers feel compelled to deny the placing of that guard. It is not because there is anything improbable in it, but because the presence of the guard renders it incredible that the body disappeared in any way compatible with the theories of unbelief. To deny a fact which is reasonably well attested for no other purpose than to get it out of the way of a theory, is convincing proof that the theory is false.

2. While few infidels have made serious attempts to account for the disappearance of the body of Jesus, many have tried to account for the other admitted fact, the belief of the disciples that he arose from the dead. The theory that all the witnesses labored under a hallucination has already been examined, and found to be without the slightest ground of evidence. As a cause of the belief in question it would be inadequate even if it were a fact. Men and women who are hallucinated firmly believe that what they see and hear in this state of mind is real while the hallucination continues, but as soon as it passes away the belief passes away with it. No sane man, for instance, continues after waking to believe in the reality of what he saw in his dreams; and no man who has suffered from delirium tremens believes, after his delirium has passed, that the serpents and hobgoblins which he saw were realities. It is contrary to the experience of hallucinated persons, therefore, that the disciples, if they were in this state of mind when they thought they saw Jesus, continued to believe that they saw him after they returned to their normal mental condition. The permanency of their belief is a complete refutation of this theory.

Not content with the bare statement that the witnesses were hallucinated, skeptics have undertaken to trace the exact process by which they were led to believe that they had seen Jesus. As this attempt is made more in detail by Renan than by others, we shall take up his remarks on the subject as the representative of all. In regard to Mary Magdalene, he follows the account given by John in every detail except that of seeing the angels, up to the point when she spoke to the supposed gardener; then he says that she thought she heard her name called: she thought it was the voice of Jesus; she cried, "O my Master!" and threw herself at his feet, when "the light vision gives way, and says to her, Touch me not." "Little by little the shadow passes away," and she believes that she has seen Jesus.[4] Now this is so near the whole story as told by John, that it leaves no room for the theory which Renan would make it support. If Mary thought she heard her name called, why should we think that she did not? And if, on hearing the voice the second time, she recognized the voice of Jesus, looked upon the person who spoke, and fell at his feet because she recognized him as Jesus, why should we doubt that it was he? She knew him as perfectly as one human being can know another; and how could she be mistaken in his identity when she both heard his voice and looked upon his person? Even if he did "little by little" disappear—an assertion made without evidence—this detracts nothing from the reality of his appearance before he began to disappear. This theory differs from John's account in only one particular—in supposing that, instead of seeing Jesus, Mary saw a "shadow" which she mistook for Jesus—a supposition as thin as the shadow which it conjures up.

---

[4] "Peter and John having departed from the garden, Mary remained alone at the edge of the cave. She wept copiously; one sole thought preoccupied her mind: Where had they put the body? Her woman's heart went no further than her desire to clasp again in her arms the beloved corpse. Suddenly she hears a light rustling behind her. There is a man, standing. At first she believes it to be the gardener. 'Oh!' she says, 'if thou hast borne him hence, tell me where thou hast laid him, that I may take him away.' For the only answer, she thinks that she hears herself called by her own name, 'Mary.' It was the voice that had so often thrilled her before. It was the accent of Jesus. 'Oh, my Master!' she cries. She is about to touch him. A sort of instinctive movement throws her at his feet to kiss them. The light vision gives way, and says to her, 'Touch me not!' Little by little the shadow disappears. But the miracle of love is accomplished. That which Cephas could not do, Mary has done; she has been able to draw life, sweet and penetrating words from the empty tomb. There is now no more talk of inferences to be deduced, or of conjectures to be framed. Mary has seen and heard. The resurrection has its first direct witness." (*Apostles*, 60.)

The author of *Supernatural Religion* makes an attempt to improve on this explanation, by observing that if Mary had turned away at the instant in which she thought the person who spoke to her was the gardener, this inference would have remained and have been erroneous; from which, he says, we might argue, that if still further examination had taken place, her second inference might have proved as erroneous as the first.[5] To put this in familiar form, it means about this: you met a gentleman, and when he first called your name you did not recognize him; but on hearing the voice a second time you recognized it as that of an old friend. You then looked at him, and recognized his person, and held out your hand to him. Now it is suggested that if you had looked at him a little closer you would have seen that he was not your old friend at all, but a shadow conjured up in your own imagination! Such reasoning reverses all experience, and shows how desperate are the straits to which learned and ingenious men are driven when they attempt to explain away the testimony for the resurrection. Baur realized the weakness of their cause and his own at this point, and consequently, while assuming with the writers just quoted that the change in the disciples from unbelief to belief in the resurrection was the result of an "inward spiritual process," he utterly repudiates their attempts to explain the process, by asserting that "no psychological analysis can show what that process was."[6] This is the candidly expressed judgment of one of the most learned and acute of all of the men who have written against the evidence of the resurrection.

In regard to the other women, Renan first misrepresents their testimony by saying that they did not claim to have seen Jesus, and then tries to account for their claim to have seen and heard the angel, by saying: "Perhaps it was the linen clothes which had given rise to this hallucination"; and "Perhaps, again, they saw

---

[5] *Sup. Rel.,* iii. 497, note.

[6] "The view we take of the resurrection is of minor importance for the history. We may regard it as an outward objective miracle, or as a subjective psychological miracle; since, though we assume that an inward spiritual process was possible by which the unbelief of the disciples at the time of the death of Jesus was changed into belief of his resurrection, still no psychological analysis can show what that process was." (*Church History,* i. 42.)

nothing at all, and only began to speak of their vision when Mary of Magdala had related hers."[7] As to the former of these two perhapses, the supposition that four or five women, entering a tomb to put spices on a dead body, and finding only the grave clothes there, would take those folded pieces of linen for a young man in dazzling apparel, and think they heard him say to them, "He is no longer here; return into Galilee; he will go before you; there you shall see him," appears incalculably more like the working of a disordered brain than anything these artless women ever did or said. The other supposition, that they saw nothing, but only told their tale after Mary had told hers; that is, that they made up a lie to keep Mary from excelling them in telling big tales, is the more reasonable of the two, and it would doubtless have been adopted in preference but for the fact that a real belief in the resurrection is admitted, and this would be accounting for its existence by denying that it existed at all. How much more rational to believe the whole story told by the women, than to believe this absurd effort to explain it away. In accounting for the belief of the Twelve, Renan succeeds no better. After the assumption already cited (page 123), that they mistook a current of air, a creaking window, or a chance murmur for the voice of Jesus, he says they immediately decided that Jesus was present, and "some pretended to have observed on his bands and his feet the mark of the nails, and on his side the mark of the spear which pierced him."[8] This is, in the first place, a false representation of the testimony. The testimony is, that when they heard the voice, instead of instantly believing that Jesus was in their midst, they were "terrified and affrighted, and supposed that they beheld a spirit"; and that it was not until he showed them his hands and feet, and ate a piece of broiled fish in their presence, that they were sure it was he (Luke 22.36–43). This is the testimony to be dealt with, and not the imaginary representation which Renan substitutes for it. With this before us, we can at once see that either they told the truth, or the assertion

---

[7] *Apostles,* 62.

[8] *Apostles,* 67, 68.

made by Renan about some of them is true of all, they *pretended* to have seen his wounds; and this means that their story is a falsehood. Here again the theory of hallucination breaks to pieces in the hands of its advocates, and turns into the theory of intentional falsehood. That it does so is proof that there is no middle ground between charging the witnesses with conscious fraud, and admitting the truth of their testimony.

As to the origin of Paul's belief, after stating the theory of delirious fever which we have already noticed (page 123), Renan says that while a prey to these hallucinations Paul saw Jesus, and heard him say to him, "Saul, Saul, why persecutest thou me?" and that instantly his sentiments experienced a revulsion as thorough as it was sudden; "and yet all this was but a new order of fanaticism."[9] If there were any reason at all for thinking that Paul was at the time suffering from delirious fever, it would be possible to suppose that in this fever he was possessed by such a hallucination; but that he would have believed this hallucination to be a reality after he recovered from the fever is preposterous; it is contrary to all the experiences of persons who have had fever. The absurdity of the supposition appears more glaring still, when we remember that Paul's disbelief in Jesus as the Messiah was based on his deliberate judgment as to the meaning of the prophesies on that subject found in the Old Testament; and there could be no possible connection between a hallucination experienced in fever and the exegesis which had led him to his conclusions.

Baur follows in the train of those who hold Paul's vision of Jesus to have been a subjective experience, but he repudiates the hypothesis defended by Renan, that a thunderstorm bursting from the sides of Mount Hermon was the immediate cause of the tran-

---

[9] "And what did he see; what did he hear, while a prey to these hallucinations? He saw the countenance which had haunted him for several days; he saw the phantom of which so much had been said. He saw Jesus himself, who spoke to him in Hebrew, saying, 'Saul, Saul, why persecutest thou me?' . . . Instantly the most thrilling thoughts rush in upon the soul of Paul. Alive to the enormity of his conduct, he saw himself stained with the blood of Stephen, and this martyr appeared to him as his father, his initiator into the new faith. Touched to the quick, his sentiments experienced a revulsion as thorough as it was sudden; and yet all this was but a new order of fanaticism." (*Apostles*, 173–174).

sition.[10] He holds that the account of that miraculous light is nothing but a symbolical and mythical expression for the real presence of the glorified Jesus; and he says: "However firmly the Apostle may have believed that he saw the form of Jesus actually and, as it were, externally before him, his testimony extends merely to what he believed he saw." This last remark is unquestionably true; and the only question is, Did he see what he believed he saw, or was he mistaken? As we have said before, if there occurred within him, from some unnatural state of mind, the conviction that he was seeing and hearing Jesus, this conviction would have passed away with the unnatural mental state which brought it about; and consequently the fact that he continued to believe that he saw and heard with his physical senses is the best of proof that he did.

Strauss, dismissing with Baur the theory of a thunder storm, makes a somewhat different attempt to account for Paul's belief psychologically. He says: "Apart from the blindness and its removal by Ananias, as also the phenomena seen by the attendants, we might look upon all as a vision which Paul attributed indeed to an external cause, but which, nevertheless, took place in his own mind." In another place he speaks in more positive terms of Paul's conviction, saying: "It is certain that in doing so he considered the ascended Christ as really and externally present, the appearance as in the full sense an objective one"; but he claims the right to be of a different opinion from Paul.[11] He attempts to account for this singular mistake of an inward for an outward vision by supposing that Paul, in hours of despondency, when thinking of the tranquility of the disciples under persecution in contrast with his own troubled feelings, began to question himself as to whether, after all, he might not be wrong and they right; and that an ecstasy coining on him—that is, in plain terms, an epileptic fit—Jesus

---

[10] "The well known modern hypothesis, so often repeated, that this light was a flash of lightning which suddenly struck the apostle and laid him and his companions senseless on the ground, is really a mere hypothesis; and as it not only has no foundation in the text, but is also in manifest contradiction with the meaning of the author, we shall make no further mention of it here." (Baur, *Paul*, i. 68.)

[11] *New Life*, i. 414, 417.

appeared and spoke to him.[12] Here, by the necessity of his attempt to show that Paul mistook the working of his own mind for the miraculous appearance of Jesus, he falls into the supposition which we have already so fully exposed as absurd, that Paul was demented at the time of his conversion. Christian Baur repudiates all these theories of his fellow infidels, and declares concerning Paul's faith as he does concerning that of the older Apostles, that it can not be accounted for in any such way.[13]

As a final exposure of the futility of all of these attempts to account for Paul's belief without admitting the reality of the appearance of Jesus to him, we cite the fact of the blindness, which resulted from the brilliancy of the light that shone around him. Strauss felt that this blindness was in his way, as appears from the qualifying clause with which he introduces his theory: "Apart from the blindness and its removal by Ananias, we might look upon all as a vision."[14] But the narrative can not be considered apart from this blindness and its removal. The latter is an essential part of the story, without which all that is said about Paul's conversion in Acts breaks to pieces. It is necessary either to get rid of the blindness, or to believe the whole story; for if the blindness was real, the theory of a mere mental change in Paul without an external cause must be dismissed; and so must the hypothesis of an ecstasy, for an ecstasy does not make men blind. It also sets aside the supposition of an optical illusion and that of a falsehood, for neither optical illusions nor falsehoods make men blind. The blindness and its removal stamp the whole story with the in-

---

[12] *Ib.*, 420.

[13] "We can not call his conversion, his sudden transformation from the most vehement opponent of Christianity into its boldest preacher, anything but a miracle; and the miracle appears all the greater when we remember that in this revulsion of his consciousness he broke through the barriers of Judaism, and rose out of the particularism of Judaism into the universal idea of Christianity. Yet great as this miracle is, it can only be conceived as a spiritual process; and this implies that some step of transition was not wanting from one extreme to the other. It is true that no analysis, either psychological or dialectical, can detect the inner secret of the act in which God revealed his Son in him. Yet it may very justly be asked whether what made the transition possible can have been anything else than the great impressiveness with which the great fact of the death of Jesus came all at once to stand before his soul." (*Church History*, i. 47.)

[14] *New Life*, i. 414.

delible marks of truthfulness and reality. Baur, realizing this, attempts to get rid of the blindness. After referring to what is said of the visit and the remarks of Ananias, he says: "Is not, then, the 'to be filled with the Holy Spirit,' which was wont to follow the laying on of hands, in itself a healing of blindness, an *a]nable<pein* in a spiritual sense; and does not the expression, 'immediately there fell from his eyes, as it were, scales,' seem to indicate that they were no real scales, that there was no real blindness, no real cure?"[15] These questions would have plausibility if the statements of the text about the blindness were at all ambiguous; but they are not so. Luke says that when Paul opened his eyes after the vision "he saw nothing"; and that he was "three days and nights without sight"; and Paul says: "When I could not see for the glory of that light, being led by the hand of them that were with me, I came into Damascus." In regard to the restoration of his sight Luke represents Ananias as saying to him, "The Lord hath sent me that thou mayest receive thy sight and be filled with the Holy Spirit." Two purposes are here declared: that he might receive sight is one, and that he might be filled with the Holy Spirit is another, and it is totally distinct from the first. Neither of these purposes was at all dependent on the other; for Paul might have been restored to his sight without receiving the Holy Spirit, and he might have received the Holy Spirit had it been in accordance with God's subsequent purposes concerning him, without receiving his sight. Furthermore, Luke says: "And straightway there fell from his eyes, as it were, scales, and he received his sight." The expression "as it were scales," shows of course that they were not real scales, but it does not show that they were nothing. They were doubtless obstructions to sight which had formed on the eyes, and they resulted from the inflammation caused by the intensity of the light. Paul's account is that Ananias said to him, "Brother Saul, receive thy sight"; and he adds: "In that very hour I looked upon him." Only on the supposition that these several statements of Paul and Luke are false can any of the questions propounded by

---

[15] *Paul,* i. 72.

Baur be answered in the affirmative except the last, which is thus answered in the text itself. Let it be noted, too, that the only reason why infidels can wish to get rid of the fact of the blindness is because it proves the reality of the miraculous light which caused it, and of the miraculous cure which removed it. Now, if in the accounts of it given in the text of Scripture it had the appearance of being lugged in to artificially support the evidence of these two miracles, this would justly excite suspicion of its reality; but no such artificiality is charged, and there is not the slightest indication of it to be found. It must stand as a fact; and while it stands, it stands as an impassable barrier to the attempts of skeptics to throw doubt on the reality of Paul's vision of Christ glorified. It was largely owing to this fact, perfectly well known to the unbelieving friends of Paul during the three days of its continuance, that he "confounded the Jews who dwelt at Damascus, proving that this is the Christ" (Acts 9.22).

We now see that all attempts to break the force of the evidence for the resurrection by adverse theories concerning the disappearance of the body of Jesus, and of the origin of the belief of the disciples that he had risen, are as futile as those to invalidate the testimony of the witnesses by various charges against them. The case, then, is the third of those mentioned at the beginning of the chapter (132–133). These two facts are to be accounted for. The resurrection of Jesus accounts for them adequately, and on no other hypothesis can they be accounted for at all; therefore we are confined to the actual resurrection as the true and only cause of the admitted facts.

TWELVE

The Resurrection of Jesus: The Testimony of the Witnesses

The writers through whose reports the testimony of the witnesses comes to us having been named, and their authenticity vindicated, we next proceed to inquire into the qualifications of the witnesses themselves. We have considered these to some extent in the last chapter, but only in the way of inquiring whether the witnesses are liable to certain charges which have been preferred against them by their enemies. We now take up the inquiry as an original question, and will conduct it as it should be conducted in regard to any witnesses of important events.

The force of human testimony depends on three things: first, the honesty of the witnesses; second, their competency; and third, their number. We ascertain whether they are honest, by considering their general character and their motives in the particular case. Hence, in attempting to impeach a witness in a court of justice, it is common to call on men who know him, to testify as to his general reputation for veracity; and also to inquire whether he is personally interested in establishing the facts to which he testifies. Competency is determined by considering the opportunities of the witness to obtain knowledge of that to which he testifies, and his mental capacity to observe and remember the facts. The requisite number varies with the degree of probability attached to the facts. The testimony of two honest and competent witnesses makes us feel more sure than that of one; and that of three, than that of two; but a limit is soon reached beyond which those who are convinced feel the need of no more, and those who are not yet convinced realize that more would not convince them. When this number has testified in any case, the number is sufficient, and a greater number would be useless.

Applying these tests to the witnesses of the resurrection of Jesus, we find that their general character, judged by all that we know of them, is good. The sentiments uttered by the principal witnesses are those which to this day guide the consciences of the most enlightened men in the world; and no teachers have ever insisted more strenuously than they on the duty of strict veracity. As to their motives in testifying to the fact of the resurrection, they are above suspicion. The motives which prompt men to false testimony are fear, avarice, and ambition; fear of some evil to themselves or others, which is to be averted by the testimony; desire of sordid gain; and ambition for some kind of distinction among men. Can any of these motives have prompted the Apostles to falsely testify that God had raised Jesus from the dead? It is impossible to see any threatened calamity which they or their friends would have escaped by this testimony if it is false. On the other hand, they must have anticipated much danger to themselves if they should publicly proclaim it; for to publicly proclaim it would be to proclaim the chief priests and Pilate murderers, convicted as such by the act of God in raising from the dead him whom they had slain. For such an offense they could not expect anything but the severest punishment; or, if they hoped at first to convince these rulers, and to bring them to repentance, the hope was soon dissipated; for it was on account of this very testimony that they were arrested, thrown into prison, scourged, and pursued with all manner of persecution. Really the Twelve suffered the loss of all that men ordinarily hold dear in consequence of persisting in this testimony; and the honesty of no set of witnesses was ever so severely tested, or so clearly demonstrated. This is especially true of the Apostle Paul, who suffered more than any other witness. The demonstration is so complete that it has won the acknowledgment, especially with reference to Paul, of the most determined foes of the Christian faith. Thus the author of Supernatural Religion says: "As to the Apostle Paul himself, let it be said in the strongest and most emphatic manner possible, that we do not suggest the most distant suspicion of the sincerity of any historical statement he makes."[1] Being honest, the witnesses believed that of which they testified; and if they believed it, it must be true unless they were mistaken. Whether they can have been mistaken or not, depends on their competency, and this we are next to consider.

Of the opportunities which these honest witnesses enjoyed for knowing that of which they testify, we are informed by their own statements. Of their mental capacity we have already spoken in full while discussing the charge that they were hallucinated. Under the head of competency, then, we have only to examine their several statements, and see whether their opportunities were such as to insure that they were not mistaken. We shall do this by considering, first, the testimony of the women; second, that of Cleopas and his unnamed companion; third, that of the Twelve; and fourth, that of Paul.

The women who went to the sepulcher on the third morning were Mary Magdalene, whose excellent character is sufficiently attested by the fact that she was the most intimate and devoted female friend of Jesus; Mary the mother of James and Joseph, of whom we only know that she was one of the company of Jesus; Salome, the honored mother of the two Apostles, James and John; Joanna, the wife of Herod's steward, who, considering her relation through her husband to that murderer of John the Baptist and persecutor of Jesus, could have become a follower of the latter only through the most disinterested motives; and "other women," whose names are not given because, perhaps, they were not conspicuous in the church at the time that our Gospels were written,

---

[1] *Sup. Rel.*, iii. 496.

or because it was thought by the writer that the names given were sufficient in number. All that is said in our Gospels to have been seen and heard by these women was of course derived from them by the writers, and it is their testimony.

On reaching the sepulcher and finding it open they claim, as we learn from Mark and Luke, to have entered into it—a circumstance of which Matthew says nothing. On entering they found the tomb empty, and soon they saw within it two angels, though Matthew and Mark mention only one of them, the one who had opened the tomb and who immediately speaks to the women. His words, only partly reported by any one writer, when put together in their natural order, are these: "Fear not: for I know that ye seek Jesus who hath been crucified. Why seek ye the living among the dead? He is not here, for he is risen, even as he said. Remember how he spake to you while he was yet in Galilee, saying that the Son of Man must be delivered up into the hands of sinful men, and be crucified, and the third day rise again. Come, see the place where the Lord lay. And go quickly, and tell his disciples he is risen from the dead; and lo, he goeth before you into Galilee; there ye shall see him: lo, I have told you." As they ran from the tomb to carry this message, Jesus himself met them, and saluted them with the word, "All hail." "They came and took hold of his feet, and worshiped him." While doing this, again they hear his voice: "Fear not: go tell my disciples, that they depart into Galilee, and there shall they see me."

While the three synoptic Gospels give jointly the details just recited, that of Mark, without explanation, informs us that Jesus appeared first to Mary Magdalene, which implies that before the appearance to the women just mentioned she had separated herself from the others, for had she been with them they would have seen him as soon as she did. The fourth Gospel accounts for this separation, and gives the particulars of the appearance to Mary. It informs us that when she saw that the stone was removed from the tomb she ran to John and Peter, and said: "They have taken away the Lord out of the tomb, and we know not where they have laid him." As she had not entered the tomb, she inferred that the body had been removed from the mere fact that the tomb was open. From this passage we gather that her separation from the other women, implied in Mark's narrative, took place at the moment when they saw that the tomb was open, and that she did not go into the tomb with them. This circumstance Matthew failed to mention; consequently his narrative reads as if she continued with them. On hearing Mary's statement, Peter and John ran to the sepulcher, and Mary followed them. After they departed she stood for awhile weeping, and "as she wept she stooped and looked into the tomb." When she did so she beheld the two angels who had showed themselves to the other women, but not to the men, and she observed that one of them sat at the head and the other at the feet of where Jesus had laid. She knew these spots not by having seen the body after it was laid in the tomb, but from having seen Joseph and Nicodemus take it in, and observing whether it was carried in head foremost or feet foremost. Her observation and her memory were very accurate. She testifies that the angels said (one of them of course doing the speaking): "Woman, why weepest thou?" She answered: "Because they have taken away my Lord, and I know not where they have laid him." At this instant, for a reason which she does not give, she "turned herself back" and beheld Jesus standing near, but mistook him for the gardener. He said: "Woman, why weepest thou?" And she answered: "Sir, if thou hast borne him hence, tell me where thou hast laid him, and I will take him away." She evidently thought that the gardener would be glad to be relieved of the dead body. For an answer she hears her own name. "She turneth herself," being only partially turned toward him before, recognizes him, and exclaims, "Rabboni." He says to her: "Touch me not; for I am not yet ascended unto the Father: but go unto my brethren, and say to them, I ascend unto my Father and your Father, and my God and your God."

With this testimony before us, we ask, Did these women have good and sufficient opportunity to know beyond question that they saw what they claimed to have seen, and heard the words which they reported? When the male disciples heard it all, they believed it not; but their disbelief arose not from considering deliberately the question which we have just propounded, but from the foregone conclusion that Jesus was not to rise, the very reason why some in our own day will not believe. But when they considered the evidence maturely they accepted it as true, and so must every one today who considers it without prejudice.

To the testimony of the women in regard to the absence of the body from the tomb is added that of Peter and John. Luke says that after the report of the women, Peter ran to the tomb, stooped and looked in, and saw the linen cloths by themselves. John, in his more minute account, adds to this the statement that both he and Peter went into the tomb, and saw the linen cloths lying, and the napkin that was upon his head not lying with the linen cloths, but rolled up in a place by itself. This testimony not only shows that the body had disappeared, but it furnishes strong evidence that it had not been removed in any of the ways suggested by unbelievers. If some of the disciples had taken it to bury it in Galilee, they would have taken it with the shroud still around it; so of the gardener, and so of the Jews. Only in ease the body went forth into life would it have been divested of the shroud in which all dead bodies were then buried.

Our records leave it in some uncertainty whether the Apostle Peter, or Cleopas and his unnamed companion, was the first among the male disciples to see Jesus after he arose; but it is certain the latter are the first whose testimony is reported. Of the appearance to Peter nothing is said except the mere fact. Their testimony is given more in detail than that of the previous group of witnesses. In substance it is this: that as they were walking to Emmaus, a distance of seven and a half miles from the city, Jesus joined them; and appearing as a stranger, opened conversation by asking what communications they were having with each other as they walked; and on learning, he proceeded to show them out of the Scriptures that it behoved the Christ to suffer all that Jesus had suffered, and to enter into his glory. They say their eyes were "holden" that they should not know him; and they say that while he was speaking to them by the way their hearts were burning within them. In answer to his first question, they said, among other things: "Certain women of our company amazed us, having been early at the tomb; and when they found not his body, they came, saying that they had also seen a vision of angels who said that he was alive." In this they confirm what is said of the testimony of the women. They add: "And certain of them that were with us went to the tomb, and found it even so as the women had said: but him they saw not." Now this last statement is entirely independent of Luke's statement in the previous paragraph, that Peter ran to the tomb, and saw the linen cloths by themselves; for they speak in the plural number, showing that they refer to more than one person. Their reference can be only to the visit of Peter and John described in John's Gospel, and yet it includes that of Peter mentioned in Luke. Here is an undesigned coincidence of an unmistakable kind, and it furnishes strong evidence that the story of Cleopas, who is the speaker, is reliable. He and his companion proceed to state that when they reached their destination the supposed stranger, after earnest solicitation, went in with them, that he sat down to eat, took bread, blessed, broke, and gave to them, and then vanished. Just before he vanished they recognized him as Jesus, their eyes at the instant being "opened." Who could have invented this story? Who, wishing to invent a story of having seen Jesus, could possibly have put it into this shape? And who, coming to them as this apparent stranger did, could possibly have given the instruction which he gave? There was not another man on earth who at that time possessed the ideas which were imparted. A conscious restraint upon their vision, which did not excite their suspicion at the time, but which was distinctly remembered after the interview was ended, accounts for their failure to recognize him sooner. If, on this account, their opportunity to know him was not so good as that of the women, the consideration just mentioned counterbalances this disadvantage, and leaves their testimony free from doubt.

The testimony of the Twelve is presented in two distinct forms in the New Testament, one in the closing chapters of the Gospels, and the other in the book of Acts. The former is their testimony as mere men to the one fact of the resurrection; the latter, their testimony as inspired men to the glorification of Christ in heaven, which involved his resurrection as a necessary antecedent. We shall consider the two divisions of the subject separately.

Their testimony as found in the Gospels is connected with five distinct interviews held with him—three in Jerusalem, and two in Galilee. The first in Jerusalem is described by Mark, Luke and John, but omitted by Matthew. All told, the details are these: Ten of the Apostles, on the evening after the resurrection, were in a room securely closed for fear of the Jews. The two from Emmaus had been admitted and had told their story, which was received with discredit. The company were "sitting at meat." The two had scarcely completed their story when Jesus stood in their midst without having passed through the door. His first word was, "Peace be unto you." At the first moment they were "terrified and affrighted, and supposed that they beheld a spirit." He said: "Why are ye troubled; and wherefore do reasonings arise in your hearts? See my hands and my feet, that it is I myself: handle me, and see; for a spirit hath not flesh and bones as ye see me having." He also showed them his side. They still "disbelieved for joy," and they still wondered, till he asked if they had anything there to eat, and receiving a piece of broiled fish he ate it before them. They were then glad "when they saw the Lord," that is, when they saw it was the Lord in reality. He upbraided them for their unbelief and hardness of heart, because they believed not them who had seen him after he was risen. He closed by saying, "Peace be unto you: as the Father hath sent me, so I send you." And when he had said this, he breathed on them and said unto them: "Receive ye the Holy Spirit: whosesoever sins ye forgive, they are forgiven unto them; whosesoever sins ye retain, they are retained." How he disappeared at the close of this or of any other interview except the last, we are not informed; and this is one of the marvels of this wonderful testimony. It shows that the witnesses were not aiming to tell a long story of irrelevant particulars, but to state simply and briefly the facts on which faith in the resurrection must rest. As regards these facts, does their story admit of the possibility that they were mistaken? Can they be mistaken as to the fact that it was Jesus whom they had seen, with whom they had conversed, whose wounds in the hands and feet and side they had beheld? Can they have been mistaken as to his having entered without opening the door, which they had securely closed for fear that an enemy might enter? Surely the story must be a series of conscious falsehoods, or it must be true: there is no middle ground.

At the second interview, which occurred just one week, as we count time, after the first, eleven were present, and this interview seems to have been granted especially for the benefit of Thomas, who was not present at the first. When he was told of the first interview he exclaimed: "Except I shall see in his hands the print of the nails, and put my finger into the print of the nails, and put my hand into his side, I will not believe." His idea evidently was that the ten had seen some one whose person and voice so closely resembled those of Jesus that, like twin brothers, they could not be distinguished; and as for the wounds, he thought that his brethren should have felt them as well as seen them before believing. The wounds he would admit as conclusive evidence if they were real, for he knew that it was impossible for another man perfectly like Jesus in every other particular to also bear those wounds, and to be going about alive. The eleven were in the same room, with the doors closed as before, when Jesus a second time stood suddenly in their midst, and exclaimed: "Peace be unto you." Then, addressing Thomas, he says: "Reach hither thy finger, and see my hands; and reach hither thy hand, and put it into my side: and be not faithless, but believing." Thomas exclaimed, "My Lord and my God"; but whether he put his finger and his hand into the wounds or not, we are not informed. It appears rather that the sight of the wounds was more convincing than he had supposed, and that this, with the other evidence of his eyes and his ears, was enough. Jesus said to him: "Because thou hast seen, thou hast believed: blessed are they who have not seen, and yet have believed." This ended the interview; and surely if the truth is told about it there was no chance for Thomas or any of the others to be mistaken.

The next interview was with seven of the disciples, including six of the Apostles. It was on the lake shore, and early in the morning. They were in their boat fishing, and he was about one hundred yards distant on the shore. The first evidence that it was he was the fact that at his command to drop their net on the right hand side of the boat, they caught an immense draught of fishes where they had fished all night and caught nothing. This caused them to hasten ashore. There they found that he had prepared for them a breakfast of broiled fish and some bread, which he deliberately distributed among them. He then entered into an elaborate conversation with Peter in their presence, at the close of which he walked away. Here there was none of the wild excitement which arose at his appearance to them on previous occasions; but all was calm and deliberate from beginning to end. No company of men ever met a friend unexpectedly and spent an hour in conversation with him, who could be more certain that it was he than these were that it was Jesus with whom they conversed. A mistake on their part is inconceivable.

The next appearance to the eleven was in Galilee, on "the mountain where he had appointed them." Matthew says: "When they saw him they worshiped him; but some doubted." If this last remark means, as it has been construed by some skeptics, that they doubted all through the interview, we have one instance in which the evidence was not convincing to all who were present: but is this the meaning? The remainder of the account shows that it is not. The very next clause is, "And Jesus came to them and spake to them," which shows that at the moment of the doubt he was not very near to them and had not yet spoken to them. There is no difference, then, between the doubt on this occasion and on the first, when they thought for a time that he was a ghost. Let us observe, too, that the very admission of this doubt is an indubitable mark of naturalness and truthfulness in the narrative; for it could certainly not have been thought of had it not been true; and even though true, it would have been omitted if the author had been more anxious to make the case a strong one than to tell it as it was. After coming to them as stated Jesus said to them: "All authority hath been given to me, in heaven and on earth. Go ye, therefore, and make disciples of all the nations, baptizing them into the name of the Father, and of the Son, and of the Holy Spirit: teaching them to observe all things whatsoever I commanded you: and lo, I am with you always, even to the end of the world." These are the words of the commission, under the authority of which they proceeded to labor and suffer all the rest of their lives. To have been mistaken in thinking that they had heard them would have been a fundamental mistake; and to have been doubtful would have given weakness in place of the strength which they ever afterward exhibited. Their opportunity for both seeing and hearing was too good to allow the supposition that they could have been mistaken.

The last of these interviews occurred in Jerusalem on the day of the ascension. Its incidents must be collected from the last six verses of Mark, verses 45–53 of the last chapter of Luke, and verses 4–11 of the first chapter of Acts. He pointed out more fully than before the prophecies which must needs be fulfilled in him; and he opened their minds that they might understand these Scriptures. He showed them particularly that his death and resurrection were in accordance with these Scriptures, and that "repentance and remission of sins should be preached in his name to all the nations, beginning at Jerusalem." He commanded them to go into all the world and preach the gospel to every creature, and promised them power to work signs and wonders in his name. He charged them, however, not to depart from Jerusalem until they should be clothed with power from on high, which he explains by the words: "Ye shall be baptized in the Holy Spirit not many days hence"; and he calls this "the promise of the Father." They were bold enough to ask him, "Dost thou at this time restore the kingdom to Israel?" but were told that it was not for them to know times and seasons. They were told the order in which they should carry their message to different communities: to Jerusalem first, then to Judea and Samaria, and then to all the earth. While this conversation was in progress he had led them from the city out across the Kedron, up the slope of the mount of Olives, and past the nearer summit of this mountain to the vicinity of Bethany; and as he concluded he lifted up his hands to bless them, and was himself lifted up till a cloud received him out of their sight. They stood gazing into the sky where he had disappeared, until two angels stood by them, and told them that he would return in like manner as they had seen him go into heaven. Now here is the most protracted interview of all those described in our books; it was the most free and unconstrained on the part of the Eleven; and even were there ground to suppose in previous interviews too great excitement on the part of the latter for reliable observation, there certainly can be none in this. We conclude that all these accounts were given by men and women guilty of conscious false-hood, or that they all describe real events. The honesty of the witnesses precludes the former alternative, and we have therefore no choice but to accept the latter.

The testimony of the Apostles as given in Acts begins with the scenes of Pentecost; for that which we have just considered from the first chapter is a mere supplement to Luke's Gospel. On the next Pentecost after the resurrection, the testimony of the Apostles was first given to the public; and it was given by all the Twelve; for they all stood up with Peter, and he was their spokesman. Peter approached the testimony by an argument from the prophecies of David, intended to remove from the minds of his Jewish hearers the antecedent improbability of the resurrection (vv 22–31), and then he presented the testimony of himself and his companions in these words: "This Jesus did God raise up, whereof we are all witnesses." This testimony to the fact of the resurrection is subordinated in the sermon to that concerning the glorification of Jesus in heaven. The account shows that

Peter was now qualified to speak on this latter subject; for we not only have Luke's statement that he and all the Twelve were now filled with the Holy Spirit and spoke in all the tongues known to the assembled multitude, but, what is more to the point of our present argument, we have the testimony of Peter and those for whom he spoke, to the same effect. He explains the phenomenon which had astonished the multitude by telling them that it was the fulfillment of Joel's prophecy, that the Holy Spirit should be poured forth upon men so that they should prophesy (16–18); and he solemnly declares to them that this gift of the Spirit had been sent down from heaven by Jesus, who had been exalted by the right hand of God and had taken a seat on his throne (32–36). Now, whatever may be thought of the possibility of the audience being mistaken as to the nature of the gift bestowed on the Twelve, it is certain that they could not be mistaken in thinking that they heard them speaking in the various tongues with which they were familiar. There is perhaps nothing in human experience in which a man is less liable to mistake than in recognizing his native language when he unexpectedly hears it spoken. And it is equally certain that the Apostles were not mistaken in thinking themselves the subjects of this phenomenon. It was a matter of consciousness to them; so here again we have a case in which the alternative is to charge these honest witnesses with a most stupendous fraud, or to confess not only that Jesus arose from the dead, but that he was exalted to such a position and authority in heaven as to send forth the Spirit of God to continue the work which he had himself begun on the earth. This testimony was repeated again and again, and it was the chief burden of the Apostolic preaching to the unbelieving world, as well as the chief cause of all the persecutions which they endured. See Acts 3.13–16, 20, 21; 4. 1–2, 18–20; 5.17–18. 30–32, 40; 10.38–42. It is all epitomised in the closing statement of Mark's Gospel: "And they went forth and preached everywhere, the Lord working with them and confirming the word by the signs that followed." When our first three Gospels were written, this work was in full progress, and the strongest evidence to the people that Jesus had risen from the dead was not the personal testimony of those who saw him between the resurrection and the ascension, but the testimony of the Twelve who were going about among the people proclaiming Jesus as the glorified ruler of heaven and earth, living at the right hand of God, and by his own power performing the signs, wonders and miracles which they continually wrought in his name. This accounts for the meagerness of the evidence of the resurrection arrayed in the closing chapters of the Gospels—meagerness in the number of appearances of Jesus reported in each, but not in the conclusiveness of the evidence which is given. In the presence of more convincing and comprehensive evidence, it was not important to elaborate that which was less so.

In addition to all that we have cited from Acts and the Gospels, we have separate testimony from Peter and John in their own writings. In the first Epistle of Peter, there are repeated references to the resurrection of Jesus as an established fact, and to his present living power in heaven. See 1. 3–4, 7–8, 12, 21; 3.18, 21; 4. 11, 13. He gives none of the details of the interviews with Jesus by which he had gained a certainty of the fact of the resurrection; but he indirectly affirms what Luke says of him in Acts, by saying that he and others had preached the gospel "by the Holy Spirit sent forth from heaven" (1.12), thus affirming his inspiration, and his consequent power to speak authoritatively of things in the heavenly world. The Apostle John, in the opening of his first Epistle, bears the following testimony: "That which was from the beginning, which we have heard, which we have seen with our eyes, which we have looked upon, and our hands have handled, of the Word of life; (for the life was manifested, and we have seen it, and bear witness, and show unto you that eternal life, which was with the Father, and was manifested unto us;) that which we have seen and heard declare we unto you, that you also may have fellowship with us; and truly our fellowship is with the Father, and with his Son Jesus Christ. And these things write we unto you, that your joy may be full." No doubt there is reference here to the manifestation of the "Word of life" both in the natural life of Jesus, and in his life subsequent to the resurrection; but the reference is more particularly to the latter; for otherwise the employing of ears, eyes and hands in identifying him would not be so insisted on. The passage is a reiteration by John in person of the testimony given in the gospels; and it renders the possibility of having been mistaken completely out of the question. In the opening statements of the Apocalypse, the same Apostle gives fresh testimony by describing a new appearance of Jesus to him, which occurred after the close of all the testimony given by the other Apostles, and after their death. He declares that Jesus appeared to him in a glorified form which he minutely describes, showing that he saw him distinctly; that notwithstanding the glory of his form he was "like unto the Son of man"; that he himself, overpowered by the sight, fell at his feet as a dead man; that Jesus came to him, laid his "right hand" upon him, and declared himself to be he who was dead, but is now alive forevermore; and that he then dictated in an audible voice seven epistles to seven of the churches in Asia (2.9–18). This testimony, let it be remembered, is admitted by infidels to be the genuine testimony of John; and as it is admitted that he was an honest writer, the only question about it is, Can he have been mistaken? We think that every unbiased mind in the world would promptly answer that the story was either made up from the imagination of the writer, or it describes a reality. This is the concluding section of the testimony of the original witnesses, as given in the New Testament. Let the reader judge, as he will answer to God, whether it establishes as a fact the resurrection of Jesus from the dead, and his ascension to the right hand of God in heaven.

The testimony of Paul given in his Epistles furnishes none of those details by which we can judge whether he or the other witnesses of whom he speaks could have been mistaken; but it is a reiteration of the main fact in very positive terms. He presents the witnesses in solid array as follows: "I delivered to you first of all that which I also received, how that Christ died for our sins according to the Scriptures; and that he was buried; and that he hath been raised the third day according to the Scriptures; and that he appeared to Cephas; then to the Twelve; then he appeared to above five hundred brethren at once, of whom the greater part remain until now, but some are fallen asleep; then he appeared to James; then to all the Apostles; and last of all he appeared to me also" (1 Cor 15.3–8). Like the Gospel writers, he selects for mention a certain number of the appearances of Jesus, and omits the others; but he mentions more of them than any other writer, and he mentions one—that to James—omitted by all the others. This passage shows that he had already made the Corinthians familiar with this evidence, having made it the foremost subject matter of his preaching, and this accounts for the absence of those details which are so carefully given in the Gospels and in Acts. But the chief value of Paul's testimony in the Epistles is found in what he says of the powers which he had received from the risen Christ. Whatever may be thought of his being mistaken about miracles wrought by other persons, he could not be mistaken in his claim to work them himself. On this point his testimony is explicit. To the Romans he says: "I will not dare to speak of any things save only those which Christ hath wrought through me, for the obedience of the Gentiles, by word and deed, in the power of signs and wonders, in the power of the Holy Spirit; so that from Jerusalem, and round about unto Illyricum, I have fully preached the Gospel of Christ" (Rom 15.18–19). Here, by "the power of signs and wonders" and "the power of the Holy Spirit," he unmistakably means the miraculous powers exercised by the Apostles. To the Corinthians he says: "Truly the signs of an apostle were wrought among you in all patience by signs, wonders and mighty works" (2 Cor 12.12). Here there are three things to be noted: first, that his expression for the miracles which he had wrought is precisely that which was used by Peter in his sermon on Pentecost for the miracles of Jesus; that is, signs, wonders and mighty works, which shows that he speaks of the same class of works; second, that these were then known to the Corinthians as "the signs of an apostle"; that is, the indispensable proofs that a man was an apostle, and that all the Apostles were known to be workers of such miracles; third, that this language was used in writing to a people who knew whether he had wrought such miracles among them, and a part of whom were his personal enemies, denying that he was an apostle; under such circumstances it is inconceivable that he should have claimed to work miracles among them if he had not. We have this evidence in addition to the admitted veracity of Paul, that he wrought these miracles in the name of Christ, and that therefore Christ was not only alive, but in the possession of infinite power.

The testimonies which we have now considered combine to prove that Jesus certainly arose from the dead, and ascended up to heaven. In thus establishing as real the great miracle of the New Testament on which all the others depend for their value, all ground and all motive for denying the latter are removed. If Jesus rose from the dead it was because he was what his disciples represent him to be, the Son of God; and from this it follows that he was possessed of all power.

There is no need, therefore, that we go back over the accounts of miracles in the Gospels, and look into the evidence for these in detail; the whole ground is now covered, and we are brought to the conclusion that the New Testament writers are credible when writing about the miraculous as well as when writing of the natural and the ordinary.

THIRTEEN

The Messiahship of Jesus

The Jews of the time of Jesus, and after, believed that in the writings of Moses and the prophets there were predictions concerning a great ruler and deliverer yet to come, called the Messiah in their language, the Christ in Greek. They expected him, as we have stated in a former chapter, to be a son of David, to restore the kingdom of David, to settle all difficult questions of doctrine and worship, and to abide forever. This expectation was embodied in the remark of Philip concerning Jesus: "We have found him of whom Moses in the law, and the prophets did write, Jesus of Nazareth, the son of Joseph" (John 1.45); and it is alluded to in the remark concerning Simeon, that he was looking for the consolation of Israel; and in the statement that the aged Anna "spoke of him to all that were looking for the redemption of Jerusalem" (Luke 2.38). The same expectation and hope are more fully and beautifully expressed in the song of Zacharias:

> Blessed be the Lord the God of Israel;
> For he hath visited and wrought redemption for his people,
>   and hath raised up a horn of salvation for us
> In the house of his servant David
> (As he spake by the mouth of his holy prophets which have
>   been since the world began),
> Salvation from our enemies, and from all that hate us;
> To show mercy toward our fathers,

And to remember his holy covenant,
The oath which he swore unto Abraham our father,
To grant unto us that we being delivered out of the hands
      of our enemies,
Should serve him without fear
In holiness and righteousness before him all our days.

(Luke 1.68–75)

When John the Baptist appeared on the banks of the Jordan, and with preaching of unprecedented power stirred the hearts and consciences of the whole people, we are told that they "were in expectation, and reasoned in their hearts concerning John, whether haply he were the Christ" (Luke 3.15); and the leaders in Jerusalem went so far as to send to him priests and Levites to ask him pointedly this very question (John 1.19–20). So when John had passed away, and Jesus engrossed the popular attention, during the whole of his ministry the great and absorbing question was, Is he the Christ? True, the question whether he was the Son of God became prominent also, and especially toward the close of his career; but the former was ever the foremost question of the two. In the course of our discussion we have reversed this order; for to us the question of his sonship stands foremost both in importance and in the order in which we most naturally consider it. Having settled this, we have prepared the way for the other question, and have made its settlement a very easy task.

The question of the Messiahship turns on the fulfillment in Jesus of the predictions concerning the Messiah. He claimed while he was living that there were such predictions, and that they were fulfilled in him, saying on one occasion: "Ye search the Scriptures, because ye think that in them ye have eternal life; and these are they that testify of me." "Think not that I will accuse you to the Father: there is one that accuseth you, even Moses on whom ye have set your hope. For if ye believed Moses ye would believe me; for he wrote of me" (John 5.39, 45). After his resurrection, in conversations with his disciples he taught the same thing with greater fullness. When addressing the two on the way to Emmaus, "beginning from Moses and from all the prophets, he interpreted to them in all the scriptures the things concerning himself"; and to the Twelve he said: "These are my words which I spake to you while I was yet with you, how that all things must needs be fulfilled which are written in the law of Moses, and the prophets, and the psalms, concerning me" (Luke 24.27, 44). This was also the leading theme with all the apostles when addressing Jewish audiences. Peter, in his second recorded discourse, after speaking of the sufferings and resurrection of Jesus, says: "But the things which God foreshowed by the mouth of all the prophets, that his Christ should suffer, he thus fulfilled." . . . "Yea, and all the prophets from Samuel, and those who follow after, as many as have spoken, they also told of these days" (Acts 3.18, 24). Thus the Apostles spoke in Jerusalem at the beginning; and in Rome, at the close of the record of apostolic preaching, we learn of Paul that when he had gathered the unbelieving Jews of the city together in great numbers, "he expounded the matter, testifying the kingdom of God, and persuading them concerning Jesus, both from the law of Moses and from the prophets, from morning till evening" (Acts xxviii. 23). These citations show that it was the settled doctrine of both Jesus and the Apostles that many predictions in the Old Testament written concerning the promised Messiah were fulfilled in Jesus, thus proving him to be the Christ.

There is no attempt by any of the New Testament writers to cite all the predictions thus fulfilled. While the general terms which they employ imply that there is a large number of them, the number which they quote is comparatively small. Matthew deals more in this kind of argument than any other, but even he leaves the specifications chiefly to the intelligence of the reader. While Matthew cites many along the line of incidents in the life of Jesus, beginning with genealogy and the scenes of the infancy, the author of Hebrews cites chiefly those respecting his exalted dignity in heaven as the Lord of angels and the high priest for men. But Jesus, Peter and Paul, in their preaching, concentrate their attention on those respecting his death, resurrection and exaltation; and as these have been proved to be realities by our previous course of evidence, it is sufficient for our purpose now to show that these were characteristics of the Christ, in order to identify Jesus as that personage.

In his first sermon, Peter rested the whole of his argument for the Messiaship of Jesus on the fulfillment of two predictions by David. The first is quoted from the sixteenth Psalm, in the words, following the Septuagint: "Moreover, my flesh also shall rest in hope: because thou wilt not leave my soul in Hades, neither wilt thou give thy Holy One to see corruption. Thou madest known to me the ways of life; thou shalt make me full of gladness with thy countenance." This is certainly a prediction of a resurrection from the dead; for if one's soul is not left in hades, and his flesh does not see corruption, it is because the soul and body are brought together again by a resurrection. But the Psalmist could not have been speaking of himself, as Peter correctly argues; for his flesh saw corruption, and his soul has remained in hades. The soul of Jesus, however, did not remain in hades, but returned into his body before the latter saw corruption; and this is true of no other eminent person; consequently, he is the person of whom the prophet spoke. He is the Christ of prophecy.

The second prediction is taken from the one hundred and tenth Psalm, in the words: "The Lord said to my Lord, Sit thou on my right hand till I make thine enemies thy footstool." This Peter had just proved by the testimony of the Holy Spirit had taken place with Jesus, and certainly no other human being ever sat on the right hand of God; consequently this is another proof that Jesus is the person of whom the prophets did write. Paul, in his sermon at Antioch of Pisidia, uses the former of these two predictions in the same way. He says: "As concerning that he raised him up from the dead, now no more to return to corruption, he hath spoken on this wise, I will give you the holy and sure mercies of David. Because he saith also in another psalm, Thou wilt not give thy Holy One to see corruption. For David, after he had in his own generation served the counsel of God, fell asleep, and was laid unto his fathers, and saw corruption: but he whom God raised up saw no corruption" (Acts 13.34–36). On these two predictions, then, together with many others which readily occurred to their hearers, these two apostles rested the argument for the Messiahship of Jesus, in connection with other and still stronger proofs that he was the Son of God; and these are sufficient to make out the case. Indeed, if the Jews, or any other people who believe in the prophecies of the Old Testament, are convinced that Jesus rose from the dead and ascended to the right hand of God to reign as a king, they need no other or better proof that he is also the Messiah of the prophets. It is for this reason, doubtless, that the apostles, after proving the former proposition, paid comparatively little attention to the proof of the latter.

We are now prepared to close this part of our inquiry, with the conclusion that Jesus is the Christ, the Son of the living God, and that therefore the system of religion which he established in the earth is of divine origin and authority. The other questions of credibility with which we started out, having reference to the thorough reliability of the record which we have of his sayings, and of the revelations which the apostles claim to have received, remain to be discussed in Part Fourth.

PART IV

The Inspiration of the New Testament Books

ONE

The Promises of Jesus

The term inspiration, when applied to the sacred books, designates the characteristic which they are supposed to have derived from the inspiration of their writers. When applied to the writers, it means the supposed miraculous action of the Spirit of God in their minds, by which they were caused to write as God willed. The term in its substantive form is not used in the New Testament; but it occurs in its adjective form (*qei<pneustoj, God-inspired*), and in this form it is applied to the Scriptures of the Old Testament (2 Tim 3.16).

The inquiry whether the New Testament books possess this characteristic, may be prosecuted in two ways: first, by considering what the writers themselves have said on the subject; and second, by considering the question whether such books could have been written by uninspired men. We have laid the basis for the first in Part Third, by finding that these writers are thoroughly credible in all their statements. Whatever they say, therefore, on the subject now before us we can believe implicitly, and we will take up this branch of the inquiry first.

If there is any kind or degree of inspiration which believers must affirm and defend, it is that which is set forth in the New Testament books themselves. It would be irrelevant to the subject of Evidences of Christianity, and useless in itself, to discuss any other. But before we can determine whether to defend it or not, we must ascertain precisely what it is. This is to be done, not, as many writers on the subject seem to have supposed, by formulating a theory of inspiration, and then searching the Scriptures to find support for it; but by studying the Scripture presentation of the subject, and accepting that as our theory. Now it so happens that the subject is presented in the New Testament in a way quite favorable to successful investigation. We are furnished, first, with a number of promises of inspiration made by Jesus to the Apostles; second, with some very explicit statements made by the Apostles and others, which show the fulfillment of these promises; and third, with many facts and statements which help to define the limits of the inspiration thus set forth. We shall consider these in the order in which we have named them.

The first promise of Jesus on the subject is quoted by Matthew in the following words: "But beware of men: for they will deliver you up to councils, and in their synagogues will they scourge you; yea, and before governors and kings shall ye be brought for my sake, for a testimony to them and the Gentiles. But when they deliver you up, be not anxious how or what ye shall speak: for it shall be given you in that hour what ye shall speak. For it is not ye that speak, but the Spirit of your Father that speaketh in you (10.17–20). The same promise is quoted by Mark and Luke, with the variation in the latter, "for the Holy Spirit shall teach you in that very hour what ye ought to say" (Mark 8.11; Luke 12.12). Here we have first a prohibition, "Be not anxious"; and it has reference to two things: first, how they shall speak; and second, what they shall speak. Under "how" is included the manner of speech; that is, the style, diction and arrangement; under "what," the matter; that is, the thoughts and facts. They are told not to be anxious about any of these, even when their lives depended on what they would say. It is impossible that mortal man should be free from anxiety under such circumstances, without supernatural aid. It follows that the reason which Jesus proceeds to give for this prohibition is the only one that could be given by a rational being. It is this: "For it shall be given you in that hour what ye shall speak:

for it is not ye that speak, but the Spirit of your Father that speaketh in you"; "for the Holy Spirit shall teach you in that hour what ye ought to say." This assurance would be sufficient to free them from anxiety, if they could only implicitly believe it; but what an implicit faith it required! How different from the feeble faith which now staggers at the thought that such a promise as this was ever realized!

In the words, "It is not ye that speak, but the Spirit of your Father that speaketh in you," we have an obvious instance of the well known Hebrew idiom by which in comparisons the absolute negative is put for the relative. They did speak, as appears from the fact that the Holy Spirit was to teach them what they ought to say; but as their speaking was to be controlled by the Spirit in them, it was not they only or chiefly that spoke, but the Holy Spirit.

The second promise is reported by Luke alone. Jesus, after telling the disciples in his prophetic discourse on the destruction of Jerusalem, that they should be delivered up to synagogues and prisons, and be brought before governors and kings, continues: "Settle it therefore in your hearts, not to meditate beforehand how to answer: for I will give you a mouth and wisdom which all your adversaries shall not be able to withstand or to gainsay" (21.12–15). Here the prohibition advances from anxiety to premeditation. A courageous man, after proper premeditation, might make a speech on the effect of which his life depended, with comparative freedom from anxiety; but who could enter upon such a speech without anxiety and at the same time without premeditation? The Apostles were not only told to do this, but the order is made emphatic by the words with which it is introduced: "Settle it therefore in your hearts." These words, while emphasizing the order, suggest also that it was to be the settled purpose of their hearts to carry the order into actual use. Such an order would have been but idle breath to these men, had it not been accompanied with the only assurance which could possibly make it practicable, the assurance that Christ would give them wisdom ample for each occasion; and he was to give it, as they knew from the previous promise, by the power of the Holy Spirit within them.

The third promise was made in the memorable discourse delivered on the night of the betrayal. The items of it are found in several distinct passages of the speech: "I will pray the Father, and he will send you another Advocate, that he may be with you forever, even the Spirit of truth, whom the world can not receive; for it beholdeth him not, neither knoweth him: ye know him, for he abideth with you, and shall be in you." "These things have I spoken unto you, while yet abiding with you. But the Advocate, even the Holy Spirit, whom the Father will send in my name, he shall teach you all things, and bring to your remembrance all that I have said to you." "I have yet many things to say to you, but ye can not bear them now. Howbeit, when he, the Spirit of truth, is come, he shall guide you into all the truth: for he shall not speak from himself; but what things soever he shall hear, these shall he speak: and he shall declare unto you the things that are to come" (John 14.15–17, 26; 16.12–13). In this promise Jesus assures the disciples, first, that the Holy Spirit would be with them and in them always, as a substitute for his own presence. Second, that he should teach them all things, and bring to their remembrance all that he had spoken to them. Third, that he would guide them into all the truth. Doubtless, by "all things," and "all the truth," we are to understand all that was needful for the discharge of their office as Apostles; and by all that he had said to them, all that was needed by them, and that they did not already remember; but these are the only limitations which we could dare to assign to the very explicit words employed.

The fourth promise was given on the day of the ascension. After charging the disciples not to depart from Jerusalem till they received the promise of the Father which he had previously mentioned, he tells them: "Ye shall be baptized in the Holy Spirit not many days hence"; "Ye shall receive power when the Holy Spirit is come upon you: and ye shall be my witnesses both in Jerusalem and in all Judea and Samaria, and unto the uttermost part of the earth" (Acts 1.5, 8). Here that same gift of the Spirit previously promised is called a baptism in the Spirit—a figure which designates the subsidence of their own mental powers in those of the Holy Spirit when he should come upon them; and he assures them that they should then receive power, and be his witnesses in every land. The power necessary to be such witnesses, as we learn from the sequel, is both the power to work physical miracles and the power to speak with absolute knowledge concerning the exaltation of Jesus, and concerning his will in all things on which he had not spoken in person.

If these several promises were fulfilled to the disciples the latter were endowed as follows:

a. The Spirit of God came upon them with such power that their spirits were figuratively immersed in it, and it abode in them to the end of their days.

b. It gave them, or taught them, what to say and how to say it, in such measure that on the most trying occasions they could speak with unerring wisdom, and yet without anxiety or premeditation. It was not they that spoke, but the Holy Spirit that spoke in them; that is, the Holy Spirit, and not they, was the responsible speaker.

c. To the end of enabling them thus to speak, it recalled to their memory, as fully as was needful, all that Jesus had in person spoken; and as the words he had spoken were intimately blended with the deeds he had done, it undoubtedly recalled these also. This was especially needed when they were to speak or write concerning his earthly career.

d. To the same end, it guided them into all truth yet untaught, which it was the will of Christ that they should know and teach. This was needful in order that their utterances concerning those items of God's will which they alone have revealed, that is, their statements concerning things in the spirit world and in the future of time and eternity, might be received as the word of God.

It is not uncommon to hear it said that the authors of our four Gospels do not claim to have written by inspiration. It is true that Mark and Luke set up no such claim for themselves, but it is far otherwise in reference to Matthew and John. In setting forth these promises of Jesus, as all four of these writers do, they mean either to assert that Matthew and John, who were of the Twelve, experienced their fulfillment, or that they remained unfulfilled. No matter what we may think of the truthfulness of these writers, we can not suppose they meant the latter, and thereby meant that their Master made promises which he failed to fulfill. Unquestionably they intended to convey the thought that every one of these promises was fulfilled; and they wrote at a time when the fulfillment was a fact of their own past experience or observation.

TWO

Fulfillment of the Promises as Stated in Acts

We have seen in Part Third that while the book of Acts has been more confidently assailed by unbelievers than any one of the Gospels, its credibility has been completely vindicated. This vindication is the more remarkable from the fact that this book occupies such a relation to the others, and especially to Paul's Epistles, as to subject it to a greater variety of tests than any other. We come to its testimony on the subject of inspiration, therefore, with full confidence that in its statements we shall find nothing but the truth.

After a few introductory paragraphs, the body of this narrative opens with a detailed account of the fulfillment of the promises of Jesus in regard to inspiration. The author having referred to these promises in the close of his previous narrative, and also in the introduction to this, purposely and formally opens the body of his work with the account of this fulfillment; so that it comes in not incidentally, but formally and prominently. He represents the Twelve as waiting for it and expecting it till it comes; and he declares that it came on the first Pentecost after the resurrection of Jesus. He says that on the morning of that day they were all together in one place, and suddenly "there appeared to them tongues parting asunder, like as of fire; and it sat upon each one of them. And they were filled with the Holy Spirit, and began to speak with other tongues, as the Spirit gave them utterance."

He adds that there were men there from fifteen provinces of the Roman Empire, which he names, representing almost as many tongues and dialects, who heard these Galileans speaking inthe tongues of all these countries, and that they were amazed and confounded by the fact, and inquired with one voice, "What does this mean?" He further states that one of the Twelve, Simon Peter, arose, together with his eleven companions, and declared that this miracle was the fulfillment of a prophecy uttered by the prophet Joel, which he proceeds to recite in their hearing, and that Jesus, who had risen from the dead and ascended to the right hand of God, had sent upon them the Spirit whose power his hearers were witnessing (Acts 2.1–33).

Now here was the fulfillment of the promises of Jesus in almost every particular. First, the Twelve had no premeditation, and they felt no anxiety. No amount of either could have helped them to speak in tongues; and for premeditation they had no opportunity. Second, both the "what" and the "how" of their utterances were given to them, and both were given by giving them the words; for, the words being unknown to them, they were not suggested by the thoughts which were conveyed to the hearers. In this was fulfilled almost absolutely the words: "It is not ye that speak, but the Spirit of your Father that speaketh in you." Third, the Spirit led Peter into truth hitherto unknown; for it enabled him to declare the law of remission of sins under Christ, and to make known the exaltation of Jesus, which had recently transpired in heaven. It is highly probable, too, that it brought to his mind the predictions both of Joel and of David, and enabled him to give an interpretation to both which he had not conceived before that hour. Fourth, such a complete possession of their minds by the Holy Spirit fully justified the metaphor by which the transaction was called a baptism in the Spirit. By the miracle of speaking in tongues it was now demonstrated, both to the multitude and to the Apostles themselves, that a power had taken up its abode within them fully able to perform all that Jesus had promised, and that this power was the Spirit of God sent down from heaven by Jesus himself.

That the power thus bestowed on the Twelve on the great Pentecost continued to abide in them according to the promise, is set forth in Acts in several ways. In the first place, the author makes formal mention of it a few times, and then leaves us to infer that as it was thus far, it continued to be till the end. For instance, when Peter was first arraigned before the Jewish Sanhedrim, the writer, as if to call attention to the fulfillment of the promise, says: "Then Peter, filled with the Holy Spirit, said unto them" (4.8), and proceeds to quote his speech. When the Apostles, being forbidden to speak any more in the name of Jesus, had prayed, he says: "They were all filled with the Holy Spirit, and they spoke the word of God with boldness" (4.31).

In the second place, he quotes the Apostles themselves as affirming the continuance of this power. He quotes Peter, the second time that he appeared before the Sanhedrim, as saying: "We are witnesses of these things; and so is the Holy Spirit whom God hath given to them who obey him" (5.31–32). This was an echo of the promise. "When the Advocate is come, even the Spirit of truth which proceedeth from the Father, he shall bear witness of me: and ye also shall bear witness, because ye have been with me from the beginning." Again, he quotes Peter three times as affirming that the miraculous gift of tongues bestowed on the Gentiles in the house of Cornelius was the same as that bestowed on the Twelve at the beginning, thus reasserting the event of Pentecost (10.44–47; 11.16–17; 15.8). Finally he quotes the Apostles and elders who were in Jerusalem at the time of the conference about circumcision, as introducing the decree by the words, "It seemed good unto the Holy Spirit, and to us, to lay upon you no greater burden than these necessary things" (15.27–28), thus affirming that their decision was the decision of the Holy Spirit, which it could have been only because they were guided in it by the Spirit.

In the third place, the author himself makes the same representation, by mentioning many miracles which the Apostles wrought, which were at once a proof and an exhibition of the presence of the Holy Spirit within them. This he does by his account of healing the lame man at the beautiful gate of the temple; that of many such persons healed after the death of Ananias and Sapphira; that of Eneas at Lydda, and the raising of Tabitha from the dead in Joppa. We should especially note also, in this connection, that peculiar exhibition of the Spirit's power by which, when the device of Ananias and his wife put it to the test, Peter looked into the secrets of their hearts and exposed their inmost thoughts. Here was a most startling and unmistakable exhibition of a mental power which the divine Spirit alone could impart.

In the fourth place, the Apostles are represented as actually imparting the gift of the Holy Spirit in its miraculous manifestations to other disciples. Only one instance is formally described, that of its impartation by Peter and John to disciples in Samaria; but the gift was possessed by Stephen, by Philip, by Agabus, by Barnabas, by Symeon called Niger, by Lucius of Cyrene, and by Manaen; and it was doubtless conferred on all of these in the same way. If there were any doubt on this point, it would be dissipated by what we shall yet learn from the practice of the Apostle Paul. Now this impartation of the Spirit to others is a demonstrative proof that the Apostles still possessed it themselves, and that the promise, "He abideth with you," was fulfilled.

In the fifth place, all that is affirmed in Acts on this subject concerning the Twelve is in every particular affirmed of Paul after he became an Apostle. He was filled with the Spirit at the time of his baptism; he was a prophet; he wrought many miracles; he imparted the Holy Spirit to others; and he was even led by the direct power of the Spirit into proper fields of labor when his own judgment as to where he should go would have led him less wisely (Acts 16.6–8).

The sum of the evidence in Acts concerning the fulfillment of the promises, we can now see, is the sum of the promises made by Jesus. The two stand over against each other as the two sides of an equation; and they combine to show that there abode permanently in the Apostles, and in some of their companions, a power of God's Holy Spirit equal to their perfect enlightenment and guidance in all that they sought to know and say; and that it did, as a matter of fact, guide their thoughts, their words, and the course of their missionary journeys. Not only so, it enabled them to speak of things in heaven, on earth, and in the future, concerning which, without divine enlightenment, men in the flesh can know nothing. A more complete inspiration for their work of speaking, of writing, and of directing the affairs of the church, is beyond conception. We can add nothing to it in thought, and we should not in thought be willing to take anything from it.

THREE

Fulfillment of The Promises as Stated in the Epistles

As the keynote on this subject for the whole book of Acts is sounded in the second chapter, so for the Epistles it is sounded in the second chapter of First Corinthians. Paul introduces the subject by saying: "My speech and my preaching were not in persuasive words of man's wisdom, but in demonstration of the Spirit and of power; that your faith should not stand in the wisdom of men, but in the power of God." By "demonstration of the Spirit and of power," he means the working of miracles which demonstrated his possession of the power of the Holy Spirit. When the people on such evidence believed, their faith rested not in philosophy, but in the power of God. After thus repudiating the wisdom of men as a source of his power and of their faith, he admits that he speaks wisdom among the perfect, but not the wisdom of this world. On the contrary, he speaks the wisdom of God, a wisdom concerning things which men had never seen, heard or conceived; "but," he says, "unto us God revealed them through the Spirit: for the Spirit searches all things, yea, the deep things of God." Here is an express assertion that he received revelations through the Spirit; and this agrees with the promise to this effect recorded in the Gospel of John.

In the next place, after remarking that the Spirit searches all things, even the deep things of God, and knows them, he says:

"We received, not the spirit of the world, but the Spirit which is of God, that we might know the things which are freely given to us by God." This is an assertion that the Spirit through which God revealed things to him and his fellows, had been received by them from God for the very purpose of making these revelations.

Paul next speaks of the words in which the things revealed by the Spirit were spoken. He says: "Which things also we speak, not in words which man's wisdom teacheth, but which the Holy Spirit teacheth; comparing spiritual things with spiritual." In this last clause the term "combining" would express the meaning better than "comparing." They combined the spiritual things with spiritual words.[1] Than this, there could not possibly be a more explicit assertion that the inspired men were guided by or taught by the Holy Spirit, as to the very words which they employed.

Finally, the Apostle ends this invaluable series of statements by saying of the same class of whom he has spoken from the beginning, "We have the mind of Christ"; by which, in the light of the context, we must understand that in all their official utterances their thoughts were the thoughts of Christ, or the very thoughts which Christ would have them to utter.

These affirmations made by Paul are as explicit and as comprehensive as those made by Luke in the second chapter of Acts; and if any one regards the words of an Apostle as more authoritative than those of the Evangelist, he ought the more readily to accept the latter because they are thus reaffirmed. Let it be remembered, too, that even those rationalists who deny the genuineness and credibility of Acts admit the genuineness of the Epistles to the Corinthians, and consequently they admit that Paul actually wrote these affirmations. These, then, must be held both by believers and unbelievers as setting forth the apostolic teaching on this subject.

If this passage stood alone in the apostolic writings, all that we have just said would be true; but it does not by any means stand alone. Every thought which it contains is echoed again and again in

---

[1] See Thayer's Grimm (Gr. Lex. N. T.) and Meyer, Com. *in loco.*

other utterances scattered through the Epistles. In regard to receiving revelations through the Spirit, Paul says of his knowledge of the Gospel, that he neither received it from men, nor was he taught it; but that it came to him "through revelation of Jesus Christ" (Gal 1.12). He says concerning the mystery of the call and the equal rights of the Gentiles, that it was made known to him "by revelation"—that "it hath now been revealed unto his holy apostles and prophets in the Spirit" (Eph 3.1–5). He introduces his prediction concerning the great apostasy, with the words, "But the Spirit saith expressly, that in the later times some shall fall away from the faith" (1 Tim 4.1). He says concerning his journey from Antioch to Jerusalem with Barnabas, "I went up by revelation" (Gal 2.2), thus affirming, as Luke in Acts affirms, that on some occasions his journeyings were controlled by the guiding power of the Holy Spirit (Acts 16.6–8). Finally, he declares to the Corinthians that his thorn in the flesh, "a messenger of Satan to buffet him," was given him to prevent him from being "exalted overmuch by the exceeding greatness of the revelations" which he received (2 Cor 12.7).

The assertion, "We have the mind of Christ," is echoed in another part of the same Epistle, as follows: "If any man thinketh himself to be a prophet, or spiritual, let him take knowledge of the things which I write to you, that they are the commandment of the Lord" (1 Cor 14.37). Here he not only asserts that what he wrote was the command of the Lord, which it could not be unless he had "the mind of the Lord," but he assumes that any man in the church who was a prophet or a spiritual man, that is, possessed of a spiritual gift, could know that what he wrote was in reality from the Lord. And let it not escape our notice here that this affirmation is made concerning what he wrote, and not concerning what he spoke. It shows that although, in the promises of Jesus on the subject of inspiration, reference was made especially to the speeches of the Apostles, Jesus did not intend to make a distinction between what they spoke and what they might write; but that speaking was put for all their utterances, whether with the tongue or the pen.

In regard to the "demonstration of the Spirit and of power," mentioned in our key passage, the affirmations elsewhere are abundant. Speaking in tongues was in itself both a demonstration of the Spirit's power, and an instance of speaking in words which the Holy Spirit taught; and on this point Paul says to the Corinthians, who prided themselves on the possession of this gift, "I thank God, I speak with tongues more than you all" (1 Cor 14.18–19). He claims also to have imparted to the Corinthians miraculous gifts of the Spirit, including the gift of tongues, and to have done the same among the Galatians. (1 Cor 1.5–6; 12.7–11; 27–31; 14.1–5; 15–17; 22–23; Gal 3.5). Moreover, he claims to have wrought wonders, signs and mighty works in support of his preaching, throughout the whole field of his labors (2 Cor 12.12; Rom 15.18–19). About the physical miracles he could not have been mistaken, and they were the demonstration, both to himself and to others, that he was not mistaken in claiming to be inspired.

The Epistles of the other Apostles are so much less voluminous than those of Paul, that we have not the same means of knowing what they asserted on this subject, apart from their words already cited from Acts; but what they do say, taken in connection with these other sources, is decisive. Thus Peter, speaking of the Old Testament prophets, says: "To whom it was revealed, that not unto themselves, but unto you, did they minister the things, which now have been announced to you through them that preached the gospel to you by the Holy Spirit sent down from heaven; which things angels desire to look into" (1 Pet 1.12). John, in almost the very language of the promise, that the Spirit of truth, when he came, should bear witness of Jesus, says: "It is the Spirit that beareth witness, because the Spirit is the truth. For there are three that bear witness, the Spirit, the water, and the blood: and the three agree in one" (1 John 5.7–8). Likewise, the author of the Epistle to the Hebrews, an apostolic writer, even if he were not the Apostle Paul, says that the great salvation which was at first spoken through the Lord "was confirmed unto us by them that heard, God also bearing witness with them, both by signs and wonders, and by manifold powers, and by gifts of the Holy Spirit, according to his own will" (Heb 2.4). Words are here multiplied, as if for the purpose of carefully covering all the ground which we have just gone over. More evidence than we have now presented could scarcely have been given, and certainly more should not be required. He who can not receive this, must deny the testimony of the Apostles, both as to their own experiences, and as to the promises which they claim to have received from Jesus.

FOUR

Inspiration of Mark, Luke, James, and Judas

Thus far the evidence of inspiration, explicit and doubly reiterated as it is, applies only to the Apostles. We have now to inquire to what extent it may be affirmed that Mark, Luke, James, and Judas, the other New Testament writers, were also inspired. It is well known that concerning the inspiration of these we have no explicit statement as in case of the Apostles; and that if there is evidence of their inspiration, it must be of an inferential kind.

To begin with Luke, it is often said that he expressly disclaims inspiration, by asserting for himself, in the preface to his Gospel, a different source of information. It is true that he does claim a different source of information; but this is not disclaiming the Holy Spirit's aid in composing his narrative. The Apostles are not represented as obtaining their information by inspiration; that is, their information about the earthly career of Jesus; but as being guided by the Spirit in recording it. If, then, Luke was as fully inspired as they, he still must have resorted to eye-witnesses for his information, while like them he would have been aided by the Holy Spirit in discriminating between what was accurate and inaccurate in the information, and in writing just that, no more, no less, which God willed that he should write. Indeed, the Apostles were themselves dependent on eye-witnesses other than themselves for information about some matters, but this detracts nothing from their claim to inspiration; and the difference between them and Luke in this particular is one only of degree. Luke, then, does not by any means disclaim inspiration.

The implication in Luke's preface really looks in the opposite direction. He avows the purpose of his narrative in the words, "That thou mightest know the certainty concerning the things wherein thou wast instructed"; and he avows this in the face of the preceding statement, that many had "taken in hand to draw up a narrative concerning those matters which have been fulfilled among us, even as they delivered them to us who were eye-witnesses and ministers of the word." Now there must have been something attached to the person of Luke, on which Theophilus could rely for the certainty in question—something which distinguished him in point of reliability from the previous reporters of the same original testimony. What could this have been unless it were the fact known to Theophilus, that Luke was inspired, and that those other writers were not? If it be answered that it was the fact of his having "traced the course of all things from the first," we reply that he does not deny this qualification to the previous writers; for he includes these with himself in the words, "even as they delivered them to *us* who were from the beginning eye-witnesses and ministers of the word."

The principal grounds for believing that Mark and Luke were inspired men are these: first, they both belonged to that class of fellow-laborers of the Apostles on whom they were accustomed, as we have seen in our citations from the Epistles and Acts, to confer miraculous gifts of the Spirit; and it is in the highest degree improbable that in the bestowment of these gifts these two men were slighted. Such gifts were bestowed on many, as in the church at Corinth and others, who sustained no such relation of intimacy with the Apostles as did these two. Second, had these men not possessed such a gift, it is highly improbable that they would have undertaken, like the writers to whom Luke refers in his preface, to compose these narratives: they would have left such work, as becoming prudence and modesty would have prompted, to others who were more competent. Finally, all the evidences of inspiration based on the unique character of our Gospels, marking them out as writings characteristically different from all others in the range of literature, support as strongly the inspiration of these two writers as they do that of Matthew and John. For these reasons both believers and unbelievers have classed these two Gospels with the other two in respect to inspiration, unbelievers pronouncing them all alike uninspired, and believers pronouncing them all alike inspired. Among all the theorists on the subject no party has been formed holding to the inspiration of Matthew and John, and denying that of Mark and Luke.

As to James and Judas, all that we have said about Mark and Luke may be said of them, and more besides. James, the author of the Epistle which bears his name, is the very James who, together with Peter and John, sent forth the decree concerning the Gentiles, and said in the introduction of it, "It seemed good to the Holy Spirit and to us," thus claiming to decide and to write by the guidance of the Holy Spirit. This is a direct claim of inspiration for James. Furthermore, it is incredible that he could have occupied the position of authority which he did in Jerusalem for many years if he had not been credited with full inspiration. As to Judas, he was a brother of James, and also a brother of the Lord; and it is incredible that in the distribution of miraculous gifts by the Apostles he was overlooked or slighted.

Now if to any one the evidence for the inspiration of these four writers shall appear unsatisfactory, he may still accept their writings as the uninspired productions of good men, thoroughly competent, so far as uninspired men could be, to write reliable narratives concerning Jesus. Much in the way of truths and facts which they have written is also contained in the writings of Apostles; and this much rests unquestionably on inspired authority. The rest, while void of this authority, would still be as credible as any mere human productions could be. So, then, the practical difference between the matter of the faith of the man who can not receive the writings of these four as inspired, if such there be, and that of him who receives all, amounts to but little, and is not worthy of much serious discussion.

FIVE

Modifying Statements and Facts

We have thus far followed the statements of the New Testament in a direct line of evidence, without paying attention to some which might have modified our view of particular passages, or led us to different conclusions. Some of the latter statements, while they may not materially change our conclusions, may broaden our view of the subject; and there are a few which have been thought to contradict some of the conclusions which we have reached. To the former class we now direct attention, and the latter we reserve for consideration in a separate chapter.

Among the most conspicuous of these modifying facts is one observed by all intelligent readers, that every writer has his own peculiar style, the result of his education and his mental endowments. In this respect the New Testament writers do not differ from writers without inspiration. They not only have their distinctive styles, but, being all Jews but one, they employ Hebraistic forms and idioms in writing Greek, just as modern Germans often employ German idioms in writing English. This shows plainly that the Holy Spirit did not to any perceptible degree change their natural modes of expression. It shows that the promise, "It shall not be ye that speak, but the Spirit of your Father that speaketh in you," did not contemplate mental inactivity on their part; and that Paul's statement, "Which things we speak not in words which man's wisdom teacheth, but which the Holy Spirit teacheth," does not mean that the Holy Spirit gave them a new vocabulary or imparted to them a new style. It chose, on the contrary, by leaving each to his own style to secure in the inspired books that variety of style which makes them at once more pleasing to the reader and more effective of good. That there was wisdom in this, no one will perhaps deny.

Not only is the natural style and diction of every writer apparently preserved in the sacred books, but we also observe in many of them, especially in the Epistles, the natural play of the feelings of the writer. True, the synoptical Gospels are wondrously free from everything of this kind, the personality of the writers being out of sight, and the Gospel of John and the book of Acts are almost as much so; but in the Epistles of Paul one can trace all the currents of his deep flow of feeling, and almost feel the beating of his heart. To such an extent is this true that of all the writers of the whole Bible Paul is the best known in his inward experiences. This shows that if in any instance the Holy Spirit restrained the inspired men in regard to the expression of their feelings concerning the things of which they wrote, in many instances there was no such restraint. The feelings thus expressed were of course all human feelings, and they must therefore be regarded as a human element in the inspired books. The Holy Spirit allowed them a place in the record for the evident purpose of enabling the reader to know how the writers felt under the circumstances. That this was wise is clearly demonstrated by the power for good with which these intense exhibitions of feeling affect the souls of thoughtful readers. Without them the Bible would have been a comparatively cold and powerless book. That this is in harmony with the promises of Jesus, and the declarations of the Apostles which we have cited in the preceding chapter, is obvious.

The quotations which the New Testament writers make from the Old Testament furnish a series of facts which still further illustrate the manner in which the Holy Spirit exercised his guidance over the minds of the inspired men. In making these quotations they were under the necessity of either quoting from the Septuagint, the only Greek translation then extant, or making new renderings for themselves directly from the Hebrew. In the majority of instances they did the former; and if they had not been inspired it is probable that all except Paul would have done so uniformly; for it is quite doubtful whether any except he was acquainted with the Hebrew of the Old Testament, which was not studied in that age except by the learned. Out of the 181 quotations which are collected and tabulated in Horn's Introduction, that laborious author sets down 74 as agreeing exactly with the Septuagint, or varying from it in insignificant particulars; 47 as being from the Septuagint "with some variations"; and 31 as "agreeing with the Septuagint in sense, but not in words." Thus 152 out of the 181 quotations agree substantially with the Septuagint, while a majority of them agree with it literally. In some instances, estimated as eleven by Horn, the quotations differ from the Septuagint, but agree nearly or exactly with the Hebrew, showing clearly that in these instances the writers made a new translation of the passages for themselves. A remarkable instance of this is the following:

Hebrew: Love covereth all sins (Prov 10.12).

Septuagint: But friendship covereth all them who are not contentious.

1 Peter 4.8: For love shall cover the multitude of sins.

In some other instances the quotations vary in words, and more or less in thought from both the present Hebrew text and the Septuagint. The following is an example:

Hebrew: Thou hast ascended up on high, thou hast led thy captivity captive, thou hast received gifts among men (Psa 68.18).

Septuagint: Having ascended on high, thou hast led thy captivity captive, and received gifts in the manner of men.

Eph. iv. 8: When he ascended up on high he led his captivity captive, and gave gifts to men.

In this instance the obscure expression of the Hebrew, "received gifts among men," is rendered by the Greek translators, "received gifts in the manner of men," and by Paul, "gave gifts unto men." This is a change of the Old Testament text in thought; but it only carries the original thought to its ultimate aim; for the gifts which Christ received were not for himself, but for men, and this is brought out in the words, "gave gifts to men."

From these observations it appears that the New Testament writers quoted the Old Testament freely. In a majority of instances they departed from its phraseology, and in a few they varied the thought by either expanding, or contracting, or expounding it. In all these latter instances, if they were guided by the Holy Spirit at all, we must understand that he guided them to make variations on his own words and thoughts previously expressed through the prophets. Or, if we suppose that in these matters he left their minds free from guidance, we must conclude that he did so because the writers without special guidance wrote that which he approved. In other words, if the Apostles have not falsified the fact of their inspiration, their quotations are just what the Holy Spirit would have them to be.

Another class of modifying facts, closely related to the last mentioned, consists of citations of facts from the Old Testament, not in the form of quotations, in which the Septuagint account is followed instead of the Hebrew, or in which there is a departure from both. Of the former we mention three specifications: First, Luke's citation of Cainan as son of Arphaxad and father of Shelah, this name being omitted in the Hebrew text (Luke 3.35, cf. Gen 11.12). Second, Stephen's statement of the number of Jacob's family when he migrated to Egypt at seventy-five souls, after the Septuagint, whereas the Hebrew has it seventy (Acts 7.14; cf. Gen 46.27). Third, Paul's statement that the law came four hundred and thirty years after the promise, as compared with the statement of the Hebrew text that the sojourning of the Israelites in Egypt was four hundred and thirty years (Gal 3.17; Ex 12.40). Paul follows the Septuagint version of Exodus, which says: "The sojourning of the children of Israel, which they sojourned in the land of Egypt, and in the land of Canaan, was four hundred and thirty years." In all these instances the writers followed the version which they constantly read, without knowing, perhaps, that it differed from the Hebrew, just as scholars at the present day often quote from our English version without stopping to inquire whether it is accurate or not. Even if Luke, Stephen or Paul had stopped to inquire which text was correct in the places cited, it is not at all probable that they could have decided the question by their unaided powers. It is clear that the Holy Spirit could have guided them, as it did other writers in other instances, to follow the Hebrew instead of the Greek text; and it follows from the fact that he did not, that he desired the facts to be stated as the people read them in their Bibles, rather than to raise questions of textual criticism among a people unprepared for such investigations. Such a procedure would not have been admissible if the argument of the writer in either case had depended on the correctness of the name or the figures; but as it did not, there was no need of decision between the two texts. At the present day the most accurate of scholars are in the habit of quoting passages from our English version that are inaccurately translated, without stopping to correct the renderings except when the use which they make of a passage depends on rendering it correctly. To do otherwise would overload discourse with irrelevant matter, and expose one to the charge of pedantry.

Instances of departure in matters of fact from both the Hebrew and the Greek of the Old Testament are not numerous, but we mention three which are conspicuous: first, the substitution of Abraham for Jacob as the purchaser of the piece of land from Hamor in Shechem (Acts 7.16, cf. Gen 33.19); second, the substitution of Abiathar for Abimelech as high priest when David ate the shewbread (Mark 2.26, cf. 1 Sam 21.1–6); and third, the citation of the passage about the thirty pieces of silver from Jeremiah instead of Zechariah (Matt 27.9–10, cf. Zech. 11.12). The first two are obvious verbal mistakes, and the only question is whether they were made by the sacred writers or by early transcribers. When we consider the unexampled accuracy of the sacred writers in all such matters, and add to this the consideration of their inspiration, and then consider on the other hand the certainty of clerical errors even in the very first copies made by transcribers, we ought not to hesitate how to decide this question. All probability is in favor of the supposition that some copyist originated the error. As to the name Jeremiah, it must be disposed of in the same way and for the same reasons, unless, as some learned writers have supposed, Matthew here used the name Jeremiah because the manuscript roll of the prophets, which in many Jewish copies began with Jeremiah, was referred to instead of the particular prophet.[1] Only in case it were certain that these three errors were committed by the inspired penmen could they have any bearing on the question of inspiration.

Some of the predictions quoted from the Old Testament as fulfilled in the New demand attention in this connection. While many of the predictions thus quoted appear from their context in the Old Testament to have direct reference to the events by which they are fulfilled, there are some which have no such apparent reference. Two representative examples are brought together by John as being fulfilled in the death of Jesus. When the soldiers, in breaking the bones of the crucified, passed by those of Jesus in disobedience to orders, and one of them pierced his side with a spear, John says there were fulfilled the two predictions, "A bone of him shall not be broken"; and, "They shall look on him whom they pierced." The former of these was originally written with respect to the paschal lamb; and it was given as a rule forbidding the Jews, in preparing and carving and eating the lamb, to break one of its bones. This was a very remarkable prohibition, requiring great care to observe it; and certainly no Israelite, throughout the ages in which it was observed, could have discovered an adequate reason for it. It appears equally certain that no Christian after the death of Jesus could have seen and affirmed the connection pointed out by John, until by the guidance of the Holy Spirit it was discovered that the paschal lamb was a type of Christ (1 Cor 5.7); and then the mysterious prohibition was

---

[1] See the discussion of this question by Canon Cook in *Additional Notes on Matthew's Gospel, Speaker's Commentary*.

understood. The latter prediction, quoted from Zechariah 12.10, is obscure in the original context; but it occurs in a passage which speaks of Judah and Jerusalem, and it is probable that no reader of the passage, either before or after the crucifixion, would have supposed it had any reference to the piercing of the side of Jesus, without the Apostle as a guide; and how could he have thought so without the Holy Spirit as a guide? Such uses of the Old Testament, unless we regard them as the vagaries of unlicensed interpretation, and this is the light in which they are regarded by those who deny miraculous inspiration, contain further proofs of the inspiration of the New Testament writers, seeing that they exhibit deeper penetration into the meaning of the Scriptures than we can credit to the unaided powers of the Apostles. They show that the Holy Spirit, in the prophetic writings of the Old Testament, had reference in his own mind, in various utterances which he prompted, to far different events from those to which the minds of the prophets were unavoidably limited. It shows also that to the inspired minds of the New Testament the Holy Spirit revealed much of the significance of words employed by those of the Old, which the latter did not themselves understand. Thus he was fulfilling the Savior's promise of guiding the Apostles into all the truth, by making known old truth that had been hidden, as well as by revealing much that had never before been spoken. The remarks suggested by these two predictions apply with equal force to a number of others quoted in the New Testament, which in the original context have no apparent reference to the events in which they were fulfilled.

On comparing the quotations made by the four Evangelists severally from the words of Jesus and others, we find that in quoting the same remark they sometimes vary the wording of it in much the same way as they vary the words of Old Testament writers. The following are familiar examples. The words heard at the baptism of Jesus are in Matthew: "This is my beloved Son in whom I am well pleased"; in Luke and Mark: "Thou art my beloved Son; in thee I am well pleased." The words of the first temptation are in Matthew: "If thou art the Son of God, command that these stones become bread"; in Luke: "Command this stone that it become bread." The reply of Jesus to this temptation is in Matthew: "It is written, Man shall not live by bread alone, but by every word that shall proceed out of the mouth of God"; in Luke: "It is written, Man shall not live by bread alone." Similar variations are found in many places; but in none of them is there a material change of meaning. They show that in bringing to remembrance what Jesus had said to the Apostles, the Spirit always brought to them the thought, but not always the exact phraseology; and as this is true of some which we can test by means of parallel reports, we may presume that it is also true of some others; and that in speeches recorded by only one Evangelist there is not always a verbatim report, but often one that preserves the thought with variations in the words. So far as the Spirit's guidance had reference in all these cases to the words, it either guided or permitted the writers to vary the phraseology, yet it always prevented such a license as would involve a change of meaning. When we consider how difficult it is to change the words of a writer or speaker without changing his meaning, we can see that the Spirit's controlling power even in these instances was not inconsiderable.

The ignorance of the Apostles concerning the admission of the uncircumcised into the church, up to the time of the baptism of Cornelius, is another modifying fact, and the more interesting from the consideration that it involved a misunderstanding of the words of Jesus in the great commission, and of Peter's own words in his address on Pentecost. It shows that when Jesus said, "I have many things to tell you, but you can not bear them now," he had reference not only to the time then present, but to some years in the future, even after the first impartation of the Holy Spirit; and it shows that the promise immediately connected with this remark, "When the Spirit of truth is come, he will guide you into all the truth," contemplated not an immediate illumination on every point, but a gradual illumination according as God should will. The same is true of their expectation concerning the second coming of the Lord. If, as many scholars suppose, they at first thought that this great event was to occur in their own generation, this was in accordance with the declaration of Jesus: "Of that day or hour, knoweth no one, not even the angels in heaven, neither the Son, but the Father." If it ever did become known to the Apostles, it must have been by a special revelation of which we have no knowledge. Yet it is quite certain that to Paul it was revealed that a great apostasy would take place before the second coming (2 Thess 2.1–12); and to Peter, that after "the fathers fell asleep," that is, after the generation to which the prediction was given had passed away, "mockers would come with mockery, saying, Where is the promise of his coming?" (2 Pet. 3.3–4). This again shows a progressive leading into the truth, although in this instance the exact time of the event was still withheld. It has been argued from Paul's use of the pronoun "we" in speaking of those who would be alive at the second coming of Christ (1 Thess 4.15, 17; 1 Cor 15.51–52), that he expected it before his own death; but his statements concerning the great apostasy which was to occur, ushering in the career of the "man of sin" (2 Thess 2.1–12), show that he uses "we" in a general sense for the saints who will then be alive, and not for those of his own generation. Before dismissing this topic, we may remark that although Peter did not know until the baptism of Cornelius that uncircumcised Gentiles were to be admitted into the church, he himself uttered on the day of Pentecost words which we can see did most clearly include that thought. He said: "For to you is the promise, and to your children, and to all that are afar off, even as many as the Lord our God shall call unto him." From this it appears that under the impulse of the Holy Spirit he uttered words the full import of which he did not understand, until in God's good time their full meaning was made known to him by a special revelation. This is an unmistakable instance of being led to employ words expressive of a meaning which was in the mind of the Spirit, but not in that of the speaker; an instance, in other terms, in which the inspiration affected the words and not the thoughts of the speaker. It is much like those predictions of the older prophets in which there was a reference in the mind of the Spirit which was not perceived or thought of by the prophet. See 1 Peter 1.10–11.

We find both in Acts and in the Epistles that the inspired Apostles, though possessing and exercising all the wonderful powers of the Spirit promised by Jesus, were still imperfect men in heart and life. This is apparent not merely from such exhibitions of it as Peter's dissimulation and the contention between Paul and Barnabas, but also from John's confession: "If we say that we have no sin, we deceive ourselves, and the truth is not in us"; "If we say that we have not sinned, we make him a liar, and his word is not in us" (1 John 1.8, 10). This shows that the inspiration of the Apostles was not a purification of their spiritual natures, so as to free them from sin; but an enlightenment of their minds, so as to enable them to teach the truth. The two conceptions are often confounded, but they are widely different, and either may exist in a person without the other. It is doubtless true that to be the subject of inspiration was calculated to elevate men spiritually; and that God usually elected only good men for this heavenly gift; but still to be inspired and to be spiritually good are two distinct conceptions never to be confounded.

We find in the Epistles, and especially in those of Paul, many remarks of a personal character which do not contribute to the doctrinal purpose of the documents; such, for example, as Paul's many salutations of persons not conspicuous in the history, and such as his request of Timothy to bring to him his cloak, his books, and his parchments, which he had left at Troas with Carpus (2 Tim 4.13); and for all these he needed no aid from the Holy Spirit either to know them or to express them. In such instances it appears that the guiding power exercised by the Spirit was at its minimum, and yet even in these instances there was room for its exercise. One of the most puzzling questions to the author of a serious document, on which the welfare of others depends, is what of all that he knows relating to the subject and the persons he should insert, and what he should omit. It is often more difficult to make a wise selection than it is to obtain the knowledge. This problem would certainly have confronted Paul if he had enjoyed no supernatural guidance, and he would probably have omitted these apparently small matters from his Epistles, and written them, if at all, in an accompanying note. Especially would he have done so if he had anticipated that his Epistles would be read in distant nations long after his decease. But if he had omitted them, how much the world would have lost. We should have known nothing of that warm-heartedness toward his fellow workers, and that tender gratitude toward his benefactors, which are revealed in his personal salutations and messages. We should not have known that in his Roman prison, when winter was coming on (2 Tim 4.21), he anticipated the need of that cloak, that he wanted his books to read in those lonely hours, and that he desired his parchments in order to do more writing. By the introduction of these matters a cord of sympathy has been drawn out from the heart of Paul to the hearts of millions of believers the world over, and an incalculable amount of spiritual good has been thereby accomplished. This shows the consummate wisdom of the arrangement by which not his own shortsighted judgment, but the divine Spirit who foresaw all the future, guided him as to what he should insert, and what he should omit.

Conclusions

We have now gone over the ground of the statements and facts relating to the inspiration of the Now Testament writers, and we are prepared to sum up the results. We state them numerically as follows:

1. The promise of the Holy Spirit to abide permanently in the Apostles with miraculous power was made by Jesus, and it was realized in the experience of the Twelve from and after the first Pentecost following the resurrection. The Spirit was also from time to time and in divers places imparted by the Apostles to other faithful persons. This was their inspiration.

2. The Spirit thus abiding in the inspired, brought to their remembrance, to the full extent that was needful, the words and the

acts of Jesus. It guaranteed, therefore, a record of these words and acts, precisely such as God willed.

3. It brought to the inspired persons revelations concerning the past, the present and the future; and when occasion required, it revealed to them the secret thoughts of living men. For this reason we can rely implicitly on the correctness of every thought which these men have expressed on these subjects.

4. The Spirit within them taught them how to speak the things thus revealed, by teaching to the full extent needed the words in which to express them; yet, in quoting others, not always the exact words; and it demonstrated this fact to lookers-on by causing the inspired at times to speak in tongues which they had never learned, but which were known to those who heard. This affords a perfect guarantee that these revelations were really made, and that they are expressed in the most suitable words.

5. By thus acting within and through the inspired men, the Spirit enabled them to speak on all occasions, even when life was at stake, without anxiety as to how or what they should say, and to speak with consummate wisdom, yet without premeditation. It brought about the fact expressed in the Hebraistic formula: "It is not ye that speak, but the Spirit of your Father that speaketh in you."

6. The Spirit enabled the inspired on all suitable occasions to demonstrate the presence of its power within them, by manifestations of it in the way of physical "powers, signs and wonders"—a demonstration which the human mind has ever demanded of men claiming to bear messages from God.

7. From the fact that these men spoke and wrote as the Spirit willed, it follows that what they wrote out of their own personal experience and observation, as well as that which was revealed to them, has the Spirit's approval as a part of the record.

SIX

Objections Considered

Various objections have been urged against the conclusions enumerated at the close of our last chapter, some of them involving a general denial of inspiration, and some a denial of particular conclusions. Several theories of inspiration, which conflict more or less with these conclusions, have also been propounded, and these demand attention in order that the whole subject may be before the mind of the student. We shall consider first the objections, and afterward the adverse theories.

Paul makes some statements in the seventh chapter of I. Corinthians, which have been interpreted to mean that he wrote that chapter without inspiration. In the course of the chapter he discusses three questions: first, the wisdom of marriage under existing circumstances, and of the temporary separation of husband and wife by consent (1–9); second, the propriety of separation from an unbelieving husband or wife (10–24); and third, the wisdom under existing distress of giving virgins in marriage (25–40).

After concluding his answer to the second branch of the first inquiry he says: "This I say by way of permission, not of commandment." This has been understood to mean that he was permitted to say this, but not commanded; and that therefore he said it on his own human authority. But the context clearly shows that the distinction is between his permitting and his commanding the *husband* and the *wife*. The remark, then, has no bearing on our question, unless it be to show that Paul's authority was so supreme that he could give commands or grant permission to the disciples, as each appeared proper.

In discussing the second question he introduces one precept with the words, "Unto the married I give charge, yea, not I, but the Lord"; and another with the words, "But to the rest say I, not the Lord." Here he has been supposed to give one precept by the authority of the Lord, and the other by his own authority, without the Lord's. But the real distinction is between what the Lord had taught in person while in the flesh, and what Paul teaches as an apostle. This is proved by the fact that the one precept is found in the sermon on the mount, and the other is not found in any of the Lord's personal teachings. It is also proved by the fact that after giving the precept in question he says: "And so I ordain in all the churches" (17).

In discussing the third question he starts out by saying: "Now concerning virgins, I have no commandment of the Lord: but I give my judgment as of one that hath obtained mercy of the Lord to be faithful. I think, therefore, that this is good by reason of the present distress, namely, that it is good for a man to be as he is." He proceeds to state at length his judgment, and then concludes with the words: "But she is happier if she abide as she is, after my judgment: and I think that I also have the Spirit of God." Here, after beginning with his human judgment, he ends with the words, "I think that I also have the Spirit of God." Does he mean to express a mere opinion, with attending doubt, that he had the Spirit of God? If so, it follows that on this one point he was not certain that he was guided by inspiration; and as he expresses no such doubt on anything else in his writings, it would follow that on this alone did he have any such doubt. But if Paul thought he had the Spirit, why should we think that he had not? Surely he had better grounds on which to form an opinion than we. But even this consideration does not bring us to the end of the matter. In the words, "I think that I also have the Spirit of God," the second I is emphatic, as appears from the fact that instead of being understood from the person of the verb, as the rule is when there is no emphasis, it is expressed (δοκῶ δέ κἀγὼ πνεῦμα θεοῦ ἔχειν). The term *also* (καί) connected with it adds to the emphasis; and the effect of the whole is to emphasize the fact that he also had the Spirit as well as somebody else. There were men in the church at Corinth with spiritual gifts; and it is probable that their authority, or that of some other Apostle, had been arrayed by misrepresentation against his; so, in order to silence any such plea for disregarding his teaching on the subject, he closes the discussion with the modest but very emphatic reminder that *he* spoke by inspiration, whether others did or not. This passage, then, furnishes not the slightest ground for doubt of its own inspiration.

In writing to the Corinthians, Paul speaks of one matter in which his memory had failed. After mentioning the names of some among them whom he had himself baptized, he says: "Beside, I know not whether I baptized any other" (1 Cor. 1.16). This lapse of memory is held as proof that lapses of memory in general, and consequently other mistakes of a like nature, are not inconsistent with the inspiration which the Apostles claimed. But they did not claim that the Holy Spirit was to bring *all* things to their remembrance; the promise was limited to the things which Jesus had taught; and the reference here is to something that Paul had done. Doubtless we may understand that the promised aid implied a remembrance of all, whether spoken by Jesus or not, that might be necessary in any manner to their official work; but in the instance here mentioned there was no such necessity, seeing that his argument was complete without it; and it is for this reason, perhaps, that the Holy Spirit did not supply the missing facts, or that Paul did not refresh his own memory by making proper inquiry.

The fact that Paul rebuked the high priest, not knowing who he was, and then, on learning, apologized (Acts 23.1–5), has been used by some as evidence against inspiration. It is held that, if inspired at all, he would have known who the man was whom he rebuked, and that he would not have made a speech for which he owed an apology. But this is to assume, as in the last instance, that it was the work of the Spirit to make known to the inspired man everything that he did not know. We must keep in mind that its work was not this, but to guide them into just that amount of truth and knowledge which was needful for the work to which they were called. If now we inquire whether the Spirit guided Paul sufficiently on this occasion, without revealing to him that the presiding officer was the high priest, I think we shall answer in the affirmative. When the person in question commanded that he be smitten in the mouth for merely saying, "I have lived in all good conscience before God until this day," it was proper that he should be told, "God shall smite thee, thou whited wall." And when Paul, after saying this, was told that the man was the high priest, it was certainly most becoming in Paul, without retracting a word, to say to the bystanders, "I knew not, brethren, that he was the high priest: for it is written, Thou shalt not speak evil of a ruler of thy people." It is probable that the Holy Spirit withheld the information from him that he might not feel restrained from littering a rebuke which was greatly needed on the occasion, and which was in reality a judicial divine sentence. The promise was that, when brought before governors and councils, the Spirit should give them what to say; and surely no one can pretend he did not on this occasion say the very best thing that could have been said.

It has been charged that Paul reasoned erroneously, and that this refutes the claim of inspiration. The instance most usually cited is the following: "Now to Abraham were the promises spoken, and to his seed. He saith not, And to seeds, as of many; but as of one, And to thy seed, which is Christ" (Gal 3.16). It is alleged that Paul here argues from a false premise in assuming that if God meant more than one seed he would have used the plural number, whereas the word seed in Greek and Hebrew, as in English, is a collective noun, and is used in the singular form whether the reference is to one or many. But Paul could not have been ignorant of this usage; for he was both a Greek and a Hebrew scholar, and a mere tyro in the grammar of either language would know this much. If special proof that he knew it were needed, we have it in verse 29 of this very chapter, where he uses the singular number of this word to include many, saying, "If ye are Christ's, then are ye Abraham's seed, and heirs according to the promise." Moreover, he was writing to Greek-speaking people, every one of whom with the least intelligence was acquainted with this usage.

Paul's real purpose in the passage is to teach that although God used a term which, as every Hebrew scholar knew, could convey the idea of plurality, it was not plurality that he meant. In other words, he teaches that God did not mean all of Abraham's offspring, although he used a term which might be so construed. The passage is an authoritative interpretation of the mind of God in a promise which was purposely made obscure by the use of an ambiguous term, and left so until the time of the fulfillment, when its obscurity was cleared up by this inspired apostle. And it must be conceded that were it not for this interpretation, no human being could to this day know that such was God's meaning. So far as Paul employs argument in the case, it is used not to prove that his interpretation is correct, but to show that his interpretation is not precluded by the terms which God employed. If God had said seeds instead of seed, the interpretation would have been inadmissible, whether the phraseology employed had been grammatical or not; for it would unquestionably have expressed the idea of plurality. Whether it would have been grammatical or not, depends on the question whether reference was had to individuals or to *kinds* of offspring. In the latter case the plural is rightly employed in English, as when we say, a dealer in seeds; and we have at least one instance in which Paul himself employs it in Greek. In his argument on the resurrection (1 Cor 15.37–38), he says: "That which thou sowest thou sowest not the body that shall be, but a bare grain, it may chance of wheat or of some other kind; but God giveth it a body even as it pleased him, and to each of the seeds (ἑχάστω τῶν σπερμάτων) a body of its own." Here, by "each of the seeds," he means not each individual grain of wheat; but, having specified wheat or some "other kind," he refers to the different kinds of bodies which he gives to the different kinds of seeds. The Septuagint version, Paul's Greek Bible, has five instances of the same use of this word in the plural (Lev 26.16; 1 Sam 8.15; Psa 125.6; Isa 31.11; Dan 1.12, 16), and the Hebrew text has one (1 Sam 8.15). Did Paul then refer to kinds of posterity? He certainly did; for in this chapter he makes believers in Christ one kind, being children of Abraham by faith in Jesus, though not children literally; and in the next chapter he makes Isaac and his descendants another kind, being children by promise and also children literally; and he makes Ishmael and his posterity still another kind, being children of the flesh and not of the promise (4.23; 28–29). So, then, here are at least three kinds of children of Abraham, making three kinds of seeds clearly distinguished from one another, and furnishing ground, if such had been the will of God, for the use of the plural, "seeds."

One of the most common grounds for denying the inspiration of the New Testament writers, and especially such inspiration as could guard them from error, is the allegation that they contradict one another, and that they also contradict known facts of history and science. But while this charge is boldly and confidently made, it has never been made good. We have considered in a former chapter the most plausible efforts to make it good, and found them all fallacious; and we shall therefore give it no further consideration here.

The same class of men who deny inspiration on account of the alleged contradictions between the writers, also deny it on account of their agreements. The striking agreements in many passages between the three synoptic Gospels, agreement in minute details and even in words, is held to be inconsistent with their guidance by a common Spirit, and to demand an inquiry into the common human sources from which they obtained their information. It is very clear that John and Matthew needed no human sources except their own remembrance of events which they had witnessed, together with direct information from other witnesses of a few incidents which did not come immediately under their eyes. As for Mark and Luke, they must of course have derived their information from others. The question, then, as to how it happened that Mark and Luke have so much matter in common with Matthew, while it is one of curiosity, can not, by any answer which may be given, affect the inspiration of any one of them. If they copied largely from some original document, or if they adopted much from what had been orally repeated by the early preachers, they may have done either under the guidance of the Holy Spirit. The first preacher was Peter; and he was led to present such aspects of the career of Jesus as were known by the Spirit to be best calculated to convince and win the first hearers of the Gospel. The others, seeing this effectiveness, were doubtless led by their own judgment, as well as by the promptings of the Spirit, to follow in his track. Even Paul, when preaching to the Jews in Antioch of Pisidia, used much of the same matter employed by Peter on the day of Pentecost; and if this is true of the Apostle to the Gentiles, how much more certainly would all of the original Twelve and the preachers who started under their instruction do the same. In all ages since, when a great religious movement has been started by the preaching of a small number of men acting in concert, both they and their first co-laborers have uniformly employed for a considerable time the same arguments and illustrations which were found effective at the beginning. It is but a dictate of common sense that they should do so. Why should it be thought strange, then, or inconsistent with their inspiration, that the first gospel writers followed largely the same line of narrative? Doubtless if either had known what the other two had written, and had been left to his own impulse, he would have avoided repeating so much; and on this supposition there is need of adding the supposition of an overruling power just such as the Holy Spirit exercised. On the other hand, if they all wrote independently, the Holy Spirit may have led them to choose so much matter in common for the very purpose of securing to the world, without the knowledge of the men employed for the purpose, this threefold presentation of a certain portion of the Lord's life. In any view of the facts, then, they contain nothing to throw doubt on the Saviour's promise of inspiration, or on the apostolic testimony that the promise was fulfilled.

The varieties of style employed by New Testament writers, of which we have spoken in chapter iv., is held by many as proof that the Holy Spirit exercised no guidance over the words of the inspired; and by some, as proof that there was no miraculous inspiration at all. It has been assumed that if the writers had been guided by the Holy Spirit they would all have written in one style, the style of the Spirit. But this is to assume that the Holy Spirit either could not or would not guide each within the range of his own style and his own vocabulary. Either assumption is baseless, and therefore the conclusion is illogical.

With still more confidence it has been urged that the departures from literal quotation which we have already noticed in quoting both the Old Testament and the words of Jesus and his interlocutors, disproves inspiration with respect to the words. If it does, it also disproves it with reference to the ideas; for, as we have seen, in varying the words the ideas are also varied in some instances. But this objection can have force in either direction only on the assumption that if the Spirit guided at all he would allow no free quotation of the sense in different words, and that he would never quote his own previously expressed thoughts with variation. To point out these assumptions is to set aside the objection.

The question has been asked, What could be the utility of giving an infallibly correct text, seeing that it has been corrupted by the mistakes of transcribers, and that God knew it would be thus corrupted when he gave it? It is admitted that so far as the text has been corrupted beyond possibility of correction, it has been rendered useless; but what is the extent of such corruption? We have seen in Part First that we now possess nine hundred and ninety-nine thousandths of the text precisely as it was given to us, and that nearly all of the other one thousandth part has been settled with almost absolute certainty. The objection, then, is fallacious, in that it aims to spread over the whole book the shadow of doubt which really affects only a very small part, and a part which is definitely known, and which is so marked in our latest English version as to point it out to the most unlearned reader. It might as well be asked, Why keep in our clerk's offices perfect standards of weights and measures, seeing that many of those in use agree but imperfectly with them? The answer is, we want the perfect standard in order that we may regulate the instruments in use, and thus keep them as nearly perfect as possible, in like manner we need an infallible text of the Scripture to begin with, in order that we may ever correct our copies by it and keep them as nearly like it as possible; and the fact that the church has succeeded in keeping her books precisely like the original text in almost every word through eighteen centuries is one of the marvels of that divine providence which watches over all things good and true.

Again it has been asked, What is the utility of an infallible original, seeing that nearly all men have to depend on fallible translations, and then on fallible interpretations, in order to get the meaning? The obvious answer is, that if we have an infallible original, so far as we get its real meaning through our translations and interpretations, we have the infallible truth; whereas, if the original is itself a fallible document, we are still a prey to uncertainty when its meaning is obtained. Moreover, this objection, like the preceding one, assumes too much. It assumes that the fallible interpreter, with his fallible translation, is unable to obtain with certainty the meaning of the original; whereas the fact is that he can and does obtain it, with the exception of occasional passages which are obscure. While it is true that in the Bible there are some words and some sentences whose precise shades of meaning can not be conveyed with unerring certainty in other than the original tongues, and a few whose meaning is not clear to proficient scholars in the original, still it is true that the great mass of words in any language can be translated into other tongues with absolute precision. To such an extent is this true, that every translator is conscious of rendering much that he translates so as to convey the thought with unmistakable accuracy, and every reader of a book knows, in regard to the chief part of it, that he has the meaning. As a consequence, in regard to the meaning of much the greater part of the Bible there is absolutely no difference of opinion. Such a consequence could not exist if the assumption which lies at the basis of the objection were a reality. There is, then, good cause for giving us an infallible book; for we do get its meaning in the main with infallible certainty; and it so happens with nearly all men who study it with diligence and candor that the part whose meaning they obtain without fail is the part most necessary to their present good and their final salvation.

The force of these objections, whether combined or taken, singly, instead of weakening the evidence for inspiration in any of its particulars as set forth in chapters first, second and third, only tends to exhibit more fully its manifold working for our good, and to prove the wisdom of bestowing on the New Testament writers precisely that kind of inspiration set forth on the sacred pages. It meets the wants of our souls, and accomplishes the benevolent purposes of that Holy Spirit who "breathes where he listeth," and causes us to hear his voice.

SEVEN

Adverse Theories of Inspiration

Instead of propounding a theory of inspiration, our course has been to examine in detail the New Testament statements which hear directly on the subject, setting these forth as conclusions, and then searching for other facts and statements which might in any way modify the conclusions. In doing so we have come into conflict with certain theories on the subject which have found more or less acceptance among scholars, and it is now proper that we test these theories by the facts which we have collected.

1. We begin with that which is styled the Mechanical Theory. This theory has been defined as teaching that not only "the sense of Scripture, and the facts and sentiments therein recorded, but each and every word, phrase and expression, as well as the or-der and arrangement of such words, phrases and expressions, has been separately supplied, breathed into, as it were, and dictated to the writers by the Spirit of God."[1]

If this theory had been propounded to explain the miracle of speaking in tongues alone, it would seem to be adequate; for in that particular instance absolute dictation of all that was uttered certainly took place. But this is not true of inspired utterances in general. The theory fails to account for the play of the writer's human feelings; and for the obvious facts that in recalling to their memory what Jesus had said the Spirit only recalled what they

---

[1] Lee, *On Inspiration,* 33. and note.

did not already remember; and in guiding them into all truth he did not guide them into that which they already possessed. The theory is then inadequate because it can account for only a small part of the facts, and it is in conflict with some others.

Some early writers who seemed to hold to this theory have illustrated it by performance on a musical instrument. Thus Justin Martyr says that the Spirit "acted on just men as a plectrum on a harp or lyre"; Athenagoras, that inspired men "uttered that which was wrought in them, the Spirit using them as its instruments, as a flute player might play a flute"; and Hyppolitus, that they "were brought to an inner harmony, like instruments, and having the Word within them, as it were to strike the notes, by him they were moved, and announced that which God wished."[2] It is not probable that these, and other ancient writers with whom this figure was common, regarded the inspired men as always passive, as a musical instrument is in the hands of the musician, although when speaking in tongues they were very nearly so; but they probably used this figure to illustrate a single feature of the work, that of the Spirit's action and the ready response of the inspired mind. As a representation of the whole work it is clearly inadequate. It would be nearer the truth to compare the whole work of the Spirit to that of driving a well trained horse. You draw the lines to the right or the left as you see that the horse needs guidance; you check him when he would go too fast, and urge him forward when he would go too slow; but he usually keeps the road and maintains the desired gait and speed of his own accord; still your hand is ever on the lines, and its pressure on the bit is constantly felt, so that you are controlling the horse's movements when he is going most completely at his own will. Indeed, the horse is all the time going very much at his own will, and yet he is never without the control of the driver.

This illustration, however, although it covers much more of the ground than the former, is still defective, for you can not drive a horse over precipitous hillsides, nor can you make him trot with-

---

[2] See these and other citations in Lee *On Inspiration*, Appendix S; Westcott's Introduction, Appendix B.

out touching the ground; but the Spirit enabled the inspired to do things comparable to these—to speak in tongues never learned, and to look into the secrets of the spiritual and the eternal world. In this last respect alone does the comparison to performance on a musical instrument seem appropriate; and lest we disparage it below its merits, let us remember that as the exact tone brought out by the performer depends on the character of the instrument as well as on the skill of the performer, so when the Spirit acted on the inspired the words come forth in the style and vocabulary of the writer.

2. At the opposite extreme from the preceding is the theory of ordinary inspiration, so styled because it recognizes only an ordinary, as opposed to a miraculous, exercise of the Spirit's power. It holds that the action of the Holy Spirit on the minds of the inspired was not different, unless it be in degree, from that influence which it exerts on the uninspired Christian.[3] This theory, which is semi-rationalistic, is not defective merely, but it is contradictory to all the statements adduced in former chapters which set forth the miraculous nature of the Spirit's action. We dismiss it, therefore, without further consideration.

3. We next consider the theory which assumes different degrees of inspiration. Certain Jewish writers of the middle ages originated this theory, and applied it to the Old Testament books, which were divided into three classes according to the degree of inspiration supposed to be possessed by their authors. In more recent times it has been accepted and applied to the New Testament by some Christian writers.[4] The essential objection to it is that inspiration is a fact, and not a quality which admits of degrees. It is the fact of an active force exerted by the Spirit. This *force* may have different degrees, but the *fact* can not. The movement of the air called wind is a fact, whether the movement be rapid or slow. The *force* with which it moves may vary in degree, but not the fact that it moves. So, the degree of intensity with which the Spirit acted on the inspired might differ, as it doubtless did, being great-

---

[3] Lee, *On Inspiration*, 34, Appendix C; Farrar, *Essay on Inspiration*, Sec. 4; Curtis, *On Inspiration*, 51, 218.

[4] See citations by Lee and Farrar, referred to in last note.

er when the inspired man spoke in tongues than when he mentioned incidents in his own experience; but the inspiration itself was one and the same fact throughout. As a theory of inspiration, then, even if it were confined to the degrees of power exercised by the Spirit, it would express no more than one obvious feature of the Spirit's work, and would leave all the rest out of sight.

4. Still another theory, which has been styled the essential theory,[5] teaches that the sacred writers were guided by the Holy Spirit in all matters essential to the great purposes of revelation, such as matters of doctrine, morals and faith; but that in all other matters they were left to their natural powers, and that therefore they were, in regard to these, as liable to mistakes as other men. The chief objection to this theory, in the light of our collation of New Testament statements, is that a very large portion of the matter found in the speeches of the apostles, and in their writings, to which reference is made in the promises of Jesus, consists of just such matter as is excluded by the theory from inspiration; and thus the theory contradicts the divine promises which are mentioned by the sacred writers as having been fulfilled. It is also obvious that if the apostles were liable to error in matters of ordinary knowledge, in regard to which we have the means of testing them, this would necessarily throw discredit on all that they say of things in which we can not test them. Really our confidence in what they say of doctrine, of the will of God, and of moral and spiritual truths and facts, is based on their perfect reliability concerning things within the range of our investigation. And as to their liability to make mistakes, inasmuch as they do not avow such liability, the only way that we can know that it existed is by discovering mistakes which they have made: this, we have seen in Part Third, has not been done.[6] This theory, then, with its other defects, makes a gratuitous admission unfavorable to the inspired writers, and it must for this reason, if for no other, be rejected.

---

[5] Farrar, *l. c.;* Alford, *Prolegomena to Commentary*, see vii.

[6] "That they did so err, I am not so irreverent as to assert, nor has the widest learning and the acutest ingenuity of skepticism ever pointed out one complete and demonstrable error of fact or doctrine in the Old or New Testament." Farrar, *Lecture on Inspiration*, sec. 6.

5. The theory most commonly accepted by scholars who are not inclined to be rationalistic on the subject, is styled the dynamical theory. It is defined by Lee as the theory "which implies such a divine influence as employs man's faculties according to their natural laws."[7] F. W. Farrar says of it: "It holds that Holy Scripture was not dictated by, but committed to writing under the guidance of, the Holy Spirit."[8] Westcott, in defining it, says: "The human powers of the divine messenger act according to their natural laws even when these powers are supernaturally strengthened"; and in regard to the word dynamical, with which he expresses some dissatisfaction, he says: "It is used to describe an influence acting upon living *powers,* and manifesting itself through them according to their natural laws, as distinguished from that influence which merely uses human *organs* for its outward expression; as, for instance, in the accounts of the demoniacs." He might have added, as also in the account of the Spirit's action on King Saul. He adds to his definition, as still further setting forth his conception of the subject, the following statements: "It supposes that the same providential power which gave the message selected the messenger; and implies that the traits of individual character and the peculiarity of manner and purpose which are displayed in the composition and language of the sacred writings, are essential to the perfect exhibition of their meaning." . . . "It preserves absolute truthfulness with perfect humanity, so that the nature of man is not neutralized, if we may thus speak, by the divine agency, and the truth of God is not impaired but, exactly expressed, in one of its several aspects, by the individual mind."[9]

This theory is an attempt to state the method in which the divine Spirit and the human soul were united in producing the sacred writings, and thus far it harmonizes with the facts which we have collected from the Scriptures. But it goes no further than this; it leaves us still dependent on the promises and their fulfillment, together with the modifying facts which we have Collected

---

[7] Lee, *On Inspiration,* 39.

[8] *Lecture on Inspiration,* see. 4, ii.

[9] *Introduction to Study of Gospels,* 39, 41.

from the Scriptures, for the details of the outworking of this combination. We may safely say, then, that no theory which has been
propounded covers correctly the whole ground of the Spirit's work
in inspiration; but that the subject as a whole can be understood
only by taking into view, and keeping in view, all the facts and
statements which have formed the conclusions laid down at the
close of chapter v.

EIGHT

Confirmatory Evidence

The direct and positive evidence of inspiration is that which we have given in previous chapters, especially in the first three. In addition to this, there are considerations based on the characteristics of the writers, which, though they might not suggest or prove inspiration, if considered alone, furnish strong confirmatory evidence to support the Scripture statements. While the fact noted in a former chapter, that these writers were left each to his own natural style, does not militate against the conclusion that they were all inspired, yet we should naturally suppose that if the Holy Spirit guided them they would possess in common some peculiarities of style resulting from this guidance. This supposition accords with the facts, as we shall now proceed to show.

We mention, first, the purely dramatic form in which all of the New Testament writers depict the characters of men. They allow all of the actors in the scenes which they describe to play their several parts without a word of comment, without an expression of approval or disapproval, and entirely without those attempts at analysis of character in which other historians indulge. We believe that they stand alone in this respect; and the fact is the more remarkable when we consider the great variety of striking characters which figure upon their pages.

Next we notice the unexampled impartiality with which they record facts, speaking with as little reserve concerning the sins and follies of themselves and their friends as of the wicked deeds of their enemies; as freely, for instance, of Peter's denial of his Lord, as of the malice and cruelty of Caiaphas. This characteristic is so prominent that it has not escaped the notice of any thoughtful reader.

Not less striking is the imperturbable calmness with which they trace the current of history, relating with as little apparent feeling the most wonderful and exciting events, as those the most trivial; as calmly, for instance, the final sufferings of Jesus as the fact of his taking a seat on Peter's fishing-boat to address the people. They appear to have been restrained by some supernatural power from giving natural utterance to the intense feeling which burned within them, or to have been lifted above all human weakness, so as to speak like him,

> Who sees with equal eye, as God of all, A hero perish, or a sparrow fall; Atoms or systems into ruin hurled, And now a bubble burst, and now a world.[1]

We next observe the unaccountable brevity of the New Testament narratives; and first, their brevity as whole books. Never were men burdened with a theme so momentous in their own estimation, or so momentous in reality, as that of the four Evangelists. Never were writers so oppressed, if brevity were aimed at, by the multitude of the details before them, and the difficulty of determining what to leave out when the welfare of a world depended on what should be written. One of them shows the

---

[1] "What reader has failed to notice how the cold sententiousness of Tacitus expands into tenderness, and warms with passion, when he turns aside to weep over the last moments of Agricola? But compare with this natural outpouring of feeling the record of the evangelists. There no expression of human sympathy accompanies the story of the agony in the garden, the awful scene before Pilate, the horrors of the cross. No burst of emotion attends the Master's body to the grave, or welcomes his resurrection." Lee, *On Inspiration,* 229.

"Their history, from the narrative of our Lord's persecution to those of Paul, the abomination of the Jews, embraces scenes and personages which claim from the ordinary reader a continual effusion of sorrow, or wonder, or indignation. In writers who were friends of the parties, and adherents of the cause for which they did and suffered so great things, the absence of it is, on ordinary grounds, incomprehensible." Bishop Hinds, *On Inspiration,* 83. See Gaussen, *Origin and Inspiration of the Bible,* 289–292.

oppression of his own mind by these details, when he is forced to exclaim in hyperbolic style: "If they should be written every one, I suppose that even the world itself would not contain the books that should be written." What then could have led these four writers, thus pressed by the copiousness of their matter, the importance of their theme, and their burning desire to defend and exalt their Master, to compress their accounts into an average of fifty-four small pages of long primer type? What, but some overruling and superhuman power? As to the book of Acts, the argument is the same in kind, and perhaps greater in force; for this writer had to deal with the widespread progress and ever-varying fortunes of the church through a period of thirty years, the most thrillingly interesting period of all its history; and yet he condenses all into about the same number of pages. When, secondly, we notice their brevity as to particular incidents, the wonder continues the same. The baptism of Jesus, for instance, accompanied as it was by the descent of the Holy Spirit upon him, and his formal acknowledgment by God in an audible voice from heaven, is disposed of in twelve lines by the first Evangelist, in six each by the second and third, and in a mere allusion quoted from another person by the fourth. Of the appearances of Jesus after his resurrection, of which there were twelve in all, only two are mentioned by the first Evangelist, only three by the second, only three by the third, and only four by the fourth. In Acts, the dispersion and apparent destruction of the only church then planted is recorded in four lines; and the death of the Apostle James, a calamity of fearful magnitude, is disposed of in eleven words. If it were truly said of Jesus, "Never man spake like this man," it could be as truly said of his historians, Never men wrote as these men; and the logical inference is that they wrote, as he spoke, from the fullness of the Spirit of God.

The argument from the brevity of the narratives is not seen in its full force until it is viewed in connection with the remarkable omissions by which it was brought about. For example, by Mark and John the whole of the first thirty years of the life of

Jesus is left blank; and by Matthew and Luke all between his infancy and his thirtieth year is omitted, except a single incident recorded by Luke. By the Synoptists all of the visits of Jesus to Jerusalem except the last are omitted, and by John all of the Galilean ministry, except a single miracle and a conversation which grew out of it. From Acts are omitted nearly all the labors of ten apostles, and from the career of the one whose labors are most fully recorded many of the most thrilling incidents are omitted. Who, unconstrained by some higher power, could have omitted from the narrative the details of those heart-stirring incidents in the life of Paul, which are merely mentioned by him in the eleventh and twelfth chapters of Second Corinthians? And who, while inserting the detailed account of the voyage from Caesarea to Rome, could have been willing to omit the account of Paul's trial before Nero?

We mention next their angelology. Among men of all nations there has existed a fondness for depicting invisible beings; hence the demigods, fairies, genii, and sylphs of ancient and modern story, all either grotesque, childish, impure, or malicious. In contrast with these, the angels of the New Testament and of the whole Bible are holy, mighty, humble, compassionate, self-poised, and every way worthy to be the messengers of God. This character is uniformly maintained whenever and wherever angels appear in any part of the book. "Unlike men, they are always like themselves." Nothing like them was ever conceived by any other class of writers, or depicted in any other literature. They are so unlike the creations of human imagination, that the latter has not allowed the divine picture to remain as it was; but Christian poets and painters have falsely and persistently given to angels the form of woman. It is incredible that all of this is the product of the unaided powers of shepherds, fishermen, herdsmen, and publicans of those early and dark ages, and of such men among just one people, and that not the most imaginative. Supernatural aid is clearly implied, and the doctrine of inspiration alone accounts for the phenomenon.

In the seventh place, we notice the air of infallibility which the writers of the New Testament everywhere assume. Though they speak on some themes which have baffled the skill of all other thinkers and writers, such as the nature of God, his eternal purposes, his present will, angels, disembodied spirits, the introduction of sin, its forgiveness and its punishment, the future of this earth, and the final destiny of us all; on all subjects and on all occasions they speak with unhesitating confidence, never admitting the possibility of a mistake. They were the most arrogant of men, next to Jesus himself, in whom this characteristic was preeminent, if they were not inspired.

Finally, we mention the inherent power of the New Testament to convince the reader of its own divine origin, and to move him to holy living. That it has such power in a most remarkable degree is the testimony from experience of every believer. As to its self-evidencing power, it is the testimony of a vast multitude that it has been the chief cause of turning men from unbelief to belief; and its power to move in the direction of holy living is attested by the whole host of the good and pure in every Christian age and country. This was the expectation of the writers, one of whom expressly declares that his purpose in writing was that his readers might believe, and that believing they might obtain eternal life; and it was also the expectation of Him who promised them the Holy Spirit; for he said: "When he is come, he will convince the world of sin, of righteousness, and of judgment." Now it is not of the nature of error or of falsehood to effect such beneficent changes in human character: these are the product of truth alone; and herein is a final and conclusive evidence that the writers of the New Testament books wrote as they were moved by the Holy Spirit.

We have now completed four of the inquiries which we undertook in the beginning of this work. We have found that the original text of the New Testament has been preserved in such a way that the many errors of transcribers which crept into it in the course of ages have, by the diligence of Christian scholars, been discovered and corrected to such an extent as to guard both the Greek scholar and the English reader from being misled thereby. We have found, in the second place, that all of the separate books of the volume are traced back by satisfactory evidence to the authors to whom they are credited—that they are genuine writings. In the third place, we have found ample evidence that all of their representations of the personal career of Jesus are thoroughly reliable, and that he is, therefore, the Christ of the Old Testament prophets, and the real Son of God. We have found, lastly, that these writers were guided in all that they wrote by the Spirit of God, imparted to them for the very purpose of such guidance; and that what they have written was written precisely as God willed. We have thus gone over all the ground of evidence necessary to the proof of the divine origin and authority of the Christian religion, and of the infallibility of the records of it contained in the New Testament; and while the remaining inquiries which we proposed at the outset are necessary to the vindication of the whole Bible, the line of evidence now before the reader is complete in reference to the Christian religion as distinguished from the Jewish and the Patriarchal.

HERITAGE
OF FAITH LIBRARY

The **DeWard Publishing Company Heritage of Faith Library** is a growing collection of classic Christian reprints. DeWard has already published or has plans to publish the following authors:

• A. B. Bruce
• Atticus G. Haygood
• H. C. Leupold
• J. W. McGarvey
• William Paley
• Albertus Pieters
• B. F. Westcott

Future authors and titles added to this series will be announced on our website.

www.deward.com

DeWard
for your journey

www.ingramcontent.com/pod-product-compliance
Lightning Source LLC
Chambersburg PA
CBHW020147090426
42734CB00008B/726

9 781947 929029